"I will tell our story to the world; that every day we shared was special."

An unforgettable memoir about a romance that will make you smile, laugh, and cry – not always in that order

---

Seized with grief at the loss of his beloved and vibrant wife, Barbara, after a thirty-year battle with breast cancer, Marc Gellman does the only thing he finds he can do. He starts telling stories. This unique memoir is much more than a tribute to a departed love. Their story shows how a cancer journey seamlessly entwines through a four decades-long love story.

A lifelong raconteur and jokester, Marc spent their forty-six-year relationship making Barbara laugh. (Most of the time it was intentional.) He'd do anything to make Barbara's gorgeous face break into the cute, dimpled smile he first saw once upon a time, in 1964, when a fourteen-year-old boy from Brooklyn met a twelve-year-old girl from The Bronx and they fell in love.

Surrounded by family and friends for seven days of sitting Shiva, Marc recounts his fairytale love story with Barbara, from their teenage meeting in the 1960s Rockaways summer scene, to being early marrieds in New York City, to suburban parenting, and to life as an urban couple relishing their empty nest. Once it appears, Barbara's courageous, grueling, determined, hope-filled fight against a brutal disease is unflinchingly depicted.

With candor and humor, laughter and tears, Marc shares the tales of a life both wildly charmed and excruciatingly challenging. Theirs is a life full of parties and singing and celebration, and a life of hard work raising three lively children while managing two demanding, deeply rewarding careers. It's a life of playful adventures and hijinks, of making the most of every silly moment in even the most serious of times. A life of standing up to every challenge together, and dancing close whenever they can.

Observing their singular, remarkable romance through "Shiva Eyes," Marc uncovers a depth to their love he'd never fully grasped, and a strength in Barbara he'd never fully understood. For all the trials that cancer brought into their lives, he discovers a happily-ever-after born of laughter, devotion, faith, and above all, a teenage puppy love that only grew with each passing year.

In the years since losing Barbara, Marc has often been asked: "Do you believe in God?" His answer is always the same: "Of course, I believe in God. I have to. How else can I hope to see my wife again?"

SEVEN DAYS of
SHIVA

Forty-six years of puppy love

SEVEN DAYS *of*
SHIVA

Forty-six years of puppy love

"…and she'd show me how to keep my chin up,
accepting all of my *zany silliness* that I never outgrew."

MARC GELLMAN

The stories in this book reflect the author's recollection, perception, and interpretation of events. In several instances, names and identifying characteristics have been changed, to protect the privacy of those depicted. Dialogue has been recreated from memory.

In loving memory

Barbara K. Gellman

September 12, 1951 – August 2, 2011

A husband's gift: I will tell our story to the world; that every day we shared was special. I am thankful for the love that we have. A love that is not limited by a measurement of time and so, our love will continue on forever.

CONTENTS

Part Two: Stories from the Second Day of Shiva

Part Three: Stories from the Third Day of Shiva

Part Four: Stories from the Fourth Day of Shiva

Part Five: Stories from the Fifth Day of Shiva

Part Six: Stories from the Sixth Day of Shiva

Part Seven: Stories from the Seventh Day of Shiva

Part Eight: After the Seventh Day of Shiva

PROLOGUE

Over the years, I've talked about writing a book and have often heard people say that their lives have been either so outrageously interesting, crazy, or wild, that they could write a book. I always wanted to be able to say to those people, "Well, I did!"

My first idea for a book was based on my growing-up years, in the 1950s and early '60s, in the East New York section of Brooklyn. Back then, I witnessed the gradual changes in the neighborhood demographics and, as a young kid, the neighborhood chitchat I overheard was interesting to me. There was much gossip about the perceived unscrupulous lifestyle of the new residents moving in and the rumors about supposed muggings and break-ins by these new residents were in full force. Longtime residents were fearful of the effects of the change on schools, crime, and real estate values.

The goings-on left an impression on me. The dynamics of what seemed to be causing change, with people panicking to sell their homes, were confusing to me. In the late 1990s, I began to research and write a book about the 1950s/'60s Brooklyn.

I didn't get very far with that book. I had a demanding job and a family. Writing a book, which I intended as a study project and a learning experience, was too demanding on my already busy schedule. Beyond my time constraints, my obsessive-compulsive disorder made writing a book impossible for me back then. Working with an editor might have made the project doable. But I couldn't work with anyone, since I needed to stress over every sentence and detail to make sure that my writing was accurate, and my grammar and punctuation were perfect.

So, the idea of my writing a book wasn't a new one thirteen years later, when my daughter, Kristen, urged me to write of stories about Barbara and me, after I lost Barbara in August 2011. I figured that a book of stories would be an easy project and not too time-consuming. After I lost Barbara, I developed DGASD (Don't Give a Shit Disorder), which toned down my OCD. Also, I had more time to devote to writing a book. And there would be no studying or learning, just writing the facts. It seemed simple, quick, and doable. And through the stories, my grandchildren could get to know their grandmother.

With the subject of the book set to be stories for my family, I started to write the first chapter. As my grief-laden emotions took over, it quickly became obvious to me that writing this book wasn't going to be easy at all. The first chapter became an introduction and I skipped ahead to write the end of the book. I decided that I could write more effectively about what I was going through at the time, having just lost my wife. It felt easier to describe my then-current state of mind, and my emotions and challenges at living alone for the first time and sleeping alone after forty years.

I dropped my preconceived ideas of what the book was to be. From that point on, my emotions guided my writing. My focus became the anguish I was experiencing, facing life without Barbara, which brought to mind the many memories of our lives together. What started out to be a simple book of stories for my family became a work of creative nonfiction.

When I started to tell people I was writing a book, it seemed to me that some of them thought I was delusional. They attempted to offer encouragement but sounded doubtful, like, "Oh, yeah ... sure. That's nice." I wasn't at all discouraged. I knew Barbara would have had confidence in me. And I was reminded of my son Jonathan once saying to me, "Dad, you're the only one I know who could take two sentences and make an incredible ten-minute speech out of them." I started off with three thoughts, which were so powerful and took me much further than a ten-minute speech.

I loved my wife.

She was a courageous woman.

I miss her.

My wife's passing marked the second time in my life I was faced with looking through "Shiva Eyes," the eyes of mourning and pain. The first time was seven years before, with the passing of my dad. Once again, it felt like my eyes were connected to my broken heart and through them I saw darkness, no matter how bright the sun was shining.

During the first few days of the Shiva, it was comforting to reminisce with guests about the incredible person Barbara was and the beautiful life we had. However, during the latter days, the number of guests was dwindling away. As I gazed into space, looking through Shiva Eyes, I became introspective. Even with the few people around me, I felt so alone.

I viewed my life differently during this time of sorrow. Through Shiva Eyes, I saw a view of having my loved one ripped away from me, of being alone and searching for answers. Writing through the sorrow and grief of Shiva Eyes made writing this book the most difficult project in my life. I had never before made such a commitment to any other project.

I wrote this book always looking through Shiva Eyes as I searched for answers to understand if Barbara had a good life, to identify her ability to overcome hardships, to learn if I had done all that I could for her, and to determine if, as she closed her eyes for the last time, she felt good and complete about her life.

I could have written only about the good things in Barbara's life. But if I'd done that, I wouldn't have been able to determine if the good outweighed the hardship. Writing about the hardships and how Barbara endured them gives proof of her courage and greatness. Despite hardships, we enjoyed a run that kept our life rich and exciting, with much talk, celebration, accomplishment, and no time for being bored. At times, a little boring might have felt good.

So often, I hear people say that their lives are boring. They tell me they get up in the morning, give the kids breakfast and send them off to school, and leave for work. They come home in the evening and have dinner, watch some TV, go to sleep, wake up the next morning and start the routine all over again. Well, when they describe their lives that way, I agree: life sounds boring. If those people opened their eyes and ears and took a moment to look and listen to the sights and sounds around them, if they deliberately and occasionally diverted from their routines, they would start to see their lives much differently.

I find it difficult to accept that anyone goes through days and weeks without something interesting happening that they can talk, laugh, or cry about. Even the simplest things, like giving the kids breakfast. Did the kids say something cute, funny, new, or unexpected that's worth remembering and laughing about with your spouse, parents, or friends? Is it worth remembering and telling the kids about when they are older?

I'm reminded of a time, more than twenty years ago, I was walking on DeKalb Avenue in Brooklyn, toward Flatbush Avenue. I saw a guy who was about 150 feet in front of me slip and fall to the ground. I ran to him to help. As I got to him, he was getting up from the ground. I asked if he was okay.

"Thank you, I'm fine."

"What happened? How did you fall?"

"Oh, I slipped on that banana peel," he answered.

"You slipped on a banana peel! That only happens in the cartoons!" We both laughed.

There were no cell phones back then and I couldn't wait to get home to tell Barbara I saw some guy slip on a banana peel. It's been more than twenty years and I'm still talking about it. Not everyone witnesses such a happening and I'm not making a case that witnessing someone slipping on a banana peel makes a person's life interesting and not boring. It's just good, fun conversation and that's all it is.

What's important is for people to realize there are things they witness, or do, or have happen to them, all the time. Rather than taking in an experience with a quick glance and moving on, take a pause and look what's happening around you. Barbara and I found that paying attention to different kinds of experiences, whether funny, strange, or weird, gave us the spice in our lives and the material to smile, laugh, and talk about. Open your eyes like Barbara and I did and perhaps you will be lucky enough to see some guy slip on a banana peel or even better, step in dog shit.

With three kids and busy schedules, it was easy for Barbara and me to fall into periods of humdrum, repetitive routines that would weigh us down, especially on weekdays. To shake us loose, Barbara would call me at work, like on a Tuesday, and say, "Listen, get home early tonight. I have a babysitter. We're going out!" It became a date night and we'd dress up, as we used to do as teenagers, for a date. We'd go to dinner and talk about the funny things our kids did. More importantly we'd catch up on the silly things that we'd seen and done, with no interruptions.

After dinner, we'd drive home, park in the driveway for fifteen minutes and make out in the car, just like old times. After making out, our evening was just beginning. We'd go into the house, pay the babysitter, go up to the bedroom, get naked, and fuck. These were wonderful evenings and the next morning we felt invigorated and alive. And I often noticed that my complexion had cleared up. Maybe this book can plant the idea in people's minds to open their eyes and be more flexible, to see all there is happening around them to talk about, laugh about, and cry about. Maybe this book will inspire people to take some action and not miss out on all the silly, fun, strange, and interesting things happening around them all the time.

What I miss most is being in love. The kind of love that only comes with having a wife, someone I can love and care for, and for that someone to love and care for me. I loved being married to Barbara.

She knew what true love was about. Barbara often asked, "Do you love me?" Then she would ask, "Do you care about me?" I used to say that it was kind of redundant to ask the second question. If you're in love, obviously you care for the person too. Barbara felt it was important to ask if I cared; it was a way to remind us that we were also best friends. I still think the caring part goes without saying. But Barbara liked to hear me say the words: "I care about you."

Along with the love, I miss the small things. An example: About two-and-a-half years after I lost Barbara, I had a St. Patrick's Day party in my apartment for friends and neighbors. No, I'm not Irish. But it was March and a St. Patrick's Day Party sounded like a good idea. It was the first party I had ever made, since all the house parties we'd thrown over the years were orchestrated by Barbara. All I ever did was show up. In a detour from Barbara's parties, I hired a caterer to do everything, even the party setup and cleanup. There were entertainers, a fiddler and a guitarist. I also hired a guy to play the bagpipes. But the guy called in sick the day before.

The party was a success, and everyone had a good time, I think. But on this evening, what was usually one of the fun parts of a party was a downer for me. Most often, one of the fun parts of our parties was after the guests had all left and it was just Barbara and me. It was a time when our adrenaline was still going and the two of us were left to talk and feel the satisfaction of a wonderful evening. We would continue that conversation into bed, while falling asleep.

But after the guests left my party, I was quickly reminded that I was alone. Shortly before, while the party was going on, my apartment had been filled with people, drinking, eating, laughing, and talking. But after, as I sat alone on the couch, there was no one left to talk with about how much fun the party was. I sat alone, in the quiet of my apartment, and grieved. I thought about how even the small things hurt hard and I came to realize, there really aren't any small things. It's all just one big hurt.

The hurt comes on when I remember and feel the good times too. Throughout writing this book, I could feel Barbara and me dancing.

When I closed my eyes, I could see Barbara's eyes and hear Frank Sinatra singing, "The Way You Look Tonight."

Barbara and I loved to dance, holding each other in our arms and feeling the softness of being cheek to cheek. As we danced, I felt our love and into Barbara's ear I would sing along to all of Sinatra's songs. She was the only one I ever sang to.

"The Way You Look Tonight" was a special one of mine. For thirty years, we had a black cloud of cancer over us. But on those nights when Barbara and I danced, I could look up and there was no black cloud. Those nights there was just me, and the way the most beautiful woman looked dancing. The most beautiful woman on the dance floor was always dancing with me.

I was on a high each time we danced. Today, when I'm at my lows, I see the loveliness of Barbara's glow and the way she looked every morning, afternoon, and night. As for our dancing, I thought I was doing the leading all those years. Having my first dance without Barbara, I quickly realized it was Barbara doing the leading all along. She was always good at making me feel bigger than I was.

Writing this book has done much for me. It has shown me that my life has been beautiful and so fulfilled. I have loved like so few other people have. Writing this book took over my life and it's been all I've been able to consistently think about through the years, as I grieve for Barbara. Along the way, I've wondered, do I really want to ever finish this book? Because to finish will bring about another end. I do believe that Barbara has been with me all the way. And when this book is done, I may feel like I've lost her once again ... or maybe she'll continue to be with me.

So, the book about stories became a book about the things I learned about Barbara and me. A lot of my questions have been answered. I understand Barbara better, after taking the time to reflect and think and understand things I didn't understand or pay attention to before. I understand our marriage better and realize how small I am without Barbara.

Along the way, several people have asked why I spent so much time writing this book and have pointed out that I'm not going to make any money. I wrote this book for my children. I don't think children really understand relationships between parents. They hear us argue, but never hear us making love (we think). In writing this book, I want my children to know about the wonderful life that Barbara and I had together. It may have been cut short, but we were married for forty years. In writing this book, I had the wonderful experience to relive it all.

There were so many wonderful people in our life. I apologize to those people who were so kind to us, but who are not mentioned here. This book isn't about including all the wonderful people in our life. Although I know if Barbara wrote this book, there would have been a lot more people mentioned. I set out to write the story of Barbara and me and, of course, our three children: Jonathan, Kristen, and Brian. As I wrote our story and a person would come to mind in a particular storyline, I included that person. I didn't guide the storyline to include certain people. The storyline of our life together guided me.

As I write this prologue, it is almost eight years since I lost Barbara. At this point in time, I'm feeling good having completed the introduction and all forty-six chapters. This prologue is the final piece. I feel a great sense of accomplishment and overall, I have been doing well. People tell me Barbara would be so proud of me. They say I need to find someone, that Barbara wouldn't have wanted me to be alone.

It's been difficult for me. I've not been able to accept being thrown into a pool with middle-aged women. When I looked at Barbara, I saw only the nineteen-year-old bride I married. I have found that couples who are really in love never grow old in each other's eyes.

My love for Barbara grew until I didn't think I could love her more than I already did. It would take forty years, and losing Barbara, to realize how much more I really loved her than I thought. I hope to find that kind of intense love once again and I wonder if that is at all possible.

There is no one on this earth to credit for introducing me to Barbara or for suggesting that we date. I believe we had a marriage arranged in heaven. Meeting Barbara and asking her for our first date was orchestrated by someone above. Since I lost Barbara, people have asked, "Do you believe in God?" My answer has been, "Of course, I believe in God. I have to. How else can I hope to see my wife again?"

Listening to the radio, I hear so many songs that bring me back to memories of Barbara. There is one song that brings me into the future with Barbara. And each time it begins, I stop and pause and listen closely to the lyrics to the song, "See You Again" by Charlie Puth. I think of memories of our early days, when, after work, I would meet Barbara at the Eighty-Second Street/Roosevelt Avenue train station in Jackson Heights, Queens. On those evenings, we would go out for an inexpensive dinner and a dollar movie. Yep, in 1971 there were dollar movies. And we could barely afford that, after the four-dollar dinner for both of us.

"See You Again" makes me long for the day when I'll see Barbara again. There will be so much for me to tell her, and we can reminisce about the long way we've come since those days in Jackson Heights. Also, I'll have a copy of this book with me, and we'll read it together, over and over, until forever.

I hope that anyone who reads this book about our love can become inspired by the beauty and wonder of their own relationship and love. That people will be encouraged to ignite a spark in a relationship that may need to be reawakened or reinvented, or to bring an already great relationship to a higher level. That people will be encouraged, while they can still touch that special person in their life, not to wait or put it off. Because there is only one now and there is so much that can be missed.

I hope you will enjoy reading about our love story. Through laughs and tears, I enjoyed writing about it. Be ready to smile, laugh, and feel our romance, and make sure to have a box of tissues nearby.

PART 1

Stories from the First Day of Shiva

"It's only you who wouldn't be ashamed
to be standing out there in just your underwear.
At least I had a robe on."

INTRODUCTION

The love of my life

*From a husband's view, can a forty-year marriage
still have been magical, romantic, and filled with life,
even with a thirty-year struggle with cancer?*

I arrived at my daughter and son-in-law Kristen and Stephen's home the evening before the funeral, with my sons Jonathan and Brian. The rabbi arrived a few minutes later and we gathered in the living room, sitting around the coffee table. I was reminded of the routine from when I lost my dad, almost seven years before. It didn't feel so long ago, and the feeling of loss was an unwelcome reminder.

The rabbi had a gentle way about him and a consoling smile. With kindness and sincerity, he prepared us for the funeral, talking us through each step of the next day: the chapel, the service, the cemetery, the gravesite, the burial, and the Shiva. He began asking questions about Barbara, and I left it to my children to talk about their mother.

I was overwhelmed and lost. I found it difficult to follow what was happening. I watched as my children spoke about Barbara and the rabbi took notes, but I couldn't follow what they were saying. Their voices were like one big, steady sound, like a continuous buzzing. Disoriented and unable to focus, as I glanced from face to face around the table as each spoke, I thought to myself, "What am I doing here, in Kristen and Stephen's house, on a Wednesday evening, without my wife?" I was there with all my children. Yet, I felt so alone and cold. It was August, but I felt cold, or more like a chill inside me.

There was silence for a few moments, and I noticed the rabbi was looking to me to say something. I didn't know where to begin to talk about Barbara. It had been forty-six years, exactly to the month, since I asked Barbara for our first date. After that date, we had forty-six years of puppy love. I couldn't remember my life before Barbara. My children spoke about the greatness of their mother and the thoughts buzzing through my mind were, "Why can't everyone make it easier on me and look into my face and see the words I want to say? Are you really going to torture me some more?"

Where do I begin? Which stories do I choose to tell, from our life of forty-six years? Barbara was so accomplished, and I was so proud of her. She was a loving person with charm, splendor, grace. She was filled with love and caring for people. Barbara was soft and calming with the strength and courage of a strong leader. I believe I said all of that. Well, I think I said all of that. I'm not sure if the thoughts that were in my brain were the words that came out of my mouth.

What I do remember exactly saying to the rabbi was, "My wife was president of our temple." It was like a big light turned on and the room was instantly brighter. The rabbi smiled and exclaimed, "Your wife was the president of your temple! Tell me more about that."

His response got me to smile and it brought out the silliness in me. "What? Tell you more? You're a congregational rabbi! Do you really think I have more to tell you than you already know about the tribulations and bubbe-meises (a Yiddish word for nonsense or tall tale) that come with being the president of a temple?"

The rabbi smiled. "No, you don't have to say more. I see the pride in your face."

That night, I slept in the lower section of my grandson's trundle bed. Jonah was hyper, he couldn't quiet down and go to sleep. He continually hung over the railing, looking down at me, asking questions about his grandma and where she was.

It was heartwarming and comforting to me to see that Barbara made such a loving impression on this three-and-three-quarter-year-old. But Jonah's questions that evening were killing me. How could I explain to him that memories of his grandma will become the memories that he'll never forget? The hurt inside me grew intense, as he asked, "Grandpa ... are all these people coming to our house because Grandma died?" I didn't know how to answer him, or how much he understood that he would never see his grandmother again. The cuteness of his face was distracting. Yet the thought that Barbara would no longer share in such joy, hurt.

The morning of August 4, 2011, was certainly not magical, romantic, nor filled with life. I awoke to get ready for my wife's funeral very weak, distraught, and upset. One of my kids gave me a sleeping pill the night before. I was overcome from months of stress and years of forced smiles and hope. I didn't trust walking outside the house without someone beside me. I'd spent the previous weeks lifting and helping Barbara. Now, it was difficult for me to help myself. I was concerned about how strong I would be at the chapel and cemetery and asked my children to be nearby as I walked and even to hold my arm.

The day was beyond belief. Over and over in my mind, I had the thought, "Is this funeral really for my wife? How is this possible?" The consolation, that the thirty-year struggle to beat the disease and keep Barbara alive and well was over, wasn't helping me on this day of high anxiety, as I anticipated the funeral. And yet, I thought, what was there to be anxious about? The stress and suffering were over. My worst nightmare had already happened.

Coming slowly down the stairs from Jonah's room, I held on tightly to the banister and noticed my daughter's friends in the living room. They were at the house to watch my grandchildren. Seeing these friends, whom I hadn't seen in quite a while, brought out the emotions and intensity of my grief. It made me aware of how much more difficult it was going to be at the funeral chapel, where I'd see my mom. My mom always said, "Barbara isn't my daughter-in-law, she's my daughter."

A limousine idled out front, waiting to take my family to the funeral chapel. It wasn't real to me, yet it was happening. This day I was attending a funeral for my wife, my dear wife. We arrived early at the funeral chapel and there already were people in the gathering room. As I walked in, the first person I saw was my friend Bruce. I burst out crying. Bruce and his wife Judy were comforting to my family the night that Barbara passed. Bruce knew I needed a hug, and gathered in his arms, I could feel his strength transfer to me. After losing it with the first person I saw, I felt weakened thinking about how I was going to make it through this funeral, and I so wanted to see Barbara one last time.

My mom was already at the funeral chapel. One of my kids had arranged for her to be brought by a handicapped van from her nearby nursing home. The last time I had seen my mom was more than a month before. Barbara and I were visiting her, and Barbara was showing signs of not doing well; her face was drawn, she had lost weight, and she held on to my arm while walking.

As Barbara and I were getting ready to leave the nursing home that day, my mom asked me to take a minute and go back to her room with her to help her with something. My mom and I were barely through the door to her room when she said, "Tell me about Barbara. I want to know!"

"She's on a new treatment and it's making her tired."

"Marc, I know something is wrong! Now tell me."

"There's nothing to tell, Ma. She's fine."

Barbara's prognosis was uncertain, and I couldn't bring myself to start explaining. That visit was the last time I saw or spoke with my mom, until the day of the funeral. I didn't have it in me to visit or talk with her, while Barbara needed all of me. I asked my kids to call and visit with their grandma and prepare her. Now, at the funeral chapel, seeing the pain and suffering in my mom's face was unbearable and it brought me to one of the heights of my grief.

The funeral director approached us and led us into the chapel. The casket was open. It was just me, my kids, and my mom in the room. Barbara wouldn't have wanted everyone staring at her. So, it was just us to say our goodbyes.

I never before would go up to an open casket to view a body. But this was my wife of almost forty years. I kissed her cheek. Her cheek was so cold. My warm, loving wife was gone. My children were busily filling the casket with pictures, but all I could do was stare at my beautiful wife. She looked so much at peace.

For forty years, we would kiss when leaving one another and I would say, "See you later, alligator," and Barbara would answer, "See you in a while, crocodile." As I left the casket, I said, "See you later, alligator." I waited for a response, but this time there wouldn't be one. "See you in a while, crocodile," I said.

As we walked out of the chapel and into the gathering room, I was overwhelmed at seeing the crowd. More than three hundred people attended the funeral service. I went to the nearest seat and people surrounded me in all directions. The funeral director attempted to direct people into the chapel. But most of them wanted to speak with me. It was unbelievable how all these people, from the different times of our lives, were there.

Finally, the only ones left in the gathering room were me and my children. The rabbi recited a prayer and cut a garment that we wore. The tearing of clothes at a funeral is a Jewish tradition of demonstrating grief and anger at the loss of a loved one. After, we followed the rabbi into the chapel. The chapel was full, and the casket was closed. We found our seats in the front row.

The rabbi began the service and called me to the podium to speak. As I stood up from my seat, I felt light-headed. I was concerned I would have difficulty making it to the podium. As I passed Stephen in the row, I asked him to walk with me and stay with me at the podium.

Looking out from the podium, I was startled by the number of people in the chapel. It was one of the larger funeral chapels in New Jersey and all the seats were full and people were standing in the back and along the side aisles. Even with more than three hundred people, the chapel was so quiet. As I settled in at the microphone, all I could hear was the sobbing and sniffling.

As I was getting myself ready to begin to speak, I became rattled by the way people were looking back at me. The expressions on their faces seemed more than expressions of mourning. There were also expressions of shock and surprise, and I began to think that I must look like shit. It was understandable; I had lost over thirty pounds. Also, I felt like shit. Guilt crossed my mind for being so vain at such a moment. After all, I was at the podium, in front of all these mournful-faced people, about to deliver a eulogy for my wife, and I was thinking about the way I looked. But the quick thoughts of my vanity reminded me of Barbara's nickname for me, "silly." I remembered how she would say to me that my silliness was filter-less and could come out at any time, regardless of circumstance and at the strangest of places.

With the casket to my left, I wanted to cry. But with my silliness, a sudden unexpected warming memory of Barbara came over me. It loosened me up a bit, and I could hear Barbara's voice at that moment saying, "Oh, Marc, for God's sakes, you are so silly." But I still needed mental support. I held on to Stephen's hand, took a few deep breaths, and began.

I've heard people, when referring to a spouse that is gone, say that their husband or their wife was the love of their life.

When I was a young boy growing up in Brooklyn, my family would spend our summers near the beach, at the Rockaways in Queens. In the summer of 1957, I met a kid who became my summertime best friend. His name was Marc, also spelled with a 'c.' We were inseparable during the summers. For many of our younger years, our families stayed at the same rooming house on Beach Sixty-Fourth Street. When that rooming house was sold, our families went to different rooming houses. But we'd find each other at the beginning of each summer and say goodbye at the end of the summer, right after Labor Day. We wouldn't see each other again until the end of the school year, the following June. With Marc living in The Bronx and me in Brooklyn, for two kids, we were a world apart.

I went on to speak about my friendship with Marc, which lasted summer after summer. I spoke specifically about the summer of 1964, when Marc and I found we had a new mutual interest: girls! It was that summer when I first met Barbara, on a Saturday night, July Fourth. And Marc played a role in the future for Barbara and me.

Speaking about the teenage years for Barbara and me, the dating and the puppy love, I became less uneasy. I saw smiles, and heard laughs, even in the sullen atmosphere of the funeral chapel and with the casket in full view. I found my words flowed easily for me as I spoke about Barbara, a cute twelve-year-old with a pretty olive complexion, dark hair, and dimples, and me, a skinny fourteen-year-old who looked eleven. Our teenage years were a funny and witty part of the eulogy. Although I may have smiled at times, I spoke with a quiver and a cry in my voice throughout the eulogy.

I spoke about the reasons why I didn't ask Barbara out that summer and even kind of ignored her. Marc was already fifteen and I was four-teen and I didn't want to hang out with any twelve-year-old girl. Marc and I wanted to hang out on the boardwalk and find some fifteen-to-sixteen-year-olds. We were two young teenage boys with huge egos.

I went on to explain that I had no interest in Barbara that summer. And how, perhaps, I only thought I had no interest. Obvi-ously, the relationship eventually changed for Barbara and me and I spoke about our wondrous teenage years and the beginning of our puppy love.

The eulogy continued to have a light wittiness. I was grieving and people in attendance at the funeral were there to join me in my griev-ing and to be consoling. But during this time of sorrow, I wanted this eulogy to be a testament to the way Barbara and I lived our lives and how our thirty-year cancer took only its place, and nothing more than just a place, without challenging to our puppy love. With that mission, I went on to speak about our silliness, like planning for our honeymoon, and said:

It's amazing how much of my shtick Barbara put up with during our marriage and even before. Barbara had been through much difficulty during her teenage years, with her parents' divorce and then her mother's illness. A honeymoon, to get away and get a fresh start to a new life as a wife, was most important. However, Barbara's plans for a honeymoon and mine were quite different.

Many people we knew had been going to exotic-sounding places, at least they seemed exotic in 1971. So, when Barbara asked about what we were doing about a honeymoon, I said I already had a great plan. You see, I had never flown on an airplane and was not planning to do that anytime soon.

"We can go to the Poconos," I said.

Barbara looked at me. "The Poconos!"

"Yes, I did some research and have a brochure from an incredible honeymoon resort close to a nearby lake. Look at the brochure and see that it has round beds, heart-shaped bathtubs for two and mirrors all over the place."

Barbara said, "That doesn't sound so decent, who knows what kind of people go there."

"Look at the brochure," I answered. "The people in the pictures look very nice. We can drive out to Pennsylvania the day after the wedding and it will be great."

That was the first of my many shticks that Barbara would agree to. The second was the cleaning of my car. A week before our wedding, Barbara asked me to get the car cleaned, since we were going to be driving to our "romantic" honeymoon in the Poconos.

"That's a waste," I said. "I never wash or get my car washed. Anyway, it may rain this week and it'll get cleaned."

"Not the inside," Barbara pointed out.

It was actually fun and cathartic to speak about our teenage years and honeymoon. About buying our first home in Flanders, New Jersey and starting a family. Although, I never stopped having a quiver and cry in my voice.

Then I began to speak about Barbara's courageousness. I spoke about her first cancer in 1981, her second in 1984, her third in 1998, and the cry in my voice was an actual cry, as I pushed out these words:

In December 2006, the cancer had metastasized. This time, there wasn't going to be a cure and Barbara would be on some form of chemotherapy for the rest of her life. Most people couldn't notice what Barbara had and was going through. Barbara's hopeful and positive personality kept her looking well and this outlook on life carried her through the thirty years of darkness that hung over her.

I could go on talking about Barbara, describing the kind of person she was and about her strength and wonderful outlook and will to live. But rather than me talking about Barbara, I found a copy of an email that Barbara wrote to some of you in December 2006. Some of you may recall receiving this email and what she wrote is more telling of Barbara, than I can describe. She wrote:

From: Barbara Gellman

To: My Dears

Sent: Tuesday, December 26, 2006

Subject: and so, we begin ...

Hi Everyone:

Well, today was the first treatment and as the saying goes, "Today is the first day of the rest of my life" and may I add ... may it be a long, long one!!!

In the last week, I opened a fortune cookie (those of you, who know me well, know that I have opened some strange ones in the past) that said: "A focused mind is the most powerful force in the universe." Well, is that true or what? I am SOOOOOOO focused right now on defeating Mr. C. As I got this shot this morning, I envisioned it coursing through my body and attacking those nasty little cells!! I am feeling very positive and I want you all to know that. This will be a huge fight against Mr. C., and I WILL be the victor!!!

My family has told me that there are a few words I am not allowed to say. They are the words "I'm sorry" and "thank you." I promised them I would try. However, just one time, guys, please. I am so sorry to have put a damper on anyone's holiday season. I realize I have no control over these things and that it is not my fault. However, just one sorry and no more.

Also, I NEED to say "thank you" to each and every one of you. You are the strength of my being and I love you all and thank you for everything you have already done and what you will be doing in the future. I cannot even begin to express to all of you how much I love you all and how much I appreciate you in my life. You may all think that I am crazy with all this bad news to say this, but I am truly such a lucky woman to have so much love in my life. My family has been amazing, my children have astounded me with their strength and my husband, my rock and my tower of strength, is struggling to smile. But he will always be by my side with his love and his laughter. I have promised him I intend to grow old with him and make fun of him when he is a crazy old man and that is a promise I intend to keep!!

So, the battle begins ... when you see me, no tears nor looks of doom and gloom, only wishes of good things to come. Many of you have asked what you can do and my answer is to keep me in your prayers. I believe in one God and that he hears ALL our prayers. So, let our voices rise, whether they be Jewish, Catholic, Presbyterian, Lutheran, Muslim, Buddhist or any other, just keep on praying. God bless all of you with good health and happiness for many years to come.

I love you all,

Barbara

That email was tough for me to read and not easy for people to listen to. As I looked out into the chapel, I noticed the many tissues in people's hands and heard the sniffling. I wasn't sure if I could go on reading more of Barbara's words. I paused for a few seconds and began to speak about her love for her faith and her leadership in our temple.

Barbara became very active in temple and joined the sisterhood and became sisterhood president. She became a board member and in the mid-1990s, we were all so proud of Barbara when she was installed as the president of the temple. She delivered her installation speech, and talked of issues in our community, our nation, and the world. In the opening part of her speech, Barbara said:

As I stand on the bimah this evening, bursting with pride and overwhelmed with the honor of being installed as president of our temple, I'm reminded of past warm and wonderful occasions for being on this bimah.

I stood on this bimah,

As a young mother ... and felt my mother's presence at the naming ceremonies of my children and in later years at my sons and daughter's Bar and Bat Mitzvah.

As a wife ... I felt love as Marc and I received a special blessing on the occasion of our twentieth wedding anniversary.

As a Bat Mitzvah ... I felt pride, at the age of thirty-six, for being part of the temple's second Adult B'nai Mitzvah class.

As a confirmand ... I felt maturity as I chanted from the Torah as part of the temple's first Adult Confirmation Class.

I stood on this bema,

As a grateful congregant ... and felt compassion and the inability to hold back the tears of joy when I returned to temple and received a special blessing after recovering from a serious illness.

As a participant in many special High Holiday services, I felt faith in our ways.

As Sisterhood President ... I felt close relationships while representing the women of our congregation.

As a presenter to our B'nai Mitzvah students on behalf of the Board of Trustees ... I felt accomplishment in our younger generation.

Reflecting back on those memories, I must smile. I see how much I have grown.

As I went on speaking about Barbara's faith, I mentioned a song that was often sung at our temple. It was by a songwriter and composer, Debbie Friedman. The song was special and meaningful to Barbara. She loved the words and the melody. As I positioned the words to the song in front of me on the podium, I had to pause for a few moments. I hadn't planned ahead of time whether I was going to read the song or sing it. I was used to leading silly sing-a-longs at our house parties. But in the chapel, I was on stage in front of more than three hundred people. I had just finished being barely able to read Barbara's email and speech, and the words to this song are a tearjerker at any time.

The song starts with the words, L'chi lach, "Go for yourself." It is taken from the Torah, Genesis 12 and can also be understood as "Go into yourself," find within yourself the journey you are meant to have. This part of the eulogy was the most difficult for me. When I sat next to Barbara in temple, I listened to her singing it along with the congregation. Now, I wished that I didn't know the English translation, perhaps it would have been easier on me.

At the podium, with the casket to my left, I could hear Barbara's voice saying to me, "Go for yourself," and singing the song to me. I took a deep breath, squeezed Stephen's hand, braced the side of my head with my right hand, and pushed the words out of my mouth, as I sang along.

> L'chi lach to a land that I will show you
> Lech l'cha to a place you do not know
> L'chi lach on your journey I will bless you
> And you shall be a blessing, you shall be a blessing
> You shall be a blessing l'chi lach
> L'chi lach and I shall make your name great
> Lech l'cha and all shall praise your name
> L'chi lach to the place that I will show you
> L'sim-chat cha-yim, l'sim-chat cha-yim
> L'-sim-chat cha-yim l'chi lach.
> And you shall be a blessing, you shall be a blessing
> You shall be a blessing l'chi lach.

I had to stop at this point. I couldn't bear to hear the crying from the people in the chapel and my eyes were too filled with tears. After a few moments, I continued.

Barbara was a thirty-year breast cancer survivor. Throughout that time, I would often think of the next milestone in our lives and hope that Barbara would always be with me. In just a few weeks, Barbara and I would have celebrated our fortieth wedding anniversary and then two weeks later her sixtieth birthday. We didn't make those milestones. I'm so thankful for all the ones that we were together for.

There is something about being married for forty years. We were so young and over the course of forty years, our physical appearances change. Our bodies change, with wrinkles and thinning hair. But even after forty years, when I looked at Barbara, I didn't see the changes. When I looked at Barbara, I only saw the beautiful bride that I married forty years ago.

At this point, my eulogy was over. I had gotten through all that I wanted to say to my family, friends, and neighbors. More than three hundred people had listened to me speak from the podium for over twenty minutes. Now, I wanted to speak directly to my wife. Once again, I brought my hand to the side of my face and my other hand squeezed Stephen's. I closed my eyes and with my eyes closed, I could no longer see the three hundred people in front of me in the chapel. In my mind, it became just Barbara and me.

Oh, Barbara ... when I close my eyes, I can feel the warm Florida sun shining down on the two of us. And we're sitting at our favorite spot, on South Beach along the ocean's edge. And we're sitting on our sand chairs, under umbrellas to protect us from the intense sun. As we look out on the beautiful water, we talk about how blessed we are to have this time. And we tell the same stories each time we're there, stories about Jonathan, Kristen, and Brian. In recent years, you added Stephen and how you liked him from the first time you met him. I always say, of course you liked him right away. That's because he brought you that big bouquet of flowers. He didn't bring anything for me. But Barbara, Stephen is standing beside me right now, and he's holding my hand to give me the strength and courage to deliver these words. We continue to talk about how fortunate and blessed we are for having this special time together. And we're thankful, not just for the minutes or the hours or the days that we have together on that beach. Because we can add up all of the minutes, all of the hours, or all of the days and calculate the measurement of time. More importantly, we are thankful for the love that we have. A love that is not limited by a measurement of time and so, our love will continue on forever. And I know that if I wish with all of my heart, we will be together again someday, sitting beside each other on that beach, for all eternity. You are and always will be the *love of my life*.

Barbara, watch over our children. Bless them with goodness. Bless them with mercy and bless them with peace. Amen.

After the memorial service, my children surrounded and held me, as we walked out of the funeral chapel to the limo. I sat in the front seat, next to the driver, and the kids sat in the seats behind. As I looked out the front window, I stared at the hearse and could see the top of the coffin. I was oblivious to everything going on around me. All I heard was the repetitive thoughts in my mind, "Oh Barbara! Oh Barbara!" It was unbelievable to me that this funeral was for my wife and we were leaving to go to the cemetery. I was numb, frightened, and drained. As soon as the limo started to move, I fell into a deep sleep.

I awoke, hearing my children talking. When I opened my eyes again, I saw the hearse in front, recognized that we were on the Belt Parkway going through Brooklyn, and knew we still had a way to go to get to the cemetery. My thoughts were, I was heading there with my children sitting behind me and my wife in the car in front. I was in no hurry to get to the cemetery, knowing that I'd be leaving the cemetery with my children, and my wife would be left behind. I thought about my dad and wondered if he knew that Barbara would be with him soon, on the family grave site. He loved Barbara and was a real father to her.

As I began to move around in my seat, I heard one of my kids ask, "Is Daddy up?"

"Why, was I sleeping?" I asked.

"Dad, that was the best speech you have ever given," Brian said.

Jonathan chimed in. "Dad, I didn't know about those stories you told."

"Yeah, Dad, we never heard about some of those things," Kristen added.

"Mommy and I would talk about those stories often, when we reminisced. I guess we never had occasion to bring them up to you. We were so young when we met and grew up together. After so many years, there are lots of stories."

Kristen asked, "Weren't you writing a book many years ago? What happened with that? And what was it about?"

"All of you is what happened. I had the three of you, my work, and everything else. The book needed a lot of effort and I didn't have the time. It was going to be a book about my experiences growing up in Brooklyn. I started piecing together notes and ideas but couldn't find the time to do more. So, I dropped it. I don't know what became of my notes."

Kristen answered, "Well, Dad, I want you to write about all those stories. We want to know more about you and Mommy."

"Kristen, let's just get to the cemetery for now. I can't focus on anything else."

"Dad, I'm serious. I want you to write it all down."

Kristen was persistent and I finally answered, "I'll tell you what, Kristen. After the service in your house each evening, for each of the seven days of Shiva, I'll tell stories about Mommy and me that I think all of you haven't heard. Then, you can write them down. For now, let's just get to the cemetery."

At the cemetery, the limo driver drove toward the grave site and stopped, as the hearse drove farther. I saw the rabbi directing the cemetery workers as the coffin was taken from the hearse to the grave site and lowered into the grave.

We gathered at the grave site and the rabbi began with prayers. Then, the rabbi directed us to begin shoveling the soil to fill the grave. I was the first to step up to begin the shoveling. I looked into the grave and stared at the coffin for a few seconds. I did the first shovel.

Once the grave was filled, the rabbi directed relatives and friends to form two lines, so that the mourners could do the traditional walking away from the grave site, between the two lines. As people formed the two lines, I whispered to my children, "Come with me."

We walked closer to the grave. "Let's form a circle," I said. "We all know that Mommy was the peacemaker in our family. She was the one who kept our family close and together. Now, we're on our own and it's up to us to keep us together. Let's do a group hug."

We hugged and kissed and walked through the two lines, leaving the grave site.

We got back into the limo and headed to Kristen and Stephen's home for the first day of Shiva.

Brian asked, "Are you okay, Dad?'

"I'm okay," I answered.

After that, there wasn't much talking in the limo. It was over. Barbara was gone.

The house was crowded as many people came back after the cemetery. Others who had been at the funeral chapel were there too. The rabbi led the Shiva service. My children and I followed the rabbi in reciting the mourner's prayer. I had recited this prayer seven years before, for my dad, and that was difficult. But reciting the prayer for my wife, as my children recited the prayer for their mother, ripped my heart out.

At the end of the service, I gestured to the rabbi that I wanted to say a few things, as I had promised my children I would do. With my family and guests still gathered together from the service, I stood before them and spoke about Barbara and me. Some of the stories were funny and people did laugh, even though my voice cracked and I couldn't hold back my emotions.

There are some traditions for a Shiva house. One is to cover the mirrors to encourage introspective reflection and discourage vanity. Also, mourners sit low to the ground, either on special low-seated benches or on cushions, as a sign of being grief-stricken. I did neither. Not only did I not have the mirrors covered, but also I didn't avoid looking into them. But not for reasons of vanity. I tried to see Barbara in my eyes. I gazed into the mirrors looking for Barbara in my reflection, thinking, "Where are you, Barbara? Are you really gone?" No matter how long I stared into a mirror, I couldn't see her. She was gone. I could feel her in my heart. But in my reflection, I couldn't see her in my Shiva Eyes. As for sitting low to the ground to show being grief-stricken, I didn't feel the need to do that to show my grief.

In another tradition, the front door to the house was kept unlocked from the early morning into the late evening. Relatives and friends were able to come and go freely, without my family being disturbed by needing to answer a ringing doorbell. Throughout the days of Shiva, there was bountiful food on the dining and kitchen tables. Visitors brought food with them or had it delivered, provisions for my family and for many visitors who stayed for long periods of the day.

During the first few days of the Shiva, the house was often full, standing room only, between the living room, dining room, and kitchen. I spent most of my time seated on the living room couch. People would come up to me, sit beside me or near to me. I don't know what my family was doing or who they were speaking to for much of the time. The Shiva was kind of a blur. It was like a strange, disorienting event was going on around me, for all these people to be here. But why are they here? I was confused, thinking, "Why am I here with all these people, without Barbara?"

It was comforting to be with people. And it wasn't. I was continually being reminded that I was alone. Conversations kept my attention some of the time. But my mind wandered and I'd quickly go back to thinking, "Where are you, Barbara? I'm here alone with these people. And, as only you would know, I don't like some of these people." Then I'd smile; I could hear Barbara saying, "You are so silly."

In the early evening for each day of the Shiva, there was a service led by the rabbi or another official from the temple. My family and guests would gather in the living and dining room and stand for the service. After the service, everyone remained standing to listen to my stories. I told stories for each of the seven days of Shiva.

This book is a story about a "once upon a time," written while looking through Shiva Eyes. It's a once upon a time when a boy from Brooklyn meets a girl from The Bronx. They fall in love and live happily ever after.

CHAPTER 1

Girls and the Rockaways

I think I was always attracted to girls. Maybe even as far back as when I was in diapers. As a young kid, I'm not sure if it was actual attraction or curiosity. Girls were confusing to me back then. I couldn't figure them out. I'm finding that such confusion is not age restricted. Nowadays, I seem to be having the same problem.

Anyway, I remember, as a kid, wondering how a girl could find playing with dolls and baby carriages fun. With all the fun things that kids could pretend to be, why pretend to be a parent? All parents do is take care of kids, with meals and bathing, and on and on. Who would want to pretend to do all that? The answer seemed to be, it was girls who wanted to do all that.

Boys had cars and trucks and wore pants and could sit on the sidewalk and play with bottle caps. Girls wore dresses. That was another thing I couldn't figure out. Dresses never seemed practical. Also, for boys, our playtime was never interrupted by the need to pee. We would just go over to a bush and pee on it. This is also something I've always wondered about. Why do guys feel the need to pee on something? Girls had to go back inside to pee in private. As a kid, I

21

used to think, "It can't be fun being a girl." And yet, girls seemed to be content playing with dolls, pretending to be mommies, wearing dresses, and having to go back inside to pee.

As a young kid, I was surely happy to be a boy. Thinking back, I don't know why I was so preoccupied with the being-a-girl versus being-a-boy thing. But I was. Because for some reason, I was attracted to girls. I could be playing a game on the sidewalk with my friends, pitching bottle caps or playing stoopball, and be totally engrossed in the game. But when a cute girl with dark brown hair, dark brown eyes, and an olive complexion walked by, I would instantly forget about the game and stare at her. Especially if I was sitting on the sidewalk and the girl was wearing a dress. For some reason, the sight of her legs would get my attention. I didn't know why. But girls were cute, soft, and clean all the time. I couldn't ignore it, there was something I liked about them. I just didn't know what it was.

My playmates were boys. It wasn't until kindergarten that I began to have some interaction with girls. At that point, not only was I confused about girls, but also, I began to dislike them. There were these smarty-pants, or I should say smarty-dress, girls in my class. They were always so well-behaved and our teacher's favorites.

By first grade, I was getting used to interacting with girls. For the first time I began, I think, to like them. There was a particular girl with brown hair and brown eyes who was really cute. Her name was Barbara Kone. I liked her. There was something about her name too. Years later, I realized I always liked Barbaras. There have been many women I've met in my lifetime whom I couldn't stand. But I've never met a Barbara I didn't like.

Barbara Kone lived in a city housing project in Brooklyn called the Pink Houses, a few blocks away from my house. We were kind of boyfriend and girlfriend. I say kind of, because neither of us knew what that meant. At least, I didn't. But I was attracted to her for reasons, well, I didn't know. For our parents, it was a perfect match; we were both Jewish. Isn't that all that matters, according to our mothers?

My attraction to Barbara Kone lasted through the third grade at

PS 64. By the end of that school year, I felt that the whole boyfriend-girlfriend thing was annoying and leading to nowhere. Where was it supposed to lead? I didn't know. Barbara Kone and I continued to be in the same classes through Berriman Junior High School and through our sophomore year at Franklin K. Lane High School. After that, I transferred to Samuel J. Tilden High School and never saw her again.

While this boyfriend-girlfriend thing was going on with Barbara Kone, my future wife, Barbara, lived about twenty-three miles away. I guess it was kismet that my wife would be a girl with dark brown hair and dark brown eyes whose name was also Barbara, with the middle initial "K." That had to mean something. I'm just not sure what.

With twenty-three miles between us, the neighborhoods Barbara and I grew up in were much the same economically, and both were predominantly Jewish. Although Jews in The Bronx, especially those who lived on or near the Grand Concourse, thought themselves to be of a higher class than the Jews in Brooklyn. The Grand Concourse was perceived as an extension of Manhattan and was referred to as the "Park Avenue of The Bronx." And it was easy to be snobby, living on a street that started with the name "Grand."

I was born at Unity Hospital on St John's Place in Brooklyn and grew up on Atkins Avenue, between Sutter and Blake Avenues, in the East New York section of Brooklyn. There was so much on that one block: a ma-and-pa grocery store and a beauty parlor on the two northern corners, and a funeral parlor and dry-cleaning store on the two southern corners. Almost exactly in the middle of the block was  a large shul, the East New York Jewish Center. It was a close-knit neighborhood of Polish Jews and the homes, mostly two-family and four-family dwellings, often housed three generations of one family. It was a great neighborhood for a kid. Most of my friends lived on the block and the public school (PS 64) and junior high school (Berriman Junior High School 64) were just one and a half blocks away.

Barbara was born at Royal Hospital on the Grand Concourse in The Bronx and she lived on the Grand Concourse until her family moved to Jackson Heights, Queens, when she was eight. Barbara had fond memories of her early childhood in The Bronx and often spoke about her grandfather, Papa Joe, who often took her to baseball games at Yankee Stadium. In contrast to the smaller residential dwellings where I grew up, the Grand Concourse neighborhood was more densely populated with mostly four-story and six-story apartment buildings. It was a close-knit neighborhood of Russian Jews and often three generations of a family lived within a couple of blocks of one another.

I was two years old and still in diapers when Barbara was born. When I look at her baby pictures today, I see the essence of cuteness. To me, Barbara never outgrew that cuteness, and it is her cuteness that I remember most about my first impression of Barbara, on the day I met her. But how would we meet? Barbara was a Bronx girl and Brooklyn, where I grew up, was like a world apart from The Bronx in the 1950s.

I didn't have any relatives living in The Bronx. Back then, Brooklyn families had mostly all of their close relatives living in Brooklyn and it was the same for families in The Bronx. It was a tedious car ride or long mass-transit ride, through Manhattan or Queens, to travel from Brooklyn to The Bronx. Other than to visit relatives, there was little reason to travel between those two boroughs.

From 1955 to 1965, my family spent our summers near the beach, at the Rockaways in Queens. It was a beach community, a mix of bungalows and three-story rooming houses. Many Brooklyn people who left the city during the summers went to bungalow colonies in the Catskills. Those dads would stay in Brooklyn during the work-week and be with their families in the country on weekends and during vacation time. My dad preferred being with us each evening and took the long subway ride each workday from Manhattan out to the Rockaways.

My parents would rent one or two rooms in a rooming house, about a half-block from the boardwalk and beach. The norm in the Rockaways was to rent a place for the entire summer. We would begin bringing our summer stuff to the rooming house and start sleeping there over the Memorial Day weekend. From the first Saturday after my brother and I finished our last day of school at the end of June, until a couple of days after Labor Day, we would be in the Rockaways.

The summer of 1955 was our first summer in the Rockaways. We stayed at a rooming house on Beach Sixty-Sixth Street. Starting in the summer of 1956 and for several summers thereafter, we stayed at The Surfcomber on Beach Sixty-Fourth Street. It was a half-block from the boardwalk and beach, in the Arverne section of the Rockaways. Most of the rooming houses and bungalows were owned and self-operated by Jewish families as investments, aside from their full-time professions. The Surfcomber was owned by Ruth and Charlie Charkin. They lived in nearby Far Rockaway during the winter months and stayed at The Surfcomber during the summer.

Charlie was a full-time realtor in the Rockaways and Ruth took care of the day-to-day operation of The Surfcomber. The accommodations were mostly single rooms, some two rooms and a few three rooms, all with kitchenettes. Some rooms had private or semi-private bathrooms. The bathroom accommodations for most rooms were common bathrooms in the hallways, some with bathtubs. There were also outdoor, wood-enclosed showers in the rear yard of the building, which practically everyone used. It was a little inconvenient, but this was the 1950s and it was perfectly acceptable and a good way to avoid tracking sand back to the rooms after the beach.

The Surfcomber had a large lobby and front porch, where mah-jongg and poker games went on late into the evenings. My mom had her mah-jongg game and my dad his poker. My dad disliked the beach. So, during the day on weekends, he had a part-time job at a bar/hot dog/burger/knish restaurant, at Beach Sixty-Eight Street on the boardwalk. The owner, Mr. Gross, would telephone my dad each year before the season started to confirm that my dad would be available for the weekends. My dad, a former cook in the army when he was stationed in the Philippines, enjoyed working at the restaurant. It was hard work standing over the hot grills. But my dad liked the continuous interaction with the public, speaking Yiddish and kibitzing, or joking, with each customer.

In the evenings, when my parents were busy with mah-jongg and poker, they put me to bed. I stayed alone in the room. My brother was five years older and he came back to the room a little later. Alone, I would go out to the hallway and hang out with the other kids, who were also supposed to be sleeping. It was a different world in the 1950s. There were no baby cams or monitors to watch how we were doing. But there were no worries either. If a kid had a problem, he just needed to scream and to be heard down to the lobby. These rooming houses were walk-ups with open stairways and no elevators.

One evening, as I walked around in the room when I should have been in bed, I heard a voice from outside the window, shouting, "Hi!" There was no air conditioning. The windows were always open and covered by screens. I went over to the window and looked around at the darkness outside to see who was continuously shouting "Hi." After a few minutes, I spotted a kid standing at a window in the next rooming house. I realized he was calling to me. The Harmony House was next door to The Surfcomber, separated by a side yard with a fence and hedges.

"Hi!" I shouted back.

The kid answered, "Are you alone?"

"Yes, my parents are downstairs. I'm supposed to be sleeping."

"I'm supposed to be sleeping too. I'm seven. How old are you?"

"I'm six. I'm going to be seven at the end of next month."

"What's your name?"

"Marc," I replied.

"My name is Marc, too! How do you spell it?"

"M-A-R-C," I answered.

"Really, that's how I spell it too. Are you French?"

"No. I'm Jewish."

"I'm Jewish too," he said.

I spoke with Marc many evenings that summer. But we never met face-to-face. We became friends, who only recognized each other's voices. We had no clear image of what the other looked like. That kid, whose name was Marc with a "c" like me, who called out to me one evening during the summer of 1956, became my friend from speaking across the dark yard, through a window screen. Eight years later, it would be that kid who introduced me to the girl who many years later would become my wife.

My childhood summers in the Rockaways were the best. I had lots of friends at The Surfcomber, all of whom were from The Bronx. It seemed like most summertime families in the Rockaways were from The Bronx. The beautiful part was that the same families returned year after year and formed long-term summer relationships.

I got to meet Marc, the kid from the Harmony House, face-to-face in the summer of 1957, when his parents decided to rent a room at The Surfcomber. Marc and I quickly became inseparable and made the neighborhood our playground. Even at a young age, our playground, unsupervised by adults, extended far beyond The Surfcomber. We combed the neighborhood, went to the shopping avenue, visited the marina on the bay side, and roamed the boardwalk. As young as we were, it was the 1950s. Everywhere seemed safe, and the summer was continuous play and fun.

Barbara's family spent their summers at a rooming house on Beach Thirty-Fifth Street, in the Edgemere section of the Rockaways. My friends and I often walked the thirty blocks on the boardwalk down to Edgemere. Edgemere had many more attractions at the boardwalk with more food concessions, games, and activities like miniature golf. Plus, my friends and I had fun being mischievous away from our neighborhood, where we could avoid getting caught by someone who knew us.

We did so many mischievous things. On the boardwalk, we took turns pranking elderly women by trying to convince them that they knew us. When it was my turn, I would walk up to a woman, walking by herself or with her friends, and greet her with a big hello. Of course, the woman wouldn't recognize me and would stare at me, wondering who I could be. I would blurt out several names until she acknowledged her name. It wasn't that difficult to eventually guess the right name, since these women were almost always Jewish immigrants from Poland or Russia and there were so many with the names Sadie, Becky, Sophie, Fanny, or Sarah. I would quickly toss out names until I landed on the right one.

Or sometimes after I said hello, I would say, "I can't remember your name," and the woman would volunteer it. Then, I would say, "Yes. I remember you. I used to deliver newspapers to your husband."

The woman might answer, "Oh ... I lost my husband."

I would give my condolences and have a whole conversation. My friends and I took turns randomly approaching different women. The challenge of the game was to get the most women to believe they knew you.

We were bad. What we did was dishonest and mean. On the other hand, we made these elderly women, who were often widowed, happy that some young kid recognized them. Nevertheless, we were still bad, and we knew it. After each woman, we would celebrate for having fooled them. Feeling some amount of guilt didn't stop us from continuing to play the game.

It wasn't until the summer I was eight years old that I got some experience with girls. It happened in the outdoor enclosed showers in the yard of The Surfcomber. My friends and I convinced some girls to go with us to the yard, just around dusk. There was a row of showers and each of us asked a girl to go into a shower, where we closed the door. The showers were dry inside by this time. So, we didn't get wet or dirty. When we got into the shower and closed the door behind us, we just stood there in total silence. Because we had no idea what to do.

I'm not sure how the girl who accompanied me felt, but I was kind of scared. It was totally quiet, and I couldn't hear my friends in the other showers. I felt awkward, embarrassed, uncomfortable. Eventually, I built up some courage to give the girl a quick peck on the cheek and we timidly stepped out of the shower. I was relieved that the experience was over and wished I had never put myself through the torture. I never told my friends what I did, which was nothing, and they never told me what they did either. I suspect that none of us did anything but to stand there nervous, a little scared, wondering what to do with a girl when you are alone with her in an outdoor shower.

On the block with The Surfcomber and the other summer rentals, there were some city-owned housing units, with year-round apartments. Several months before the 1961 summer season, the Housing Authority placed families receiving public assistance into those apartments and ceased proper maintenance of the properties. It wasn't long before the housing became an eyesore, with garbage, debris, and old furniture on the patios. This prompted Ruth and Charlie Charkin to sell The Surfcomber. Most families decided not to return that season. My friend Marc's family and several other families decided to rent at the Breakers Hotel and adjacent Strand Hotel, located near Beach Thirty-First Street, in Edgemere.

I remember going with my parents to The Surfcomber before the summer season, to decide what to do, since friends had decided not to return for the coming summer. The new owner had renovated The Surfcomber in order to better market it. My parents were considering renting there again, since the price for the season was significantly reduced. But they decided that without the Charkins and our friends, the way The Surfcomber used to be was over and fond memories were all that was left.

I tried to convince my parents to consider the Breakers, where Marc and my other friends were going to be. But my parents decided to rent in a rooming house on Beach Sixty-Sixth Street, owned by the Pravda family. My parents knew the Pravdas and my mother's sister, Letty, was renting at the Pine House, directly across the street. It was fun seeing my aunt often that summer and I made new friends. But I missed Marc and my other friends from The Surfcomber. Although Marc and I did visit each other a few of times that summer, it wasn't the same as being together all the time.

While our summers in the Rockaways continued to be fun, our Brooklyn neighborhood, which had begun a decline in the late 1950s, was perceived to being increasingly unsafe. There were gradual changes in the neighborhood demographics, and much gossip about the perceived unscrupulous lifestyles of the new residents. Our neighbors began moving to other Brooklyn neighborhoods and to Queens and Long Island. By 1964, many of our neighbors who hadn't planned on moving decided staying in the neighborhood was no longer an option. My parents decided we wouldn't be going to the Rockaways for the summer of 1964. Instead, they began making plans for us to move the following year, after the end of the next school year, in 1965.

In 1964, July 4 was on a Saturday. The Fourth of July weekend was always so much fun in the Rockaways. Many of the bungalows with courtyards and the rooming houses had lively parties. Some of the rooming houses even had live bands performing on the porches. The streets were congested with people and traffic, and concessions along the boardwalk were packed with people. I was missing being in the Rockaways that summer, especially as that weekend approached. The morning of July 4, my parents decided that we'd take a drive to Rockaway and spend the evening there. They would stop by to see their friends and I could hang out with Marc.

Although Edgemere was pandemonium that evening, my dad luckily found a parking space pretty quickly and we agreed that I'd meet them back at the car at eleven o'clock. If they needed me earlier, they knew I'd be with Marc at the Breakers. There were no cell phones in 1964. So, being separated could be a problem.

I walked to the Breakers and spotted Marc hanging out with

friends in the front patio. He wasn't expecting me and was surprised. We hadn't seen or spoken to each other for almost a year, since the end of the summer before. But we picked up where we left off, just one year older. We quickly began talking about girls. It was obvious to both of us that the only change in us was that we both had girls on our minds. Unlike my younger years, I now understood my attraction to girls.

Marc said, "There are a lot of cute girls here this summer." Then he said, "Oh, there's one over there. Come on, I'll introduce you to her." We walked over and Marc introduced me to Barbara. She was so, so cute. Barbara had dark brown hair and eyes, and her olive complexion was already tanned, even though it was early in the summer. She was dressed up in a flower-patterned dress for the Saturday night, July 4 festivities. She was thin and tall, about my height. Also, Barbara had these cute dimples. But she seemed too young for us.

We talked for a while before I said to Marc, "Let's go."

"Okay, let's go." Marc turned to Barbara and said, "See you later."

As we walked away, Marc asked, "What's the matter? Didn't you like her? She's very pretty."

I answered, "Marc, how old is that girl?"

"She's twelve. Probably going to be thirteen soon."

"She's twelve! Marc, I don't want to hang out with a twelve-year-old girl. Let's go up to the boardwalk and find older girls."

Marc and I were typical teenage boys, empowered by our own egos. Marc was already fifteen and I was fourteen. We were confident about getting lucky and spent a couple of hours roaming the boardwalk, saying hi to girls. But the girls we approached ignored us. They were busily cruising the boardwalk looking for high school seniors.

Eventually, we gave up and walked back to the party at the Breakers. We were convinced it was a bad night. It was the Fourth of July and girls were busy. We convinced ourselves the girls we approached on the boardwalk that evening all sucked anyway. There was no way that I was about to admit I was just a skinny kid with curly hair, who looked younger than fourteen. I was at the early stage of developing my masculinity and believed I was a teenage God's gift to girls.

I had fun that evening hanging out with Marc. At about ten thirty I was sorrowfully getting ready to say goodbye, when I saw my parents hurrying toward us. I wasn't ready to leave.

"I thought I was meeting you at the car at eleven o'clock?" I said with disappointment.

"We have to hurry and get back home to pack," my mother said. "We saw a summer rental sign on a small building and decided to take it. We're moving in tomorrow."

"Where is it?" I asked.

"Right over there," my dad answered, pointing to a small rooming house almost directly across the street from the Breakers.

I turned to Marc with a big smile. He smiled back.

"Hey, I'll see you tomorrow," I said.

It was always difficult to find rentals after the season began, especially ones near the boardwalk and beach. I was so excited. The rental was three rooms and was practically across the street from Marc's rooming house. Someone had backed out of this rental at the last minute and the owner was trying to rent it quickly. My parents had been walking around the area with friends and noticed the For-Rent sign. They got caught up in the excitement of the evening and the bargain rental was too compelling to pass up.

By the next afternoon, I was back to hanging out with Marc and looking forward to the rest of the summer in the Rockaways. That evening, I went with Marc to Beach Twenty-Ninth Street, where many of the kids that Marc knew hung out. There was this girl, Sharon, who lived there, and kids would congregate around the front of her bungalow. Her parents were great and seemed to like that their bungalow was the hangout spot. Some of the boys felt that Sharon's parents liked the hangout at their bungalow because their daughter was really hot-looking. I mean really hot-looking. She wore these scant bikinis. We believed her parents must have wanted to keep an eye on her and everyone she hung out with.

Marc introduced me to everyone. While I was following him around the crowd, I noticed a girl looking in my direction as she talked to another girl. The other girl was glancing at me too.

I turned to Marc. "Don't make this look obvious. But I think a girl over there is talking to her friend about me."

"Oh, that's Shelley. Barry likes her. They hung out together for a couple of days and then she dumped him. Oh wait—don't turn around. She's coming over."

"Oh, shit!"

I was often nervous and a little shy when beginning to speak with a girl who was super cute. And, from a distance, Shelley looked super cute. She came over to us.

"Hi, Marc."

Marc answered, "Hi, Shelley. This is my friend, Marc. We've been friends for many summers."

Shelley turned to me. "Hi, nice to meet you."

Once Shelley and I started a conversation, Marc drifted away from us. Up close, Shelley was very pretty and super cute. She was thin with light brown, almost blonde hair and a bob-style haircut with bangs. She had a super cute round face with these compelling-to-pinch cheeks.

Shelley and I found we had something in common. Unlike most of the other kids, we weren't from The Bronx. Shelley was from Sunnyside, Queens. We talked and became more comfortable with each other and a little silly. Shelley told me her front tooth was a cap and she could pop the cap off. I dared her to pop it off ... and she did. I have no idea why she did that, but it did get us laughing. Even with her cap tooth off, she was still so cute.

Over the next few days, Shelley and I hung out a lot: at the beach, on the boardwalk, and at Sharon's bungalow. One evening, while walking on the boardwalk, I said, "Let's walk the beach." The beach was dark, with only some spill-off lighting from the boardwalk. As we walked along the water's edge, we came across a lifeguard stand that hadn't been pulled back closer to the boardwalk for the evening. "Let's sit on the lifeguard stand," Shelley suggested.

To me, it sounded like a fun thing to do. Although it wasn't obvious to me where this could lead. We were two young teenagers about to be sitting in the dark on a stand built for two. It was as if this lifeguard stand were intentionally set up to offer opportunity for two young lovers to happen by. Shelley and I would be those two young lovers.

Shelley was so cute, and I was so attracted to her and horny as hell. But I was naïve and oblivious to this perfect setup. The thought didn't come to me that I was about to get a girl with me in a very romantic position. Instead, I was thinking about how great it was going to be watching the ocean waves from atop the stand.

So, Shelley and I climbed up. It was a pretty sight watching the waves, while sitting high on the stand. Also, the ocean breeze was brisk and felt good, and in the darkness, we felt secluded near the water's edge. It was fun looking around and as I turned and looked at Shelley, I realized she was looking directly at me and not at the ocean. At first, I tried to ignore what I thought she wanted to do and turned away to look at the ocean. As I felt Shelley moving closer to me, I turned to her. She moved her face inches from mine, and she closed her eyes.

"Holy shit!" I thought to myself. She wants me to kiss her. Maybe this wasn't such a good idea to be secluded in the darkness, on top of this lifeguard stand. But Shelley was so cute, and I was really very horny. I so wanted to jump her bones but didn't know how to start or what to do.

I hadn't ever really kissed a girl and I didn't know if she just wanted a kiss, or she wanted more. I knew I could handle a kiss, but really making out could be a challenge. I felt so inexperienced. After all, this wasn't the outdoor showers at The Surfcomber anymore. I was now fourteen and with a girl, in the dark, on top of a lifeguard stand. It was time for me to know what to do. I wanted to rip off her clothes or just have exploratory roaming hands. The attraction was there, but not the confidence or the know-how. I was confused, wondering how to make a move and how far she wanted me to go.

Shelley was getting closer. I knew I had to do something. As she closed her eyes, I knew I had to make the move and kiss her. Her lips got closer to mine and I kissed her. My eyes were open for the entire kiss. I didn't want to just imagine kissing Shelley. I was captured by the moment and seeing her cuteness was such a turn-on. I kissed her again ... and again ... and again.

This was a first time for me. But there was no doubt, it wasn't the first time for Shelley. She wanted to make out and she confidently took the lead and moved into position. Her lips were very soft, and I could feel the passion in her kiss. I was nervous and don't know how I did, but Shelley was experienced and knew how to kiss. So, I followed her lead. I kissed her with the same softness and came up for air when she did.

That evening, Shelley and I moved to a new level in our relationship. After we were finished on the lifeguard stand, I walked her back to her bungalow. I would have kissed her goodnight, but her mom was on the front porch. Walking home that evening, I felt completely different about myself. It was as if I had just grown up. My feelings for Shelley were completely different too. I was in love with her. A feeling came over me I'd never had before. I knew it was love. I had just dropped Shelley off at her bungalow and I missed her already. I couldn't wait to see her again the next day.

A few evenings later, Shelley and I were hanging out again at Sharon's bungalow. Shelley walked away to speak with her friend. In the meantime, a girl named Marsha came up to me. Marsha knew about me and Shelley. But that didn't stop her from greeting me with a big hug. She had her hands all over me, rubbing my shoulder and back and down to my butt. I didn't make anything of it and didn't push her away, either. Shelley saw this going on and that was the end of me and Shelley.

I was heartbroken. I could barely eat or sleep. For the next few days, all I could think about was Shelley. I was truly in love with her, but it was over. I was so angry with myself for being so stupid. In the meantime, knowing Shelley was out of the picture, Marsha made her move on me. Unlike Shelley, Marsha was loose as a goose and even more experienced. With Marsha, my making-out skills improved.

After Marsha, I hung out with one or two more girls that summer. It was an incredible summer. Marc and I were old enough to learn to have fun with girls and young enough to have no cares, with all day and evening to play and no responsibilities weighing us down.

After Labor Day, I said my goodbyes to Marc and my other friends. The street was quiet as I stood on the porch of my building for the last night. So many people had already left, and the area was beginning to feel desolate. There was an end-of-summer chill in the air. I so disliked the feeling at the end of each summer. This year it seemed worse, because it was the most active, fun-filled summer I'd ever had.

As I moped around on the porch, feeling lonely, I saw Barbara and her friend walking past the building, heading to the boardwalk. I had seen Barbara often over that summer when I hung out with Marc at the Breakers. But she didn't hang out on Twenty-Ninth Street or with any of my friends and I had little interaction with her.

I thought about the other girls I had been with. After an entire summer, it was only at that very moment that I wished I had spent more time with Barbara. The other girls were fun, and I was in love with Shelley. But Barbara seemed different from the others. For some reason, each time I saw Barbara, I felt a connection to her, even though we spent so little time together.

That evening, feeling so alone on the porch, I so wished I had gotten to know Barbara. She was so sweet, always with a happy smile. But it was too late. I was leaving the next day. At that moment, I truly believed that even if I hadn't seen Barbara that evening, I would always remember her, when thinking back about my fun-filled summer of 1964 in the Rockaways. She was the cute girl with dark brown hair, dark brown eyes, and olive complexion, the girl I should have gotten to know.

The summer was over and by tomorrow night I'd be alone back in Brooklyn, with just memories of the summer, but no girlfriend or any relationships to continue. I watched Barbara walking toward the boardwalk and reflected on my regrets. I felt an emptiness, like I'd missed out on something. Any opportunity that I might have had with a really nice girl was gone. And I'd never see her again.

CHAPTER 2

Pookie ... ask Barbara

I felt I had matured over the summer of 1964, and my experiences gave me a new outlook. I wanted to have more fun and decided it was time for me to kick-start being a teenager. I started the school year off with a different frame of mind in than years past. I was still a serious student, but my intent for my sophomore year was to really have fun. I had enjoyed the extracurricular activities of school, being in the band and tutoring in math. But I wanted more.

Almost thirty years after my own high school years, two of my kids, Jonathan and Kristen, were in high school. When I showed them my high school yearbook, their reaction was, "Dad, you were in the band ... and you were a math tutor! Please don't mention this to our friends." I may not have been so cool in high school. But I didn't imagine that my activities would someday be an embarrassment to my children. I can't imagine how embarrassed they're going to be when they read the private parts in this book.

As a rising sophomore, I was feeling that my early teenage experiences had been kind of nerdy. I decided I would break away from my past routines and focus on more adventurous opportunities for fun.

Although, I didn't give up the band or the tutoring. Until then the biggest trouble I ever got into in school was being reprimanded for laughing when someone fell or got hurt. Plus, a discussion on current events in class, about some hardship in the world, would crack me up. I often couldn't hold back my laughter, and it got me sent to the assistant principal's office.

At the assistant principal's office, I would be asked how I could find people's outrageous misfortune to be so funny to cause me to laugh uncontrollably out loud. And, my answer was, "I don't know why I find those kinds of things funny. I just do." That answer would get me the strangest and most questionable look. It seemed they didn't know how to respond, other than with a lecture. I never understood what the lecture was about. It never had anything do with my laughing reflex. But I would listen attentively and try my best to hold in my laugh. Since most often the lecture was funnier to me than the original thing I'd been laughing about.

As a teenager, I found the humor in most things. It didn't take much to set me off laughing. While others would listen about an unfortunate situation and feel the hurt, I would feel the hurt, too, but also visualize in my mind the funny side of it. Otherwise, I was a good student and always followed the rules set by my parents. Basically, I was a nice Jewish boy, growing up in Brooklyn. I decided if I was really going to have fun, it was time to push the envelope and break the rules a little bit. Or maybe more than a little bit.

Being more social at school and after school became the norm for me. I joined the Y (Young Men's and Young Woman's Hebrew Association). This was a new adventure for me. After school, I had always hung out with friends close to home. Now, I was hanging out at the Y, which was about two miles away, in the Brownsville section of Brooklyn. This made studying and homework fun. Rather than doing homework at home, I went to the Y each day where I could get my work done and fool around a bit.

The social experience at the Y was new to me, especially the Saturday night dances. The entertainment was often a live band, usually made up of guys in their early twenties, who hadn't yet outgrown being teenagers. Slow dancing, holding a girl close, was all new to me. I spent much of my time spent at the Y dances outside of the building, making out with any girl who I met that night.

I was a late bloomer, and I was making up for lost time. Getting home when my parents expected me was over. I quickly realized I could get away with it. My brother, five years older, was punished when he broke the rules. Years later, when I began pulling the same things, rather than punishing me, my parents eased up on their rules. There's some benefit in being the younger sibling. I was experiencing a whole new world. At the age of fifteen, I felt like I had finally become a teenager. I attributed the change in me to the summer of 1964. My lost love Shelley, my loose girlfriend Marsha, and the Rockaways gave me a new perspective and a fun school year 1964-65.

In the meantime, my parents were busy planning our move for the end of the school year. In June 1965, we moved to Snyder Avenue and East Forty-Eighth Street, in the East Flatbush section of Brooklyn. Our apartment was one block from the busy retail street, Church Avenue. The day we moved in I began exploring the neighborhood. There were so many retail, commercial, and other facilities in the neighborhood, which I wasn't used to having within walking distance.

I came across a Big Apple Supermarket one block from the apartment. I went into the store, scoped it out, and decided it would be the place for me to work after school. Since girls were a new interest of mine, I needed pocket money. I went to the manager's office and introduced myself.

"Hi, my name is Marc Gellman. I just moved to this neighborhood today. I live right around the corner. What do I need to do to get a job here?"

The manager, Abe Ambler, was stout, bald, and intimidating, with a scowling look on his face. It matched his rough personality. Abe looked me up and down, sneered at me, growled a bit, and firmly said, "First you need to get your working papers and to do that you need to be sixteen. How old are you, what grade are you in, and which school do you go to?"

"I'll be sixteen in August and I'll be a junior at Tilden in September."

"Well, don't bother me now," he grumbled. "Come back in August, if you're really going to be sixteen by then."

I thought to myself, "Wow! This is great." My happy ears went up. I was really going to get a job. I asked, "So, there's a possibility that I can get a job here?"

Abe's voice rose with impatience. "Listen, come back when you're sixteen and I'll see. Until then, try to grow a little and look like you can lift a heavy box."

I was so young-looking and so skinny. I wasn't discouraged, because I had two months to grow. I had no alternative. If I wanted to date girls, I needed a job.

It was the summer of 1965 and after I got comfortable with my new neighborhood, I had the Rockaways on my mind. That summer, my parents decided that we would not be going to the Rockaways. That wasn't so terrible for me. It was an easy bus ride from East Flatbush to the Rockaways. Plus, my Aunt Letty, my mother's sister, was in the Twin Houses, a rooming house on Beach Twenty-Ninth Street. She had a room with a semi-private bathroom that was shared with another room on the other side of the bathroom. My aunt's good friend was in the other room and the friend wasn't there during the week. The friend offered my aunt her room for me to stay in when she wasn't there. On the other days, I commuted by bus and kept my stuff at my aunt's place.

On my first day in the Rockaways that summer, I went to the Breakers to look for Marc. The Breakers had a tall staircase leading up to the front porch. As I began walking up the steps, I noticed Barbara coming down from the porch. I took one look at Barbara and my mind screamed, "Wow!" Barbara was hot-looking, wearing skintight jeans and a halter blouse. She had certainly blossomed over the winter. I remembered her from the summer before as being cute and pretty, which she still was. But now, she was hot!

I didn't say anything to her. I wasn't sure if she would even remember me. And I thought, if she did remember me, why would she want anything to do with me? I had kind of ignored her the summer before. As we were about to cross paths on the steps, Barbara looked at me and said, "Marc is on the other side of the porch."

"Oh, thanks," I answered.

As we passed each other on the steps, I turned to get a look at her from the back. Barbara looked hot from the back too. With surprise, I thought to myself, "Wow, she remembered me. A girl who looks like that remembered me from a year ago." It made me wonder about how she felt about me.

The summer of 1965 was another great summer for me and Marc, even though we missed the hangout on Beach Twenty-Ninth Street from the summer before. Sharon now had a steady boyfriend, so there was no more hanging out at her bungalow. I did cross paths with Shelley a few times, but she didn't want anything to do with me.

Marc and I spent most of our time at the Breakers with some new kids, particularly Myrna, who became a close friend and who nicknamed me "Pookie." Myrna said I reminded her of a puppet named Pookie on the *Soupy Sales Show*. Marc's friends from Forest Hills, Queens, came often. One was Richie. Myrna fell intensely in love with Richie and they began dating. I saw Barbara often. She occasionally hung out with us, but she was a little younger and wasn't a part of our group of friends. But each time Barbara hung out with us, I never had the sense that she was interested in me. And I didn't have the courage to show interest in her and face the possibility of rejection.

Around the second week in August, my friends decided that we would all go to the movies that Saturday evening. It sounded good to me, but as the week progressed everyone was getting a date to go with them. By Thursday, I decided I wasn't going. I didn't have a date. Although I was welcome to join in, I felt a little uncomfortable being the only person without one. I called Myrna.

"Pookie, what's up?"

"I just want to let you know that I'm not going to the movies with everyone on Saturday."

"Oh, Pookie, why not?"

"I feel funny because everyone has a date, and I don't."

"Oh, come anyway. No one cares. Just come. You'll have fun anyway. Why, is there something else that you'll be doing?"

"No, I just will feel funny."

"Pookie ... ask Barbara!"

"What?"

I was caught totally off guard. I couldn't believe Myrna was suggesting I ask Barbara. Panicking a bit, I wondered, why would Myrna think I'd be interested in asking Barbara? And why would Myrna think Barbara would want to go to the movies with me? Then I thought, maybe this would get me a chance with Barbara, since I didn't have the guts to approach her by myself. While all this was racing through my mind, Myrna continued talking.

"Pookie, come on. Ask Barbara."

"No ... no, I don't want to."

"Come on. You know you like her. Pookie, wait. I see Barbara. She's walking through the lobby. Just hold on. I'm going to get her. You know you like her. You better ask her."

How did Myrna know I liked Barbara? How could she be so sure? I had never said anything to anyone and wasn't sure myself about my feelings.

"No Myrna ... Myrna! Hello? Hello? Myrna ... Myrna, are you there? Oh, shit!"

I was nervous! I was anxious! I took a deep breath and the next thing I heard was Barbara's mellow voice say, "Hello?"

"Hi ... this is Marc."

"Oh, hi."

"Everyone is going to the movies this Saturday. Would you like to go with me?"

"Yes," she answered.

Barbara answered so quickly. I was caught off guard and couldn't wait to hang up the phone. I stuttered a little, took another deep breath, and blurted out, "Okay, I'll see you on Saturday. Bye."

I was so nervous, I stood by the phone for a few minutes after I hung up, going over and over in my mind what just happened. The cute girl I knew from the summer before, who I'd regretted not getting to know better, was now going out with me that Saturday. This summer was three-quarters over. If not for this phone call, I might have missed out asking Barbara on a date.

I liked Barbara and found it hard to believe what had just happened. I realized I had been so stupid. It took someone to tell me that I liked Barbara, even though I had known that for two summers. But I liked her so much that I didn't have the guts to approach her. Barbara seemed so perfect that I was afraid of rejection. Now, I was going out with her. It happened so quickly. One minute, I wasn't going to the movies. And the next minute, I was going with this hot-looking girl.

Eventually, my friends told me they knew I liked Barbara by the way I would stare at her each time she walked by our group. They said that it was as if no one else were around and all my attention went to staring at Barbara.

Waking up Saturday morning, all I could think about was taking Barbara to the movies that night. I felt a little queasy, though. When I got out of bed, the room was spinning. I made it to the bathroom just in time to throw up. I went back into bed and lay there thinking, "Oh, shit, I'm going to screw up this date." I could tell I had a stomach virus. I used to get these once a year. The sick feeling, dizziness, and low fever wouldn't last very long, but it kept me in bed.

I went back to sleep, hoping that when I woke up, I'd feel better. But I was sure I wouldn't, and I didn't. I waited for as long as I could to see if I felt better. In the afternoon, I called Barbara to call off the date. I called the lobby phone at the Breakers Hotel. Someone answered and I said, "Hi, can I please speak with Barbara Meltzer?"

I could hear someone shouting for Barbara and then Barbara answered the phone. "Hello."

"Hi, Barbara, this is Marc. I'm so sorry, but I woke up this morning and I'm sick. I've been throwing up and all that stuff. So, I can't take you to the movies."

"Oh, I'm sorry that you're sick. Feel better."

"Thanks, I'll see you," I answered.

I was disappointed. No, I was really, very, extremely, out-of-my-mind disappointed! I felt I'd blown my chance with Barbara. I had had a very slight fever early that day. By that evening, I had no fever and just felt shitty. When I woke up the next morning, I felt fine. My mom said I probably had a twenty-four-hour bug, and I was okay to go out.

I went to the Breakers to hang out with Marc. I knew I'd see Barbara but figured I had ruined any chance with her. She probably wouldn't believe I'd really been sick, since I called her practically at the last minute to cancel.

When I walked into the lobby, Barbara happened to be there. When she saw me, she broke into a big smile and walked up to me. I was about to say, hi, sorry about yesterday. But before I had a chance, Barbara asked, "How do you feel?" Before I could answer, she gave me this big, long kiss on the lips. We were standing in the middle of the lobby, with people sitting around watching this going on.

In the middle of this kiss, I'm thinking, "Holy shit!" I didn't know what to make of what was happening. I felt a little embarrassed as people stared at us. It became obvious to me that Barbara hadn't thought I was full of shit about being sick, calling to cancel at the last minute. More importantly, I felt she really liked me. After we came up for some air from the kiss, Barbara said, "Want to hang out on the porch?"

A little shaken by the surprise kiss, I answered, "Yes!"

I was anxious to do anything to get away from everyone in the lobby staring at us. We sat on the porch for quite a while and talked. The more we talked, the more I realized how much I liked Barbara and how much I wanted to make out with her. I began to realize that Barbara must have been interested in me too. For all this time, she'd been waiting for me to have the guts to ask her out. From that day until the end of the summer, we were inseparable.

After Labor Day weekend, people began leaving the hotel. Barbara's family was planning to leave a few days after Labor Day, which gave us a little more time together. We started sneaking into the vacant hotel rooms, and these empty spaces became our hangout. It provided us with a comfortable, private, and uninterrupted haven to make out. We took full advantage of those vacant rooms over those couple of days. On our last day, we were doing our goodbyes in one of the empty rooms. As we lay beside each other on a mattress, Barbara asked, "Are we still going to go out together? I live in Jackson Heights. It's not so easy to get there from Brooklyn."

"I'll figure it out. I'll call you when you get home. I can't see you this weekend, with a lot to do for school starting on Monday. Especially since it's my first day at a new school. But I can see you next weekend. Gee, I wish we got together earlier this summer."

"Well, you never seemed interested, and it took you forever to ask me out. Actually, was it you who asked me out? Or was it Myrna who asked me out for you?"

"No, no! I asked you out."

Barbara wasn't giving it up so easily. "Would you have asked me out if Myrna hadn't forced you?"

"Myrna didn't force me. She just made the suggestion." I quickly changed the subject. "So, I'll call you when you get home. Just one more kiss ... or maybe two?"

I could tell that Barbara was purposely putting me on the spot. She didn't buy my answers. What I couldn't foresee, at that time, was that Barbara would be putting me on the spot and seeing through my bullshit for the next forty-six years. During all our years together, it was always a love game between us, and Barbara knew I never lied to her. Rather, I would attempt to play with the truth, as I did that day on the mattress in the vacant hotel room. For forty-six years, Barbara was never fooled by me, and I always knew it.

Ahead of the weekend we planned to get together, I called Barbara every day. I did get that job at the Big Apple Supermarket and I was working that Saturday. I was so looking forward to our date that night. It was a long, tedious commute to Jackson Heights from East Flatbush. My anxiety to see Barbara made the trip feel even longer, all the way to Junction Boulevard. This was the next-to-last stop on the Flushing Line.

Once I got off the train, I still had a long walk up Junction Boulevard to her building. Along the way, I passed a florist shop and decided to buy a dozen roses. I was stunned by the price and asked the florist, "Um, do you have anything else much cheaper?"

"Yes, of course, there are less expensive flowers. But are you buying flowers for someone special, like a girlfriend?"

"Yes, but I'm not sure if she's actually my girlfriend, yet."

"Okay, let me make a suggestion," she said. "Roses are very special. I can package one rose for you that will look very pretty and be more special than other kinds of flowers. And maybe that one rose will encourage this girl to become your girlfriend."

The one rose did look pretty. I kept looking at it as I walked to Barbara's building. I walked into the building vestibule and saw the apartment number on the directory. Barbara buzzed me into the lobby, and I found my way to the apartment where her mom greeted me at the door. When she saw me standing in the doorway holding the bouquet of one rose, a smile broke out across her face. "Barbara, Marc is here," her mother shouted.

Walking into the apartment and waiting for Barbara in the living room, I felt a little awkward. Barbara came in with a big smile. I didn't want to kiss her, since her parents were standing right there. But Barbara came right over and kissed me. I was only sixteen and Barbara fourteen. I continued standing there and Barbara asked, "Is that rose for me?"

"Oh ... oh, yes."

The florist was right. The rose was a big hit. After that day, Barbara was my girlfriend. I got to know that florist very well, as I often stopped by her store on my route to Barbara. When the florist would spot me entering her store, she went right to preparing a rose for me. And every so often, she didn't charge me.

Throughout my life, I've met so many kind people who've offered me guidance and mentoring. Whether it was my teachers lecturing to me to grow up and be more serious, or friends giving me a push to be bolder, or a supermarket manager hiring me for my first job, or people like the florist, whose name I don't recall, I would learn through the years that there are so many good people in this world, or at least in my world. And, there was Barbara. I have always been so very lucky.

CHAPTER 3

Two teenagers can become one

Barbara and I wanted to make out, and I dreamt about getting laid. We hadn't seen each other in a week and a half. Anxious to be alone with each other again, we hung out in her room, trying to sneak in a kiss. With Barbara's parents and younger brother in the apartment, it was uncomfortable trying to get close. We hadn't made specific plans for our date in Jackson Heights. So, we decided to go for a walk. Barbara showed me around the neighborhood and then we went to a playground across the street from her building and made out on a bench.

The evening went by too quickly and I felt like we were hardly together. It felt like one moment I was walking into her apartment, the next moment we were in her room, the next moment we were at the playground and now I was at the door saying goodbye. I wasn't going to see Barbara again for a whole week and I wanted just one more kiss. But with her family standing there saying goodbye too, a quick kiss was all I got.

As I boarded the train for my long commute back to Brooklyn. I already missed being with Barbara. And being on an almost-empty train, that late Saturday night, increased my feeling of being alone. I hoped the coming week would go by fast.

I called Barbara the next day, Sunday.

"Hi, what are you doing today?" I asked.

"Just doing some stuff with my friends."

"I wish we could be together more often than just last night," I said.

"Me too. I miss you already and don't know when I'll see you again. Can you come next weekend? Maybe you can sleep over. You can come after work on Saturday and then we'll have all day Sunday."

"Oh, yeah, like sleeping over at a girl's house will go over very well with my mother. How about you clear it with your mother first. If it's okay, I'll figure out a way to ask my mother."

The next day I spoke to Barbara and she said it was okay with her mother. Now, the real challenge was getting my mother to agree. We decided to arrange for our two mothers to talk. Barbara's mother explained how I'd be sleeping on a folding bed in the living room and, of course, Barbara's parents would always be there to chaperone. Reluctantly, my mother agreed.

Between the long week at school, working that Saturday at the supermarket, and the long, tedious commute by bus and train to Jackson Heights, it felt like I hadn't been with Barbara in forever, even though we had spoken on the phone every night.

This time, we planned a much better date. We went to the movies and afterward to Jahn's Ice Cream Shop. Since I was sleeping over, we didn't feel rushed, and I wasn't anxious about a late train ride back to Brooklyn. We got back to Barbara's apartment, watched TV in the living room with her parents, and began getting ready to go to bed.

Barbara went to her room, got into her pajamas, and came back to the living room to say good night. As she was leaving to go back to her room, I whispered to Barbara, "Maybe you can come visit me, when everyone is sleeping." Barbara just smiled. Her mom set up the folding bed for me in the living room and then it was lights out. All was quiet.

I couldn't fall asleep right away. The folding bed was uncomfortable. I felt strange trying to fall asleep in the middle of the living room, in someone else's apartment, while my hot-looking girlfriend was in her pajamas on the other side of the wall. I was almost asleep when I felt a poke on my arm. It was Barbara.

"Hi," I whispered.

"My parents and brother are asleep," Barbara whispered back.

I lifted the blanket and Barbara got into bed with me. We kissed and got really close. With Barbara wearing pajamas and me wearing boxer shorts, that night beat our times together in the vacant hotel rooms in Rockaway. Eventually, we both dozed off together in full embrace. There was no other way for us to lie together on that folding bed, which was only, like, thirty inches wide. It was perfect. After a while, Barbara kissed me and whispered that she was going back to her room. After she left, I fell right to sleep.

Back to school on Monday, I was at lunch sitting with a group of friends.

"Hey, Marc, what'd you do over the weekend?"

"I went to my girlfriend's in Jackson Heights."

Most often when guys talked about a girlfriend, it became a shit-talk session with a lot of macho, pompous-ass bragging. I didn't want to have that kind of shit-talk with my friends about Barbara. I wanted my relationship with Barbara to be private. For that reason, I was reluctant to tell anyone I had a girlfriend. I only told them so they'd know the reason for me not being interested in the girls at our high school.

As I tried to give curt answers, one of my friends went on, asking, "The whole weekend?"

"Yes. I slept over her house."

No sooner did I say that, when I realized this was the wrong thing for me to say at the lunch table, with a bunch of my other friends listening in on the conversation. I left myself wide open to all kinds of busting and wiseass comments from these jokesters, which is expected from a group of sixteen-year-old boys. The busting began when another friend asked, "So, tell us. Did you get anything?"

"Hey, guys ... leave me alone. She's not any girl. She's my serious girlfriend. So, don't start with me and shut the fuck up."

"Oh, come on. We're asking politely. Did you make out?" asked another friend.

Giving all of them a disgusted look, I answered, "Yes, okay! Enough! Or one of you is getting hurt!"

No matter how angry I got, I couldn't control or stop these wiseasses. Another friend chimed in. "Did you get any more than just making out?"

They were coming at me from all directions. I was pissed. No, I was fucking angry. I held myself back from throwing a punch. Barbara wasn't just any girl. I wasn't going to allow such cheap talk about her. No, not the girl that I was in love with. Even though I didn't understand what love was, at that time. I answered, "No—and fuck you, dickhead! Fuck all of you! I'm leaving! Goodbye!"

These guys were all new friends to me. They all had known each other for many years, going through school together. But this was the beginning of my first semester at Tilden and I had gotten friendly seeing them in my classes and spotting them sitting together at lunch. From the start they were a nice group to hang with. But at that moment I was ready to say fuck you and leave.

As I started to get up, the giggling started, and this guy, Gary, tried a different approach on me. "Marc, come on. Don't leave. We're sorry. You're new here and we're just getting to know you and want to be helpful, okay? Just tell us, were you prepared to go further? Did you have your condom ready?"

Gary was Mr. Cool in the group, with his Brylcreem hairdo and the smell of Canoe cologne emanating from him. Other than this bullshit session at the lunch table, I liked the group and didn't want to start off with enemies at a new school. I was the newbie. I sat back down. These guys were all big talkers. But they were all virgins. I was the only one who had a girlfriend. Also, I wanted to hear more about condoms, which I began to think I might need.

"I don't have any condoms," I answered.

"Wait, are you telling me that you don't carry a condom with you? Don't you keep one in your wallet? Everyone keeps one in their wallet."

"Not me. I don't have one. And I don't have a wallet."

With that, Gary took out his wallet and handed me a condom. He told me to get a wallet and always make sure to have a condom in it. This was the 1960s and it was supposed to be cool for a guy to have a condom in his wallet. I took the condom and put it in my pocket. After school, I searched my room for the wallet that my grandmother had given to me a few years before and put the condom in it. The funny thing is, after that day, I had that wallet with me all the time and I did feel cool about having a condom in it. I wasn't sure why, I just did. It was kind of a status symbol. What I didn't foresee that day was that the condom would stay in my wallet for many years. Until the day I lost it and couldn't figure out what happened to it.

Barbara and I continued seeing each other every weekend. Often, I slept over. And the after-lights-out-visits in the living room continued to get better, and we didn't get caught. But by mid-December, our teenage romance had some challenges. I had become more familiar with my new neighborhood and had friends at school. The weekly commute to Jackson Heights became tiring. Barbara was a sophomore at Newtown High School and had her own increasing social life with friends. Neither of us was taking advantage of our more convenient social opportunities and we felt like we were missing out on a lot.

That December, we had a disagreement. Our minds were on other things and we were drifting apart. We agreed that our relationship was over. I wasn't sure that I wanted it to be over. But it was.

In early January 1966, my friend Myrna was turning "sweet" sixteen and having a party. I was so looking forward to the party. It was going to be like a reunion for me. I would see some of the kids that I hadn't seen since the summer in Rockaway. A couple of problems sprung up. One was a New York City transit strike the week of the party. Myrna lived in The Bronx and there was no way for me to get there. Luckily, Myrna was able to arrange for me to catch a ride with her uncle, who would be driving her cousins to the party from Brooklyn.

Another problem was that the cousins weren't planning to stay late at the party. I didn't want to leave early and miss anything. I arranged with my friend Richie, who lived in Forest Hills, to drop me off at my Aunt Mollie's house in Kew Garden Hills, on his way home. My aunt expected me before midnight and said she would leave the front door unlocked for me and drive me back to Brooklyn the next day.

The party was on Saturday night, January 8, 1966. Myrna's apartment was at the corner of Townsend Avenue and East 171 Street. Her uncle found a parking spot around the corner. As we walked from the car and turned the corner to go to the apartment building, I saw Barbara's mother drive up in front of the building, to drop off Barbara.

I didn't know Barbara had been invited. I was surprised to see her. Barbara was a year or two younger than the other kids and not really part of the group. I waved hello and waited as Barbara got out of the car. I felt a little awkward seeing her, since we'd broken up only a few weeks before. As we smiled and walked into the building together, I remembered how much I liked being with Barbara and began to hope she felt the same way about me. When we got into the apartment, we went our separate ways to hang out with the other kids. Several times, I glanced at Barbara as I mingled. Two times I caught her glancing back at me.

It was a fun party. When the dancing started, somehow Barbara and I drifted to each other. We danced very close and talked. Eventually, we left the living room for Myrna's room. I closed the door and we sat on the bed. I took a gulp of air and confessed. "I didn't really want to break up. Did you?"

"I didn't want to break up either. Did you miss me? Because I missed you."

"Yes, I missed you and wished I could have seen you over the holidays, when school was closed."

Barbara and I spent some time in Myrna's room. We talked, made out, and made up. After, we went back to the party in the living room. It was obvious to everyone that we were back together.

"Where did you two disappear for so long?" kids asked us.

I boastfully answered, "We were in Myrna's room. That room gets a lot of action."

When it was time for Barbara to leave the party and meet her mother in front of the building, I told everyone I was walking with Barbara to her mother's car and would be right back. Before we walked out of the building, I stopped and turned to Barbara. I didn't know what to say. It felt like we had made up at the party, but I wasn't quite sure what came next.

"I really missed you."

"I missed you too."

"So, can I call you?" I asked.

"Yes," Barbara answered with the sweetest smile on her face.

As we walked out from the building, her mother was double-parked out front. I noticed she had a big smile. Barbara and I were holding hands. It must have been obvious to her mother that we had made up.

It was an incredible night. The party was fun, I saw so many friends, and Barbara and I were back together. There was only one problem. Richie and I continued to party way past the end of the sweet sixteen get-together. We didn't get to my aunt's house until two thirty. Richie dropped me off in front of the house and was waiting for me to go in before leaving. When he saw me turn and start walking back to the car, Richie rolled down his window.

"What's up?"

"Shit," I said. "The fucking door is locked. My aunt probably figured that I wasn't coming, when it got so late."

"You can sleep over my house."

"No. I can't walk into your parents' apartment in the middle of the night to sleep over and I still have to get back to Brooklyn tomorrow.

There's a road behind the house that leads to the driveway. Maybe I can get into the house that way, without disturbing anyone."

Richie drove around back. The back door to the basement happened to be unlocked. I turned and gave thumbs-up to Richie and went into the house. I slept in the basement that night with Flash. Flash was my aunt's dog, who slept in the basement.

The next morning, I heard my aunt in the kitchen and walked up from the basement steps into the kitchen. My aunt turned around. "Where did you come from? I thought you weren't coming. I waited for you until it was late."

"My friend dropped me off around two thirty and I got in from the back door and slept in the basement."

My aunt had this great laugh that she let loose. "So, you slept in the basement!!"

"Yes! It wasn't so bad. Flash enjoyed my company."

Barbara and I were together again, still very much attracted to each other. When together, we would make out continuously and when on the phone, we mostly talked about making out.

I would ask Barbara, "Are you hot?"

"Yes, are you?"

"I'm always hot," I would answer back.

We kind of had phone sex, without knowing what phone sex was. Fortunately, we each became involved with our own social activities, with our own friends from school, which distracted our hormones from going too crazy, until we could see each other again. I began putting in more hours at the Big Apple Supermarket, working each day after school and on Saturdays. I kind of had my own business going on at the supermarket. The money I was able to earn, in addition to my minimum-wage salary, was too compelling for me to give up and, for me, making money took priority over hanging out with friends.

The supermarket had a customer base that extended to nearby neighborhoods, beyond walking distance. Since there was no parking lot for the supermarket, these customers parked on nearby streets. They used the store's shopping carts to get their groceries to their cars, leaving the carts on the nearby sidewalks. When Abe, the store manager, saw a customer walking out of the store with a cart, he would frantically call for a stock boy to chase after the customer and bring the cart back, after the customer finished with it.

Abe knew he could depend on me to come running when he called. I would continuously hear over the loudspeaker, "Marc, come up front, now!" When I got up front, he would scream, "Follow that cart and bring it back!" At the beginning, I would do just that. But eventually, I learned how to hustle the customers for tips. I would run to the customers as they reached the door and say, "Let me help you with this." Then, I would push the cart to their car and load their groceries. For this, I would almost always get a tip, usually a dime or fifteen cents and sometimes the big tip, a quarter.

One day, Abe called for me to follow this elderly woman to her car. As I pushed the cart, I kept asking the woman where her car was. She kept answering, "Just a little farther." Finally, when we were a block-and-a-half from the store, she said, "This is my house right here." I brought her groceries into her house. For this I got my biggest tip: fifty cents. I was ecstatic. But when I got back to the store, Abe screamed at me. "Where the hell were you all this time?" When I tried to answer, he screamed again. "Get back to work!"

A week later, the elderly woman saw me in the store and asked if I could help her home again. I told her I had been gone too long last time and got screamed at by the manager. Her face fell in disappointment.

"Well, I'll tell you what we can do. When we walk out of the store, you can give me the key to your house. Then, I'll run with the cart and put everything in your house. On my way back, I'll give you back your key."

From that day on, she only did her big shopping when she knew I was in the store. She was my biggest customer, and I had many other regular customers too. I was earning a minimum wage of something like $1.25 an hour and earning almost one-and-a-half times that from my own business. I never told the other stock boys what I was doing.

They wondered why I was always exerting extra energy chasing after customers who were leaving the store with shopping carts.

Barbara and I had the same work ethic. When she turned sixteen, she began working as a cashier at a nearby supermarket on Junction Boulevard, the border of Jackson Heights and Corona in Queens. Louis Armstrong, the legendary singer and musician, lived in Corona and his wife shopped at that supermarket. One time while Louis's wife was shopping in the store, another cashier pointed her out to Barbara. When Louis's wife was approaching the cashiers, Barbara called out, "Mrs. Armstrong, please come to my aisle." After that day, Louis's wife would only go to the cashier aisle where Barbara was working.

This was so exciting for Barbara, especially the first time Louis Armstrong came with his wife and she introduced him to Barbara. Barbara described Louis Armstrong as having this big smile on his face and saying to her, "So glad to meet ya." I had fun often asking Barbara what Louis Armstrong said to her, because she would imitate him in that coarse voice. "So glad to meet ya." As for her work ethic, Barbara gave her paycheck to her mother each week to help with family expenses, and never asked to keep any portion for herself.

At the start of the summer of 1966, it was back to the Rockaways for my friends. My parents decided that we weren't going to the Rockaways that summer. I got lucky. My paternal grandmother rented a room on Beach Thirty-Fourth Street and invited me to stay with her. The room was furnished with an extra bed and was just three blocks away from my friends. When I knew that my grandmother would be visiting friends and not in the room, Barbara and I had fun in that room, all summer long.

I went back to Brooklyn on Thursday evenings, in order to work at the supermarket on Friday and Saturday, and returned to Rockaway Saturday night. This gave me pocket money for the week.

This summer was particularly exciting. I was going to be seventeen and would have my driver's license by the third week in August. My dad had already bought an old car, an Anglia, known as an English Ford, that I would share with my brother. My brother was in the

Navy and when he was on leave would have first dibs on the car. But when he was away, which was often, the car was mine.

On my birthday, I went to the motor vehicle office in downtown Brooklyn to get my driver's license. I drove straight to pick up Barbara for our first ride together and to celebrate my birthday. That day, Barbara surprised me with an initial ring. I often talked about getting such a ring, which was a fad in the sixties. I didn't expect her to get me such a great present. I put that ring on my right pinkie finger on August 22, 1966 and I've been wearing it every day since then. The ring has always been so special to me. I haven't figured out which one of my kids I'm going to leave it to.

After the summer, I started my senior year and Barbara began her junior year. The tedious commute by train was now a pleasant car ride between East Flatbush and Jackson Heights. My parents were a little nervous for me being a new driver and often reminded me to make sure to always have money on me for a phone call, in case of an emergency.

Thinking back, I'm reminded of the time when I got into the car after a date and noticed that the gas gauge was on empty. I panicked and checked my pocket. I had thirty-five cents. I breathed a sigh of relief, realizing I had enough money. I drove to a nearby gas station on Northern Boulevard and put in twenty-five cents worth of gas to get me back to Brooklyn. Easily doable in 1966. Plus, I still had ten cents for a phone call, in case of an emergency.

For two teenagers who couldn't keep our hands off each other, my car made it easy for us to be together more often. We had much more freedom and saw each other more often, including during the week, after school. We faced only one problem, and it was a major one. I was seventeen and Barbara was fifteen. And our relationship was worrying Barbara's parents.

We were kids getting increasingly comfortable with displaying our affection for each other. We still were within the definition of being virgins, according to "our" definition. But when Barbara's parents saw us together, we were most often holding hands, or I had my arm around Barbara. When we sat at a table, our chairs were always close.

When we watched TV, we lay cuddled up beside each other on the couch. Our feelings for each other showed. Our lust for each other showed and we weren't shy about a kiss every so often. Barbara and I were oblivious to any concerns that her parents or anyone else had from witnessing our relationship. I would later learn, when I became the parent of teenagers, that these are the things that drive a parent of a teenager to worry.

Barbara's parents thought we were a little too comfortable and touchy-feely for being virgins. They began to grill Barbara about our sexual activities and pressured her to stop seeing me so often. Her parents liked me and were happy with us dating. They weren't against the possibility of us someday getting married. But they lectured Barbara that she needed to do more dating with other boys. They warned her that marriage that arose from exclusive teenage dating ended in divorce. It was an honest concern. We were still kids, and our future was still uncharted.

We had to cut our dating down to once every other week, and only on weekends. We couldn't see each other during the week. Barbara started to date other people and so did I. We continued to speak often over the phone, and we always had a lot to talk about. Sometimes, we talked a little about our dating other people. I would lead the conversation about our separate dating lives, trying to be as silly as I could.

"Do you have a date this Saturday with the same guy you went out with two weeks ago?"

"Yes, I do."

"I thought your parents wanted you to date many different guys."

"For now, I'm dating just two," Barbara answered.

"You're dating two guys! I know of the one from two weeks ago. Who's the other guy?" I asked.

"It's you ... you, silly."

"Oh, right. I forgot about that for a minute. What does this guy look like?" I asked.

"He's tall and he's big."

"Oh, so he's fat."

"Shut up! He's not fat."

"Is he good-looking?"

"He's kind of good-looking."

"Oh, so he's ugly. It sounds like he's fat and ugly."

Barbara ignored me. "Tell me about who you're dating?"

"Well, you didn't deny what I said. So, I guess he's really fat and ugly. So, now I'll tell you about the girl I'm dating. She's hot!"

"Is that all that you're going to tell me about her?" Barbara paused. "Do you kiss her?"

As thoughts raced through my mind, I was at a loss for how to answer. The question caught me off guard. It knocked the silliness right out of me and reminded me how much I missed seeing Barbara more often. The other girls that I knew or was kind of dating I really didn't care for, not in a way I would a girlfriend. When I was with other girls, in my mind I was always comparing them to Barbara. And there was no girl who came close. I hoped Barbara felt the same about me.

An empty feeling came over me, a sense I was losing Barbara. I didn't want to ask if she had kissed someone else. I didn't want to know the answer. I thought if I answered her question by saying, "Yes, I do kiss her," it would surely distance us. So, I was about to answer, "No, I haven't kissed her."

But I did kiss other girls. I didn't know how to tell Barbara the truth and yet let her know my true feelings. I had to push the words out. In my most sincere tone of voice, I softly answered, "Yes, we kiss. But it's not like you and me."

In a voice just above a whisper, Barbara said, "I miss you too."

After that phone call, I sat and stared at the phone for a while. This dating arrangement challenged our feelings for each other. It could have ended our teenage romance. But it didn't. Because each time we were together, we felt the excitement of a new beginning, as if it were a new romance. Each kiss was as warm and as fresh as our first. Barbara and I had so many new beginnings together. No matter how many times we did things together, things we had done before, we felt excitement as if it were a first.

Fifty-two years later, as I write about this teenage time in our lives, it is so natural for me to have the feelings I had back then. I feel the thrill and attraction that made me quiver each time I looked at Barbara. I feel the hurt that came from being apart. It's all so natural for me because, well, I had these feelings throughout our dating, our engagement, and our forty-year marriage. Even now, I quiver as I picture her smile in my mind. And the hurt which comes from being apart doesn't go away.

If it was just puppy love back then, I couldn't tell when it changed over to true love. Perhaps it was when our feelings grew into a love that transformed the two teenagers we were into being one. I'm not exactly sure when that happened, because it was seamless. I so believe that from puppy love even two teenagers can become one. Barbara and I certainly did. Our hearts bonded from a romance that always ignited at the feeling of our lips and bodies touching each other's.

CHAPTER 4

Going all the way

During my senior year in high school, 1966-67, I was busy deciding where to apply to college. I was always interested in construction and the design of buildings. It was at a very young age that I first showed interest in being an architect. As a young kid, I used to visit construction sites in my neighborhood and watch the progress, from the ground excavation, to the building starting to take form, all the way through to completion. A friend and neighbor of my parents was an architect and he used to give me blueprints. It was fun looking through the plans and visualizing the spaces.

There was one particular out-of-town college I was excited about, which had a recognized school of architecture. I applied and was accepted. Upon receiving the letter of acceptance, I immediately responded and confirmed I would attend. My parents and I started to get the paperwork ready to send back to the college.

At this point, the love between Barbara and me had grown solid. Barbara was happy for me, but she also knew our always-being-together was going to end. I had similar thoughts, but I was all caught up in the excitement and novelty of going away to college. Together, we needed to face that I would be leaving in September. It was time to discuss our future and how we would have a long-distance relationship ... or not.

One afternoon in the spring of 1967, I was with Barbara in her room. Her parents and brother were away. As we lay beside each other on her bed, we talked about being apart. As teenagers in love, we had overcome so many challenges, and now I was leaving. With the expense of long-distance phone calls, we wouldn't be able to talk over the phone as often. As we looked into each other's eyes, Barbara said, "So, you're leaving for college in September. Are you excited or scared?"

"I'm a little scared about being away and on my own for the first time in my life. But I am excited about the whole thing."

"Will you miss me? Because I'll miss you."

"Yes ... I'm going to miss you a lot."

"You'll probably forget about me, as soon as you meet some college girl who'll go all the way."

"Whoa!" I thought to myself. That statement hit me right between the eyes. I wasn't expecting it at that moment and Barbara was so blunt. I was taken aback a little. Actually, I was taken aback a lot. I wondered if she was expecting me to be a horny teenage guy at college, who'd jump at the first opportunity with another girl. Because I wasn't like that at all. Well, that's not exactly true. I was a horny teenage guy. But it was Barbara I wanted. Then a thought came to me. Maybe this would be a good time to seize the moment.

"Um ... you may be right," I answered. "We're all alone here and I still have that condom in my wallet. We should probably go all the way right now. You know, we should do it a lot of times, before I leave in September. That way we can talk about it over the phone and the part of our brain that reduces our horniness after sex will be fully engaged until we're together again. And we won't need anyone else."

"Don't be so silly," she answered.

"I'm not being silly. It makes a lot of sense!"

For sure, I wanted to get laid. And I was stalling, trying to avoid facing the real question: Will this be the end for us or not? And then, Barbara put it to me.

"Do you love me? Because ... I so love you."

The moment was becoming too heavy for me to deal with. I could feel my heart beating and my love for Barbara, as I looked into her warm, dark brown eyes. She looked so sweet. I didn't know how to avoid the question. I continued to try to cover it up with silliness, and I laughed. "So, I guess we're not going all the way right now. And you still want me to say that I love you?"

As we continued to look into each other's eyes, we kissed. Sadness came over us. With few words needing to be spoken, we both knew that our puppy-love romance was going to come to an end. I couldn't expect Barbara, at sixteen years old, to sit home and not date. She would be a senior in September. Surely, she'd have many offers to go out with other guys. Barbara knew I'd be living in a dorm, with new college friends and new dating opportunities. We seemed to be communicating these thoughts to each other in our eyes. I needed to give her an answer about my love for her.

Finally, with a teary voice, I answered, "Yes ... I do love you ... and I think about you all the time. That will never change, even though we'll be doing our own thing, separately. You have to promise me that it will never change for you too."

"I promise," Barbara answered.

"In the meantime, September is a long time away and we have all summer to be together."

With that, the sadness and tears in our voices faded away. I could feel my devilish smile coming on, as I asked, "Are you sure we're not going all the way right now?"

"Positive!"

My college plans were all set, until the night I overheard my parents talking in the living room. They were facing some challenging decisions. My dad had started a new job the year before in The Bronx, near the Whitestone Bridge. Commuting to The Bronx from East Flatbush not only was exhausting, but also it was expensive, with the wear and tear on his car. Only two years earlier, they had incurred the expense of a move from East New York to East Flatbush. Now, they realized another move might be necessary. On top of this, they were facing my college expenses.

My parents were talking low, so as not to be heard. The door to my room was closed, but I was near the door when I overheard my mother's question and began to listen in on their conversation.

"Ben, how are we going to pay for college?"

"It'll be okay, we'll do it," my dad replied.

"What about your commute to work? How much longer can that last? We need to move again."

"We don't need to move. I'll just do the commute. It's fine. Don't worry, I'll figure it out. Let him go to college where he wants."

Reality hit me hard. I didn't know what to do. My parents couldn't afford to send me to an out-of-town college. I knew it and I'd always known it. I was so caught up in the excitement and absorbed in myself that I hadn't considered the stress on my parents. They were so proud and excited telling relatives and friends of the news that I would be attending this college. But they were too proud to admit that sending me to an out-of-town college was going to be a financial struggle for them.

For the next several days, I kind of moped around, wondering if being accepted to this college really was wonderful news, considering the burden it would put on my parents. I tried to convince myself that the financial burden was minimal compared to how happy and proud they were. But I knew this was selfish thinking on my part.

Over the next several days my mother asked if something was bothering me. Each time, I told her all was fine. But she could sense that something was wrong. Finally, after a few days, at dinner one evening, I blurted out, "I don't think that I want to go away to college."

"What are you talking about? What do you want to do?" My parents jumped at me and asked at the same time.

"There is a school of architecture in Manhattan and I think that I want to go there. I checked it out and it has a great reputation. Also, the school is part of the City University of New York and the tuition is free, except for charges of twenty-eight dollars a semester. I'm going to think about it over the next few days and decide."

They looked at me. Concerned, my mom asked, "Are you sure? Listen, take your time, do the right thing, and decide what is best."

My dad seemed kind of pissed at me and added, "No one asked you to think about the costs. I want you to make up your own mind and do what's best for you."

But I had already decided I wasn't going to that out-of-town college. I felt good about the decision. I told my parents a few days later. After, I could see that they were less anxious and a little more at ease and I knew I was doing the right thing. As I write about this decision more than fifty years later, I can honestly say that I've never had regrets. I had Barbara.

It would be several years later when I fully understood my parents' will to sacrifice and struggle for me. With our own children, Jonathan was first in college and Kristen followed two years later. We had a two-year overlap of college tuition payments. And when Kristen graduated, Brian was starting.

I'm reminded of an evening Barbara and I were in the family room watching TV. I was also looking through the tuition bills. Jonathan was a junior and Kristen was a freshman. I turned to Barbara.

"Oh my God, Barbara! Oh my God. Please tell me that you've been stealing from me all these years and you have all the money hidden in our mattress."

With this big smile, Barbara laughed, making believe she had no idea what I was referring to. In an innocent voice, she asked, "What's the matter, dear? Are we having a cash flow problem?"

I caught on to her laugh and with silliness answered, "No, we only have a partial cash flow problem. There is no problem with the cash flow going out, just with the cash flow coming in."

Still laughing, she said. "Well, sorry to disappoint you, my dear. I have not been stealing from you. And there is no money in our mattress."

"Shit, Barbara. Seriously, couldn't you just lie to me for tonight and tell me you have been stealing? So that I can enjoy the rest of the evening."

Barbara answered, "We love our children."

"Oh, really. What the fuck does that mean, with these bills?"

Then, I laughed too. While sometimes Barbara's abstract answers in response to my woes confused me, Barbara was always able to make things seem better. With her smile and laugh, she'd get me to loosen up and chill.

Oh, Barbara ... at my most worrisome times, you made everything feel simply okay. You could always make me feel like we'd make it through, and we'd be fine. And then, we were.

Barbara and I weren't going to be apart, which did make my college decision easier. I planned that when I broke the good news to Barbara, we would go out, celebrate, and go all the way. But that's not quite what happened. We went out and we celebrated. As for going all the way, that didn't happen.

Going into the winter of 1967-68, my parents decided that we really did need to move. My dad's commute was too difficult. They didn't want to move to The Bronx and decided that neighborhoods nearby, to the Queens side of the Whitestone Bridge, would work best. This was great news for me. I would be closer to Barbara. As they looked at various areas like Bayside and Flushing, I was pushing for Jackson Heights. On one of my parents' outings, I got them to go to Jackson Heights to see Barbara's parents' apartment, which was in a cooperative complex called Southridge. My parents liked the building and the apartment and said they would consider an apartment there.

A couple of weeks later, Barbara's mother called my mother and told her about an apartment in Southridge that had just come on the market. I went nuts with excitement. Barbara lived on Ninety-Third Street and the apartment was around the corner on Ninety-Second Street. My parents liked the apartment, immediately put down a deposit, and closed on the apartment. We moved in on April 9, 1968. Barbara and I were flying high.

In the spring of 1968, Barbara was graduating from high school.

She was two years younger than me, but one grade behind. She had skipped one grade in junior high school, in an S.P. class. That class completed the seventh and eighth grade in one year. I was always attracted to smart girls. Our son Jonathan would inherit that trait of mine.

I was finishing my first year of college. With our move to Jackson Heights, I had to give up my job and side business at the Big Apple Supermarket. I began thinking about what kind of job I wanted. My head was swelled about being a college man now. I felt the need to strive for something more challenging; a professional job, where I would need to dress up in a suit.

As a high school graduate, Barbara felt the same way about the kind of job she ought to seek. She decided to search for a job as a clothing model, for a company in Manhattan. Even though she had no prior modeling experience, Barbara planned the day to pursue it. She got all made up, took the train into Manhattan, and searched for job leads, going from building to building in the Garment District, knocking on doors and talking to elevator operators. Barbara didn't expect to get lucky so quickly. However, she was passionate about finding a modeling job and came across several opportunities on her first day.

Barbara chose a job as a model for a company called F.A. Blunget, a clothing manufacturer. I was kind of concerned about my girlfriend being a model in New York City, having to promenade and pose in front of wiseass old men. On the other hand, I was enamored with my girlfriend being a model. It was a total turn-on for me, and Barbara knew it. When we were alone together, I would egg her on to walk around the living room like a model. She would kind of spice it up and feel extra sexy. It was the best foreplay for both of us. Although we still weren't going all the way.

Deciding on the kind of job I wanted to pursue came easy. Growing up in the East New York section of Brooklyn, I had witnessed the dynamics of realtors working the neighborhood, as many families planned to move. When my family prepared to sell a four-family house, I followed the interview and negotiating process, and observed the techniques of the realtors. It was all so interesting to me. I figured I could do something in the real estate field.

I answered an ad for a sales position in a real estate office in The Bronx and got an interview. Almost immediately, I hit it off with the broker and was offered a sales position. I applied to the city and took the exam for my license. At eighteen years old I became a licensed real estate salesperson. The office, Royal Key Realty, was located on White Plains Road and 229th Street in The Bronx.

The sales position was on a commission-only basis, which didn't scare me. Compared to other kinds of sales jobs that offered a salary, it was a gamble. But at my age and with my lack of experience, I felt the realtor job gave me the opportunity to earn significantly more money.

I worked my ass off, running around trying to get listings and showing people houses. It was summertime and the weather was shitty for getting dressed up in a suit and canvass through neighborhoods. But I survived. I was hungry to make money. I was like a broken record, going from house to house knocking on doors and saying, "Hi, I'm Marc Gellman from Royal Key Realty. Are you interested in selling your home?"

This was the 1960s and most stay-at-home moms, then referred to as housewives, were home during the weekdays. I had a lot of doors slammed in my face, and I mean, slammed. The first few times it happened kind of stunned me. Then it became a challenge I grew to enjoy. The harder the doors got slammed the more humorous and fun the whole experience was. I learned a lot and got very familiar with the predominantly Italian neighborhood in the northeast Bronx. I knew about all the parishes and Catholic schools.

Barbara had a lot of fun that summer. She built up her self-confidence and was very much liked and treated well modeling for the company. She did have to put up with bullshit from clients, especially the old perverts who came on to her. Barbara dealt with it fine and the only pervert she gave in to was me.

I did well that summer too and sold a few homes. By the end of August, I had money in my pocket and in my bank account, which was perfect timing. Barbara's seventeenth birthday was coming up on September 12. I wanted to get her something over-the-top special. There was a jewelry store on the next block from the real estate office on White Plains Road. I went over to see if I could find something.

The merchants in the retail stores along White Plains Road were predominantly Italian and lived in nearby neighborhoods. I was surprised to find that this jeweler was a young Jewish guy from Scarsdale. The day I went into the store, he had his five-year-old son with him.

"Hello, how I can help you?" he asked, as soon as I walked in.

Seconds later, his son repeated, "Hello, how can I help you?"

We laughed and I said, "I'm looking for a birthday present."

"Who is the present for?"

"My girlfriend."

"Nice. Look through that display case."

I didn't see anything that caught my eye in the display case he suggested. I strolled around the store looking at the other cases. A wristwatch caught my attention. It was a formal watch, a Longines-Wittnauer with a white gold band and some diamond chips.

"This watch looks nice," I said.

"I'll show you the price on that. It's kind of expensive. Did you have a certain amount that you planned on spending?"

"I haven't thought about it much. I just know that I want to get something special."

He took out the watch from the display case and held it in front of me as he told me the price. Yep, he was right, it was expensive. But I liked it. I continued staring at it as I tried to overcome the sticker shock. The jeweler could read the surprised look on my face. He put the watch back into the display case.

"What's your name?"

"Marc."

"Marc, talk to me like I'm your big brother."

With that, his son repeated, "Talk to me like I'm your big brother."

Again, we laughed. With a friendly smile, the jeweler asked, "Marc, how old are you and your girlfriend?"

"I'm nineteen and my girlfriend is going to be seventeen."

"I'm not trying to discourage you from buying this watch, but you may want to consider that this kind of gift gives out a certain message. This is an expensive present to give to a seventeen-year-old girlfriend and definitely sends a message more than just a birthday gift. You just walked into my store, so I don't know you. But I already feel comfortable to give you some big-brotherly advice. So, tell me, where are you going with this girl and what's in the future for the two of you?"

"Wow," I thought to myself. No one had ever asked me such a question about my future plans with Barbara. We were in love and our parents accepted that we were serious boyfriend and girlfriend. I don't think anyone assumed it was a slam dunk that we would be married someday. We were way too young for such an assumption. In fact, most people told us we'd mature at different stages and eventually go our separate ways.

Barbara and I expressed our love for each other, and we were always in sync, whether walking, talking, or dancing. We were one. But there had never been any talk beyond where we were at this point. We never talked about marriage. We were too young for that. The future for Barbara and me was always about our next date, the next time we'd be together, and about graduating from college. We were too young and having too much fun to think beyond that. "Beyond that" meant we'd have so much responsibility, which we were in no way ready for. Now, for the first time, someone was asking about our future.

As I looked into the jeweler's eyes, I saw a stranger trying to help. Then, for the very first time, the words rolled off my lips.

"I'm going to marry this girl."

The jeweler smiled and said, "You look and sound very certain."

"I am!"

"Gee," I thought. "I didn't gulp or wobble." I was so very certain. Those words came out of me so easily and felt so good. I grew up at that very moment and stood proud and tall. And I was steadfast in buying that watch for my future wife.

After negotiating a large price reduction, I bought the watch. The jeweler engraved on the back:

9/12/68

To Barbara

Love

Marc

The jeweler was right. From the moment I gave Barbara that watch, our parents and everyone else accepted that we were two young kids who were going to be married someday. Exactly when that would be? No one had that figured out yet. We were still working on making it through college. But it quickly became clear and certain that a marriage would happen. For Barbara and me, and our love for each other, the watch was the preamble to the engagement ring.

CHAPTER 5

Those two words

No, we're not getting married yet. No, we haven't picked a date yet. No, we're not engaged yet. Why so many questions? We're happy! Leave us the fuck alone.

To some people, by the spring of 1970 it seemed like Barbara and I had been going together forever. There were many times when Barbara's elderly great aunt, Fanny, said to us, "When are you two going to get married? It's not healthy to be going together like this for so long."

Barbara and I would just listen and smile back at her. After one of those times, I said to Barbara, "Your Aunt Fanny keeps saying the same thing each time she sees us. What does she mean that it's not healthy? She probably thinks that we've been fucking our brains out and you're going to get pregnant. Next time we see her, we should say, 'Aunt Fanny, we want you to know that there is no need to worry. We haven't been fucking and are waiting until we're married. Be assured that there has been no penetration.'"

Sarcastically, I continued. "Barbara, unless you've had a change of mind and want to go all the way? In that case, it wouldn't be right for us to tell Aunt Fanny that we aren't fucking, if we really are. We shouldn't lie to her."

Barbara laughed. "Would you shut up with saying that? You're crazy. How about we just let Aunt Fanny say whatever she wants, and we just listen."

"I don't agree. I think she'd like us to tell her not to worry. I get it that you don't want to use the word 'fucking.' How about we just say that we're not going all the way. Is that better?"

"How about you stop being so silly?"

"Silly is me. And come on, wouldn't you love to see the look on Aunt Fanny's face if we told her something like that? Anyway, do you think Aunt Fanny calls it fucking?"

"She probably calls it 'schtupping,'" Barbara answered.

"Okay, how about we tell her we haven't been schtupping."

"How about you shut up about Aunt Fanny and stop being so annoying, already."

At this point, I was holding my stomach, rolling over on my side on the couch, laughing hysterically. "No—I can't stop. It's too funny. Just one more thing. Barbara, think about this. What kind of sounds do you think old Jewish women make while having sex? You think they scream out, 'Oy ... Oy ... Oy'?"

I loved having conversations like this with Barbara. She put up with my silliness. I had fun annoying Barbara by not letting go of a silly conversation. Instead, I'd go on and on. Eventually, Barbara would get very annoyed, and I loved the look on her face when that happened. She would give me this serious stare, with this cute look on her face, and I would smirk back until she would crack up and laughingly plead, "Okay, enough already! I can't take any more." Barbara was so wonderful. I knew there was no other girl who would put up with my silliness.

That spring, I sold a two-family house in the Baychester section of The Bronx. The deal closed in May and the sales price was $38,000, the most expensive house I had sold and the biggest commission that I had ever earned. As soon as the broker handed me the commission check, I looked at it and knew what I was going to do; buy an engagement ring for Barbara.

I was twenty years old and Barbara was eighteen. I was finishing my third year of college and still had two more years to go. But it was time to become engaged and begin planning our future. We were too young to get married, but I figured that we'd had a long courtship and we'd have a long engagement too.

I looked through the classified section of the Sunday newspaper and noted that there were many jewelers on Canal Street in Manhattan advertising engagement rings. One jeweler's ad in particular caught my attention: "Jay of Diamonds." One day after classes, I took the train down to Canal Street and found the store.

"Hi, how can I help you?" asked one of the saleswomen, as I walked into the store.

"I'm looking for an engagement ring, with a pear-shaped diamond."

She showed me several and I said, "These diamonds all look very small."

"Pear-shaped tends to look smaller, because of what is lost in the cut. How much do you want to spend?" she asked.

"I haven't thought about it much. I just know that I want to get something special." That was my typical answer to kick off my chiseling-the-price-down routine.

"You will get a larger-looking stone when the diamond is round. Let me show you some rings with round stones," she answered.

While she gathered some rings, I looked around the store and noticed a large pear-shaped diamond ring in a display case behind the counter. But first, I let the saleswoman go through her routine of showing me several rings, none of which I liked.

When she finished showing me all that she wanted to, I asked, "How about that ring?" I pointed to the large, pear-shaped diamond ring.

"Oh, that ring is about two and a half carats, a little expensive."

As she took the ring out of the display case and held it in front of me, I asked, "What's this tag on the ring? Is that the serial number?"

The look on the saleswoman's face was laughable. It was a cross between disgust, impatience, and thinking I was an idiot. She couldn't tell I was playing with her, and that was good. Because the more I could play with her the more her desire to get rid of me would increase.

From my real estate sales experience, I learned the way to get rid of an annoying customer was to sell them something quickly. Sometimes an ignorant shopper can get more than an informed shopper. You just have to wear down the salesperson to believing that no matter what they say, you aren't going to understand their point.

Now annoyed, the saleswoman answered, "No, that's the price."

I knew I had her going and would have to drive her a little crazier. Sounding naïve, I asked, "Oh ... really ... wow! Is that the list price or the sales price, and does that include the sales tax?"

"Yes, yes, and no." By this time, she'd had enough of me and said, "Let me ask the jeweler to come over and see what he can do."

"Perfect," I thought to myself. That was exactly the person I wanted. Someone who had the authority to sell me that ring at the cheapest price possible. The jeweler came over and said, "Hi, so you're getting married."

This guy obviously wanted to take the let's-get-personal sales approach. "Perfect," I thought. "I'll befriend him and then drive him crazy too." I thought his question was stupid. Of course, I'm getting married. Why the fuck else would I be in this store looking for an engagement ring? So, I smiled, began to humor him, and answered, "Well, I want to get engaged first."

He laughed. "This is an exceptionally nice ring and there can only be little movement on the price. How much were you expecting to spend?"

Again, I went with my standard answer. "I haven't thought about it much. I just know that I want to get something special. And that ring looks very special, just too expensive for me."

He studied me for a moment. "How old are you and your girlfriend? I see that you're carrying books. Are you still in school? You look very young to be getting married."

He was getting personal again. I knew I was sucking him in.

"I'm twenty and my girlfriend is eighteen. I have two more years at City College and then we can get married."

The jeweler offered me a small price reduction. The ring, I told him, was still too expensive for me. He suggested I consider one of his other rings and began presenting me with alternatives. "You're young," he told me. He suggested I settle for a more affordable ring for our engagement. I could come back to him in the future, when I had more money, and trade in the ring for a larger one. But although the ring was beyond my budget, I had already made up my mind. I was determined to buy it.

I figured the best approach was to let the jeweler go through his spiel about the other rings. I purposely kept comparing each ring to the one I wanted. I was extremely patient. I had no other plans and a lot of time to wear him down. I spent about two hours being juggled between the saleswoman and the jeweler. It had become a fun afternoon for me. They gradually reduced the price of the ring, until the last price reduction came close within my reach. The jeweler, getting impatient with me, finally said, "Listen. If you want this ring so badly, you're going to have to tell me what you'll pay for it so that I can know if I'm wasting my time."

So, I did just that. I finally told him what I was willing to pay. When he heard my offer, the look on his face turned sour. At that moment, I knew I had annoyed him beyond his limits. I quickly offered to split the difference between my offer and his last offer, as long as it included the sales tax and I could come back with Barbara to have the ring properly sized to her finger, at no additional cost.

After he sighed, took a deep breath, and made sure that I wasn't going to ask for anything else, we shook hands on the deal. I told him I only had a morning class the next day and would be back with the money. He promised to hold the ring for me until noontime the following day.

The next day, while taking the train from school down to Canal Street, I imagined the jeweler and the saleswoman would have an attitude about seeing me again, considering the ordeal I put them through the day before. But when I walked into the store they broke into big smiles. They were genuinely excited for me and looking forward to meeting Barbara, when we would return to have the ring properly sized. I guessed that they must have felt they were helping out a young kid who didn't know what he was doing. I was always good at giving that impression at the right time.

I hid the ring in my clothing for my train ride to Jackson Heights. I was wearing a T-shirt under my shirt and I placed the ring box in my shirt, against my belly button. Nervous about getting mugged and having the ring stolen from me on the tedious train ride up to Grand Central Station and changing for the Flushing line, I continually checked that the ring box was positioned against my belly button.

Barbara only had morning classes that day. I was so anxious about proposing to Barbara. With her brother at school and her mother at work, we'd be alone in her mother's apartment for me to propose.

Finally, I was at her building, being buzzed into the lobby. I didn't have the patience to wait for the elevator. I ran up the stairs and to her door. Barbara opened the door for me and as I walked into the apartment and stood in the foyer, she said, "What's up? You have a funny look on your face. How come you're home early today?"

I laughed a little too hard. "I only had morning classes today ... and did you say I'm funny-looking?"

"Well, why are you laughing? What happened that's so funny?"

"I'm not laughing," I answered as I continued to laugh. It was a nervous laugh.

Barbara walked up to me, put her hands on top of my shoulders, looked me straight in my eyes, and said, "Tell me what is so funny."

I put my hands on her waist and kissed her. With our eyes only inches apart, I teared up a little. I gulped, stuttered a little, and with a quiver in my voice I whispered, "I bought something for you."

"Really? What did you buy me?" Her voice was innocent and naïve.

With my left hand, I felt for the ring box and with my right hand, I pulled the front of my shirt and T-shirt up and reached for the box. Holding the box in my hand, Barbara stared at it for a few seconds. "Is that—"

There was total silence in the apartment. It was just Barbara and me and at that moment our smiles turned serious. As I opened the box, I whispered, "Yes."

It was a Thursday afternoon, May 21, 1970, when we stood there staring at the ring in the box for a few seconds. Barbara looked like she was about to cry. I took out the ring, lifted Barbara's hand, and slid the ring onto her finger. "Oh, Marc," Barbara said as tears cluttered her eyes and filled her voice. We kissed. That was all she said.

So often throughout our next forty-one years together, at happy times and difficult times, Barbara said to me, "Oh, Marc," always with a tear in her voice. She did it upon the birth of each of our children, on the day of their Bar and Bat Mitzvahs, at their high school and college graduations and at the too many times when we were confronted with another cancer. At those times, those two words said everything about what was in our hearts. Nothing else needed to be said.

As I write this looking through Shiva Eyes, I continue to hear Barbara's voice and those two words echo in my ears. On May 21, 1970, we didn't say another word as I slid the ring onto her finger. At that moment, it was those two words, the silence around us, and our gaze into each other's eyes that sent our love quivering through our bodies.

After a few seconds, Barbara asked, "Who knows about this?"

"No one, just you, me, and the people at the jewelry store."

"Your parents and my mom don't know?"

"Nope, no one knows."

Barbara rushed to the phone. She called my mother and told her we were going to be sitting on a bench alongside the building and suggested that she walk over. My mother joined us there a few minutes later. Barbara sat beside my mother and made a point of gesturing with her hand as she spoke. But no matter how hard Barbara tried, my mother was oblivious to the ring on Barbara's finger.

At last, my mother asked, "What's that on your finger?"

"Finally!" Barbara exclaimed. "I was waiting for you to notice it. Marc gave it to me about an hour ago."

In complete surprise, my mother took Barbara's hand and looked at the ring. "It's beautiful." With this incredible, glowing smile, she looked back and forth from Barbara to me.

Barbara said to her, "You're the first to know. We're going to surprise my mom when she gets home from work."

"Okay, I'm not going to tell anyone until your mother knows," my mother answered.

Barbara and I waited in her apartment for her mother to come home that evening. Barbara and her mother had a very loving, close relationship. She wanted to plan out how to surprise her mom. We went through all kinds of ways. Should we be sitting next to each other on the couch? Should we be watching TV? Do we want to run to her mother as soon as she walks in and say, look what we have? We were so very excited and couldn't sit still, getting on and off the couch. All of our planning quickly went by the wayside when her mother walked into the apartment. Barbara walked toward her. Almost immediately her mother asked, "What's that on your finger?"

Her mother wasted no time getting on the phone to call my mother. Then, she wasted no time in calling the world. The very next day, Barbara's mother contacted *The New York Times* to place an announcement of the engagement. In the Sunday issue, on June 14, 1970, the announcement ran, with a picture of Barbara.

That weekend, we all got together to discuss our future: Barbara's mother, my parents, and of course Barbara and me. It was an easy decision that the wedding would happen after we both graduated. Barbara was to graduate in two years from Queens College with a degree in education and I was to graduate in two years from City College of New

B30 • SUNDAY NEWS, JUNE 14, 1970

She'll Marry City College Man

The engagement of Barbara Karen Meltzer, a Queensborough Community College senior, to Marc Gellman was announced by her mother, Mrs. Constance L. Meltzer of Jackson Heights. Her fiance, son of Mr. and Mrs. Bernard Gellman of Jackson Heights, is an architecture student at City College.

York, School of Architecture. So, we planned a wedding date for August 1972. In the meantime, since the wedding was a long way off, Barbara's mother wanted to have a big engagement party. My parents agreed.

Our parents worked quickly in sending an announcement of our engagement, which included an invitation to our engagement party on July 11. The party was held in the recreation lounge of the cooperative building where we lived. It was almost like a wedding, with assigned table seating, centerpieces, a full buffet, and dancing to a three-piece band: an accordionist, clarinetist, and drummer.

Barbara and I decided we wanted to get married in a temple. At every chance we had, we toured the temples throughout Queens. Once we decided on the temple, we brought our parents. By the end of July, everyone knew we were engaged, we'd had a successful engagement party, and all the arrangements, from the temple to the caterer, the band and flowers, were set for us to be married in August 1972. Ten months later, those arrangements were cancelled.

CHAPTER 6

Every girl deserves to be a bride

Barbara's mother, Connie, having been divorced for a couple of years, had been dating Sam on and off for over a year. In December 1970, Connie and Sam got married. Barbara was thrilled for her mother to be remarried, after a bitter divorce from a horrible first marriage and years of putting up with what Barbara described as the craziness of her father.

All seemed wonderful. But Connie began to feel tired, sluggish, and lethargic. This was so unlike her. Connie was always on the go and filled with energy. Barbara was concerned. I joked with Barbara, saying things like, "There's nothing to be worried about. Your mom is probably just exhausted now that she has Sam to go 'at it' with every night. She's not used to having to put out."

About a year before they were married, Sam had noticed a lump in Connie's breast, which her doctor quickly dismissed as a fatty cyst. But at the end of January 1971, there was swelling developing on the side of her neck. Connie had a cousin in New Jersey, a surgeon at

Newark Beth Israel Medical Center, Dr. Marvin Cohen. She went to him for an evaluation. Marvin determined from his physical examination that Connie's condition was severe. He scheduled her for surgery and further tests to confirm his determination.

By the end of February, the prognosis wasn't good. Connie had cancer and it had spread to lymph nodes in her neck. Marvin reviewed the results with Connie and Sam, making certain they understood everything, with complete understanding that this cancer would take her life in the very near future. His advice to them was to enjoy the time Connie had left.

As a last effort, Connie's family doctor in Jackson Heights recommended cobalt treatments to her neck over a period of two months. The treatments were several times a week. Between Barbara, her grandparents, me, my mother, and neighbors, we took turns taking Connie to the hospital in nearby Forest Hills for treatment. Connie was weakened from the treatments, eventually requiring a wheelchair, and often said, "I can't wait until the summer to know whether or not I'm going to live through this."

At the time, I felt that the doctor had advised Connie and her family poorly. He gave us all false hope. I questioned, "What good does hope do, when faced with an impossible long shot?" But I've come to believe it is hope, along with a wish and a prayer, that can make for a better chance that a person is the one in a million to receive a miracle.

As I write this chapter, I'm thinking ahead to forty years after Barbara's mother faced a terminal cancer diagnosis in 1971. In 2011, it would be Barbara. And once again, after so many times, Barbara and I reached out for hope. A couple of weeks before Barbara passed, she knew the end of her life was near. Yet, when a nurse asked Barbara if she wanted to continue with the strenuous chemotherapy treatments, Barbara answered emphatically: "Yes!" She was a three-time breast cancer survivor, and our wishes and prayers might have helped, over the course of the thirty years of recurring cancers she survived. But there would be no more miracles for Barbara. Perhaps

Barbara benefited from her share of miracles and the time had come for others to have a turn.

Connie's condition continually worsened. By May, Barbara's grandparents began commuting back and forth each day from their apartment in Far Rockaway to Jackson Heights to help out and be with their daughter. Many relatives came during this month to visit and help out. The only no-shows were Barbara's uncle and his wife, Arthur and Helen. Arthur was Connie's brother, her only sibling. Arthur had a cancer surgery on his stomach a couple of years before. He later explained that he didn't visit because he couldn't bear to see his sister dying, knowing that he could be facing death too.

Each day, Connie's condition became worse. Barbara's grandparents arranged for their rabbi to visit and offer prayers. The rabbi gave Connie a new name, "Alta," a Yiddish word which means old, and the rabbi offered prayers for her to grow old. But by the middle of May, the doctor notified the family that he would be making a house call and asked that the family be present. My mother was there, too, to give support to Barbara. The doctor examined Connie. After, he gathered the family in the living room and delivered the news. Connie had only six months to live.

I was at school when the doctor made the house call. There were no cell phones for text messaging in those days, no way for Barbara to let me know the outcome of the doctor's visit. After school, I went directly to Barbara's apartment.

As I walked into the apartment, Barbara ran to me. She took me immediately into her room. She closed the door behind us and started to cry, hugging me as she said, "Oh, Marc." As she cried, I tried to figure out what had happened since that morning, when I had stopped by to see her on my way to school. Finally, Barbara said, "My mom is not going to get better. She only has six months." I was stunned. I had no words to say. We stood there for quite a while in a full embrace.

I went home. Hearing me walk into the apartment, my mother called me into the kitchen. As I walked into the kitchen, my mother was sitting at the table looking pale and shocked. She said she had been sitting there for quite a while, just thinking and waiting for me to come home. I told her I'd just come from Barbara and I had some bad news. She said she already knew and had been with Barbara while the doctor was there.

We looked at each other for a few moments in silence before my mother said, "Sit down, we have to talk. Well, this news changes everything. Sam will probably stay in the apartment for now and move out immediately after Connie is gone. He's been married to her for only five months and has no ties to her family."

This prediction about Sam wasn't a surprise. During the five months that he and Connie had been married, he'd made no effort to bond with Barbara and her brother. There would be no reason for him to stay after Connie was gone. My mother continued. "Listen, Barbara is only nineteen years old. She can't be left to live alone until next year. You're going to have to change the wedding plans and get married when the time comes. I called Daddy at work and he agrees. You were marrying Barbara anyway. So, it'll be a year sooner. You need to tell this to Barbara soon ... tonight, so that she knows not to worry. She has enough on her now. You need to make sure she knows that you're getting married and she won't be alone after her mother is gone."

I sat there and listened to my mother, a little unsure and very nervous. Our wedding was scheduled for fifteen months away. We would have had time to plan where to live. By then, Barbara and I would have graduated from college and been working. Now, my mother was talking about me getting married a year sooner. Without it being said, I got the feeling that my mother believed Connie would be gone much sooner than the six months. Barbara was still nineteen and I was twenty-one. We weren't ready. But whether we were ready or not, my mother was right. There was no alternative. I didn't want Barbara to be alone. She couldn't be alone, with her thirteen-year-old brother. And I said to my mother, "Okay, I'll talk with Barbara later."

The six-month prognosis turned out to be totally incorrect. Connie passed away almost two weeks later. The last weekend in

May was Memorial Day weekend. My parents left for a weekend in the Catskills and Barbara's brother was staying with a friend for the weekend. On Saturday, Barbara and I decided to get away for the afternoon and go to The Bronx Zoo, leaving her mother under the care of her grandparents and Sam. First, we stopped by my parents' apartment to pick up some things and headed to my car, which was parked by Barbara's apartment building. As we got to the car, we saw Sam running out of the building. He explained that Connie was in terrible pain and the doctor had called in a prescription to the pharmacy. We told Sam to go back to the apartment and we'd go to the pharmacy.

By the time we got back to the apartment, Connie's condition had gotten worse. As she lay in bed, she was in dreadful pain, saying, "I'm dying ... I'm dying." We were all panicked, confused, and didn't know what to do. Who do we call for help? Should we scream in the hallway for neighbors? Should we call the police? Should we call emergency for an ambulance? We were crying as we paced in different directions, in and out of the bedroom.

It was painful for Barbara to stay in the bedroom, watching her mother suffer. But each time she left the room, her grandmother would shout out, "Barbara, come in here. Your mother wants to see you." As we all stood beside the bed, Barbara turned to me. "Call my Uncle Arthur and Aunt Helen and tell them they need to get here."

I went into the living room to make the call. Helen answered the phone. I explained what was going on and I heard her say, "Arthur, Connie is dying. We need to leave now." To me, she said, "We're on our way."

They were not going to make it in time. As I hung up the phone, I heard coming from the bedroom the most horrific sound that I'd ever heard in my life. Connie had just passed and her mother, Barbara's grandmother, was screaming in a shrieking voice, over and over, "Connie, talk to me ... Connie, talk to me. I'm your mother ... Connie ... I'm your mother. Talk to me ... talk to me."

Barbara came running out of the bedroom and into my arms. We cried as we held each other in the tightest embrace and listened to the repeated screams. "Connie ... talk to me... I'm your mother." As I write this, tears fill my eyes and I can still feel the emotions of that moment. Since then, I have never witnessed a person's life ending with such pain or heard shrieks so heart-wrenching. It was a horror. The sound of those shrieks has never left me. Even at this very moment, I find it difficult to write about. Because as I write, my fingers stop on the keyboard, my mind wanders, my eyes close, and I relive the horror. Barbara was totally broken, shaking with fright. The sight of Barbara watching her mother take her painful last breath and the sound of her grandmother's shrieks are still so clear to me. I can still feel and hear them resonating through my entire body and I quiver at the coldness of the moment, with a chill going through me. Barbara's mother was only forty-three.

About an hour later, Arthur and Helen arrived. As they walked into the apartment, Barbara ran to Helen, while Arthur consoled his parents. Barbara's grandmother was on the phone with the rabbi, informing him of Connie's passing and asking him to officiate at the funeral. This had been an incredibly stressful several-month experience for Barbara, and she wanted all arrangements to happen quickly. Hearing her grandmother on the phone with the rabbi, Barbara urged for the funeral to be as soon as possible, like, the next day, Sunday. But the rabbi advised that the funeral could not be until Tuesday because of the Jewish holiday of Shavuot on that Saturday, Sunday, and Monday.

Arthur and Barbara's grandfather left to go to the funeral parlor to make the arrangements. Helen consoled Barbara and said Barbara's brother would come to live with them in Long Beach. Barbara's brother, Mark, was only thirteen. He wasn't in the apartment for this ordeal. It was Memorial Day weekend and his friend's family invited him to come along with them to upstate New York for the weekend.

Barbara gave me her mother's telephone book and asked me to call all their friends and relatives. When Arthur and Barbara's grandfather returned from the funeral parlor, Arthur asked the six of us to gather around the dining table: me and Barbara, her grandparents, and Helen and him. As we all sat at the table, Arthur turned to me and blurted out, "How much money do you make selling real estate?" My instant thought was, "Why is that any of his business, and do I really have to tell him?"

Barbara and I had just been through hell and Arthur had marched into the apartment like a hero. Actually, more like a schmuck. He stood tall with his chest sticking out. When he asked me how much money I made, I was intimidated by his obnoxious forwardness. Reluctantly, I told him how much I earned. He answered, "That's good and enough for the two of you to live on. I'll arrange for the two of you to get married in my rabbi's chamber."

I so regretted telling Arthur my earnings. It was none of his business. I regretted not telling him off at that point. He hadn't shown up for months while all this suffering was going on and now, he was a big shot. I always had the impression Arthur thought of himself as a big shot. To me, he seemed to be enamored with being a college graduate and a lawyer. I don't believe he ever practiced much law. A cousin of Arthur's once mentioned to me that they believed Arthur made his living from bootlegging recording song tapes. So, it could be that Arthur not only didn't practice law, but also didn't obey the law. It appeared to me that other family members didn't think much of him. His cousins talked about him as being smug and condescending. His cousin Ann would say about Arthur, "I can buy him, sell him, and when I'm finished, I can throw him in the garbage."

I quietly sat at the table and held back my feelings, and held myself back from saying, "You pompous-ass son of a bitch. Who the fuck do you think you are?" But I said nothing and sat and listened to the rest of his bullshit plans.

Barbara and I decided not to call my parents, since they were away for the weekend and the funeral wasn't until Tuesday anyway. Instead, on Monday, we waited in my parents' apartment for them to come home. As soon as they walked into the apartment and saw the look on our faces, my mother immediately asked, "What's the matter?" We told them. My mom got very upset and we stayed with my parents until they calmed down a little. Then I walked with Barbara back to her apartment.

Later, I went home and filled my parents in on the details of all that happened on Saturday, including what Arthur had said about arrangements for Barbara and me to be married. My parents had a lot of pent-up disgust about Arthur and Helen. They were about to let it all out. My mother was first.

"Oh, so now the two of them finally show up. They weren't around when his sister was dying, to give support to his elderly parents who were losing a child and watching her die. They don't have the brains to think that their nineteen-year-old niece and thirteen-year-old nephew could have used their support. Listen to me," my mother shouted, "you're not getting married in his rabbi's chamber or anyone's chamber. Every girl deserves to be a bride and have a real wedding. I don't believe in this rabbi's chamber business. Barbara is going to be my daughter-in-law and she will be a bride and have a wedding. Who the hell do they think they are? They act like they have so much money and the best they can do is something in their rabbi's chamber and to make such a plan without discussing it with me and Daddy. Do they think that they're better than us?"

My father added, "I don't give a rat's ass who they think they are. Mommy and I discussed the whole thing while you were walking Barbara home. We will be making all the arrangements and paying for the wedding. The funeral is tomorrow and then people will be coming to the apartment all this week. I'll make an appointment for next Sunday to meet with the caterer at the shul and we'll see what dates he has available to move the wedding up one year sooner. Tell this to Barbara and keep it all to yourselves. Let's get past the funeral and this week. Is this okay with you?"

"Yes, I'm going back to Barbara later and I'll tell her everything."

The funeral was Tuesday, June 1, 1971. Between the funeral and the rest of that week with the apartment filled each day with visiting friends and relatives, plus Barbara's grandparents sleeping over in the apartment, it was difficult for Barbara and me to get alone time together. But when we had the opportunity to be alone, I had my arm around Barbara, as we stared into space. Barbara would ask, "Everything is going to be all right ... right?"

That was the first time Barbara asked me that question. It would be a question she asked me many times, in many different situations, over the next forty years. It would be years later that I began to better understand its meaning and our relationship, at the times she asked this question. Back then, I simply answered, "Yes."

I was relieved that Barbara accepted an answer of just, "yes." Because I didn't know how to answer. I figured that a "yes" was what she wanted to hear. I was young and inexperienced about life. I was totally unsure about how everything was going to be. Rather than answering with yes, a more accurate answer would have been, "I don't know." Because I didn't know.

This was an incredibly challenging time for us as a young couple. Having no relationship with her father and faced with the loss of her mother at nineteen, Barbara was a teenaged orphan, and soon to become a full-fledged adult, a wife. Even though we had planned to be married so young, Barbara was depending on her mother, to whom she was so close, to guide her and walk her down the aisle.

I was overwhelmed and confused about what was expected of me. I was twenty-one, had one more year of college, and was soon to take on the responsibility of being a husband. How was I to know if everything was going to be all right? I was a Jewish boy, still living at home with mommy and daddy. Although I knew how to wipe my ass, that was about all I knew. Also, it was 1971. Husbands were expected to be the primary breadwinners. And we were still virgins. What if Barbara became pregnant? Do I quit college and get a full-time job? It was all happening too quickly for the two of us. We found our comfort amid the tumult when being alone, with my arm around Barbara, as we stared into space.

The afternoon of the funeral, Barbara's father, Morty, came to the apartment to offer his condolences. He walked over to Barbara's grandfather and extended his hand, prompting her grandfather to shout, "Get out of my sight! You ruined my day!" The apartment was filled with people. It was kind of embarrassing but broke up the solemnness in the apartment. It also gave Barbara and me a little laugh in the midst of our sadness. Later that evening, we joked about the ridiculousness of that statement. I said to Barbara, "I guess your grandfather was having a good day up until your father approached him. Even though it was the day of his daughter's funeral. Sounded to me like his day wasn't ruined until he saw your father. That's pretty incredible shit."

Barbara didn't have any love for her father. She often described the awful experiences of her childhood. Barbara heard the arguments when her mother would get her dad to fess up to the details of his unscrupulous activities. She described the time her father took the household money and tried to cover up for the missing money with a false story of a robbery. He staged the robbery and even called the police to investigate. Another time, Barbara heard her father bragging that he used his paycheck to hire prostitutes and how he was able to get young girls. Barbara talked about how frightening it was for her. During one of the arguments she witnessed, her father ran into the kitchen and came out with a large knife and threatened to kill himself.

Connie's surgeon cousin from New Jersey, Marvin, also came to pay his condolences the afternoon of the funeral. This prompted another scene in the apartment. Barbara's grandmother shouted, "Marvin, why did you tell Connie that she was dying? You never should have told her. She was so very frightened. There was no reason for her to know." Marvin was a professional and handled that outburst very well. I could see in his face the sincere understanding of her grandmother's pain, having lost her daughter. Marvin calmly and gently answered, "Doctors always have to tell their patients the truth."

"You shouldn't have told her. There was no need for that." Barbara's grandmother wouldn't let up.

Barbara and I felt so badly and embarrassed for Marvin. We had spoken to Marvin several times after he diagnosed Connie's condition. Even with his busy schedule, he always made time to talk with us and the talks were never rushed. He was patient and kind. Marvin's reputation with family and extended family was that he was always supportive of their medical needs.

As people visited that day and for the rest of the week, Barbara's grandmother took them on tours of the apartment and pointed out everything she had bought for Connie over the years, noting how much each thing cost. Her grandmother even opened drawers and the cabinets in the kitchen to point out items. Her prize item to show off was a large vase, filled with an expensive artificial flower arrangement, which sat atop the television in the living room. She went on and on talking about the type of vase and flowers and what each cost. She also made sure to let everyone know how much she did for her daughter over the years, while never mentioning how much her daughter did for her.

It was sad to see Barbara's grandmother grieving the loss of a loving and devoted daughter, and talking only about material things. Barbara and I couldn't figure out if her grandmother truly understood what her loss was. Was her loss that she would no longer be able to do things for her daughter that would get her a thank you? She was a domineering person who had to be in control and looked to be thanked for everything she did. Or was her loss that she would no longer be able to brag about the things she did for her daughter?

After so many stressful months, it was painful for Barbara to sit by and quietly watch as these scenes went on. Together, under our breath, we kind of joked about the goings-on of that week. There was some humor in it all. But through the forced joking, I could see how much it all hurt Barbara. She was always a people person; she wanted to be with family and friends. But it all had been too much, and she so wanted it all to be over, for everyone to be gone and for the two of us to be alone.

As predicted, Sam moved out of the apartment the day after the funeral. Arthur and Helen came a few times that week and Barbara's grandparents left on Saturday. As difficult as the situation seemed, things quickly got worse. Barbara quickly realized that her mother, grandparents, uncle, and aunt had made no plans or preparations for Barbara and her brother upon Connie's death. Barbara was left with almost no money for household expenses and bills to care for herself and her brother.

Connie had lived from paycheck to paycheck, along with the child support and alimony she could get from Morty and, from time to time, any assistance she could get from her parents and brother. But at this point, no one from Barbara's family was stepping up and offering any assistance. Rather, everyone ran for the hills. Her grandparents had suffered through the months of caregiving and watching their daughter die. They talked about how much they had done in the past for their daughter and never spoke about the future and the needs of Barbara and her younger brother. They packed up and left the apartment on Saturday morning, as if they had done enough and there was nothing else they needed to do.

On Sunday morning, I went with my dad to the caterer to discuss wedding plans, leaving my mother with Barbara. Some people were still coming that day to pay their respects. Unfortunately, the caterer had no earlier dates. He called an affiliate caterer, who had a date available in August. He stressed that we would be very satisfied with the wedding at this other synagogue, which was a nice congregation in Hewlett, Long Island. We left and went directly to the other synagogue to meet with that caterer.

As soon as my dad and I drove on to the parking lot at Congregation Beth Emeth, we had a good feeling. The synagogue had a nice, comfortable look about it. Going into the building had a nice feeling. The caterer was expecting us. When he heard us enter the building, he came out of his office to greet us and introduce himself. He started off taking us on a tour of the building, showing us the ballroom for the cocktail hour and dinner, the sanctuary, and the bridal room. After, we went to his office. He started with offering his condolences and then said, "I understand this has been a tough time for you. I'm not usually happy that I have an open date available so near in advance. But I guess it was meant to be that I haven't been able to engage an affair on this date. I have Sunday evening, August 29 available."

My dad turned to me and asked, "Are you available on August 29?"

"Yes."

My father answered, "Good! Because you're getting married on that day."

In under an hour, my dad made all the wedding arrangements, menu, flowers, band, and signed the contracts.

When we got back to the apartment, there were a couple of people still there. My dad told me not to say anything until everyone had left. As soon as the people left, my mother asked, "So, Ben, how did you do?"

My dad looked at me. "Tell Barbara."

I sat next to Barbara on the couch. "If you still want to marry me, we'll be getting married on August 29 at Congregation Beth Emeth in Hewlett."

With a big smile and her first happy voice in months, Barbara answered, "We're getting married in less than three months!"

"Everything is all done," my dad said, sounding pleased with himself.

My mother interrupted. "Ben, what are you saying? It's not all done! We need to order and mail invitations. We need clothes for the wedding and most important a wedding gown and veil and other things. I'm going to call my friend Beatty. Her daughter got married recently. I'll see if we can borrow her wedding gown."

"I'll call my cousin, Rose," Barbara said. "Her daughter, Marsha, wore a beautiful veil at her wedding."

My dad turned to my mom. "Okay, Dottie, let's go. You want to start making calls and plans. Let's leave the kids alone to talk."

Finally, after this long ordeal, Barbara and I were completely alone. As soon as my parents walked out of the apartment, the tears poured down Barbara's cheeks. I put my arm around her, and she laid her head against my shoulder. "Oh, Marc. There's been so much talking this week all about the past; my grandfather screaming that ridiculous thing at my father and my grandmother picking on Marvin and conducting tours around the apartment. The days of mourning and people offering words of support are all meaningless to me now. Now that everyone is gone, I feel even more that my mom is gone, and I miss her so much already. Your mother has been with me ... and I need her ... but she can't replace my mom."

"I know that my mother can't replace yours. She's just here for you and that's all. It's just you and me now and we can talk about what we want."

"I have so much to do," Barbara said. "I have to move forward and figure out plans for my brother. My aunt said that he'll live with them. But I haven't heard any more about that during this past week and don't know what to do. My childhood ... my childhood was watching my parents having such an awful marriage. I want a good marriage, with our children growing up in a happy home. I know it's going to be a rough start for us."

"Not so rough. We'll figure it all out and do things on our own, the way we want."

I didn't understand what it was or how it came about. But suddenly, I felt everything was going to be all right. Nothing had changed. Barbara was still nineteen and I was twenty-one. We both still had one more year of college. Somehow, suddenly, I believed our start was not going to be so rough for us. Everything was going to be all right. I didn't understand what came over me. It felt like I was wearing big-boy pants for the first time. It was the first time I had such confidence about taking on so much responsibility. But everything was going to be all right. I had Barbara.

Barbara couldn't stop the words spilling out. "You know that my grandparents controlled my mother's life and my uncle put in his two cents, too, in return for the help they gave to her. But they were all paid back with my mother always responding to their every beck and call. I never want it to be that way for me. I want to be my own person with my husband. That's you, silly. I don't know how we're going to do it. But we have to, Marc ... we have to. I need you so."

My head was resting atop hers. For the first time in several months, the apartment was so quiet. Everyone was gone and the silence was comforting. We spoke to each other just above a whisper. "Barbara," I said, "we'll figure everything out, just the two of us. I didn't ask for anyone's approval to get engaged. I bought your ring on my own and totally paid for it myself. Y'know, we should take a ride up to The Bronx and I can show you the house that I sold to pay for your ring."

"I'd like to do that. Can we knock on the door and I can thank the people for my ring?"

"No, I don't think so."

Snuggled up together on the couch, with my head still resting atop Barbara's, we were beginning to feel the calm in the apartment. Everyone had left. It felt good being alone. There was no one to console us and no one for us to console. The tears were over. We were loosening up. We laughed, talking about knocking on the door of the people I sold the house to in The Bronx. We were each with the only person we wanted to be with. Our talking gradually drifted to a stop. Our eyes closed. We dozed off to the sound of each other breathing.

We may have dozed off for about fifteen minutes, when I heard Barbara ask, "Are you sleeping?"

I laughed. "Not anymore, silly head. Barbara, listen, from now on, it's just you and me. My parents are going to pay for our wedding. After, we'll be on our own and we will never ask anyone for money or help. Your life in the past is all over. We're starting off new and it will be our way and we'll never have to answer to anyone except to each other."

Barbara answered, "I love you. One more thing that we haven't talked about. Can we go on a honeymoon?"

"Um ... I have been thinking about that. Give me some more time on that one."

As much as I thought that I couldn't love Barbara any more than I already did, at that moment, as we whispered to each other with the total silence around us, it felt like our love had risen to a new level. Although her eyes were filled with tears, Barbara was so strong. She had survived a difficult childhood and was now facing the loss of her mother. Yet, she wasn't quitting. She was determined to move forward. Barbara wasn't going to let her past life experiences hold her back. She was a survivor and so resilient. Barbara knew what she wanted and intended to get it all.

Barbara turned to face me and as I looked into her eyes, I saw the strength and courage in her that I doubted I could ever have. I was a little scared at this point. About thirty minutes before, I felt like I was wearing big-boy pants. But this was 1971. As a husband, I was expected to be a man who would be strong and protect and provide for my wife. Barbara was everything to me. I wondered if I could be everything to her.

In the coming years, this sweet and soft nineteen-year-old girl would be the rock of our family. Today, I know that it was Barbara who led us through a forty-year marriage, overcoming so many difficult times along the way.

I noticed tears again. "Smile for me, Barbara," I whispered. "Can you smile for me?"

She forced a smile. "Am I smiling?"

"Yeah, that's kind of a smile. Now, there's one more thing that we haven't talked about."

"What's that?"

"Those fucking artificial flowers in that vase on top of the TV. Can I throw them down the incinerator?"

"You're so silly," she answered.

CHAPTER 7

Something about the two of us had changed

It was the summer of 1971 when, somehow, someway, something happened that resulted in a change in the both of us. I don't know what it was. But it was a pivotal time for us, a game changer. Something came over the both of us at the very same moment and we felt changed. I'm not sure how to explain it or what exactly changed about us. We just felt differently about ourselves and about us.

Maybe it was the result of experiencing one thing after the other: losing Barbara's mother, experiencing the funeral and the period of Shiva, and the struggles with wondering about making plans for her brother's care. And we were planning our wedding. We were getting married! Barbara was nineteen and I was twenty-one. We were going to be a big girl and boy. So much happened over a short period of time. Could it have been all that? I'm not sure what it was. But suddenly, everything felt different. Like suddenly, we could take risks and deal with them. The summer of 1971 made us stronger and drew us even closer together. We felt we could accomplish anything.

The sun was once again shining down on Barbara and me. Everything was coming together. We were surrounded by the smiles and happiness of everyone who knew of our wedding plans. My mother took Barbara to mom's friend Beatty to try on the wedding gown, which fit perfectly. Barbara picked up her Cousin Marsha's veil. The invitations were ordered. My mother and sister-in-law made appointments to go dress shopping.

In the meantime, I was brainstorming what to do for our honeymoon. We knew so many couples who'd recently gotten married and had gone on exotic honeymoons. Well, they were exotic for the 1970s. The big problem for me: I was afraid to go on an airplane. I had never flown. The thought of it terrified me. I wanted to find a honeymoon destination within driving distance.

I came across an advertisement for a honeymoon resort, high in the Pocono Mountains, in Lakeville, Pennsylvania, only a few hours' drive from Jackson Heights. It was advertised as being located close to a lake. I called the resort and requested a brochure be sent to me.

To a horny twenty-one-year-old who was still a virgin, the brochure was compelling. It showed pictures of the suites with mirrors on the walls around the round bed and on the ceiling above the bed. There were Roman-style bathtubs, with mirrors all around them, too. The floors had shag carpeting, even in the bathrooms. I planned to keep my eyes open for all the love making and see as much of Barbara as possible. Hoping, she'd want to see as much of me too. All I had to do was convince Barbara this place was as great as I thought it was.

With brochure in hand, my sales pitch planned, I went to Barbara's apartment. As soon as I walked in, Barbara saw the smirk on my face, and she knew something silly was up.

"Let's sit at the table. I have something to show you. I have a brochure about a great honeymoon resort. Everyone we know goes to the same places. I think we should do something different and more special."

Barbara looked at me with a suspicious smile. She knew I was a prankster, making up things that I would try to get her to believe, and joking around with the silliest of ideas. In a curious and cautious voice, Barbara asked, "Okay ... so ... is that the brochure you're holding, with the cover toward you? Is there a reason why you're not showing it to me?"

"I'm just trying to set the scene for presenting a plan to you for an incredible honeymoon."

Barbara started to laugh. "Okay, silly, I can already tell that this is going to be a joke. So, tell me your plan."

"Yes, my plan. So, okay. Well, we'll come back to the apartment after the wedding and the next morning, we leave—"

"Stop right there," she interrupted me. "No! We're not coming back to the apartment after the wedding. We're going to your parents' apartment and picking up our luggage, which will be packed and ready for our honeymoon. I know it will be late Sunday night. So, we'll stay overnight near the airport at the Sheraton Inn at La Guardia. The next morning, we will leave for our honeymoon from there. When we come back from our honeymoon, we're going straight to our apartment and you'll carry me over the threshold. That's the plan. Does any of that interfere with your plan, which I can't wait to hear?"

Barbara threw off my thoroughly planned sales pitch. It almost burst my bubble and I got a little ruffled. I had to digest all that information for a few seconds. I became preoccupied with the idea of carrying Barbara over the threshold. I weighed, like, 145 pounds and was five feet, ten inches tall. I wondered if I could lift her. Barbara was thin, but about five feet, six inches tall. A little shaken by all that information, I tried to regain my momentum. I began to feel a little insecure that I would be able to sell Barbara on the Poconos.

Trying to find my way back to what I'd planned as my grand presentation, I timidly answered, "No ... that's fine. It doesn't interfere at all. But you want me to carry you over the threshold? I'm not sure I can carry you."

"You better start working out. Because that's what you're going to do."

I was seeing a new side of Barbara. She put me in my place. It caught me off guard. I felt that Barbara was a strong person, having survived her life's experiences so well. And I believed her to be a stronger person than I was. We weren't married yet. She already sounded like my wife. And, you know what? I liked it! I liked it! My sweet, soft, beautiful, future wife could come on like a powerhouse. And I liked it. I laughed, watching the dimples in her face, as she told me what I better do.

"When did you start being so bossy?" I asked, grinning from ear to ear.

"Right now, as I can't wait to hear your plan." She was laughing too, when she added, "Is this really going to turn out to be a joke?"

Saying that, Barbara loosened up a bit on me and I regained my momentum.

"Nope! Here's the brochure. It's an incredible honeymoon resort."

Barbara glanced though the brochure. "Marc, the rooms have shag carpeting, even in the bathrooms, with mirrors all over the place and big bathtubs."

"Those aren't bathtubs. They're Roman tubs that you step down into and the mirrors are there so we can see more of each other from every position. It's all geared for honeymooners and fucking, which, you'll agree, we need to catch up on."

Barbara looked at me with her sweet, dimpled smile. I could see in her eyes that she was fine with my honeymoon plans. I waited a few seconds, as my composure changed from a little silly to serious. I had started off presenting my plan in my typical, joking way. My joking was over. It was time to be serious. I knew this honeymoon meant a lot to Barbara. It would be the buffer between the difficult experiences of her past and the fresh start to our lives together. We were taking over her mother's apartment and this honeymoon would be a getaway from Jackson Heights. It would be like coming back to a new beginning.

I took Barbara's hand. We got up from the table, went into the living room, and sat on the couch. We kissed, smiled, gazed into each other's eyes, and kissed some more. We weren't making out, just lovingly kissing. In a soft voice, I said, "Barbara, I'm afraid to fly and I don't want to be thinking about it and nervous from now and until the wedding."

I didn't know it back then, but I suffered from OCD (obsessive-compulsive disorder). What I did know was that I would have obsessed for weeks about getting on an airplane. I continued as Barbara listened to me. "After all that we've been through, it will be so nice and relaxing to drive off in my car, the morning after our wedding. It'll be just the two of us going at our own speed. It doesn't matter about the place. We'll be together and with other honeymooners, looking for the same kinds of things as us."

Barbara stared at me for a few seconds. Then she smiled. "It sounds very exciting, and I do want to go there, because I'll be with you. Only you could come up with something like this ... and I know that you want it to be special. I love you for that, silly."

"Okay. I'll make the reservations. Now that our honeymoon plans are done, are we all set on our job and school decisions?"

For several weeks, Barbara and I had been talking about how we were going to support ourselves. We were determined that once we were married, we would be totally independent and on our own and never ask anyone for money. We decided I would finish college on schedule, while continuing with real estate, working evenings during the week and all day on weekends. Barbara was an education major and was finishing up the season of her student teaching. After the summer, we'd decide what to do about her student teaching for the fall. Our plan was for Barbara to do all the cooking for the week on Sundays, while I was working. Barbara would go back to her modeling job from the summer before and attend night classes at Queens College, delaying her graduation.

We were confident we could make it work. During one of our conversations, Barbara and I talked about the many sacrifices we would need to make, like seeing much less of each other. This was going to be new for us. Because up until this point, we weren't fully supporting ourselves financially. Neither of us had our own apartment. Money, bills, budgets were never a concern. We were able to be together all the time, with no worries. Now we would be crossing paths, rushing in different directions. But we'd have the nights together. That meant so much more than we'd ever had.

I couldn't resist making one joke. I was sitting on the couch and Barbara was standing in the dining area. I tried to put on a serious voice. "Y'know, we're going to be married and the best part about being married is that we will be able to 'do it' whenever we want. It doesn't sound like we're going to have time and you've been holding out on me for so long."

Barbara came over to the couch and sat next to me. With a smirk on her face and in a sexy voice, Barbara answered, "Listen, silly, I'm sure we'll have time for that. Why? How often are you planning for?"

"I only want to make sure that you're happy. I figure twice a day, once in the morning and once in the evening."

"You are so silly," Barbara answered.

I quickly answered, "You listen to me. We have to make up for lost time!"

By the middle of July, the invitations had been mailed and our wedding plans were all set. Also, Barbara's biggest concern, the care for her brother, Mark (with a 'k'), was all worked out, after a big setback. For more than a week back in June, Barbara placed several calls to her aunt and uncle, to coordinate a meeting with them. Often, the phone would just ring and ring with no answer. When Helen or Arthur did answer, they had excuses to delay meeting with us.

One evening, we decided to take a drive out to Long Beach and just show up at their home. We took Mark with us. It was a very short meeting. As soon as we walked in, we all sat in the living room and Arthur started the conversation off saying he had already raised his children and he wasn't interested in doing it again. His message was short and not-so-sweet. What also wasn't so sweet was his impatient tone, like he couldn't be bothered. And he said this in front of Mark.

After some small talk, Barbara and I stood up with Mark, politely said our goodbyes, and left. As soon as we got into the car, I said, "I know he's your uncle and everything. But I have to say, he can kiss my ass."

"Unbelievable," Barbara fumed. "Why did my aunt make the offer to begin with? They must have discussed it beforehand. What changed their minds?"

"I don't think they had discussed it at all. Probably, your aunt didn't know what to say when she saw you and just blurted it out, but never really meant it. Your mother always said that your aunt is a phony. As for your uncle, I think he's a dickhead."

As I looked into the rearview mirror, I noticed the sorrowful look on Mark's face. I realized this was not a good conversation to have while he was sitting in the back seat, very upset. I felt badly for him and for what I had said. Mark was only thirteen. I wasn't helping by trying to come up with a solution in front of him. What we needed to do was to make sure Mark understood that his well-being was not being overlooked and that he'd be all right. I waited a few seconds and said, "Let's just get back and not talk about this right now."

When we got back to Barbara's apartment, Mark went to his room and Barbara and I talked in the living room. Barbara asked, "What are we going to do? With my mother always working, I played sister/ mom to my brother. We're going to be so busy. Who's going to make sure he's being taking care of? He's only thirteen."

"It's not like we're rushed to make arrangements for your brother. We're taking over this apartment and he has his own room. It's not like we're moving out."

Shaking her head from side to side as if to say, no-no-no, and with a frowning, worried look on her face, Barbara said, "Oh, Marc, how could he live with us? He'd be on his own from early morning until the evening with no supervision. How are we going to do this?"

"You didn't have a relationship with your father, but your brother got along with him well. He's living with his girlfriend in Greenpoint, Brooklyn. But we don't actually know if your father has straightened himself out or what kind of woman he's living with."

"I know what I'm going to do. I'm going to call my father tomorrow and tell him the situation. I'll say I'm concerned that Mark is going to be unsupervised a lot. Let's see what his response is. The only way that I can allow Mark to live with my father is if I'm satisfied that my father has straightened himself out and his girlfriend has been a good influence on him and is a good person, ready to be a stepmother. I don't want to get involved with my father, if this has no chance of working out."

"Okay. Let's take one step at a time."

I went home, where my parents were waiting to hear what had happened with our meeting with Arthur and Helen. After hearing about Arthur's pronouncement, my father said, "Okay. We're not surprised. Mommy and I have no use for those people anyway. We've talked about it. You're getting married and moving out. Mark can move into your room and live with us. This way, he will just be moving around the corner, keeping all of his friends and going to the same school."

"Okay, that's a good alternative," I answered. "But first, Barbara is going to call her father and find out what is going on in his life with his girlfriend. It may work out that Mark gets reunited with his father."

My mother spoke up. "If that's what Barbara is going to do, you and Barbara need to go to see Morty, see where and how he's living, what kind of home his girlfriend has, and what she does. And see if they are ready and capable of caring for a thirteen-year-old kid, before sending Mark off to them. Otherwise, he'll live with us."

I was surprised to hear my parents make that offer. They had raised my older brother, who was married, and me, who was getting married. I figured they were looking forward to being on their own. I had heard so much about their plans for converting my room into a den with a couch and TV. Now, they were prepared to take on the responsibility of a thirteen-year-old kid. As surprised as I was about this offer back then, as I write about it today, I'm not surprised at all. This offer was so my parents. They would have loved raising Mark.

The next day, Barbara waited until I got to her apartment before she called Morty. She wanted me to be on the extension phone in the bedroom, so we could both talk to him. Barbara was crazed with worry for her brother. She wouldn't abandon him or pass him over to just anyone. She wanted me to help her listen and screen every word from her father. She questioned herself, did she even want to give her father the option of caring for Mark? Although Morty appeared to have straightened himself out, he was still the father she had little respect for. To Barbara, Mark was not only her brother, he was her mother's child. She asked herself, "What would my mother have wanted me to do?" We needed to figure this out.

It turned out, Morty and his girlfriend, Roberta, had been discussing plans for having Mark live with them. Morty explained that he had been living with Roberta for quite a while. She couldn't have children and would welcome having Mark live with them.

But all that wasn't good enough for Barbara. She told her father to hold on for a few minutes. Barbara put the phone down and came into the bedroom, where I was on the extension. As Barbara began to whisper to me, I put the phone down too. We went into the other bedroom to talk.

"Marc, I'm not comfortable with this. I can't do this quickly. Maybe, I can't do this at all. He is my brother. If anything, I need to spend some time with Roberta and my father and see where and how they're living."

"Barbara, you're the one in control, not your father. Tell those exact words to your father and tell him everything else that's bothering you. Let's see how far he'll reach for your brother. And still in the end, you control the decision. Tell him that too. This isn't a done deal just because he wants to have a family with his girlfriend."

After going through all the steps, tests, and drills that Barbara demanded of her father and Roberta, this story did have a happy ending. Barbara was very happy with Roberta. Roberta was a lovely person and a good influence on Morty. Within a couple of weeks, Roberta and Morty made plans to be married in mid-September, a few weeks after our wedding. They also began apartment hunting in Jackson Heights and quickly went under contract at nearby Northridge Cooperative, for a September occupancy. Most importantly, Mark was happy being reunited with his father. Also, most importantly, Barbara was smiling and confident her brother would be well parented.

So, here we were. It was the middle of July. Our wedding day was just six weeks away. Barbara and I were in the apartment, busily doing chores to convert her mother's apartment into what was going to be a newlywed couple's apartment. For Barbara, a high priority was the bedroom.

Barbara didn't want the bedroom to remind her that this was the room where her mother died. It needed a striking, overhauling change. We stripped apart the bedroom, discarding her mother's furniture, carpeting, and window treatments. We ordered new furniture and carpeting. I painted the room and hung wallpaper on the wall behind the bed, an orange and yellow paisley print. We ordered bright orange shag carpeting. Today, our decorating choices might sound outrageous. But in 1971, the bedroom looked like it was right out of a decorator's magazine. Barbara and I were so proud. It was our first decorating creation.

We were often alone in the apartment in July and up until our wedding weekend. With each new thing that we did in the apartment, we were smiley, giggly, sometimes touchy-feely and kissing. I was almost finished painting the living room wall behind the couch, orange. Barbara wanted the apartment to be transformed into a bright and cheerful apartment. That's what I was doing. Again, this was 1971 and an orange wall in the living room looked nice. Barbara said, "I just realized. I need to decide who is going to walk me down the aisle."

"Whoa! Hold on," I said as I came down from the ladder. "Is there anything to decide? It should be your father. He's been out of your life for several years, but he's back now and your brother is going to be living with him."

"My grandparents will have a fit. It'll probably be too much for them just to see my father at the wedding with Roberta. I think I should ask my uncle to walk me down the aisle."

"Are you kidding me? Are you fucking kidding me? Do you really want to give that pompous ass that honor? Do you really need him to walk you down the aisle the way he does, with his shoulders back and chest out looking like a big shot and giving everyone the impression he contributed to this wedding?" I said, as I strode across the living room, imitating the way her uncle walked.

Laughing as she watched my imitation of Arthur, Barbara sarcastically answered, "Well, tell me how you really feel. I'm getting the impression you're angry with my family."

With a smile, I answered, "Yeah! Fuck them!"

Her sarcasm calmed me down. "Barbara, I thought that we were going to be our own selves, doing things on our own and the way we want, without anyone telling us what to do or having any control over us. We can do things in a way that will make people happy. But, if people aren't going to respect the way we want to do things or the decisions that we make, that's just tough on them."

"I'm so used to being controlled by my relatives. I need to break loose," Barbara replied.

"I have a great idea how you can take a major step in breaking loose," I answered with a smile.

"You are too silly. Okay, I can't wait to hear what you're going to come up with."

"We should take those artificial flowers and throw them down the incinerator, now ... right now! Let's do it!"

Barbara looked unsure. "Really?"

"Yes! I'm doing it and you'll feel totally free of all the bullshit. First, give me a few minutes to finish painting the wall and clean up, and we'll move the couch back."

I took the vase from the top of the television, placed it on the floor, and started to rip out the flowers. Barbara joined me. "I can't believe I'm doing this," she said. It was so much fun. We laughed hysterically as we bundled all the flowers and took them out to the incinerator. Barbara opened the chute and I tossed them down. Back in the apartment, Barbara asked, "What about the vase?"

"We'll keep that in the closet. It'll be a good thing to hold various nails, screws, and bolts, and things like that."

As I continued looking at the vase, Barbara came up to me and put her hands on my shoulders. "I love you."

"Do you feel better?"

Barbara didn't answer. Instead, we kissed and made our way to the couch where we lay down. For both of us, the moment together felt different than any before. Like, something about the two of us had changed. Like, we became emboldened, or something like that. It may have been the new responsibilities that were thrust upon us, and the sorting out and working through challenges that quickly matured the two of us. It may have been the decisions we needed to make and how we were strong together, moving forward totally in sync. Whatever it was, something had changed. We could feel the change together and see it looking into each other's eyes. Whatever it was, we didn't know. But something about the two of us had changed.

We continued to kiss and soon began to peel off some of our clothes. Our love, passion, and uncontrollable lust for each other had never been so intense than at that moment. Gradually, we were totally undressed. We were both virgins, for the first time feeling completely free, confident, independent, and responsible for ourselves. The moment was so uninhibited and there was nothing to stop us from the love we were headed for. This was our first time.

After, we continued to kiss. And then I noticed Barbara's tears. "Why are you crying?"

"Oh, Marc. I always promised my mother that I'd wait until my wedding night. Now she's gone and I broke my promise."

"Well, you did pretty well with your promise. We're getting married in like six weeks. You came very close and I'm very proud of you."

Weeping, Barbara answered, "Oh, don't be silly. It wasn't right. I wanted our wedding night to be special; to be the first time. Let's not go all the way again and be good until then. Okay?"

Barbara composed herself and we got dressed and back to doing our chores. The thought of not doing it again until our wedding night sounded easy at that moment, after we had just finished. But that thought wore off quickly and we didn't hold off very well at all. It was only about two hours later and we were going at it again.

Barbara was okay with it after the second time. There were no tears, since she had already broken her promise to her mother the first time we did it. But she continued to insist on a sex moratorium. "Okay, silly, now, no more until our wedding night." That didn't work. We continued going all the way, many times, over the course of the next six weeks. Each time was special, and each time felt like it was the first.

For so many years, it had been drilled into us that having sex before marriage was wrong. That saving ourselves for our wedding night would be the best kind of sex. Well, for Barbara and me, that proved to be total bullshit advice. We found that it was over-the-top arousing to be doing something that was supposed to be wrong to do. For us, it was knowing of the disapproval of our premarital sex that made for the best sex. Anyway, all the past lecturing didn't matter anymore. Barbara and I were doing things our way.

Two days before our wedding, on Friday, August 27, I was in my room finishing up things and getting ready to move out, when I heard my mother shout for me to come to the kitchen. I thought to myself, "Shit! What could she want now? Just two more days and I'm out of here." My mother was wonderful, and she made a good home for our family. But she was strict and demanding and I was really anxious to move out.

In those years, in the Jewish community where I grew up, a grown child didn't dare move out of their parents' home before marriage. Much worse was for a child to move in with their girlfriend or boyfriend. Exceptions to this rule were rare occurrences. But when it did happen, word would quickly spread through the community by way of the neighborhood yentas (a Yiddish word for a woman who gossips). People relished such gossip and categorized this lifestyle as socially unacceptable, disgusting behavior. Even if parents could find their way to accepting the lifestyle their children chose, they were embarrassed, knowing for sure that the yentas were gossiping about them. Because they would recall how in the past, they themselves would take part in the gossip, when it was someone else's child.

Nowadays, yentas have fallen on hard times to come up with community news to yenta about. Even information about someone's child pregnant before marriage is no longer yenta-worthy news. So much has become socially acceptable and, for this, I feel badly for yentas. Nevertheless, I don't believe that yentas will become extinct. There will always be yentas around and perhaps a conscientious effort needs to be made to make the important role of yentas understood by each community. I truly believe that no neighborhood is complete unless it has at least one good active and productive yenta, spreading the latest piece of gossip. In the East New York section of Brooklyn where I grew up, the yentas were a fabric of the community.

My empathy for the plight of yentas comes with some sarcasm. When Barbara and I lived in the suburbs, we'd hear of some of the gossip about us, such as the gossip about our walks together around the neighborhood. Barbara and I would walk, side by side, with our arms around each other. We would hear from sources that neighbors were saying, with disdain, "The way the Gellmans walk the neighborhood with their arms around each other. Do those two think they're still in high school, or are they just putting on a show?" Nevertheless, we couldn't have cared less about such gossiping behind our backs. We demonstrated our devotion and love for each other the way we wanted, with no concern about the gossip from the suburban yentas.

Barbara and I were certainly aware that high school was well in our past. We weren't putting on a show, but we sure did feel like we were still in high school. It's unfortunate that many people are unaware there's more to puppy love than they'll ever understand. If those married couples had the frame of mind to sustain a young romance and love, even for them, then high school puppy love wouldn't have to end. Instead, I so often hear couples talk about the wonder of growing old together. For Barbara and me, as we grew older in years, we talked about the wonder of staying young together.

So, moving out of my parents' home before marriage wasn't an option for me and my brother. My mother made that clear. "My children don't move out of the house until they get married," she would say, often. That's why I jokingly like to explain that I got married so young, because it was the only way I could move out of my mother's house. But at that moment, as I was summoned to the kitchen, I was still living in her house. I respectfully went to the kitchen. My mother began by saying, "Sit down. I want to talk to you."

I sat down, thinking, "Two more days and I'm out of here." I listened, as my mother continued. "In two days, you and Barbara will begin a new life as a married couple. From then on, all the major decisions that will affect your future happiness will be made by the both of you. You will have a wife and will be taking on the responsibilities of a husband. There are certain things that you should know in order to be a good husband." My mother began to list her "commandments" for being a good husband.

Number 1: As a husband, you should learn to keep your mouth shut.

Number 2: Your wife should be in charge of running the household.

Number 3: It's not your place to plan the dinner meals. Your wife should plan that, and you should be happy with it.

Number 4: Your wife should be in charge of the checking account.

Number 5: Your wife should be in charge of paying the bills.

Number 6: You should not cash your paycheck on the way home. Bring your check home, uncashed.

Number 7: You should turn down invitations from your friends at work to go out after work.

Number 8: You should go directly home after work to your wife.

Number 9: You shouldn't concern yourself with what other people have.

Number 10: You should be satisfied with what you and your wife have.

When my mother was finished with her list, she said, "So, you understand what I'm saying?"

"Yes," I answered.

At that moment, I just listened and accepted my mother's advice. Thinking back to that moment, I've come to realize how difficult it was for her. I've since learned of the joy, yet also the heartfelt emotions, experienced by a parent when a child is set free and leaves home. Our hope for our children is that they take the guidance we have given them and are ready to be on their own. We encourage our children to walk out our door and into the world, looking forward and not backward. But in our hearts, when our children do look back and see us, we want them to know they will see someone who, through good times and bad, will always love them and always care.

I loved my mom and so respected her for this advice that came with experience, wisdom, and love. At the time, I took her advice for granted, but I never forgot it. I'm proud to say that other than commandment number one, I was very good at obeying two through nine and maybe even okay at number one. As for commandment number ten, I was often impatient and always wanted more. Barbara wanted more, too, but she had a way in our family of making sure that while striving for more, we were thankful for what we had.

At times when things were difficult, Barbara would say, "What's with that worried look on your face?" Then, she would put her face close into mine and smile. When Barbara smiled, with her dimples showing, I couldn't help but smile too. And with that, the worries would be gone. Because we had each other and, as per commandment number ten, we really were satisfied with what we had.

This chapter of our story has tears, laughter, and silliness. With my silliness and sarcasm, I loved writing about the yentas. My silliness is sometimes a diversion for me to step out of my search and have some fun, until I can get back to what I'm searching for.

I wish I could better explain what the something was, that changed about the two of us, that summer of 1971. As I write searching for answers, this was one experience I never understood or found the answer. Something came over us and that was it.

It was just a feeling, and I could never figure it out. It was like five years' worth of growing up and experiences happened within a moment. It was like everything Barbara and I did was right. There were no regrets, no looking back. It was like everything around us was coming together so easily. We were in unison and knew what the other was thinking and didn't have to speak. It was like all we could think about was each other. It was like we were waving our arms orchestrating and music was happening. Or ... maybe it was Barbara's mother orchestrating from above, all the music around us.

CHAPTER 8

I can't believe it's me

What does one do the day before their wedding? For the groom, that's a lot different than for the bride, I think. The answer may seem obvious. But it wasn't to me back then.

I was with Barbara, in our soon-to-be newlywed apartment, for much of Friday, before our wedding weekend. That evening, I kissed Barbara goodnight and she said, "Goodnight, I love you. I'll see you on Sunday."

"Sunday! What about tomorrow?"

I didn't have any specific plans for Saturday. I figured I'd just stop by after I picked up my tuxedo and hang out a bit. Barbara answered, "You're not supposed to see me the day before the wedding. I have a lot to do tomorrow and so do you. The next time you see me, I'll be a bride. So, goodnight." She flashed me this big smile.

"How about one more kiss?"

"Goodnight," she said as she began to push me out the door.

"Wait, wait, you said that I have a lot to do tomorrow. Other than pick up my tuxedo, what else do I have to do?"

"Goodnight." She gave me one more push and closed the door behind me.

On Saturday morning, my cousin, Norman, and his wife, Carol, came to Jackson Heights to help out that day and sleep over that night before the wedding. The plan was that Norman would sleep over at my parents' apartment and Carol at Barbara's, to help Barbara get ready and to keep me from seeing Barbara the day before the wedding. Remember, my parents' apartment was just around the corner from our newlywed apartment.

So once again, and for one night, I had a roommate. From the time I was born, I shared a bedroom with my brother, until he got married. It was nice having my own room after my brother left. But after this one last night with a male roommate, my cousin, I looked forward to having a different kind of roommate: a female one who was going to be sleeping naked next to me.

I figured it was going to be unimaginably great to be married. I would never again have to say goodnight to Barbara and then leave to go home. I could sleep naked and go to the bathroom, wearing nothing. I could take a shower and not have to dry off in the bathroom and put something on to go from the bathroom to the bedroom. Even better, I would have company in the shower, to soap up my back and do other extracurricular shower activities with me.

Norman dropped off Carol at Barbara's with all her clothes for the wedding and then came to my parents' apartment. My dad, Norman, Barbara's brother, and I went to pick up our tuxedos, stopped off for lunch and then returned home. I mentioned to my dad that Barbara had said that there was a lot I had to do today. I asked him, "Other than picking up our tuxedos, what else is there for me to do today?"

"Nothing, we just relax and hang around until tomorrow. Then we get dressed, go around the corner to pick up Barbara, and I'll drive to the shul. It's just the three of us today. Mom is with Barbara and Carol, helping out to get things done."

"That's what I've been wondering about. What things are they getting done for them to be busy all day?"

"Getting ready," my dad answered.

I wasn't getting anywhere trying to understand if I was supposed to be doing something or what, exactly, was keeping the women so busy. I was getting restless, waiting around to do nothing but relax, all the while wondering what Carol and my mom were doing with Barbara. I decided to walk around the corner, hoping to be able to talk to Barbara through the window.

The apartment was on the second floor and the windows faced out to a small park alongside the building. From the park, I called up to Barbara. Carol came to the window and asked what I wanted. When I asked to talk to Barbara, Carol told me, a groom is not supposed to see the bride the day before the wedding and until she is wearing her gown and veil. I left. Two hours later, I came back and called up to the window. Again, Carol came to the window and I asked her what they were doing. She said they were busy and told me to go away and not to come back again.

The wedding was scheduled for Sunday evening at seven o'clock on August 29, 1971. That afternoon, my mom and Norman were at the apartment with Barbara and Carol. The women were helping Barbara and getting dressed together and Norman and Barbara's brother were getting dressed there too.

A friend, who had a Super 8-millimeter movie camera, volunteered to record a movie of all the goings-on in the apartment. There was a big contrast between the hubbub with Barbara compared to the activity at my parents' apartment, where it was just me and my dad. That day, I saw something in my dad's face that I hadn't seen before. Or maybe, I hadn't noticed before.

My dad wasn't one to show his emotions. Back then, men weren't supposed to cry. But that day it seemed like he was going to, and I didn't understand why. I noticed something different about the way my dad was looking at me. I could see the emotions in his face as he looked at me in my tuxedo and helped me straighten my bow tie. It was the first time I noticed my dad really looking at me. His face showed emotions of pride, happiness, and sadness.

It would be forty-three years later, at my son Jonathan's wedding, when I would feel such pride, happiness, and sadness. It was then that I understood: with our children, we become our parents. A few minutes before the wedding ceremony, there was a ceremony in a separate room from the chapel, for just close relatives. It was a ceremony to witness the signing of the ketubah, a Jewish marriage contract, and was led by Rabbi Bill Kraus, who officiated the wedding service. He was also the hospice rabbi who visited my home and comforted my family two days before Barbara died. Jonathan and Stacey were seated at a table across from the rabbi. Stacey's parents stood behind her and I stood behind Jonathan, my hands on his shoulders.

With tears running down my cheeks, I felt proud and happy. It was 2014 and acceptable for men to cry. Like my dad, I felt sadness, thinking, "Where did the years go?" And as I witnessed the ceremony looking through Shiva Eyes, I felt further sadness, thinking, "Where is Barbara?"

Several weeks after Barbara and I were back from our honeymoon, our friend invited us to his home to watch the movie. Back then, it was a little bit of a chore to set up for watching a home movie. When we arrived, he had the movie projector and projection screen ready for us. Since I couldn't see Barbara the afternoon before the wedding, I had only heard about what went on in the apartment. It was fun watching the movie and seeing all the tumult and excitement. My mother and Carol were fussing over Barbara. Norman and Mark were getting dressed. They were all having a fun time laughing and fooling around.

It was 1971 and the movie camera didn't record sound. But viewing the movie, it was easy to get the feel of the fun, happiness, and excitement. The movie showed Barbara holding up her gown and then ... she was fully dressed. The scene changed quickly. The tumult was gone. And the silent movie seemed quieter. Barbara and I watched the movie of her looking into the mirror and seeing herself for the first time. With gown and veil, she was a bride.

The movie was silent. But looking at the movie recording of Barbara's reflection in the mirror, it was easy to read her lips. And even though silent, I could hear my bride repeatedly saying, "I can't believe it's me. I can't believe it's me." Barbara had forgotten that she had said that. Or maybe she didn't realize that she was being filmed at that moment. It was an extraordinary moment for the two of us to see her saying the words, "I can't believe it's me." I squeezed Barbara's hand.

This was the first time that Barbara was in the limelight. The first time that it was all about her, with people all around, fussing over her. Until that day, for all her life, Barbara had always been the spectator to someone else who was celebrating something incredibly special. Now for the first time, something incredibly special was happening to Barbara.

My dad and I were dressed early and anxiously waiting for a phone call from Carol, telling us it was okay to come over. Finally, it was time for me to walk around the corner and see my bride. My dad drove his car to the front of Barbara's apartment building, getting it ready to drive us to the shul. As I approached the building, there was a group of neighbors waiting out front to watch Barbara and me leaving. They cheered when they saw me. I thanked them for their support and told them we'd be right out.

As I stepped out of the elevator, I saw Norman holding the apartment door open for me. The door was at the end of the hallway. With it open, I could see into the apartment, through the foyer and into the living room. Along with everyone else, Barbara's dad and Roberta were in the apartment, too, but everyone was standing to the side. As I walked down the hallway, I saw Barbara standing in the living room waiting for me.

Our friend was recording a movie of me walking down the hallway, into the apartment, and seeing Barbara for the first time in her gown and veil. I had such a big smile on my face, that I felt like my face was going to burst. I walked up to Barbara and we kissed. I couldn't take my eyes off her. She was so incredibly beautiful. I stared at her gown and Barbara asked if I liked it. I was too overwhelmed to speak and, with a beaming smile, gave her a wink.

Arriving at the shul, we were greeted by the caterer. It was a family-owned business; husband, wife, and daughter were there to orchestrate the wedding. The daughter was doing much of the orchestration of the ceremony and rehearsed with the wedding party. Rabbi Milton Goldberg and Cantor Yechiel Rosen rehearsed the ceremony with us. The rabbi said to me, "Your parents are going to walk with you down the aisle, until you are under the chuppah, or canopy. Then, they will stand to the side and you will be facing me. When your bride appears in the aisle, you're going to hear 'oohs' and 'ahhs' from your guests and your instinct is going to be to turn around. But you continue looking directly at me. Barbara's dad is going to be walking her down the aisle. Then, they will stop. Her dad will lift up her veil, give her a kiss, come to the chuppah, and stand to the side. Your bride will be standing by herself in the aisle. When I shake my head yes, you will turn, look at your bride, walk to her, and escort her to the chuppah. Remember, wait for me to shake my head, before turning around."

"Okay," I answered.

As the guests were being seated in the sanctuary, the band played background music and then switched to the processional music as the wedding party began to walk down the aisle. Then, it was my turn to walk down the aisle with my parents.

Under the chuppah, I stood nervously staring at the rabbi. With my back to the aisle, I listened to the band continue to play the processional music. Then, I heard the "oohs" and "ahhs" and knew that Barbara and her dad started to walk down the aisle. The band began to sing the song by The Carpenters, "We've Only Just Begun."

Barbara chose that song. It was so "us," she said, and so described our story and how our lives were going to be, together. It told our story of our dreams for our wedding day. With Barbara in white lace, we'll make our promises and say our "I do's." I'll break the glass, symbolizing the absolute finality of our marital agreement. Then, we'll kiss, and our marriage will begin. Less than twelve hours later, we'll awake before the sun rises and be on our way, driving the roads to our honeymoon. As we drive on the roads, through the hills and valleys along our way, we'll be talking and planning our future and begin to live.

When the band changed from the processional music to "We've

Only Just Begun," I was tempted to turn around. But I didn't. The rabbi had been so right to warn me about hearing the guests' reaction when Barbara started down the aisle.

I nervously waited for the rabbi's signal for me to turn around. It seemed like it was taking so long. I didn't move or even flinch. I focused on the rabbi, waiting for him to shake his head yes. Finally, the rabbi signaled, and I turned around. There was my bride, waiting for me. I had seen Barbara only minutes before the ceremony began. But seeing her standing in the aisle was amazing. I thought to myself, "There's my bride. I'm really getting married to the most beautiful girl in the world."

During the ceremony, I held Barbara's hand. Through her smile, I could see she was hurting. With the wedding party standing at the chuppah with us and all the guests in the sanctuary, it was on Barbara's mind, and everyone else's, too, that there was someone missing. Her mom had passed away on May 29, just three months before, to the day. At the end of the ceremony, I kissed my bride and held her hand to keep my balance for the traditional breaking of the glass. I lifted my leg up and gave it my all, for the biggest stomp on the glass, and everyone shouted, "Mazel Tov!"

We were supposed to walk slowly, out from under the chuppah and down the aisle. Barbara whispered to me that she needed to get to the bridal room quickly. So, we rushed down the aisle. At the end of the aisle, the caterer began to say something about the reception line. Barbara quickly interrupted, saying that she needed to get to the bridal room. We barely got into the room when Barbara fell into my arms and began to cry. "Oh, Marc ... I wish my mom was here. She was so looking forward to this day and I miss her not being here with me. I'm sorry I'm crying ... I'm sorry." I didn't say anything. I just held her in my arms as she cried.

While this was going on, the wedding party was on the reception line. By the time they joined us in the bridal room, Barbara had regained her composure and started redoing her makeup. They were all on a high and entered with smiles and laughing, which quickly helped to cheer up the mood in the room. We all started joking around and laughing.

The empty feeling, because Barbara's mother wasn't there, hung over us all evening. But we did celebrate, and the wedding was beautiful. The band was called The Jesters, and they kept us partying. Barbara and I added to the tone of the celebration, with our love for each other.

As per Barbara's plan, we spent our wedding night at a Sheraton hotel near the airport. We so had fun checking in, for the first time, as Mr. and Mrs. Gellman. As soon as we walked into our hotel room, Barbara kept repeating, "I'm Mrs. Gellman ... I'm Mrs. Gellman." Then she said, "I've become your mother."

"Oh, don't say that. You're going to kill the whole effect when I see you naked."

"Well, because of you, you've already seen me naked. and this should have been our first time."

"Are you blaming me? What's that expression, it takes two to tango? Also, before you, I didn't even know how to tango," I answered.

"Is that what you want to start to call it from now on, tango?"

"No, let's still call it fucking."

Barbara smiled, with those dimples showing. "You get undressed and ready, and I'll be right out of the bathroom."

"Let me go in there first. I've been holding it in and have had to take a piss for a while," I said as I dashed into the bathroom.

As I closed the door to the bathroom behind me, Barbara shouted, "Thanks for that announcement. I guess we really are married now."

I waited with anticipation. Barbara came out wearing a sexy, sheer negligée. She lay down beside me. As we kissed, Barbara whispered, "Well, at least this is the first time that you're seeing me wearing something like this."

I whispered back, "Why are you so hung up about it not being the first time? You know, this is a first. It's the first time that everyone knows that we're doing it. Even my mother. Even Aunt Fanny."

That night was special for us. Not only because of the great wedding ceremony and reception. It was that extra special way we felt, as we looked at each other and smiled, when the hotel clerk said, "Hello, Mr. and Mrs. Gellman. Welcome to the Sheraton." For the first time out on our own, we were who we wanted to be. The clerk was the first person who only knew us as Mr. and Mrs. Gellman and that felt so good. For Barbara and me, our wedding night was our first. What we didn't know that night was that our love would grow, but stay forever new and forever young and, for the next forty years, each time would always be like our first. After all the talking about our first time, on our wedding night, it was our first time ... again.

The next morning, Monday, we checked out of the hotel, loaded up the car, and started our adventure to our honeymoon. For two city kids, it was fun to see the countryside of western New Jersey and eastern Pennsylvania along the way. In a few hours, we came to the lake and knew we were getting close.

It felt so good to get out of the car when we arrived at the resort. We stretched and headed to the office to check in. At the office, we were advised that we needed to meet first with the resort manager. As we waited, Barbara said to me, "I wonder what the manager needs to talk with us about."

"Barbara, this is a resort for young honeymooners and many of them may not be knowledgeable about what to do," I answered in mock seriousness.

Barbara got silly. "You mean they are going to tell us how to put it in?"

We were both laughing as I said, "No, silly. They may just want to make sure that we are well informed about what to do. Maybe they want to make sure that we have condoms or maybe give us a quick instruction on what to do or show us a quick instructional movie. As soon as we walk in, we should advise the manager that we don't need any instructions, that we're fully prepared, and have been fucking since the middle of July."

We were getting sillier and sillier as we waited. We finally got into the manager's office and heard the bad news. The resort had overbooked, and we couldn't get into our room until Wednesday. We would have full use of the resort facilities and activities and it would be like we were at the resort. But for our first night we had to stay at a small motel down the road. For the second night, we would move into a cabin on the grounds of the resort and finally move into our room on the third day.

Although this was a disappointment, the resort was nice about it and made it up to us big time. But I had a fit. I felt responsible, since I convinced Barbara to go to this place. I felt like I'd let her down. Barbara took it in stride and calmed me down. "Marc, the room is not the important thing. We're only sleeping there. We still have everything that is going on and we'll only be down the road for tonight."

The manager added his two cents. "You have my word. We'll make it all up to you. And your wife is right. You have the use of all of the facilities and you're only sleeping there."

"This is our honeymoon! Who told you that we're only sleeping there?" I answered.

"Oops, oh—yes." The manager sounded flustered, and Barbara had an embarrassed look on her face.

That may have been the first time I said or did something that was embarrassing for Barbara. But after a few years of marriage, there was little I did that surprised Barbara, and any embarrassment rolled off her shoulders. Barbara enjoyed entertaining friends, hosting house parties, and preparing all the food herself. I viewed Barbara's parties as an opportunity to take advantage of a captive audience. I'd do a stand-up routine and lead the guests in singing a popular tune to which I'd made up my own words. I knew it was easy for me to be a sure hit, since it was our house and our food. The first time I did something like this, Barbara was embarrassed. Over time, she came to expect that I would always have something outrageous planned, and so did our guests.

We drove down the road and easily found the motel. The motel manager was expecting us and brought us to our room. The room was tiny. Barbara said, "I can't stay here. There's no window in this room."

The manager showed us to another room. This time Barbara said, "Wait! This room has no air conditioner." The manager explained that the rooms with a window didn't have an air conditioner and the rooms with an air conditioner had the unit in the space that was the window. I asked Barbara which one she wanted. She chose the room with the air conditioner.

The room was tiny with a regular, full-sized bed and a small dresser. There was so little room between the foot of the bed and the wall that it was easier to climb over the bed to get to the bathroom and the other side of the room. We didn't want to waste much time there. We quickly changed and went back to the resort for the day.

Later that afternoon, we returned to the motel to shower and dress for dinner. As we undressed, I started to get touchy-feely. There was very little open floor area in the room. It was almost impossible not to get touchy-feely, while getting undressed at the same time. "How about we take our first shower together?" I asked.

"Marc, did you look at that shower in the bathroom? It's disgusting!"

"Are you saying that you're not showering?"

Barbara answered, "I'm showering, but I don't want to touch the walls or that shower curtain, and the shower is barely big enough for one person to fit in."

"Don't be a silly head. Come on, we'll fit. I'll step in first, then you come in and I'll reach over you and close the shower curtain."

Barbara was right, the shower was small and very skeevy. It was an old shower, with tin walls on three sides and an old shower curtain. But so what? We were young and horny. Well, I was horny, at least enough not to let the condition of the shower discourage me.

I stepped in first and as Barbara squeezed in and up against me, I reached over her and pulled the shower curtain closed. Barbara complained that the disgusting shower curtain was touching her. I was crammed in and couldn't reach the handle for the water. Barbara was able to turn on the water, but accidentally only turned on the hot water. It was fine at first, but the water got scalding hot. My quick reflex was to push Barbara, and she went flying through the shower curtain. I followed her out of the shower.

"I told you this wasn't going to work," Barbara said.

"Of course not, you only turned on the hot water, silly. Let's get back in. But this time, let's turn the water on first and let it run."

We did get back into the shower together and the experience was too silly to do anything sexual. It was our first shower together and very memorable. The fact that Barbara went along with me in that disgusting shower was a sign that I was married to the only woman who would put up with my silliness. We quickly got dressed and went back to the resort for dinner.

We had a fun evening and then came back to the motel for the night. This was our second night of marriage and we started to get romantic again. That little intermezzo in the shower earlier hadn't fulfilled us. We got ready and into bed and found another problem. The mattress sagged in the middle. It had been fine for sex but would be difficult for sleeping. Trying to fall asleep, we kept sliding to the center of the mattress and against each other. I asked Barbara, "Are you all right?"

She laughed. "I'm looking forward to being married to you, because I think it will never be boring. There'll always be something."

"Maybe it would be better if I just sleep on top of you. The room has air conditioning."

"Just tell me you love me and say goodnight," she answered.

"I love you. Goodnight."

The next morning, we packed and moved into the cabin. The cabin was nice, decorated as an early American cabin, with a king-sized bed and a large fireplace. There was a note in the room stating that in order to use the fireplace, we needed to stop by the gift shop. They would deliver a fire log.

It was the last night in August and chilly in the Poconos, a perfect night to have a fire. When we got back to the cabin, the log had been delivered and placed in the fireplace. We got undressed. Barbara was wearing a sheer negligee and I was in boxer shorts. As Barbara sat on the floor in front of the fireplace and watched, I opened the screen to light the fire and then turned the lever that opened the flue. The only problem was the staff had already opened the flue when they delivered the log. So, I closed the flue.

Within seconds, smoke began to pour into the room. I screamed to Barbara that we had to get out quickly. Barbara grabbed a bathrobe and ran out. I followed in my boxer shorts and we stood outside, in front of the cabin on the dirt in bare feet. It was freezing outside, so we embraced each other to stay warm. Someone spotted us and ran over to the gift shop and from there they sent help. After the staff reopened the flue, they brought over a fan to air out the cabin.

After all the smoke was gone, the staff left. We went back inside. Barbara went back over to the fireplace and sat down. She started laughing, as she said, "Well, the fire sure is nice, now that the smoke is going up the chimney."

As I cuddled up beside her, I replied, "Yeah, it is nice, especially after being out in the cold." I noticed Barbara was still laughing and asked, "What's so funny?"

"Oh, Marc," she answered, "you're hysterical. The look on your face when you screamed, 'Let's get out of here,' was so funny. At first, I was scared. But after realizing that you didn't burn down the place and seeing you out in the cold ... It's only you who wouldn't be ashamed to be standing out there in just your underwear. At least I had a robe on. Then, everyone leaves, and you continue on like nothing happened. Something like this can only happen to you."

"Are you making fun of me?" I laughed.

"Marc. We've only been married for forty-eight hours and during that time our reservation was screwed up. We had to stay in a room with no window, on a bed with a broken mattress that sagged in the middle, and bathe in a shower made of tin. Then tonight, this happens. I can't wait for what's next."

"I think the excitement is over for tonight," I answered.

"Good. Do you love me?" she asked.

A seriousness came over me. "Barbara," I asked, "why do you always ask me if I love you?"

There was total silence as Barbara paused for a few seconds. The feeling changed. It was as if I had said something wrong. As Barbara's smile turned to tears, she slowly whispered, "Because, nothing in my life has ever felt secure ... until I met you."

I put my arm around Barbara, as we gazed at the fire. I thought to myself, "Wow, she feels secure with me." That was pretty incredible for Barbara to say, right after I almost burned down the cabin. The way Barbara always smiled, when she looked at me, and the way she treated me, made me feel like her hero. I liked feeling that way; a man feeling that he's the protector and the stronger. I know it's a silly ego "man thing," and I admit guilt. We were newlyweds and I had just turned twenty-two a week before. Even through our teenage years, Barbara always made me feel like a man, her man. And she would continue to make me feel this way throughout our forty-year marriage. Even though we both knew, it was Barbara who was the stronger.

The rest of the week went fine. Well, except for the very next night, when the resort moved us to our next room, the one with the Roman bathtub with mirrors all around and the round bed. That afternoon, I stopped off at the gift shop to get bubble bath. After dinner and dancing at the casino, Barbara and I were anxious to take advantage of the Roman tub. I started filling the tub with water and told Barbara to get in, as I poured in the bubble bath.

"How much of this shit do I use?"

"Use half and we'll have the rest for tomorrow."

"You know what, I'll get another one for tomorrow and just use this up for tonight."

The bubbles started overflowing, up the mirrors and out from the tub. I quickly turned off the water, but the more we moved around in the tub the more the bubbles started to rise. In seconds, bubbles covered the bathroom floor carpeting and crawled up the mirrors. Barbara couldn't stop laughing, watching me panic as I tried to control the bubbles.

Then there was the horseback ride we took later in the week that went sideways. Barbara and I had never been horseback riding. It was fun and we followed the lead of the staff around a trail, until one of the staff riders said that we would be heading back to the stable. I happened to shout something like, "Okay, horse, take me back to the stable!" I didn't know the horse would understand me. With my shout, the horse took off, running back to the stable. I kept shouting, "Whoa! Whoa!" But the horse kept its stride and got me back to the stable. The group arrived a few minutes later and when Barbara saw that I was fine, she couldn't stop laughing, along with some of the other honeymooners.

The week was so much fun and we were sad when it was over. The car ride back to Jackson Heights was calming. We talked about how our honeymoon was perfect. It was a good transition from the past months of one ordeal after another and being anxious about the wedding. It was a beautiful, sunny day and we felt like the sun was shining down on us. Barbara was so looking forward to having me carry her over the threshold.

As I unlocked the apartment door, I turned to Barbara. "So ... you really want me to carry you?"

Barbara just smiled and I said, "Okay, I will."

I can't say that my carrying her over the threshold was as dainty as you see in the old-time movies. But I took a deep breath, lifted her up, carried her over the threshold, and put her down as soon as we were clear of the door.

It felt good to be in our apartment. Everything that we had was now ours and we would have our first night in our new bedroom. We were tired from all the excitement of the past week. We fell asleep, cuddled up so close.

The next morning, I woke up first, facing Barbara. Barbara was facing me, still in a deep sleep. As I stared at her, under my breath, I whispered, "I can't believe it's me." I couldn't believe, not only that I was married, but also that I was married to someone so beautiful.

We made it to this point, never concerned with the occasional negativity that we heard along our way from divorced people we knew, who were ten or fifteen years older. They would tell us of their experiences, as high school sweethearts. They lectured us that we were too young, didn't understand love, would grow apart, and get caught up in the momentum to get married. And like theirs, our marriage would end in divorce. This advice was always unsolicited. On those rare occasions, Barbara and I would politely pay little attention, let such advice roll off our backs, and instantly forget what we'd heard. We considered it to be, "Misery loves company." We knew we weren't them and wouldn't be joining their divorce club.

When Barbara and I told these same people of our honeymoon experiences, they couldn't understand how our honeymoon was so wonderful, considering the last-minute snafus that occurred. This was an example, and a sign, of how our marriage would differ from theirs and how we weren't them. Because for Barbara and me, our honeymoon snafus, and things like that, were just bumps in the road that added to our silliness, made us laugh, and would become our fond memories.

As I continued to stare at Barbara, I thought that maybe people were right. That we were still kids, pretending to be grown-ups. But Barbara and I believed that some people, although well intentioned, didn't understand our love. Maybe their misunderstanding was based on the possibility that they had never experienced true love themselves. Or maybe, they couldn't recognize a puppy love that would grow. Because, for Barbara and me, it was our puppy love that kept our marriage young and our true love that kept our marriage everlasting. And it was simply that, which would prove those naysayers wrong.

As I lay in bed beside Barbara, I thought about my married friends. To me, I had a love stronger than any of theirs. I never stopped believing I was the luckiest guy. I thought of my last night in the Rockaways, in the summer of 1964, when I watched Barbara walking to the boardwalk with her friends. I thought I would never see her again. And then, the next summer at the Breakers Hotel, I was caught by surprise and awe as we crossed paths, when I was going up the stairs to the porch and Barbara was coming down. Back then, I could never have imagined that Barbara would someday be the one. And now she was.

CHAPTER 9

I made one big mistake

In September, two days after we were home from our honeymoon, a dear neighbor who lived in the building, Mollie, invited Barbara and me to join her and her husband, Nat, for dinner. The invite was for Thursday evening. Barbara and I had been home since Sunday and were busily getting settled into our new life. The invitation was a welcome break for us.

Having moved to Jackson Heights from Brooklyn, Mollie and Nat were relatively new neighbors in the building, living a few floors above us. They were in their mid-fifties and had three married sons. They became friends with my parents and Barbara's mother.

Back in February, when Barbara's mother was diagnosed with cancer, the word quickly spread to friends and neighbors in the complex of six cooperative buildings. Mollie was one of the first to reach out to Barbara. I was with Barbara, in her apartment, a few days after her mother was diagnosed. The phone rang, and Barbara answered. It was Mollie, asking if Barbara had some time to come up to see her. I heard Barbara say, "I can come up now, if that is okay. Marc is here too."

Mollie answered, "Even better! Bring Marc too."

On our way upstairs, Barbara and I felt a little uncomfortable. We didn't know Mollie and Nat very well and they were even older than our parents. Plus, we thought, what could they possibly want to see us about? From the moment we walked into their apartment, they helped us to feel at home and like family. They gave us a tour of their apartment. We sat in the living room and they told us about their children and the home they had sold in Brooklyn.

I sat on their couch, alongside Barbara. Mollie and Nat sat opposite us on living-room chairs. I wondered what this was about. It wasn't until Mollie changed the subject, from about them to about Barbara and me, did I realize that they had been getting us comfortable to be with them.

"So," Mollie said, "we didn't ask you here to talk about us. We want to open our home to you. The next few months may be very difficult and we're just an elevator away. If you need someplace to get away to, you're welcome here. If you need someone much older than you to speak with, we're here for you."

I didn't know how to respond. Barbara and I hardly knew them at that point. And we had no idea about how difficult the next few months were going to be, or what we could need. Almost together, Barbara and I answered, "Thank you."

Mollie replied, "I know that you have many friends in the building. Just keep in the back of your mind, that you can always knock on our door."

That was so nice. They came across so very sincerely. It was a very sweet gesture, from two very sweet people. They asked about our schoolwork and part-time jobs. Barbara and I continued to talk about us. As we left their apartment and took the elevator back down to Barbara's apartment, we smiled at each other. For us, it was a nice, pleasant happening, a refreshing break. That's all we thought of the visit at the time. We didn't know that we'd be taking them up on their offer many times over the next seven months. There would be many friends and neighbors being of help. It would be Mollie and Nat who kind of adopted Barbara.

By September, we had developed a close relationship with Mollie and Nat and enjoyed their company. We were looking forward to having a casual dinner with them; nothing formal, just jeans. We figured that they wanted to talk about how much they enjoyed being at our wedding and hear about our honeymoon. Plus, Mollie was a good cook.

They set up for dinner at the kitchen table. It was really nice, with tablecloth, china, and stemware. As we sat down at the table, Mollie began, "Both of you are very dear to us. Nat and I want you to know that we are always here for you. We're very convenient, living just a couple of floors above. And, if we can be of any help, you should feel comfortable to come to us."

As I look back over the years and write about this, I think about how we learn from our parents during our growing up years, following their leadership and guidance. If we're fortunate during our lifetime, along the way, we meet other people, too, who we learn from and who will offer their support and guidance. Barbara and I were so fortunate to have known so many people like Mollie and Nat. People who shared with us their experiences and offered us opportunities during our early married years, which helped us and positively influenced our future.

As Mollie spoke, I listened attentively trying to catch looks at Barbara. I was certain Barbara was about to burst out in tears. I could see on Barbara's face a look of disbelief as she listened to Mollie. Mollie's words weren't ones Barbara was used to hearing. No one before had ever spoken directly to her like Mollie had, with such caring and sincerity.

Barbara's family had disappeared, out-of-sight. There were no offers of anything from them. Not even a check-in over the months since her mother died, like, "How are you doing?" We had been back since Sunday. This was Thursday. There had been no word from her grandparents or aunt and uncle. Barbara had my parents and my cousin, Norman, and his wife, Carol. She heard from her two cousins, Rose and Ann. But from her immediate family, she heard nothing. I hurt for Barbara, as I felt the quiet hurt inside of her. And, what Mollie had said was over-the-top sweet. I held back tears, as Barbara responded.

"I'm going to say this and try not to cry. Thank you for thinking of us and inviting us tonight. Throughout these past few months, both of you have reached out to me with concern and advice. You've been like an aunt and uncle, so supportive and so easy to talk to about so many things that I've been going through, and I am going to take you up on your offer."

There were a lot of emotions around the table. I looked at Nat, who had been quiet. He looked like he was about to cry. I figured everything had been said and now it was time for dinner. With all this emotional talk, I was getting hungry. For me, the diversion for dinner would be a welcome transition to move on, to talk about fun things. Also, I wanted to the conversation to end before I started to cry. In reaction to the seriousness of the moment, my silliness was coming over me. I thought to myself, "This conversation is pretty heavy shit and I'm hungry."

But Mollie wasn't finished. She seemed nervous. And I thought, "Uh oh! What's next? Here comes the real, heavy, serious shit. I love these people. But I guess we're not eating yet."

Mollie stood up to speak and clasped her hands together to control a slight tremble of nervousness. As she stood over us, it was if she was about to make a proclamation.

"The both of you are so sweet and we think of the two of you like our extended children. But if aunt and uncle is better for you, that's okay too. Well, without you asking, I did something that may be of help. But you have no obligation, and you shouldn't feel obligated to do this. I think you know that I work for Merrill Lynch in Manhattan. Well, a job opportunity came available this week in my office. It's for a sales assistant to a few stockbrokers. When I heard about the job, I told my office manager to hold off looking for someone. That I have a lovely young woman, who just got married and would be perfect for the job. I can get you an interview for early next week. But you shouldn't feel obligated at all. You may already have plans of your own."

With all our talk and planning over the past couple of months, Barbara and I believed we were all set and going to be able to get along fine. I was doing well selling residential real estate and we had a small savings from our wedding gifts. But we were headed for hard times. Barbara and I knew it. But we ignored it. We proceeded with a hope and a prayer, believing, "We'll do what we have to do." We were a married couple. But we were twenty and twenty-two and in love and figured our love was going to pay the bills. Yes, we believed our love was going to pay the bills. Full of piss and vinegar, we believed we'd make it. I only got paid sporadically, upon the sale of a property. I was a commissioned salesperson with no steady income or guarantee of any income. Barbara was an hourly employee. Neither of us had any kind of health insurance.

This new opportunity from Mollie was a welcome surprise. It could be a turning point in our well-being. Mollie repeatedly explained that we should feel no obligation, and take a day or two to decide what we wanted to do. Barbara looked at me with a big smile and I could see that she didn't need more time to decide. I gave her a go-for-it smile back.

"Oh, Mollie, thank you for doing this for me. I don't need more time to think about this. I will go for the interview. Just tell me where and when and I'll be there."

Barbara went for the interview. A couple of days later, the office manager told Mollie that the job was Barbara's. He asked Mollie if he should call Barbara, or if she would like to be the one to tell Barbara. Mollie told her manager that she would tell Barbara and warned her manager, "As you saw when you interviewed her, Barbara is a beautiful young woman, and I don't trust some of the brokers in this office. I want you to know that I'm going to be watching over her as if she were my daughter."

After Barbara and I moved from Jackson Heights to New Jersey, we kept in touch with Mollie and Nat, and they visited us one time before they retired to Florida. The last time we saw them was in 1975, at the Pidyon HaBen ceremony for our son Jonathan, when he was one month old. A Pidyon HaBen is a traditional Hebrew service for the redemption of the firstborn son. The ceremony is where the father redeems his son, by paying silver coins to a "Kohen" (a priestly descendent of Aaron). Nat was a Kohen and officiated the ceremony. We eventually lost touch with them.

I searched for Mollie and Nat online and learned that Nat died at the age of ninety-six on September 15, 2011, just one month after Barbara. Seven months later, on April 8, 2012, Mollie died at ninety-six.

As I write about and remember Mollie and Nat, I have regrets. They were in my category of great people who Barbara and I were fortunate to have known. They stepped into our lives to help and guide us when we needed emotional support, when Barbara's mother was dying. And again, they stepped into our lives when we needed financial guidance by providing us with a job opportunity. They weren't people of only talk. Mollie and Nat were people of action. And we were blessed with them. I wish we had kept in touch over the years. Our children would have loved them, and the love would have been reciprocated.

I've learned we surely cheat ourselves when we let such special relationships fade away. It's not as though we must be continuously in contact. An occasional letter, phone call, or visit can be all that's needed to keep a dear relationship with special people we meet along our way. Barbara and I continued to be blessed with such people throughout our marriage. We learned early on that the more people we opened up to, the more life opportunities and rewards would come to us.

Barbara's job with Merrill Lynch gave us security at a time when we needed financial stability. What's that out-of-date expression? "Behind every successful man, there is a strong woman." I never quite related to that expression. Rather, I believed that Barbara always stood alongside me, not behind. Or, possibly, I stood behind her. Barbara took on the role as breadwinner, while I was a college student. It was her job that carried us through and afforded us a secure start to our marriage. And it would turn out to be a good opportunity, a career and life-changer for Barbara. Barbara enjoyed working in business and would eventually decide to give up a career in teaching.

With Barbara's job with Merrill Lynch, we weren't going to be two young kids playing house. Our financial worries were gone, allowing us emotional security to let our love run free. The job helped us to quickly acclimate to the lifestyle of a real married couple. We had a steady weekly income. We had health insurance too. My commission checks became income to buy special things with, like furniture. Yep, we were a real married couple, in love too.

Barbara loved her new job and attended night classes at Queens College. I was back to school and worked evenings and weekends. We were busy and loving being married. And yes, we did have time for plenty of sex, just not twice a day, as we had planned. Well, really, as I had planned.

Going to and from work, Barbara took the Flushing train, at the Roosevelt Avenue and Eighty-Second Street station. It was a long walk from the station to our apartment. On the evenings that Barbara had no classes, and I didn't have a real estate appointment, I would double park at the train station and wait for her. She didn't make the exact same train each night and since there were no cell phones back then, I would get to the station a little early and watch each train go by. After each train passed, people poured from the elevated platform down the steps. I would carefully scan the crowd, looking for Barbara. Eventually Barbara's train would pass, and I would spot her among the crowd and beep the horn. When she saw me, she would smile. Once I saw her smile, my evening was made.

On those evenings, we would go out for an inexpensive dinner and a dollar movie. Even though we had seen each other that morning, our excitement to see each other in the evening was like we hadn't seen each other in days. When apart, we missed each other so. And when we were together, we were so into each other, oblivious to everything around us. We always had so much to say about our day. We started talking as soon as Barbara got into the car, and talked all through dinner, after the movie, and until we kissed good night. It was an incredible time of our marriage, a time that was all about us.

With my busy school schedule, my commission checks were very sporadic. We were thankful for Barbara's full-time job and steady income. We paid our bills on time but were on a tight budget. I remember one evening when we were snuggled on the couch watching TV and Barbara was looking through a magazine. She held up a page to show me.

"Do you like this kind of haircut for me? I really like the cut."

"Yeah, looks nice," I answered.

"If I go to a beauty parlor to have this done, it's going to be so expensive."

"Why? It's just a haircut."

"Men's haircuts are so cheap. When a woman walks into a beauty parlor asking for a specific kind of cut, it's a whole big to-do."

"For just a haircut?"

"Yes!"

"Let me see those pictures," I said.

There were pictures of a model, shown from several views, demonstrating the style cut of her hair.

"Yeah, I like it. I can cut your hair to look just like this."

"You really think you can? I have haircutting scissors, but where can we do it? There'll be hair all over the place, like in a beauty parlor."

"Yes, I can cut your hair that way. We'll do it in the bathroom. Get undressed down to your panties, so that we don't get hair all over your clothes. And put a towel over your shoulders. Also, rip that page out of the magazine, so I can follow it as I cut your hair."

We went into the bathroom to start the haircut. I taped the picture of the model onto the wall behind the toilet so I could refer to it. Barbara sat on top of the toilet seat, facing the back wall. I was about to start cutting when I stopped and said, "Just wait here, I just have to do one thing first." I went to the bedroom.

When I came back wearing only my boxer shorts, Barbara asked, "Why did you get undressed?"

"I didn't want to get hair all over my clothes, either."

Well, it became kind of an X-rated haircut and lots of fun. After, as we were giggling, Barbara was anxious to look at herself in the mirror. She said it looked good and was anxious to shampoo and blow-dry to see how it really came out. We cleaned up the bathroom, which had hair all over. There was hair all over the two of us too. So, we took a shower together.

It was our second time showering together and after, as we were drying off, I said, "Wow, that was fun!"

Blushing, with a timid look on her face, Barbara said, "Are you going to start getting silly and talk about this nonstop?"

"I'm just wondering what else we could be missing out on that we don't know about. We took a shower together on our honeymoon, which was a bust. We've been home a few weeks now and didn't think of taking a shower together. How did we miss that?"

"Okay, enough already about the shower. I just want to blow-dry my hair and see how it looks."

"Well, you don't have to scream at me. I just want to make sure that I'm fulfilling my husbandly duties."

Laughing, Barbara answered, "You are so silly. Your husbandly duties. How do you come up with these things?"

"It just comes to me naturally, when I see you naked."

The whole experience was lots of fun and we hoped that the haircut, after being washed and shampooed, would be as successful as the shower. Barbara dried her hair and the cut looked great. Barbara said, "Now that I know that I have my own in-house beautician, I'm getting my hair cut more often." And that was what happened for the first four years of our marriage.

For that first haircut, Barbara wanted bangs. After, she changed back and forth from bangs to no bangs. Even when we could afford for Barbara to have a professional haircut, I still cut her hair. It was so convenient and, more importantly, the haircuts continued to be X-rated, and showering together was always the best part. It got to the point that I often asked Barbara, "Are you sure that you don't want me to cut your hair tonight?"

"No, I don't want to take a shower," Barbara would answer.

The toughest part about our marriage turned out to be the fact that I hated to go shopping: food shopping, clothes shopping, everything except furniture shopping. I loved furnishing and fixing up the apartment. The worst was clothes shopping. I had no patience for looking at and trying on clothes. Plus, we were on a tight budget and I didn't want to spend a lot of money on clothes. Barbara would shop by herself and look for clothes for me and she was great at finding sales. When she came across something she liked for me, she bought it. Barbara even bought me pants, which she would get me to try on and then she would pin the waist, cuffs, and anywhere else that needed tailoring. Barbara would have them sewn by a tailor at the dry cleaners.

Barbara and I got along fine and had lots of friends, but we loved it most when it was just the two of us, doing our own thing. To us, we had everything we needed for a newlywed couple. It would have been nice to have more money but, more importantly, we were happy. And we were extra careful. We were having too much fun just being the two of us. Neither of us was ready to have children.

In August 1972, we celebrated our first wedding anniversary and spent a week at the Host Farm Hotel in Lancaster, Pennsylvania. We began to be able to save money and afford to do more things. This was our first vacation. By this time, Barbara had been working for Merrill Lynch for almost a year. After graduation, I started working for Mehlman Management, a real estate property management company, as the leasing agent at Kips Bay, an 1,118-unit rental apartment building in Manhattan. I was responsible for directing contractors in refurbishing the units upon vacancy, leasing apartments, coordinating the tenant move ins and outs, and tenant relations. Unlike my real estate sales job, I no longer had to wait until the sporadic house sales closed to be paid. Between the two of us, we had an okay steady income.

My dad began to suggest, that as a married man, it was important for me to have a life insurance policy. From time to time, in passing, I would mention this to Barbara. She was against it. The thought of something happening to me and her collecting money upon my death was a topic that Barbara didn't want to hear about or discuss.

We definitely had two different opinions about my taking out a life insurance policy. It was all about the difference in our personalities. More spiritual than I was, Barbara feared insurance was a jinx. She was also the stronger and worried less about potential disasters. I was concerned that we had little savings. Barbara had no family to turn to for financial help, and my parents weren't financially well off to provide help for another household. With my OCD, I obsessed that Barbara would surely be alone to provide for herself, should something happen to me. I loved her so much and the thought frightened me.

We were married a little over a year when I pushed the issue. "Listen to me. You keep on avoiding the subject that we need to talk about. I agree with my dad that I should have an insurance policy, just for your security."

Finally, I made some headway and convinced Barbara that in case something terrible should happen to me, she should have enough money to pay for a funeral. Barbara reluctantly said that it was okay, if, and only if, the policy was for an amount only enough to pay for a funeral.

"The whole subject makes me scared, and I don't want any money because something happened to you. I'll go along with a policy for you and don't want any insurance policy for me."

I called the Allstate agent who handled our car insurance and made an appointment for him to come to our apartment, to discuss our options. When the agent came, he told us about term insurance, which only pays upon death, and whole life insurance, which pays upon death, but also pays out the value of the policy upon maturity at age sixty-five.

Barbara responded immediately. "We don't want term insurance. I want a small policy that has more value if you live than if you die."

The agent suggested a policy that would pay ten thousand dollars upon death and fourteen thousand dollars at maturity, at age sixty-five. Barbara agreed, happy to have all this talk about life insurance over. After we signed all the papers, the insurance agent told us that by selling us this policy that night, it put him over a level of his sales that would earn him an award.

To that, Barbara's response was, "Well, that's a good omen, since this whole conversation made me very uncomfortable."

After the insurance agent left, Barbara came over to me with a concerned look on her face. "I need a hug and you have to promise me that nothing bad is going to happen to you and you will be around to collect the fourteen thousand dollars, okay? Promise me that."

"I promise." We kissed on that promise.

It would be forty-two years later, November 12, 2014, a little more than three years after I lost Barbara, when I got home from work and listened to a message on my answering machine from Allstate Life Insurance. The message was about my life insurance policy. I needed to call back and ask for Norma. At first, I couldn't figure out what this call could be about. Then I realized the policy was probably going to expire soon, and the insurance company probably wanted to know what my plans were. I planned to call the next day and extend the policy.

I called Norma and it was exactly as I suspected. Norma told me my policy had expired. She needed to verify my address so she could send the check.

"I have no reason to let the policy expire at this point. I'd like to extend it."

"Oh, you can't do that," Norma answered.

"Why not?"

"Because it's a policy to age sixty-five and then you collect the value of the policy. So, congratulations!" she answered.

"Okay, I understand. I just didn't expect that it couldn't be extended. It doesn't feel so long ago when my wife and I took out that policy. By the way, are you able to let me know the date that I took out that policy?"

"Yes, I can easily look it up. Just give me a few minutes and I'll be right back to you." When Norma got back on the phone, she said with a laugh, "It was November 1, 1972. You were twenty-three years old."

After I got off the phone with Norma, I vividly remembered all of the talking and convincing I needed to do to purchase this insurance policy, when I was twenty-three years old and Barbara was twenty-one. I couldn't stop thinking about the whole process. I blinked my eyes, and it was like I was back to November 1, 1972. I was twenty-three, with Barbara, in our apartment in Jackson Heights. I could see her as we sat at the table with the insurance agent, insisting that it should only be a small policy. I remembered our kiss and my promise. It brought about a shiver of grief in me. I have found through the years that it takes little to bring me back to moments with Barbara that trigger my grieving.

I sat on my couch and grieved. The memory was so clear. I wanted to be back in that moment with Barbara. After a while, I emailed my children, describing what had happened. My son-in-law, Stephen, wrote back. "Amazing what we are able to recall. How some things can still be so vivid after such a long time. It's the people that are part of the memory, that make it vivid, not necessarily how big the event is."

Barbara had been paying the premiums for thirty-nine years and I had taken over, paying for the last three. Now, it was time to collect the value of the policy. This is what Barbara had wished would happen and what she made me promise her, forty-two years before. As I think about this policy, I now see that I made one big mistake back then. I should have asked Barbara to also promise that nothing bad would happen to her and she would be around with me, to collect the fourteen thousand dollars.

But in 1972, I couldn't imagine ever losing Barbara. We were young and going to live together forever. Our marriage took off with a promising start. We both had good jobs. I liked working for Mehlman Management, getting hands-on construction, contractor, business, and legal experience. The company treated me well and I could see a good and financially secure future. But after a year, I wanted to do more complex design and construction work. In the winter of 1973, I lined up a job as superintendent of construction for a home builder in New Jersey. The builder was working on three projects, one in Boonton and two in Scotch Plains.

I began the grueling commute from Jackson Heights to New

Jersey. I would leave very early in the morning and drive across Manhattan to the Holland Tunnel to New Jersey and reverse commute back home, getting home late in the evening. It was a long day for me. Barbara and I knew we needed to move soon, and we began to look for a home. Barbara wanted to find a house in a suburb, where there were absolutely no tall buildings. Having grown up in The Bronx and Jackson Heights, she wanted something countrified.

We began our search and looked at many homes in several different areas of central and northern New Jersey. We heard about a town in far western Morris County, called Flanders, and decided to check it out. In a local newspaper, we came across an ad placed by a homeowner. Right away, we called the owner and made an appointment to see the house.

Before going to the house, we drove around the neighboring communities. Much of the area was kind of rural. We drove by horse farms and farms with cows in the pasture. It wasn't totally isolated. In the residential areas, many properties had large plots of land, with homes spaced far apart. There were no sidewalks anywhere we drove. For a girl from The Bronx and a boy from Brooklyn, this kind of suburb was not what we were looking for.

We were already in the area and decided to keep our appointment and check out the house anyway. We didn't have any alternative but to look. It was 1973, we had no cells phones to call the owners to cancel. As we drove through the neighborhood, we got a much better feeling. The houses were on only quarter-acre lots, giving us a feeling of community. And there were sidewalks! As we turned onto the street, looking for the house number, Barbara said, "Yuck. It's that house right there. The one with the ugly red shutters."

"Hey, let's look at it. I can paint the shutters. Barbara, we're looking for our first house. We don't have to be so particular. We have to be able to afford it now. We're not going to live here forever."

As soon as we walked through the door, we felt like we'd come home. An instant feeling of comfort came over both of us. Almost immediately, I knew I wanted to buy this house and I could see that Barbara did too. As the homeowner showed us around, I tried to put on a poker face, in order to negotiate the price. Barbara kept giving me the look like she wanted this house. As we went from room to room, Barbara's smile had a look of excitement. At no point did I see a look of doubt or question. Like a cute, happy puppy, Barbara had her happy ears on.

Whenever we were about to make a purchase that required negotiation, Barbara would smile and get very quiet. That was her way of signaling to me to start the dealmaking. Barbara would say that I could drive anyone up a wall in a negotiation and she would step out of the way to give me free rein.

We bought that house and painting the shutters was one of the first projects I did. As for not having to live there forever, this would be the house where we would live for the next thirty-six years and bring three babies home.

Barbara gave notice at work that we had purchased a home in New Jersey, and she would be leaving. She was doing well at her job and the brokers and the office manager liked her. They recommended Barbara for a transfer to the nearest Merrill Lynch office to Flanders, which was in Morristown. One of the brokers whom Barbara reported to, Gus, said he had a good friend, Scott, in the Morristown office. The timing was perfect, because Scott and two other brokers had been planning to look for a sales assistant to start around the time we would be moving to Flanders. Barbara interviewed at the Morristown office and got the transfer.

Barbara and I were so excited about this move to a home in what we considered the country. But we had mixed emotions. We had lived in our Jackson Heights "honeymoon" apartment for less than two years. It had been a beautiful time for us. Buying a home in the country was a dream come true, but our time in the apartment had been like an extended honeymoon we wished would never end. It was a time when we talked about our future, while we were happy to live for today, with little responsibility and lots of loving. And this is the time in our marriage that comes to my mind the most when I think of Barbara. A time that is its own story. It is our "once upon a time."

Once upon a time. When we often talked about all the unknowns in our future: where we would eventually live, buying a house, and having kids. After a busy day, in bed after lights out, we'd lie on our backs and face the ceiling. Barbara sometimes asked, "So ... how long are we going to live in this apartment?"

"How long do you want to live here?"

"Well, how long do *you* want to live here?"

"I don't know."

Then Barbara would ask, "How many kids do you want to have?"

I loved being silly when Barbara was being serious. The annoyance on her face was cutely irresistible. She would smile and get back to getting me to be serious. So, I answered, "Five or seven."

"No, silly. You always say that. We're not having five or seven kids. Just two!"

In mock seriousness, I answered, "Barbara! We can't have just two. We have to have, like, three. Two is an even number and boring. Almost everyone we know has two kids and either already lives or is planning to live in Long Island. I don't want to be like everyone we know! I want to be you and me."

"That's another thing you keep on saying. What is being you and me?" Barbara asked.

"I was hoping that you knew that. Because I don't. But that's what I want."

Barbara laughed. "You can't want something that you don't know what it is."

"Now you're being silly ... silly."

This move to the far suburbs was our next adventure. And we made the move without a worry or a concern about tomorrow. It would be several years later that our tomorrows would become a concern. For Barbara and me at this time, it was all about today. I guess we were too young and inexperienced to feel otherwise. At twenty-one and twenty-three years old, we had our love to keep us strong and confident.

We closed on the purchase of our house on June 12, 1973 and moved in on the fourteenth. I didn't want to move in on the thirteenth. Very much aware of my OCD by then, Barbara agreed to the fourteenth, knowing that I would obsess over a moving date of the thirteenth. With so many of our friends and family planning to move east to Long Island, Barbara and I took one last look back and said goodbye to our honeymoon apartment, got into the car with Pepper, our black lab puppy we'd gotten two weeks before, and headed west to New Jersey.

In doing this, we weren't being like everyone we knew. Along the way, Barbara and I were discovering what we wanted. We were discovering being us. Whatever that was.

PART 2

Stories from the Second Day of Shiva

"You know ... it's getting very close to midnight. Maybe you can try to hold off until after midnight to have the baby."

CHAPTER 10

Just the two of us

Barbara and I were quickly welcomed onto Brewster Place in Flanders. As the movers were unloading the truck, many of the neighbors came by to introduce themselves and their children. The neighbors had heard from the previous owners that we were a very young couple. But they weren't expecting us to be so young and were surprised to hear that we were only twenty-one and twenty-three. We were happy to see that our neighbors were also young, in their late twenties and early thirties.

We quickly got busy getting the things that we needed, as new homeowners: lawnmower, garbage cans, fertilizer, seed spreader, the list went on and on. The most pressing thing was a car for Barbara. She was starting work in a little over a week. Living in Jackson Heights, we only needed one car. But, in this suburban, almost rural, westernmost town of Morris County, we needed a second car.

I started looking for a used car, but they all seemed like junkers to me. I didn't know a lot about cars and was concerned about what we might get stuck with. Also, the term "used" to describe a car always turned me off. I associate the description "used car," with "abused

153

car." At least nowadays, some genius has come up with the term "pre-owned." Had cars been called "pre-owned" back in 1973, I may have bought a pre-owned car. Well, maybe not. Because now I associate the description "pre-owned car" with "abused car."

I was running out of time and Barbara was on my back. One day during my lunch break working on the Scotch Plains tract, I went to a Ford dealership on Route 22. In the center of the sales showroom was this cute, tan, shiny, new Ford Pinto. It looked like a perfect car for Barbara, except for the price. I called Barbara. "Listen, I'm not having any luck finding you a used car. I'm at a new car dealership in Watchung. I just drove the sales guy crazy negotiating a price and I don't know what I really want to do."

Barbara impatiently answered, "Marc, I need a car in a few days to get to work!"

"Barbara, I know that. I'm just a little nervous about having new car payments on top of everything else. I'm dizzy from thinking about all the things that we need to do and buy. So much so that I went to the bathroom here at the dealership and, while in the stall, I realized that I was in the ladies' bathroom."

To Barbara, me being in the ladies' bathroom was not at all surprising. She often said, "Things always happen to you, because nothing embarrasses you. If it embarrassed you, it wouldn't happen." Barbara first realized this on our honeymoon. The night I tried to light the fireplace and we had to run out of the cabin, she later said, "It's only you who wouldn't be ashamed to be standing out there in just your underwear." Barbara knew there was little that embarrassed me, and she rolled in laughter each time something like this happened.

"That's hysterical," Barbara answered.

"Yeah. I'm sitting there doing my thing, when I hear two ladies come in and start talking to each other. I had to wait in the stall until they left, to make a mad dash out of the bathroom."

Barbara kept laughing. "That didn't happen because you're dizzy. It happened because that's the kind of thing that can only happen to you. Okay, I need a car. But you decide what is best."

"Okay. Listen, you know what? I just decided. We're going to buy this car. We can pick it up tomorrow evening and we'll be done and all set. See you later, alligator," I answered.

"Wonderful! I love you. See you in a while, crocodile. Wait! Marc—Marc!

"Yes, what?"

"What kind of car is it?"

"A Ford Pinto."

"Wow. My first car is going to be brand new. I'm so excited. I love you."

The next day, we drove down to the dealership to pick up the car. It was parked right out front when we got there. The door was unlocked and Barbara got right in. I went inside the dealership to sign all the papers. All this time Barbara was in the car. When I came out with the keys, Barbara opened the car door. She had been crying. I thought to myself, "Oh, shit! She hates it, and we now own it. I wonder if they'll take the car back?"

"What's the matter?"

"Oh, Marc ... I love it."

It was a happy cry. It didn't take much to make Barbara happy. I'm not saying that getting a new car isn't much. But it was as though Barbara didn't expect good things to happen to her. When good things did happen to her, she found it difficult to believe.

I'd wonder what I could do to help her get past the damage from her childhood. I'm not sure that I ever did, other than to make her smile and laugh. I loved it when Barbara smiled. When she put me on stage for my silliness, I could make her laugh. In Barbara's smiles and laughter, I could feel her happiness. And in her happy cries, I could feel her happiness too.

While we were busy with our jobs at work, getting used to the chores of homeownership and training a new puppy, our new neighbors were obviously busy too. Brewster Place, with its green grass lawns, neatly manicured shrubbery, and trees, was a very fertile block. It seemed like every few months there was a new baby born; either someone's first, second, or third kid. Barbara and I made sure not to get sucked into the baby-making momentum. We both needed to work, and we were still loving it being just the two of us. Despite all that, living on Brewster Place, the thought of starting a family was becoming compelling.

All was going along well, and we had a fun first summer in the house. That fall, our situation drastically changed. The oil crisis of 1973 began in October, when Arab nations began an oil embargo on the United States and several other countries. This oil crisis affected everyone. For people living in the far suburbs with minimal-to-no local public transportation, it was a particular horror.

Barbara and I depended on our cars to get to work and gas stations were rationing their sales, with limited operating hours, because of limited supply. When the stations were open, there were long lines out to the roadways. When people saw a station where the pumps were open and the lines not too long, they'd stop to fill up, even if their tank was almost full. With much uncertainty about the availability of gas, most people continually topped off the gas in their tanks. Barbara was able to join a carpool with people in the neighborhood who traveled to Morristown. I alternated between driving each of our two cars to work, hoping to come across an open gas station along the way, to keep both cars filled with gas.

The economy was taking a huge hit. Home sales had slowed down. Because of the market uncertainty, banks were tightening on their mortgage lending policies. Barbara's job was solid, but mine was in jeopardy. The builder had slowed down with housing starts and wasn't committing to new development sites. My company had two construction superintendents, and I knew I was the one who would be cut.

Sure enough, I was laid off. I began to look for a job. It was rough. It was not a good job market. Now, just six months after our move, I was stuck living in a remote suburb, far from job opportunities. Barbara was working, and we started living on a very tight budget. Through it all, we faced each day as if all was fine and didn't stop enjoying what we had: our life together, our home, and our puppy.

Not wanting to worry anyone, we didn't tell any relatives; only a few of our neighbors knew of our situation. Although it was just the two of us, we never felt alone. Barbara and I had each other to depend on and we wouldn't look for help or support from anyone. We were very young and had already been through difficult situations. For me, I guess past difficulties and this current situation toughened me up for the adversities we would face in our future. As for Barbara, she was always strong, confident, and resilient.

Then I got incredibly lucky. A few weeks after I was laid off, the other superintendent, Nick, quit. The builder, Dave, could have continued on his own. But his wife was dying from breast cancer and his time was consumed with caring for his wife. Dave called me one evening.

"Hi, Marc. This is Dave. How are you doing?"

"Hey, Dave. I'm doing fine. I've been looking for a job. But no luck yet and no prospects."

"So sorry to hear that," Dave answered. "But that's good and bad. Bad that you have no prospects and good because I need you back. Nick quit and I have been trying to get along. But my wife is not doing well. I'm being pulled in different directions. I could really use you to come back."

I felt badly for Dave. But that was all I felt; just feeling badly. I didn't feel his pain at all. I needed that job and was happy to get back to work. It's only now that I feel guilt, as I write about this and reflect on how the sadness in a person's misfortune becomes another person's good fortune. Sadly, it sometimes takes experiencing our own misfortune to feel the pain of others.

"So sorry about your wife. I didn't know it was that bad. When do you want me to start?"

"Tomorrow. I can meet you tomorrow and go over everything with you and bring you up to speed. But I can only stay for a half day, for two reasons. I can't keep my mind on the business, and I need to be with my wife. Marc, not only do I need you back, but I need you to run the job and finish the tract. I can give you the support and guide you. But you will have to step up and hire and supervise all of the subcontractors."

"I'm sorry to hear about your wife, Dave. I'll be on the job tomorrow. Thank you for your confidence in me."

I wasn't sure if Dave really had as much confidence in me as he expressed. Or it was just that I was his only option to step in quickly, since I was familiar with every aspect of the project? Whatever, in this difficult job market, I was happy to be getting back to work.

This turned out to be an incredible opportunity for me. I had to step up, take on more responsibility, and learn quickly, in order to run the project. At twenty-four years old, I was basically on my own building single-family homes: hiring and supervising subcontractors, coordinating the inspections by the local building inspectors, and working with the homebuyers.

I was busy and loving the work. But I continued looking for another job.

I couldn't shake the bad feeling I had, having been laid off by Dave. I understood that he had no alternative. There wasn't enough work for two superintendents and Nick had years' more experience. But Dave called me into the construction trailer one day, let me go, and I was gone. There was no real farewell, or any severance pay. As a young married guy, who had bought a home, and moved to New Jersey to work for him, I felt no compassion from Dave.

Also, I questioned how active this builder would be going forward. The tract that I was working on would be completed in a few months. Dave wasn't actively out there looking to line up more sites. I had already learned he had no problem in laying me off. I figured he'd have no problem doing it a second time.

About two months after I returned to work, Dave's wife passed away. I still hadn't found another job, partially because I had my hands full with building the homes. I thought that after a week or two, Dave would return to full time and lay me off again. But after his wife passed away, he was a broken man, and his mind wasn't back to business. He was relying on me. He would show up at the tract, check on how I was doing, and leave.

I didn't know Dave's wife very well, or their marital relationship. I had only met her once or twice. Now, as I reflect back, I don't relate to how he became so broken. Back then, it was easy for me to not to relate. I was young, inexperienced, and needed to get my career in order. But even today, I find it difficult to relate to how Dave became so broken.

Too well, I know of the grief that doesn't go away. The grief I can't get used to. The grief I feel shivering through my body and have grown to accept. I can't imagine anyone being more in love with their wife than I was with Barbara. But maybe it's not the measure of the love that causes the intensity of our grief. Or how resilient we can be to go forward with our life with the grief. Maybe for some, the grieving eventually stops, and maybe others take it to their graves. I've thought that grieving sucks. But it does bring back to my mind the beautiful moments with Barbara. I see Barbara through Shiva Eyes, in moments that I treasure. And sometimes, I think that maybe, just maybe ... grieving isn't all that bad.

Barbara and I were married for forty years. Dave had been married for a little over twenty. Is that what the difference is? Is forty years considered to be a lifetime and twenty years not? I can easily answer that question. For me, forty years was not even close to be a lifetime.

People have told me that Barbara would be so proud of me. Is that what the difference is? Did Dave have as much support as I did? Or was the way Barbara left me different from the way Dave's wife left him? I don't have the answers to many questions, and I am a bit confused as to what the questions really are. I still have a long way to go in writing this book in search for answers. I hope to find peace with my grief. Or maybe, I don't truly want to.

With all that was going on with Dave back then, I was certain he would have little-to-no ambition to find new tracts. My résumé was pretty impressive, and I stepped up my momentum in searching for another job. By the end of April 1974, I had the tract of homes almost completed. I noticed an ad in the Sunday *New York Times*. Back then, the employment section of the newspaper was the best source for finding jobs. I came across an ad for a company looking for a staff architect. However, it was with a parking design-consulting firm, called Cosmo Parking. I didn't follow up, since I wasn't interested in working for a parking company. The following Sunday, I saw the ad again. Again, I decided I wasn't interested.

The third week, I noticed that Cosmo was looking for someone with experience in real estate. That caught my interest and changed my perspective of the company. I sent my résumé. A few days later, I received a phone call from the owner of the company, who introduced himself as Steve Roseman. His personnel manager had forwarded my résumé and he was calling to interview me. We spoke for quite some time. After I got off the call, Barbara was eager to get all the details.

"You were on the phone for a long time. It was almost like a complete interview and you were very chatty. How did it go?"

"I think it went well. The guy is the owner of the company and was easy to talk to and I think he liked me. His name is Steve Roseman. Do you think he's Jewish?"

"Are you silly? I'm one hundred percent sure that a man with the name 'Steve Roseman' is Jewish. So, what did he say?"

"He said that he will talk to his personnel manager and the manager will contact me to set up an interview."

Over the next couple of weeks, I had several interviews with the personnel manager, with Steve, and with his partner, Philip Katz. In the meantime, I also interviewed with a national property management company with its corporate office in Manhattan. That company made me a firm job offer. Since I'd had so many interviews at Cosmo, I called the personnel manager to thank him for everything. I explained I had an offer from another company, which I was going to accept. He told me Steve and Philip were very interested in hiring me and asked if I could come back the next day to meet with them again and firm up a job offer.

I really liked Steve and Philip, and after so many interviews, I felt close to them. I met with them the next day and accepted their job offer. I couldn't wait to see Barbara that evening to tell her the good news. I got home before Barbara.

As soon as she walked into the house, she asked, "Well?"

"I accepted the job. I start on June 10, which will give Dave enough time to take over the tract. Things are kind of finished anyway and he knows that I've been interviewing. There's just one more thing that I need to do to finalize getting the job with Cosmo Parking. I need to go into Manhattan tomorrow to take a test. But they said there is not going to be a problem and I could give notice to my current job."

"What kind of test is it?' Barbara asked.

"I'm not sure. I think he called it a polygraph test."

Barbara seemed stunned and gave me the strangest look of confusion and surprise. "What! Marc, do you know what that is? That's a lie detector test. Why would they need to give you a lie detector test for a job as a staff architect?"

A little confused, I innocently answered, "I don't know. But I'm going for it tomorrow."

I was perfectly fine going for this test, before Barbara got me all worked up and frightened. I tried to think about the bad things about me that could be revealed by the polygraph. Like, when I was eleven years old and was fresh to my Hebrew schoolteacher. I pushed her so far saying things, she smacked me across my face. I tried to come up with reasons to explain to the polygrapher why my big mouth was her fault. Or, how I ran my own little business behind the store manager's back at the Big Apple supermarket. Or, I had premarital sex with my wife. These kinds of things went through my mind. I couldn't stop obsessing about what the polygraph would reveal.

All of my obsessing was for naught. Quelle surprise! I passed the polygraph test. And I breathed a sigh of relief that my wiseass mouth that got me a smack in Hebrew school, my sneaky side business, and my premarital sex were not found out. I started working for Cosmo Parking. And I found out that all new employees were polygraphed, regardless of their job description.

For Barbara and me, we'd survived the small setback and were back on track. We continued living happily ever after. It was just the two of us and our dog, Pepper. We were a young couple on our own, in our home in the suburbs on Brewster Place, a fertile, landscaped block that continued to produce babies.

CHAPTER 11

I want a baby

Then came that night in bed. We were cuddled up close to each other, when, in between our kisses, Barbara smiled. "No more being careful. I want a baby."

I smiled back. "Me too."

Barbara began to figure out when we had to do it. She started off talking about her cycles, the day of the month, and the time of day. I couldn't follow what she was talking about. I planned to make myself available and do whatever she said. It turned out that Barbara's planning was perfect. We were pregnant after the first try. Barbara was all set with an obstetrician in nearby Succasunna, Dr. Robert Oshrin.

Barbara was so excited and began telling everybody. I joked about how anxious she was to make the announcement. I would say that Barbara began telling people before I had the chance to get my pants back on. An exaggeration, but almost true.

Barbara called me after her first appointment with Dr. Oshrin. "I know my due date. It's May 13, 1975."

"Oh, Barbara. I don't want the baby born on the thirteenth."

"You're so silly. There is no control over the due date."

"Yeah, but that's just an estimate by the doctor," I answered.

"No, it isn't an estimate, and you know that I'm always on time."

If you remember, I didn't want to move into our house on the thirteenth, so we moved on the fourteenth. Once again, the number thirteen came up. I'm not a superstitious person. It was the bad connotations of that number in the Bible, in the date Friday the thirteenth, and in buildings that skip thirteen when numbering the floors.

The due date was far enough away, and I felt anything could change. I didn't bring up the thirteenth again. Instead, we began to discuss my being in the room during her labor. Barbara knew that I was very squeamish about things like seeing operations on TV, scars, and anything to do with blood. And after several talks about it, Barbara suggested, "I think it's best for you not to be in the delivery room with me." She laughed when she saw me breathe a sigh of relief, as the worried look on my face changed to a smile.

Barbara signed up for Lamaze classes at Dover General Hospital. She wanted me to attend the classes with her. With last minute conflicts at work, I couldn't make the first few classes. I asked Barbara, "Do you really need me to go to the classes? I'm not going to be in the delivery room with you. Isn't that the only reason for a husband to attend these classes?"

"I'd like you there. I've been going alone and when I'm in class with all the other married couples, I feel like an unwed mother."

"Okay. I'll make sure to go with you to the next class."

Barbara and I were twenty-three and twenty-five. It was nice being in class with other young couples and having something in common; everyone was pregnant. I was doing well in the class. Even uncomfortable about seeing blood, I survived the movie on childbirth. I surprised myself by being totally fine with it. I quickly got caught up from the classes I had missed in learning the breathing exercises. Most importantly, Barbara was happy I was with her and I loved watching Barbara preparing to become a mommy. Her smile had a glow of excitement and she looked at me with those loving mommy eyes. I may have made up the expression "mommy eyes." It was my way of saying that when Barbara looked at me, she was confirming that I was the daddy.

Halfway through the class, the instructor gave us a recess. I whispered to Barbara that I was going to the bathroom. I had no problem getting into the bathroom. I had a problem getting out. I was locked in. People were fidgeting with the lock from the outside and I was doing the same from the inside. Eventually, someone found a maintenance guy and he was able to get the door open.

When I got back into the Lamaze room, Barbara had this big smile on her face. I asked why she was smiling, and she said that she would tell me later, when we get back to the car. In the car, Barbara said, "A few minutes after you left to go to the bathroom, the instructor made an announcement that we had a problem. That one of the daddies was locked in the bathroom. When I heard that, I said to the instructor, 'That's probably my husband.' I guess you really don't want to come to these classes."

"Barbara, I wasn't fooling! I was locked in the bathroom!"

"Really?"

"Yes! I went into the bathroom and locked the door behind me and when I tried to get out, the lock was stuck."

"I just knew it was you, when the instructor made the announcement. No one else gets themselves into such situations like you do. You are too silly."

Barbara was the most understanding and forgiving wife anyone could have. I don't think there was another woman who would have put up with such things. I did go to a couple more Lamaze classes with Barbara, until she let me off the hook.

The morning of May 13, 1975, my alarm clock sounded, waking me for work. As usual I pressed the snooze alarm several times before getting out of the bed. As I got out of bed and started toward the bathroom, I hadn't noticed that Barbara was awake. I heard her ask, "Where do you think you're going?"

"What? I'm going to work."

"No, you're not. You're taking me to the hospital. My water broke at three o'clock, in the middle of the night. I've been waiting for you to wake up, after watching you press the snooze button four times. I've been timing the contractions. We have plenty of time. So, go take your shower and I'll start getting ready to leave."

I don't stutter when I speak, but I did not fully understand what I'd just heard Barbara say. And I was not fully awake.

"Tell me that a-a-again! Wha-what did you say? Did you say you're in labor? Your water broke. The baby is coming. Wha-what time did your water break?"

"At three o'clock. You slept through the whole thing. There's no hurry. Get showered, dressed, and walk the dog, and I'll be ready to leave by then."

Was I married to the most considerate, loving, and caring woman in the world? Or did Barbara feel she'd be better off letting me sleep, and it would be easier on her to avoid my obsessing? Okay, let me guess. You're thinking, "Hey, Marc, the answer is yes, to both questions."

Barbara knew me very well. She patiently waited for what she knew was coming next.

"Barbara, just one thing. It's the thirteenth. I didn't want the baby to be born today."

"Well, there is no choice, silly head. This baby is coming today. I told you, I'm always on time."

At the hospital, the doctor examined Barbara and advised that the baby was going to be born breech. It would be a long labor. He considered sending us home but decided to keep Barbara in the hospital. Barbara took the news in stride and we walked the halls together to pass the time and maybe help induce the birth.

I thought I was doing fine helping Barbara. Obviously, the nurses felt differently. They suggested that there was no need for me to hang out at the hospital and Barbara needed her rest for the long labor ahead of her. That sounded like a polite line of bullshit to me. I guessed that I had given the impression I was a little nervous. Barbara was so cool about everything. One of us had to be nervous and I was nervous for both of us. I was nervous for Barbara having a breech birth. And I was nervous for me. Because I was nervous for me. The nurses suggested I go home and come back in several hours.

I went home. Pulling into the driveway, neighbors saw me and came over to ask about Barbara. I let them know the baby was breech, and it would be several hours. Since there was nothing else for me to do at home but wait, I figured it was a good time to fertilize the lawn and yard. After, I had to shower again and walk the dog.

A couple of hours passed, and I rushed back to Barbara. As soon as I got off the elevator, the nurses asked why I came back so soon and said it would still be quite a while. I spent some more time with Barbara and then they sent me home again.

Finally, around ten thirty in the evening, after Barbara had already been in labor for almost nineteen hours, the nurses said the baby would be born soon. I asked where the doctor was. They told me they would call the doctor when Barbara's delivery got closer, and the doctor would make it to the hospital no matter what the hour.

With that information, I went into panic mode. I was like, what? They were going to wait until Barbara was ready to give birth. Then, and only then, they would call the doctor! Then, the doctor would answer his phone, probably need to get dressed, and perhaps take a piss. And then get into his car to drive to the hospital. Then park his car and finally head for the delivery room. Not so calmly, I asked, "What if he doesn't get here in time?"

The nurse answered, "He will!"

I stood there dumfounded, thinking, "What kind of stupid fucking answer was that?" I was beginning to understand why the nurses kept suggesting I go home. It finally occurred to me that my OCD had been fully engaged.

In the labor room, I stood beside Barbara and held her hand through the labor pains and breathed along with her. We gazed into each other's eyes. Barbara had her sweet smile, and her dimples were so cute. The moment was so beautiful. I knew I was a lucky guy to be married to the most wonderful woman. And then, Barbara asked me, "Why are you staring at me like that?"

"I can't believe how incredible this all is, silly. You're having our baby."

"Yeah ... and it better happen soon."

I often wonder how Barbara put up with me for a forty-year marriage. She was probably the only woman in the world who would have. Fortunately, we had a marriage arranged in heaven. It was probably my side of the family who did the arranging, knowing there could only be Barbara for me. I think if it were Barbara's family doing the arranging, they would have passed me by. Because at that moment, in total seriousness, and with no second thought, I said, "You know ... it's getting very close to midnight. Maybe you can try to hold off until after midnight to have the baby."

"Oh, Marc ... don't try to make me laugh."

"I'm not trying to make you laugh. I mean it."

About an hour later, Barbara was taken into the delivery room. I nervously paced as I waited just outside the door. Often, I pushed my ear up against the door to try to hear something and wondered if we were having a boy or a girl. But I was mostly in a state of panic. It was one thing to have our minds prepared for a difficult delivery, being advised several hours in advance. But the delivery was finally happening, and I was scared.

Finally, I heard the baby cry. I gulped with pride and relief and so hoped that Barbara was okay. The doctor came out and told me the good news. Just after midnight, at 12:24 in the morning, on May 14, 1975, our son, Jonathan Scott Gellman, was born.

I was twenty-five years old. Today, I laugh about how ridiculously, truly happy I was for Jonathan to be born on the fourteenth. Over the years, I've loved telling the story about Jonathan's due date of the thirteenth and how Barbara held off to the fourteenth. Had Jonathan not been born on the fourteenth, I wouldn't have been able to thank Barbara for the next thirty-six years, on each May 14. A fond memory of a thanks that always got a smile from her.

Dr. Oshrin escorted me into the delivery room. Barbara was holding Jonathan, who was so small, at five pounds fifteen ounces. I walked up to them and Barbara asked me, "Do you love him?"

"Yes, I do. He's really cute. And thanks for holding out until after midnight."

Barbara gave me her dimpled smile, and rolled her eyes a little. "Oh, Marc ... only you could be silly enough to think that I would hold out."

A few seconds later, she said, "Marc, you know that I wanted to name the baby after my mother. Even though we have a boy, I'd like his Hebrew name to be after my mother. Okay with you?"

"Of course."

Then Barbara asked, "Do you want to hold him?"

"I don't think so. He's kind of small. I'll wait until he gets a little bigger."

With that, the nurse took Jonathan from Barbara, turned to me, and said, "Okay, Daddy, sit down in that chair and get comfortable. Because you're going to hold your son." I was so nervous as she placed Jonathan into my arms. I stared at him. It was all so surreal. I was holding my son.

I stayed with Barbara and Jonathan for a little while, until the nurse took him to the nursery. The nurse said to me, "You can't stay long. It's been a long day and Mommy needs her rest, and I think you do too."

That morning, I was back at the hospital. As I watched Jonathan through the window of the nursery, I noticed my parents coming off the elevator. They had these big smiles and looked so excited. As I pointed out Jonathan to them, my dad turned and started to approach me. I was a little confused, because it looked like he was going to give me a kiss. That would have been so out of character for my dad. Until that moment, I don't remember my dad ever giving me a kiss. I remember him carrying me when I was very young, but never a kiss.

My dad was a great father and was a well-known and respected person in our community. When he passed away, I received many compliments on the eulogy I delivered in his honor. But the eulogy was good because there was so much greatness about my dad. He was so very easy to eulogize.

But now, standing in front of the nursery, I was caught off guard. What was my dad about to do? At that moment, my dad put his hands on my shoulders, pulled me to him, and kissed me on my cheek. It felt so good. In his kiss, I could feel his pride in becoming a grandfather and his pride in me. It was such an incredible experience that, at that moment, I promised myself I would never lose the years in kissing my children and would never stop no matter how old they became. And from that moment on, I always kissed my dad when I saw him.

It was a little over a year later, after Jonathan was asleep, that Barbara and I were cuddling in bed. In between the kisses, Barbara smiled. "Let's stop being careful again. I want another baby."

I smiled back. "Me too."

Barbara's due date was May 22, 1977. The morning of the twenty-second was like déjà vu. Barbara's water broke about a half hour before my alarm clock sounded. But this time, Barbara poked me after the first ring and said, "Wake up! My water broke a half hour ago. No work for you today, you're taking me to the hospital. I'll call Annie. She's going to watch Jonathan. You get in and out of the shower quickly, walk the dog, and we're leaving for the hospital."

As our neighbor came into the house to get Jonathan, I went out to walk the dog. As we circled the block, Pepper decided to take her time peeing. When I came back on the block, I saw Barbara near the curb, leaning against the mailbox. She shouted to me, "Marc! Where were you? Hurry up! This is not like last time. This baby is coming!"

I stepped up my pace and we were off to the hospital. We made it in time. At the hospital, I held on to Barbara as she walked. We were quickly taken to the labor room. As I sighed a feeling of relief, safe in the labor room, Barbara gave out a big scream of pain. I reached out to squeeze her hand. I can't imagine the look of fright that was on my face. Barbara took one look at me, said she was okay, and told me to go back to the car and get her suitcase.

As I walked back to the parking lot, I wondered how many times the nurses were going to send me home this time. But, when I got back to the labor room with the suitcase, Barbara wasn't there. Dr. Oshrin came into the room and I asked, "Where's Barbara?"

Dr. Oshrin smiled. "Where were you?"

"I went to the car to get Barbara's suitcase. Where's Barbara?"

"Your wife is in the delivery room with her little girl," he answered.

"What ... Where is she?"

"She's in the delivery room with her little girl."

On May 22, 1977, at 10:34 in the morning, our daughter, Kristen Lynn Gellman, was born. As Dr. Oshrin brought me into the delivery room, I saw my wife and baby girl. When Barbara saw me, she began to cry. Through her tears, the first thing she said to me was, "Oh, Marc ... I so wanted a girl. I had such a close relationship with my mother and now I can have the same with my little girl. I'm so happy. But I miss my mother so much and wish she were here to see our little girl and us and Jonathan. We've come so far and have everything ... Right?"

I was caught off guard, a little in shock. It all happened so quickly. I left Barbara to get her suitcase. Now, here was Barbara holding our baby girl. Emotions came over me, hearing Barbara talk about her mom. I answered, "Yes, we do. Through everything, we've been lucky too."

I waited a few seconds, as I watched Barbara holding and staring at our baby and then I asked, "And ... you're sure that you still want to name her 'Kristen'?"

"Yes! Now that I look at her, I see her as Kristen. It's a beautiful name for my beautiful little girl."

"Okay. I'm going to go and call my parents now and tell them the good news. They'll be so happy that we had a girl. I'm not sure what their reaction is going to be to her name. They'll just have to get used to it. After all, they should be thankful that we didn't come up with a name that sounded even more non-Jewish than Kristen."

Indeed, my parents had a shocked and questioning reaction to the name Kristen. "What kind of name is that?" they asked at first. But they got over it quickly ... I think. It would be Kristen who, many years later, questioned her name. She would ask, "Why did you name me Kristen? Do you know what it was like, going to Hebrew school with the name Kristen?" But many years later, her name would become more clearly Jewish, when she married and became Kristen Lebenstein.

Over the short period of twenty-four months, we became a family, with a son and a daughter, and a dog. We traded the Ford Pinto in for a Chrysler Suburban station wagon, with simulated wood-grain finish on the sides. People told us we were now a typical suburban American family.

Hearing that annoyed me so much. I disliked that expression when it was used to describe us. I never wanted to be a typical any-thing. I just wanted to be us, different from everyone else. And we were. We were the only members of our temple who had a daughter named Kristen.

CHAPTER 12

I am incorrigible

In the spring of 1979, Jonathan was four, the age when he would repeat everything we said. Barbara often reminded me to be careful of my language and what I said in front of the kids. Kristen was only two, so she wasn't repeating things yet. But Jonathan would come out with the most outrageous things and Barbara would totally blame me. I didn't think the language I used, or what I said, was so bad. And it was funny when Jonathan repeated certain things. At least to me it was funny. Barbara's reaction was different. She often didn't think it was funny and would get on my case.

One afternoon, I was walking down the block with Jonathan. As we passed a neighbor working on his front lawn, I said hello and the neighbor said hello back. We were just about past the neighbor's house when Jonathan shouted, "Daddy, is that the man you said is an idiot?" I grabbed Jonathan's hand and continued walking quickly. I was certain that the neighbor heard Jonathan. He said it so very loud. I tried to make believe like nothing had happened and make a quick getaway.

As we continued walking, Jonathan asked again, "Daddy, is that the man you said is an idiot?"

I so wanted to have some fun and say, "Yes, that's the man. He's a real idiot and he's funny-looking too." But I knew that Jonathan would repeat it to Barbara, and she'd be all over me about it. So, I didn't. Then Jonathan asked, "Daddy, why are you laughing?"

I didn't know how to respond. "I'm not laughing."

"Yes, you are. Are you laughing because that man is an idiot?"

This was so Jonathan. He wouldn't give up on things and repeated things over and over, until he got the answer he wanted. Like the time when I was on a ladder in the garage and dropped a screwdriver. When the screwdriver fell to the floor, I looked down from the ladder at the screwdriver and said, "Oh, you bastard."

Jonathan was in the garage with me and quickly picked up on this. He asked very loudly, "Is that a bastard, Daddy?"

"No, no. That's a screwdriver," I answered.

"Daddy, you said it is a bastard."

No matter what I said, Jonathan kept calling it a bastard. I tried to distract him from the screwdriver, but he was focused on it. The door from the garage to the house was open and I knew Barbara would be able to hear him. Fortunately for me, she didn't. Or maybe she did hear him and let me slide on this one.

Or the time Barbara was out running errands and I was home with the kids. We were in the family room and I thought I smelled a dirty diaper. I didn't want to look. So, I asked Jonathan to peek into Kristen's diaper and see if it was clean. He pulled open the back waistband, looked in, and said, "The diaper is clean, Daddy. It's just a wet fart."

I treasured the funny things our kids came out with and Barbara did too, to a point. Like the time we were sitting at dinner and Brian, our third child, was telling us about watching TV that afternoon. He talked about a news flash that American troops had been attacked by "gorillas."

At first, I didn't get what Brian was talking about. I asked if the news flash showed the gorillas that attacked the troops. Getting annoyed with me, Barbara interrupted, "Marc, would you stop it! It's not funny."

"I'm not being funny. Just want to know where the troops were, that there were gorillas on the loose."

Barbara started laughing. "Are you serious? You think these were gorillas? These were obviously army guerrilla troops, not animal gorillas."

It was then I realized what the news flash was about. I looked at Brian, who was trying to follow what we were saying. I had fun listening to him continue to defend what he believed happened, with his imagination controlling his description of the event, and the cutest expressions on his face. I started laughing and encouraged Brian to tell us more. He had such a serious look on his face, and I had no intention of not taking advantage of the silliness of the conversation.

"Well, maybe it's obvious to you," I said to Barbara. "But I'd like to hear more about the gorillas from Brian."

Still laughing, Barbara answered, "No, we're not talking about gorillas."

Turning to Brian, Barbara felt it important to explain to him that it was "guerrilla" troops. But Brian didn't want to accept Barbara's explanation. He was convinced that it was real gorillas that attacked the troops. I enjoyed watching him stand his ground before eventually conceding, saying, "Mommy is right." I agreed with the importance of correcting Brian. But only to a point. For my children's sake, I thanked God for Barbara.

One evening Barbara and I were in our bedroom and in came marching Jonathan and Kristen. They were arm-in-arm and giggling, with some questions. Jonathan had learned some information about the facts of life that day and shared it with Kristen. He wanted us to confirm what he learned. I was walking out from the bathroom. As soon as I heard the topic of their questions, I turned around and went back into the bathroom and closed the door.

Barbara dutifully explained everything to them. Kristen's response was, "Ew ... you and Daddy did that three times?" After they left the room, I skulked back out of the bathroom.

"Thanks a lot for leaving me with them, coward."

"I knew that you would handle all of the questions very well and I didn't want to get in the way."

Another night, at the dinner table, a discussion of homosexuals came up. Barbara explained that some men choose to have another man as a partner. Then, the subject turned to women.

"Oh, girls do that too?" Kristen asked with a puzzled look.

"Yes, they are lesbians," Barbara answered.

And then, Kristen, my young, innocent, and adorable twelve-year-old daughter with pigtails answered, "But what can girls do? They can't butt fuck."

I loved how their young minds interpreted things, even though some things the kids said were inappropriate. Barbara loved it too. But it didn't stop her from blaming me for most of the outrageous things the kids said.

Barbara was definitely the disciplinarian in our home, to the kids and to me. I give total credit to Barbara for the great way our kids turned out. As for disciplining me, despite Barbara's reminders I was never totally careful of my language or what I said in front of the kids.

There were times in our marriage when my silliness got in the way of better judgment. When I did things a little off-color and Barbara grounded me. More often, Barbara accepted my sense of humor and went along with the laugh, even when I was being inappropriate. Barbara would say, "Okay, I give up. Have your laugh." And she'd laugh along with me. For the most part, Barbara put up with things in stride. Sometimes my silliness would become stubbornness. When we had disagreements, Barbara said that I couldn't admit to ever being wrong.

My fiftieth birthday was on a Sunday. Barbara arranged a party at a restaurant. It was our kids, friends, and relatives for an afternoon dinner party. Barbara and I were in our bedroom and finished getting dressed for the party, when in mock seriousness she asked, "So on this day of your fiftieth birthday, what confessions do you have?"

After twenty-eight years of marriage, it was, at that very moment, that I admitted to Barbara that I am incorrigible. Barbara started to laugh, came over to me, put her hands on my shoulders, looked me straight in the eyes, and said, "So, you are admitting to being incorrigible. Let me tell you something. I've always known that, but I'm happy to hear you admit to it. Good. I can use that admission. It'll make future disagreements with you easier on me."

CHAPTER 13

Something or someone was always guiding us

One morning, during the summer of 1979, I heard Barbara say from the bathroom, "Oh my ... What is this?" She came out from the bathroom with her hand on her left breast.

A little puzzled, I looked at her. "What do you mean, what is this? That's your left tit."

Then I noticed the frightened look on Barbara's face and my heart began to race.

"Oh, Marc ... I think I feel a lump. It's right here. See if you can feel it too."

At first, I said, "No, I don't feel any lump." And then, "Wait ... I think I feel something very small."

For a moment Barbara lost it. Fear spread across her face. She was about to cry. I could see the adrenaline rush of panic happening to her. I wasn't used to seeing Barbara in a state of panic. I was the one

179

who would lose it, while Barbara stayed calm. She quickly took a deep breath and began sorting things out.

"Marc, you go to work. I'll call the doctor as soon as his office opens and hopefully get an appointment. I'll call you when I know when the appointment is. In the meantime, I'll get someone to watch the kids."

"I'll stay home and wait for you to call the doctor."

"No use waiting around. He may not be able to see me today. Go to work and I'll call you."

My long commute to Newark seemed endless that day. There were no car or cell phones in 1979. As soon as I got into my office, I hurried to the phone to call Barbara.

"I'm rushing to leave right now. The doctor is going to see me as soon as I get to his office. I'll call you after."

"I'll meet you at the doctor."

"By the time you drive back from Newark, I'll already be back home."

The waiting was horrific. I was off the wall, obsessing. I had everyone in the office on alert for a phone call from Barbara and ready to track me down, wherever I was.

Finally, while I was in my office, the phone rang. It was Barbara. Almost immediately, hearing her voice, I could tell she was fine. She sounded so much better, completely calm. I could hear the smile in her voice.

"Everything is fine. The doctor is positive that it is nothing and there's no need to worry or do anything. I told him that for my peace of mind, I want it removed. So, he referred me to a surgeon. I'm going to call and make an appointment as soon as I get off the phone with you."

A few days later, Barbara had the lump removed at Dover General Hospital. Her doctor was correct. The lump was a benign cyst. That night, we lay in bed, staring at the ceiling and chilling from the stress of the last few days.

"Oh, Marc ... I was so scared."

"Me too," I answered.

"The doctor said it would be nothing, but something was telling me to have it removed."

"What is the something that was telling you? Was it guiding you too?"

"I don't know," she answered.

I set up Barbara for this opening for me to get silly. And at that moment, I so needed to get silly.

"You always say that something is telling you something or guiding you. It can't be a something telling you something. It has to be a someone telling you something. Or a someone guiding you."

"Are you being silly?"

In mock seriousness, I answered, "I'm just trying to help you figure this out about this something or someone. I don't think that I'll be able to fall asleep until we resolve your confusion with this."

"Listen, silly head, it doesn't have to be a someone. It could be a something. Maybe it was my mother watching over me."

"Do you think your mom is watching over you now? Cause we're both lying here fully naked."

At this point, I was rolling in laughter. I was, like, drunken silly. "Or maybe, it was Aunt Fanny watching over you."

Laughing, Barbara answered, "You really enjoy entertaining yourself."

"Don't blame me. I never asked your mother or Aunt Fanny to watch over us, especially when we're naked."

Still laughing, Barbara answered, "How did blame get into this conversation? Okay, enough, silly head. Let my mother and Aunt Fanny rest in peace. Whatever the something or someone was, I'm happy I had the lump removed. It would have been on my mind and I would have been constantly touching it."

With a wiseass smile, I answered, "Yeah, I would have been constantly touching it too."

Barbara smiled back. "It doesn't matter that the doctor was right. I'm always going to listen to my own intuition. I don't want anything growing on my body that doesn't belong."

Still being a wiseass, I asked, "How about the feeling of something growing in your body?"

Blushing and dimples showing, Barbara turned to me. "You are so silly."

Although I was often very silly, I couldn't help myself from being extra silly at that moment. I had been so anxious over the past few days and needed to release the tension buildup. I couldn't stop picturing the frightened look on Barbara's face, when she first found the lump. It was difficult for me to bear seeing her suffer the pain of fearing the unknown.

I continued trying to lighten up the moment for the two of us. "Well let's get really silly." And we did. That night, we put this difficult episode behind us and moved on.

One night, about a year later, while we were getting into a romantic mood, I said to Barbara, "Remember when I said I wanted to have five or seven kids and we agreed to just three?"

Barbara quickly interrupted. "I want another baby too. But we already have two kids with birthdays in the month of May. So not tonight or we'll have another 'May' baby."

"Why did you interrupt? How did you know what I was going to say?"

Barbara rolled over on top of me until we were nose to nose. "Because I saw that mischievous twinkle in your eyes."

"Yeah, making a baby still feels a little mischievous, even though we're married. Let's keep it that way. Thinking that we're being a little bad is arousing."

To the both of us, even after nine years of marriage and two kids, it still felt a little bad. And it was that feeling that would keep our love exciting and forever young. Over the next thirty-one years that we had together, Barbara and I never felt like we were growing old. For sure, growing old together in age is wonderful. But for us, during our forty-year marriage, Barbara and I stayed young together, with a lot of silliness and a lot of loving. And I know for sure, if we were able to be together into our nineties, our teenage puppy love would have gone on, unchanged by our age and our wrinkles.

In thinking more about it, our puppy love would have been incredibly romantic in our nineties. It would have been a new adventure, a new beginning to our silliness. My eyesight would probably be compromised by then, and I'd have difficulty distinguishing between the wrinkles and that thing I'd be searching for. That would make for a good laugh and something to be silly about. Barbara would be an old Jewish woman and probably be screaming, "Oy ... Oy ... Oy." Instead of calling it fucking, we'd call it schtupping. I'd probably have difficulty getting into position and require the assistance from someone to help put me on, and take me off when we finished. This would be the ultimate in our silliness and we'd experience an arousing puppy love that was beyond being bad.

We started planning for another child. Barbara had become expert at figuring out how to plan for the birth date of a baby. She wanted a September 1981 birth. Barbara's plan worked. During the summer of 1981, Barbara was nearing the end of her pregnancy.

Also, we were looking forward to celebrating our tenth wedding anniversary on August 29. I wanted to do something crazy special for Barbara, like a public announcement of my feelings after being married for ten years. At that time, we subscribed to a monthly regional Jewish newspaper called the *Morris-Sussex Jewish News*. I knew that if I placed a quarter-page announcement about our anniversary, it would be something extra special for Barbara. In the August issue, on page thirteen, the announcement read:

> To my dear wife:
> Barbara Gellman
>
> Happy Anniversary.
> The last ten years
> have been the
> happiest of my life.
>
> Love, Marc

I knew which day the newspaper would arrive in the mail. And I knew Barbara would read the paper while relaxing after dinner. I just hoped none of our friends would notice the announcement first and call, before Barbara had a chance to see it.

I called Barbara from work and said I'd be home early and suggested an early dinner. I kind of rushed the pace of dinner and led the kids upstairs to spend some time with them and get them ready for bed. I left Barbara to clean up, knowing that after, she'd go down to the family room to relax and read the paper. I wanted Barbara to come across the announcement while reading the paper in the quietness of herself.

I was upstairs with the kids. I got them in their pajamas, and we were reading stories. It had been about thirty minutes since I left Barbara in the kitchen. I was getting anxious, waiting to hear that she'd come across the announcement. Then I heard her shout, "Oh, Marc, I love you!"

I tucked the kids in bed and went downstairs to the family room. Barbara was sitting on the couch. I walked over to her. With a look of mock surprise on my face, I asked, "What's the matter?"

"You know. This announcement in the newspaper."

I sat down beside her. "Which paper are you reading?"

"Stop joking around."

"Let me see what you're talking about." Barbara handed me the paper.

Still acting surprised, I said, "Oh, this. I was wondering when it would appear in the paper."

"You're so silly. You love me so much."

"Yeah, I guess it's obvious. 'Cause this announcement was pretty expensive!"

I did love Barbara so much. I loved being married to her and I wanted everyone to know. We started to kiss and fool around, and the phone rang for the rest of the evening, as people noticed the announcement. It was exactly what I hoped would happen. Barbara was soon to give birth to our third child, and I wanted the world around her to shine. And, with the smile on her face, it surely did.

The Monday before Labor Day, I began joking with Barbara. "With Labor Day coming up, does that mean that the baby will be born then? Are you going to start off answering me with, 'something or someone' is telling you?" My joking was close. It was the Thursday morning before Labor Day weekend when Barbara poked me in my sleep to tell me her water broke. This time around, we were experienced, and all went easily as planned. Our neighbor came over to get Jonathan and Kristen. I quickly walked the dog and we left for the hospital.

A little more experienced than when Jonathan and Kristen were born, I waited outside the delivery room more relaxed, less nervous, but more emotional. Jonathan was six and Kristen, four. This time, I better understood the amazingness of being a parent. I loved arriving home from work each evening. I would walk into the house and shout, "Daddy's home!" With that, our two little kids ran to the door to greet me, so excited to see me home. Our dog, Pepper, came to greet me too.

As I waited, I kept envisioning one more set of little feet running to greet me at the door. What wasn't in my vision was whether it would be a girl or a boy. I was getting ready for either. More than thirty-five years later, my son, Jonathan, continues the tradition of "Daddy's home," when he gets home from work. My grandson, Benjamin, and my grand-dog, Brewster, run to the door to greet him.

I heard the baby cry and was wiping a tear from my eye as Dr. Oshrin came out from the delivery room to tell me that Barbara and our baby boy were doing fine. Our third child, Brian Joseph Gellman, was born on Thursday, September 3, 1981, at 11:34 a.m. Dr. Oshrin escorted me into the delivery room. I walked up to Barbara and kissed her and then the nurse handed the baby to me. As I held Brian, I announced, "This baby is sooooo cute!"

"Who does he look like?" Barbara asked.

That was a good question. As I stared at him, I couldn't figure that out and neither could Barbara. It was mostly his eyes that made it confusing. He kind of had squinty eyes, like no one else in the family.

"I don't know. Are you sure we're his parents?"

Everyone in the delivery room laughed and I added, "We already have two kids at home who don't look like brother and sister and now we have a third who doesn't look like either one of them. I'm guessing that something or someone made him in their own image, rather than ours. So, we now have three kids who look nothing alike. But we'll keep him anyway, since he's so cute."

The next afternoon, I brought Jonathan and Kristen to the hospital to see Barbara and meet the baby. It was so much fun to see the two of them excited and fussing over Barbara, when we got to her room. Brian was in the nursery and Barbara walked with us to the nursery window. I pulled up two chairs for Jonathan and Kristen to stand on. They quickly asked which baby was ours. I pointed to Brian.

"That one is our baby."

Jonathan shouted out, "I like our baby. The other babies are ugly!"

Jonathan's voice practically bounced down the long corridor. A little embarrassed, Barbara gave me a stern look. I quickly blurted out, "Listen, I don't know where he got that from. I've never said anything like that. At least, I don't think I ever said anything like that."

Barbara smiled. "You're impossible."

Barbara breastfed for about three months. Until early December 1981, when she felt another lump in her left breast. Having gone through this once before, we were much calmer this time. Once again, the doctor advised that it wasn't a concern, but Barbara wanted it removed. She scheduled the procedure with the same surgeon as the last time, at Dover General Hospital.

Since it was a minor, routine procedure, and of no concern, Barbara went by herself. She called me after and said all went well and she'd have the results the next day. We were confident of the results and took it all in stride.

The next day, I was in my office, at my desk, when my phone rang. It was Barbara. She was in a panic and crying. I had no idea what sort of bad news she had for me. "Oh, Marc ... It's not good. It's breast cancer. Come home. I need you."

"I'm on my way."

As I hung the phone, fright came over me, as I tried to process what I just heard. I felt so alone. Spiritually, I hoped if something or someone was always guiding us, that something or someone would help us now. I ran into my boss's office to tell him, and he called his business partner to come in too. They both tried to console and calm me and said that I need to take a deep breath and go home to Barbara.

When I got home, I drove into the driveway, turned off the engine, and sat in the car for a few minutes, trying to build up the courage to go into the house and see Barbara. As soon as she heard me walk in, Barbara came running into my arms. This was the most frightening thing we had ever been faced with. It was 1981, ten years after Barbara's mother passed away. For a woman, it hadn't gotten any less frightening to hear someone say, "You have breast cancer."

Barbara kept saying, "Marc, I don't want to die." My mind was racing from one thought to the next. I didn't know what to say. I felt so lost and over my head. Going through my mind was, "Is this really happening? Why Barbara? She's such a good person. When does she get to live in peace? She's been through so much in her life. Things are so wonderful for us. I love her so much. How do I comfort her? I can't lose her. It hurts so much to see her in pain. I need her. We are so much one and I won't be able to go on without her. What do I say now? What do I do? How do I make this nightmare go away? What about our children?"

We went into the family room and sat down on the couch in a silent embrace. Jonathan and Kristen were at school and preschool and Brian was napping. Barbara began to tell me about what the doctor had said: that there might not be any need for a mastectomy, since the lumpectomy removed all of the tumor, with clear margins. Also, the tumor was very small. Barbara would need more tests before the doctor would know if she needed more surgery.

After sitting there a while in silence, Barbara began to talk about when she worked for Merrill Lynch. She remembered that one of the brokers she worked for had a client who was a radiologist at Dover General Hospital. "Remember? I always talked about a Dr. B, when I worked for Scott. His name is Aaron Borsky and I remember that he's a radiologist at Dover General. He was a favorite client. I'm going to call him, and we'll see what he has to say."

It was just the two of us, continuing to sit in the silence. I felt help-less and vulnerable. This was over our heads. We needed something or someone to guide us. Who do we call? What do we do? Which doctors do we listen to? I thought that perhaps this doctor could be the someone who could guide us about what we needed to do.

"Call Dr. B, right now. Maybe he'll remember you and offer to meet with us."

Barbara called his office and Dr. B came to the phone. It had been six-and-a-half years since Barbara left Merrill Lynch, just before Jonathan was born. After they got reacquainted, Barbara telling him that we had two more children after Jonathan, she filled him in on our current situation. Dr. B said he knew very well the surgeon who had performed her lumpectomy. He would speak with him and get up to speed before the end of that day. He suggested we come to see him the following day to discuss next steps.

We met with Dr. B the next day. As he put it, seeing Barbara was a visit with an old friend who is not so old. Barbara was only thirty. He explained to us that the tumor was a small infiltrating ductal car-cinoma involving the upper quadrant of her breast and it was totally removed by the lumpectomy. He recommended more tests, includ-ing an axillary node dissection to make sure that there was no lymph node involvement. His prognosis was that all the tests would turn out fine and, if that happened, Barbara would not require a mastectomy.

Although hearing the clinical terms was overwhelming for us, Barbara and I felt comfortable listening to Dr. B. He explained everything in a very optimistic way. More importantly, we felt assured that Dr. B was going to be that someone we could rely on to give us guidance throughout the process. We felt very fortunate that he considered Barbara an old friend, who was not so old.

We met with Dr. B again after Barbara's tests. As he predicted, all was fine. He recommended a program of radiation therapy. For this type of radiation, he discussed several doctors with us. His first choice was Dr. Michael Pearson at Yale New Haven Hospital.

It was mid-December 1981 when Barbara and I traveled up to New Haven, Connecticut to meet with Dr. Pearson. He examined

Barbara and patiently reviewed the program with us. I could see that Barbara felt very comfortable with this doctor. She was smiling and laughing and was very chatty with him. At one point, when he turned away, Barbara looked at me and gestured with a thumbs up. I smiled back and nodded my head, yes.

The radiation treatments were to happen each weekday for nine weeks and were scheduled for January 5 through March 9. Driving home from New Haven, we felt such relief. We had a plan! All the medical experts had given Barbara a very optimistic prognosis. We celebrated in the optimism all around us. We only had two more difficult details to overcome for the nine weeks of therapy: how to care for Jonathan and Kristen and how to find temporary housing for Barbara and Brian in New Haven.

We got incredibly lucky. Barbara was able to hire a neighbor from down the block. The plan was for Eileen to pick up Jonathan and Kristen each weekday morning. She had two children of her own. For nine weeks, Jonathan and Kristen would become part of Eileen's household, as if she had four children. I would pick them up after their dinner. With this taken care of, we still needed to find temporary housing in New Haven.

I was very fortunate to have an incredibly caring employer. Philip and Steve wanted to be kept up-to-date about each step in Barbara's treatment and its effect on our family, and they closely monitored how I was doing. I vividly remember the time Steve said to me that he had a luncheon meeting scheduled for the next day in Manhattan on Fifth Avenue, near the Metropolitan Museum of Art. He wanted me to come along with him to the meeting. I asked Steve if I needed to prepare. "No," he said. "Just come to the meeting with me."

The next day, I drove with Steve into Manhattan. The meeting was a lovely lunch with a business friend of Steve's. I wasn't sure of the purpose for the meeting and my mind wandered a lot, thinking about Barbara. When we got back into the car, I asked Steve, "Sorry, but I was having trouble focusing on what that meeting was about. Is there something that I need to do to follow up?"

Steve answered, "Nope. It was just a friendly lunch and I thought that you would enjoy it. I could see your mind drifting in and out of the conversation. This was just a little diversion for you."

That was very kind and thoughtful of Steve and a much-needed diversion for me. In the meantime, and unknown to me, Philip was working on finding temporary housing in New Haven. He reached out to his daughter Deborah's in-laws, Naomi and Alvin Bloom. They lived near Yale New Haven Hospital. That afternoon, Philip called me into his office to tell me of his conversation with Naomi and Alvin. Barbara and the baby were welcome to stay with them in their home for the entire period of her treatment. Philip suggested that Barbara call Naomi and visit the Blooms to make sure she would feel comfortable staying with Naomi and Alvin.

I called Barbara to tell her.

"Wonderful! I'll call her right now and call you back after I speak with her."

I waited impatiently by the phone. It seemed like it was taking too long for her to call me back. Finally, about a half hour later, Barbara called. She was happy and, like, out of breath excited. There had been so much pressure on us to find temporary housing. Barbara was concerned and I was obsessing about what we'd have to settle for. As Barbara started to talk, I sat back in my chair and listened.

"Marc, I am so happy! Naomi is so, so nice! I'm going to visit her the day after tomorrow. Tell Philip, thank you, thank you, thank you!"

Barbara traveled to New Haven and had a nice visit with Naomi and Alvin. After, Barbara told me Naomi and Alvin made her feel so comfortable and welcomed to stay with them. Naomi even called to speak to me and the kids, so we could feel assured that Barbara was going to be in safe keeping. After the call, I remember Kristen saying, "I like Mrs. Bloom. She's nice!"

I saw Naomi and Alvin several times over the years that followed, after those nine weeks Barbara spent in their home. But it would be one year after I lost Barbara, and almost thirty-one years after Barbara stayed with them, that I received a note from Naomi, in which she described the first time she met Barbara.

August 9, 2012

Dear Marc,

Hopefully this finds you well in your "new" residence, and your children and grands are fairly close by.

Every evening I sit in my den and read on the lamp table and to my left is a clear crystal cube that Barbara brought me when she came here with your five-month-old baby.

She put that baby on the top of the washing machine to change his diaper and I knew she was scared but relaxed and we would have a wonderful visit together. And, we did!

If you have the inclination and time, I'd love to hear about you and yours, and maybe a new picture.

My best to you all,

Fondly,

Naomi

A few months after I received that note, I received another note from Naomi, in which she described the conversation she had with Philip, thirty-one years before.

January 9, 2013

Dear Marc,

Thank you so much for your remembering me with the beautiful card and your good wishes. It brought back many memories.

I recall so vividly when Philip Katz called me and said the wife of an employee of his was diagnosed with breast cancer and needed specific treatment. She researched hospitals in New Jersey, Philadelphia, New York City and liked New Haven best. Could I possibly find her a room within walking distance of New Haven Hospital? When I said, "She'll stay with me," Philip responded with, "Not so fast, she comes with a five-month-old baby." And I responded that we have grandchildren in common. I have all the accoutrements and it would be my pleasure to have them here. It took Barbara and me less than five minutes to become friends!

Today, as I look at our lives in retrospect, it's amazing how at difficult times, Barbara and I always knew people to help us. Or we knew someone who could introduce us to people to help us. It's as if something or someone was always guiding us in a direction to take and a decision to make, and in choices for friends and relationships.

In our early years, Barbara and I were very fortunate in our choices of employers. Perhaps it really was that something was always guiding us, and we were blessed with good work environments and viewed our workplaces as being so much more than places where we went to get a paycheck. These were places where we learned, grew, met people, and built relationships; relationships that enriched our lives.

I often hear the expression about a person having had the ability to become successful, because he or she had a good rabbi. The definition of "rabbi" is teacher. I believe that the definition of a "good" employer should also include teacher. I was very fortunate that all my employers had that in common. They were good teachers. They were people who, at different times, became my rabbi, taking me under their wings, guiding me, teaching me about the job I was to do, the work ethic I needed to do the job well, and making me think about my future and life priorities.

At Cosmo Parking, Philip and Steve were not just good teachers, they were great teachers, who took employees under their wings. So, it wasn't by chance that Barbara and I had the good fortune of being introduced to Naomi and Alvin Bloom. It was because of the choices we made in employers that we had such people to guide us.

At a time when we had so many challenges and needs, Naomi and Alvin took Barbara and Brian into their home and made them family. I was doing some research on the Internet as I wrote this chapter and found something very interesting about Naomi that Barbara never knew. Naomi was born on April 1, 1926, April Fool's Day. This information came as a surprise to me, and I was struck by a powerful coincidence. Barbara's mother was born on April 1, 1928. Naomi was like a surrogate mother to Barbara, during those nine weeks. Perhaps having the same birthday as Barbara's mother wasn't a coincidence at all. Because something or someone was always guiding us.

During the nine weeks, Barbara headed up to New Haven on Sunday evenings and came back home on Friday evenings. The first Sunday evening that Barbara left began the most difficult of the nine weeks. We all cried. That week, Jonathan, Kristen, and I settled into the routine. I got up early to shower and dress and then wake the kids. I got them dressed, gave them breakfast, and they were ready for Eileen to pick them up for school. I picked them up in the evening from Eileen, after they had dinner. Then it was getting the kids showered, in their pajamas, and a call to Barbara before bedtime. The weekdays were a tedious, humdrum, day-to-day routine.

Our only source for a refreshing break was our calls with Barbara every night. Each evening, as soon as we walked into the house, the kids started asking, "Can we call Mommy now?" But although talking with Barbara was the high point of our evening, the calls were all about hearing Barbara's voice and asking, "How many more days until you come home, Mommy?" After the call, there was sadness and my attempts at playtime weren't the same without Barbara. My children needed Barbara. I needed Barbara.

Of course, the best part of the routine was Friday evenings, as the three of us waited for Barbara to pull into the driveway. It was a difficult time. We tried to make the best of the weekend. It became all about the five of us being together. But the weekends flew by too quickly. Like, within a blink, we were saying goodbye on Sunday.

The nine weeks were emotionally, physically, and mentally exhausting for me. I hit the bed hard and early those weeks. But I couldn't sleep. Being alone in bed brought me down. I found out how lonely I could be without Barbara and would lay awake into the night. Each day, we all counted the days until March 9. For Barbara and me, March 9 meant our lives would begin again. For our kids, Mommy would be coming home, for good.

Barbara's last treatment at Yale New Haven Hospital was on Tuesday morning, March 9. It was a celebratory day for our family and especially for Barbara. We all glowed with happiness and excitement in our smiles.

Yet there was sadness for Barbara in saying goodbye to Naomi and

Alvin. Barbara couldn't thank them enough and promised that their dearest relationship would continue. Naomi said, "I hope you'll invite us to Brian's Bar Mitzvah. We'll be two old people by then. But we'll be there, even if we're walking with canes." Barbara kept in touch, with occasional visits, and Naomi and Alvin attended all three of my children's Bar and Bat Mitzvahs. Also, Naomi was at Kristen's wedding. Alvin had passed away a few years before. They are examples of the guiding someones in our lives.

So, Barbara packed up the car and headed home with our five-month-old baby. As she got onto Interstate 95, Barbara felt a good omen happening. When she turned on the radio, the theme from *The Greatest American Hero* started playing. The lyrics to the song so described Barbara's feelings, as she was heading south on Interstate 95, back to New Jersey. She felt only good things happening to her at that moment; so good that it was hard for her to believe. It was a new day for Barbara. She felt like she had broken out of the darkness and all her dreams and wishes would, for sure, come true.

Barbara described her drive home listening to that song as invigorating. It was her moment of starting over fresh and new, with a new chance on life and a future of only good things ahead. Barbara said she couldn't help singing along out loud, even though Brian was asleep in the back seat. After the song was over, she continued to hear it over and over in her mind and sang it out loud, over and over, all the way home from New Haven, Connecticut to Flanders, New Jersey.

Our world was wonderful again. We were thankful for the something or someone that was always guiding us. At a time when Barbara needed her mother, Barbara met a surrogate mother. Whether it was Barbara's mother orchestrating the process or something else, we believed it to be something. We knew we couldn't have made it through alone. Through all our experiences, we seemed to have had a guiding hand from either above or on this earth.

Barbara and I had already experienced our share of difficult times. And yet, we looked to our future with innocence, a little wounded, and with a puppy love unspoiled by the past.

CHAPTER 14

Tears filled my eyes too

Until 1973, a little more than the first two-thirds of our lives, Barbara and I were city people. By 1983, we had been living in New Jersey for ten years and had acclimated to the suburbs, near rural areas of the northwestern part of the state. We had our routines and schedules in sync. During the week, I tried to get home in time to have dinner as a family. But it was difficult with my late work hours and the long commute home. Most often, Barbara would give the kids their dinner and try to keep them up until I got home, before putting them to bed. She waited to have her dinner with me.

One evening in the spring of 1983, I got home and the kids were already asleep. It was a quiet dinner for just the two of us. We chatted about our day and Barbara told me about what the kids did in school and some of the funny things they did and said after school. Almost as soon as I swallowed my last bit of food, Barbara asked, "Marc, are you ready?"

"Oh? Ready for what?

I had just about finished taking my last bite and had no idea what was up. Barbara had kind of a smile on her face. So, I figured it had to do with something possibly good. But the way she asked, "Are you ready?" and the timing, waiting to finish dinner, it had to be some kind of startling news. Being silly, I was just about to ask if our crazy neighbor killed herself, as she blurted out, "I'm pregnant."

"What!"

"I'm pregnant."

"I know! I heard you the first time. I mean ...wow."

I was confused and unsure of how to react. I was totally surprised. Happy, but totally surprised. And I sensed that something was wrong. Barbara wouldn't normally have made such an announcement this way. Instead, she would have run into my arms as soon as I walked into the house and said, "I'm pregnant! Do you love me?" But she didn't, and she wasn't being her happy, excited self about this news.

Barbara and I got up from the table at the same time. I gave her a hug and we kissed. I didn't say anything else. I tried to process this news and figure out what else was up. Then, as Barbara looked into my eyes, she said, "What are you thinking?"

Confused by that question, I answered, "What am I thinking ... I'm ... um ... thinking ... I guess ...we're not good at the rhythm method, and I'm thinking we need to get a bigger house. Why?"

She began to cry, "Oh, Marc ... I'm not sure if it's going to be okay for me to have this baby, after all that radiation I had last year."

I felt an instant jolt, like my heart had dropped.

"Oh, shit, I didn't think about that. Oh, Barbara, what do we do?"

"I'm going to call Dr. Pearson tomorrow and get his opinion."

That evening, we spent some quiet time together; cuddled up watching TV, trying not to talk about the pregnancy, and holding back on getting excited. However, I couldn't stop thinking about being excited about another baby. I could tell Barbara cautiously felt the same way. As we watched TV, we would occasionally turn to each other about to say something, but just gave a smile. It was like each of us wanted to blurt out, "Let's do it." Yet, we didn't want to build up each other's hope in case of a big disappointment.

Barbara called Dr. Pearson the next day. It had been over a year since her radiation therapy at Yale New Haven. Dr. Pearson was now at a hospital in North Carolina and Barbara had flown down to North Carolina a few months before for her one-year checkup. Barbara called me at work to tell me about her conversation with the doctor. She said he was so nice to her over the phone, sensitive in how he asked her questions about our family. He asked if this pregnancy had been planned and about our other three children. He expressed his happiness to hear that our family was doing fine.

Then Barbara said, "Oh, Marc...." With that I became anxious, waiting to hear the outcome of the telephone conversation. I didn't say a word. Barbara was doing the talking and I listened.

"Dr. Pearson explained about the newness of the procedure of radiation therapy for breast cancer and about how so much is still unknown. It isn't clear about the long-term effects of such radiation on the body and future pregnancies. Oh, Marc ... there was kindness and gentleness in his voice and in his words, when he said that we have three kids and a nice family. With that said, he didn't give me his advice, just that it could be a risky pregnancy. He was clear that the decision was up to you and me. But the way he asked about our family and we talked about having three kids, I am certain that he was encouraging an abortion."

Saddened, I answered, "Let's discuss it tonight. I'll get home a little earlier."

That evening, after the kids were sleeping, we cuddled on the couch in the family room. More accepting than I was, Barbara said that it could possibly be too risky a pregnancy for her and the baby. With that said, there wasn't more for me to say. The next day, Barbara made the appointment for the abortion.

I went with Barbara for the procedure at Dover General Hospital. On our way, we talked in the car about things. What those things were? I don't remember. It just filled the time as we made the drive, giving us a feeling of calm as we discussed the matter-of-fact stuff of life. We'd brought our three babies home from Dover General. Now, we were headed to the hospital to do the opposite.

The procedure was quick and simple. After, when Barbara walked out to the waiting area, all she said was, "All done. Let's go." We went back to the car. We drove about a block from the hospital and I heard Barbara say, "Oh, Marc."

I turned to Barbara and saw the tears running down her cheeks, as she cried out uncontrollably. I took a deep breath. Slowly, I pulled over and turned off the engine. I didn't know what to say or do. With no experience, our knowledge about abortions was that it was a quick and simple procedure. Barbara had proved that out. But we were unaware of the emotional aftereffects we would suffer. The almost immediate feeling of guilt. We had taken an unborn life. In the car, it felt like we were running away from the scene of the crime. Tears filled my eyes, too, and I felt that we had suffered a loss.

Barbara and I had always been pro-choice. But this was about the two of us. And the abortion didn't feel right. This decision wasn't about our political point of view, or what's right or wrong, or what's good for everyone. It was all about what was right for us. And what was right for us was difficult for us to understand. Because it was our decision and afterward, it was a decision we immediately doubted. It was our decision to take a life and for us, that was too difficult to accept. Regardless of the risk, for Barbara and me, having the abortion felt wrong and left us with a heart-wrenching feeling of remorse.

When we regained our composure, Barbara said, "We need to be careful. I never want us to have to make this choice again. Let's go home to our children." Throughout our marriage there was never any decision that we doubted with such remorse as that abortion. But after that day, we never discussed it again and, for us, it was forgotten. Or maybe for each of us, with such remorse, it was too painful to be forgotten. It was an unborn life, and it was gone. I carried the guilt around with me, too painful to talk about. I never did find peace with this abortion. I don't believe Barbara ever did either.

That day, we kind of moped around the house, did some chores, ran some errands, and cared for Brian, all to fill the time waiting for Jonathan and Kristen to come home from school. I also bumped into a local realtor, Jay, with whom I'd become quite friendly. Each time I happened to see Jay, he was always trying to recruit me to work for him. I always explained that I sold homes while in college and was on a different career path. His rebuttal was always, "You seem like an active person. You can do it part-time." To get him off my back, I suggested that he recruit Barbara. And he did.

Barbara began to work for Zissen Realtors in their Randolph, New Jersey office on January 1, 1984. Barbara was a natural. She took off running out-of-the-gate to make sales, while she juggled being a mom and a wife. When I was home in the evenings and on weekends, somehow and some way, I became her assistant; answering phone calls when she was out and putting up her For Sale and Open House signs. Our lives quickly changed. We became a very busy family. It was a good time for us. Barbara loved her new career with Zissen Realtors, one that would last more than twenty-seven years.

Most importantly, we loved being a busy family. With Jonathan and Kristen in school and Brian in daycare, they were making new friends. Through our kids and Barbara's job as a local realtor, we were making new friends too. We were constantly on the go with fun things: attending the kids soccer team games, partying with friends, attending charity events and local events in our town. We knew so many people in our town. Wherever we went, we always met someone we knew. We were doing better financially too. I even hired someone to mow the lawn. After eleven years, I'd had enough of grass. It was all good and all fun.

One beautiful, sunny Sunday in August 1984, Barbara invited her cousin's family over to spend the day and have a barbecue. It was a fun day and that evening we got the kids to bed early. After walking the dog, Barbara and I relaxed, watching TV for a while before deciding to turn in early too.

When we got into bed, we didn't want the weekend to end without some loving and started to go at it. We were just starting and suddenly, I thought I felt something in Barbara's left breast. I must have been touching that spot in a certain way that made Barbara suspicious and she put her hand there and felt it herself. "Oh, Marc ... is this a lump?"

"I'm not sure."

"Oh shit, this can't be."

This was the same breast that had received the radiation treatment. We were concerned, but we were cool about it. The probability of a recurrence, so soon after the radiation, was very low. The next morning, Barbara made an appointment to meet with the surgeon. At the appointment, the surgeon confirmed a small lump in her left breast. Considering the radiation that she had to that breast two and a half years before, the surgeon expected this lump would not be a problem. To be certain, he scheduled the procedure to have it removed.

I went with Barbara to Dover General Hospital. Dover General Hospital, the hospital where, in our lives, we celebrated the highest of our highs and experienced the lowest of our lows. We brought three babies' home with us from this hospital. We were back, once again.

We arrived at the hospital early in the morning, not expecting any surprises. Barbara was happy and smiling as I gave her a kiss and wished her luck before she was taken into surgery. I went downstairs to wait in the lounge. I was in the lounge for about thirty minutes, thinking that the doctor would come by soon to tell me that all went well. But I began hearing Dr. Borsky being paged a few times over the hospital's public address system. I became concerned, wondering if the page had anything to do with Barbara. A few minutes later, I was being paged. I knew for sure it wasn't good.

When I got to the surgical room, Dr. Borsky was already there, standing beside the bed and consoling Barbara. I couldn't make out what had happened. When I left Barbara, she was smiling without a care and the surgeon was smiling too. There wasn't supposed to be a problem. This surgery was supposed to be a confirmation that all was fine. Instead, Barbara was crying hysterically. Stunned and confused, I walked up to her and held her hand as she began to speak.

"Oh, Marc. The surgeon and I were laughing and joking. But as soon as he made the incision, I saw the look on his face change. I knew it wasn't good. He said the tissue didn't look normal and that he'll know very soon. But I know it isn't going to be good news. I asked the doctor to find you and Dr. B."

With that, the surgeon came back into the room. As the surgeon began to speak, I felt a weakness come over me and asked for a chair. I sat beside Barbara and she squeezed my hand as the surgeon spoke. I was in shock and couldn't concentrate on what he was saying. I believe I heard him say something about a frozen section and the results weren't good. He described that this was a local recurrence in the same breast and that Barbara would need more tests to confirm that the cancer was local in the breast and had not spread.

Then Dr. B began to speak in a consoling voice. "Barbara, you know that you're going to need the surgery now. I suggest that you call Dr. Pearson and tell him what has happened. Because of the radiation you had, he will probably recommend a specific surgeon for you."

Dr. Pearson recommended a surgeon at a hospital in Philadelphia. A few days later, we drove down to Philadelphia for her first appointment. After examining Barbara, the surgeon recommended a left radical mastectomy and a prophylactic simple right mastectomy. He explained that since this was a recurrence in the left breast, the prescribed treatment was to remove the entire breast, underlying chest muscle, and lymph nodes. As a further preventative measure to reduce the risk of another recurrence, he recommended removal of the right breast.

This was shocking news. We weren't expecting a double mastectomy. The doctor said, "Take some time with your decision. There is no hurry on this. You can get back to me in a few days or even a week."

Barbara got off the examination table and walked over to me. The doctor and his nurse looked like they were busy with something, but they probably turned away to give us some privacy. I reached out and put a hand on each side of Barbara's waist. I so wanted to hear her say that she wanted to go ahead with the double, rather than just the single, mastectomy. As much as I hoped that's what Barbara would say, I felt that it needed to be her decision.

When she said, "Both sides, right?" I wasn't sure if she was asking me or telling me. I didn't have to answer, because Barbara could nearly always read the look on my face and read my mind. I could rarely hide anything from her. Then she said to me, "Okay ... both sides."

Barbara turned to the doctor. "Both sides." And with that, her surgery was scheduled for the following week.

It was a long, stressful week. Several evenings while getting undressed for bed, I caught Barbara staring at herself, for a few moments, in the floor-to-ceiling mirror we had in our bedroom. It was as if she was preparing herself to accept the changes that were going to be. The night before we left for the hospital, as Barbara stared into the mirror, I walked up behind her and put my arms around her waist, clenching my hands together in front of her. With the side of my head against the side of hers, together we stared at our reflections in the mirror. With tears in her eyes, she whispered, "Oh, Marc, it's going to be very different for us."

As tears filled my eyes, I whispered in her ear, "Nothing's going to change for us."

"I'm going to be okay, right?" she asked.

Barbara was asking if she was going to be okay. But I knew that wasn't her question. Barbara was really asking if we were going to be okay. The question that she didn't ask was, would we still have a marriage? My honest answer could have been, I don't know. Because I didn't. Barbara feared the statistics in the rate of divorce after mastectomy. So did I.

I regret that I answered Barbara with a simple "Yes," to her question that she'd be okay. I regret that I didn't say that our marriage, love, and bond are too strong. So of course, everything would be okay. But I didn't. Because I didn't know. Looking through Shiva Eyes, I struggle with the question: At that moment, how could I have doubted that my love for Barbara wasn't strong enough to overcome anything?

The next morning, the day before the surgery, we drove down to Philadelphia. The surgeon wanted Barbara admitted to the hospital that day to do some preparation for her surgery the next morning.

I stayed with Barbara into the early evening. As it was getting late, Barbara said, "You should leave now. You have a long drive home and have to turn around and come back early tomorrow morning."

It was difficult for me to leave. I leaned over to kiss Barbara and after a kiss, I kissed her again and again until she whispered, "I'm okay. Go home. See you in the morning."

"Okay ... see you later, alligator."

And Barbara answered, "See you in a while, crocodile."

It was a lonely drive home. I kept trying to remember the look on Barbara's face when I left her. I wondered, was she smiling, was she calm, was she scared, should I have given her another kiss, did I give her a hug? She seemed more worried about me than about herself. Does she know how much I love her? She usually asked, "Do you love me?" Why didn't she ask? I wish I had given her one more kiss and said, "Love you." But I didn't. And I felt so empty, as if I were losing her.

The drive home went quickly, even though I didn't make it home in any record time. My mind was going from one thought to the next and it seemed like the car found its own way home.

I got up early the next morning to get on the road. Several friends had offered to go along with me and keep me company in the waiting room during the surgery. I didn't take anyone up on their offer. I just wanted to be with Barbara and have some alone time during the surgery.

As I got off the elevator on the hospital floor, a nurse spotted me and grabbed my arm to hurry me along. They had decided to take Barbara into the surgery room a little earlier. Barbara was crying and told the nurses that she couldn't go into the surgery until she saw me first. I got to her room as they were getting ready to take her to surgery.

I walked alongside the bed, holding her hand, as they rolled the bed through the corridors. Barbara was crying and trembling, as she squeezed my hand tightly, until we got to the point where I was not permitted to go any farther. I gave Barbara a kiss and heard her cries as I watched her being wheeled away from me to behind closed doors.

When the doors closed, I could hear Barbara's cries for a few seconds, until the sound faded away. Barbara was on one side of those doors and I was standing alone on the other. I continued to stand there and stare at those closed doors for several minutes. The intensity of my stare at those doors made my mind blank. I thought of nothing. I didn't know why all my thoughts were only about staring at those doors. It was all I could do in that moment.

The doctor told me to wait in the waiting area by the elevators; he'd come to see me after the surgery. There was no one else sitting in the area. I sat alone and stared around, watching as people waited for or got off the elevator, feeling so alone and scared. I regretted not taking someone up on their offer to be with me. Tears filled my eyes and I held myself back from crying while sitting in that lonely area. I would have cried had there not been people continually walking by and getting on and off the elevator.

Then, the elevator doors opened. I saw my friend Doug. It was such an incredible sight to suddenly have him in front of me. For a quick moment, I felt like I was seeing God. Doug came over to me and gave me a big, tight hug. I so welcomed Doug's presence and I so needed that kind of hug.

Barbara and I met Doug, and his wife Cheryl, twelve years before, when we were on vacation in Lancaster, Pennsylvania celebrating our first wedding anniversary. They lived in a suburb of Philadelphia. I called Doug earlier that week to let him know what was going on with us and when the surgery was scheduled. I knew they would want to visit Barbara while she was in the hospital. Doug offered to be with me during the surgery and I told him it would not be necessary. Doug ignored me and showed up anyway. I was so happy that he did.

As we sat and talked, I continuously checked the time on my watch, anxiously waiting for the surgery to be over. It was taking so long. Finally, I spotted the doctor walking toward us. He wasn't smiling. Immediately, I felt a shock wave through my body. I feared that I was about to hear bad news. But he smiled when he got closer to me and explained that all went well, and Barbara would be in the recovery room for a while, before being moved to her room. The surgeon was quick and brief. That was fine with me, I heard what wanted to hear. It was over.

Doug said, "Let me take you to lunch. You can relax now. The hard part is over." I stood up, stretched, and felt better. I did feel better, since the doctor said that the surgery went well. It was so good to have Doug as company for lunch. At one point Doug said, "This whole ordeal is a shock to the two of you and a part of Barbara's body has been removed. Look at it this way, she still has the most important part of her body." Some people probably would have considered that remark inappropriate. But this comment was so Doug and what I needed at that moment. I couldn't hold back a laugh.

After lunch, I waited for Barbara in her room. As the nurses brought her in, she was smiling. When we were alone, I sat beside her on the bed.

"The doctor said that it all went well. I'll be here for several days and then I go home. How are you doing?"

"Okay. Doug surprised me and was with me in the waiting area. As soon as the doctor came out of surgery and said that all went well, Doug and I went to lunch, while you were in recovery."

"Oh, that's so nice of him. He's a good guy."

"Sure is! I was sitting alone by the elevators and all of a sudden the doors opened and there was Doug."

I stayed with Barbara until she fell asleep for the night. The next morning, I went to work for a few hours, before I planned to head down to Philadelphia. I was at work about an hour when I received a phone call from a nurse who said that she was putting Barbara on to speak with me. I could hardly hear Barbara, as she sounded out of breath and was straining to speak.

"Oh, Marc. I don't have any energy to talk."

I had to hold the phone tightly against my ear to hear her and understand what she was saying, as fright quickly came over me.

"Marc, I'm bleeding internally, and they keep giving me transfusions. But the bleeding isn't stopping. I'm feeling faint and I think I'm dying."

For a moment, I couldn't see straight and felt faint myself. It was difficult for me to process what Barbara had said. Then I heard her say, "Marc ... I love you."

Those were three words I so dreaded hearing at that moment. It was like hearing her say goodbye. I felt so helpless. I needed to get to Barbara. I blurted out, "I'm on my way. I love you too."

As I raced down the New Jersey Turnpike to Philadelphia, I found myself hoping I would be stopped by the police, so that I could plead for an escort to get me to the hospital quicker. But it felt like something more powerful was looking over me and guiding me there in record time. I even got lucky in quickly finding convenient parking.

I ran to Barbara's hospital room. There were two doctors working on her, the surgeon and another doctor, plus two nurses. They had just removed the bandages from her chest, exposing the surgery. Her chest cavity had swollen, filling with blood.

I could see the pain in Barbara's face; not from the surgery or the fear of dying, but from me seeing her raw scars. Barbara feared that it wasn't a pretty sight. It was painful for her that I was seeing her scars for the first time in the middle of such tumult. And, although she wasn't crying on the outside, it was obvious to me she was crying on the inside.

It saddens me to know how Barbara interpreted the look on my face. But whatever look my face displayed, it wasn't from seeing the scars. It was from fearing that I was about to lose her. To me, the scars were nothing. I could only see the beautiful person who was my wife.

I watched as the doctors reapplied the bandages. I heard them say to Barbara, "We've wrapped you very tight in these bandages and are testing your blood. You will be fine. Your husband is here now. You have nothing to worry about. We now have the bleeding stabilized and under control."

As they left the room, I sat on the bed beside Barbara. I leaned over to give her a kiss, as she reached her hand up as far as she could to softly touch the side my face, which was quite an accomplishment after such surgery. It felt good to feel her touch, as she began to show a smile and her dimples. And then she asked, "Are you okay? I must have scared you."

That question was so Barbara. "Silly! You're asking me if I'm okay?"

"I know that you can't look at scars. How bad does it look?"

"I was only looking at your face," I answered.

"Oh, so you're telling me it looks pretty bad."

I didn't know how to answer. I was never known to be short of words. But I was lost in this fragile moment, a moment I didn't know how to handle. I didn't know what to say. All I wanted to do was look into Barbara's eyes and have her see that I was in love with her and loved her so much.

The day Barbara was being discharged from the hospital, I was nervous during my drive down to Philadelphia. I was unsure of how things would be for us and how Barbara would adjust to her physical change. During the drive back to New Jersey, I could tell that Barbara felt uneasy too. Although we both were relieved that our nightmare was over, the aftereffects of this nightmare to our marriage was on our minds. So, we tried to act like the surgery never happened and talked about our kids. Barbara was anxious to see them.

I had told our children a kids' version of the surgery and how they needed to be gentle when giving Barbara hugs. Although I tried to shelter them from the severity of the surgery, they could certainly sense the seriousness from overhearing conversations. When we got home, the kids were so excited to see Barbara. The first thing she said to them was, "I'm okay and I will be home now. I'm just a little tired and I have a bandage. But it's getting better and I'm okay and so happy to be home."

That evening, it was a little awkward for both of us in our bedroom. Barbara was quite tired and achy, and the bandages were wrapped totally around her upper body. I went downstairs to turn off the lights and stayed downstairs for a while. I hesitated to go back upstairs. I didn't know how to feel about being with Barbara. It had been awkward in the car during our drive home. Barbara was my wife, the love of my life, and I felt uncomfortable.

When I returned to the bedroom, Barbara was already in bed and under the covers. I noticed that she was wearing pajamas. I wasn't sure what to do or say. We had always slept in the nude. This was a big change for us. I got undressed to my undershorts and went into the bathroom to wash up. When I came out, I was still wearing my undershorts and got into bed and under the covers.

"How come you're wearing your undershorts?"

I moved closer to Barbara and turned onto my side. "Well ... how come you're wearing pajamas?"

She answered, "It is crazy enough to have gone through all of this. I'm not planning to be constantly reminded every time I walk by a mirror and I thought you'd feel more comfortable, not having to look at bandages. So, I'm only wearing a top."

I lifted the blanket for a peek and saw that she wasn't wearing the bottom to the pajamas, and said, "Oh, wow!" as I stared down her body.

Barbara laughed. "How long do you intend to look down there? You are too silly."

With that said, I got out of bed, took off my undershorts, put on a T-shirt, got back into bed, and cuddled up next Barbara. "Now we match."

We kissed. I felt awkward and sensed some awkwardness from Barbara too. It was as if we had become distant from each other. But we needed each other too much. That awkwardness soon wore off as we began to make love, with a love that had no distance between us. And after, as I lay on top of Barbara, I saw tears run down her cheeks as she cried.

I was reminded of the first time we made love on the couch in the living room in the Jackson Heights apartment, a month before our wedding. I asked, "Why are you crying? Are you still thinking about the promise that you made to your mother about having sex? We're married now, remember?"

Gazing into my eyes, Barbara took a breath, let it out slowly, and with a tear in her voice, she whispered, "I thought that you wouldn't want me anymore. I now see that this surgery hasn't changed your feelings. You don't care about the surgery. And ... you still want me."

I didn't expect to hear these words from Barbara. She was so direct and honest. Barbara spilled out her fear to me. I wasn't sure what to say. I was about to say that I loved her no matter what. But I figured that wasn't what she wanted to hear. I did love her. But at that moment, Barbara wanted to be loved as a woman. A woman I wanted because of her sexual beauty. A woman whose femininity wasn't lessened by a mastectomy. Barbara wanted to know that this spontaneous, heat-of-the-moment sex had been because I found her to be irresistible. And, because I was so attracted to her.

It took me a few seconds to answer. As I quickly thought about Barbara's statement, I figured there was little for me to add. She had said it all. Now, it was time for some silliness. "Well, at lunch the other day, Doug reminded me that you still have the most important part of your body. And I just confirmed that he was right."

Her tears turned into a laugh. "That's what Doug said? He's crazy ... and I love you."

It was so difficult for me to see my wife go through a double mastectomy and, although she braved the surgery, to realize the pain in her eyes was the worry about losing me and feeling less of a woman and unwanted. Our love and caring for each other carried us through this ordeal.

That night, Barbara and I each made peace with the surgery and what fate had dealt us. For me, I still had my wife. For Barbara, she still had her husband, and we weren't going to become a statistic of divorce after mastectomy. From that night on, Barbara always wore just a top to bed. I went back to sleeping in the nude. We still had the most important part of our bodies: the hearts we shared with each other.

CHAPTER 15

That special spirit

Barbara was anxious to get up and about quickly and get back to normal. She decided that she wasn't giving up on wearing a bra. "Starting to wear a bra was a special event for me as a young teen." So, almost the first thing that she did, after the surgery, was to buy falsies. But that would be a temporary fix. Her priority was to have additional surgery: bilateral reconstruction with implants. "As a young girl, I looked forward to developing breasts," Barbara told me. "I want the horror of losing them behind me and don't want to be reminded of it each time I look in the mirror."

Although Barbara nearly died from internal bleeding from the surgery, this wouldn't preclude future surgeries. Blood tests at the hospital revealed Barbara had a mild factor XI deficiency. Although she never had prior bleeding complications, this deficiency caused abnormal bleeding due to a shortage of a protein involved in blood clotting after the surgery. With this new information, Barbara was fine to go ahead with surgery, as long as she was pre-treated for the factor deficiency.

By the early winter of 1985, Barbara was all healed and ready for reconstructive surgery. The first time she met with the surgeon, I waited outside the examination room. Barbara came out with a big smile on her face and, kind of laughing, said, "I like him. So, I scheduled the surgery."

"Wonderful! What's so funny?" I asked.

"Nothing. I'll tell you later."

We had taken separate cars into Manhattan, so we could both go straight to work after the appointment. Barbara seemed happy and I felt good about that. That evening, after the kids were asleep, Barbara cuddled up next to me on the couch.

"Okay, are you going to tell me what was so funny when you came out of the surgeon's office? I know something was funny."

"Well, first, the not-so-good news. I'm going to need two operations," she answered.

"Oh, shit! Why?"

"Because of the internal bleeding from the mastectomy, one of the muscles in my chest, necessary to support the implants, had atrophied. So, he will use a muscle from my back and, from under my shoulder, move it to my chest. I'll lose a little strength in my right arm and twisting will be a little restricted. But I'll be okay."

"Well, that sucks. So, what's the good news?" I asked.

"So, you're ready for the good news? He said that I can have any size implant I want."

"Really! Can he make you the size of Dolly Parton?"

"Yes, he can. Is that what you want?"

With a laugh, I answered, "That could be fun. We have a king-sized bed. So, there'll be plenty of room for your new big tits. You'll just need to be careful not to roll over too quickly and smack me in the face."

But that wasn't what I wanted. I just wanted my wife to be happy. It had been a couple of months since the mastectomy and our lives were totally back. The only thing that had been haunting us was another surgery. Now it had become two surgeries. I wasn't sure how important it was for Barbara to go through with this. I couldn't tell if she really wanted it for herself or if she was doing it for me.

I was attracted to Barbara the first time I met her, during the summer of 1964 in the Rockaways, when I was fourteen years old. Although, at the moment I met her, my mind was on other things. It wasn't until the end of that summer when I came to realize my feelings for Barbara.

Through the years, the attraction grew into intense love, as Barbara matured from a twelve-year-old girl into a beautiful woman. Her dimples, dark eyes and hair, and her olive complexion were so sexy to me. I couldn't keep my hands off her. The mastectomy didn't take anything away from her sexiness or change my romantic feelings for the person who was everything to me.

"Barbara ... is this whole reconstructive surgery what you really want? I get the feeling that you're only doing this for me. If you are, you need to decide if you really want to go through with more surgeries. Because we're doing pretty well."

With a serious expression on her face, Barbara was looking at me as if she was searching for something to say. My trying to find out how important this surgery was to her was going nowhere. Barbara grew up in a family where she even as a child was always doing for someone else. For me, those days were in the past and long over. Before we continued with plans for this surgery, I wanted to make certain that my wife was doing this for herself. I figured I'd break the ice with some silliness. I stood up from the couch, faced Barbara directly, and firmly said, "Barbara, I've put the mastectomy out of my mind. If you want me to prove it to you, I'll rip my clothes off right now. Go ahead, get naked. I'll screw you right here on the couch ... right now!"

I thought Barbara would laugh. She didn't. Instead, she looked up at me sadly. "We didn't really talk about it and I was so worried. I now know that I'm not losing you and you want me 'the way I am.' Yes ... I'm doing it for you ... but ... I really want to have the surgery for me."

I sat back down and cuddled up next to Barbara. The look on her face became even more sorrowful. "Marc, the doctor said that all nerve endings were cut away and that even with reconstruction, I will not have any feeling there."

"So, they are gone. Then why have the surgery? With no feeling there, why put yourself through this?" I asked.

Then, she began to cry. "Oh, Marc ... you don't understand. But you have to understand what this means to me." As she caught her breath, she continued. "I want my body back. I'm only thirty-three years old and I want my body back."

I put my arm around her and my head against hers, as she cried. There was nothing else she needed to say for me to understand. It hurt for me to hear Barbara describe herself with the words, "the way I am." I felt guilty for not realizing on my own how important it was and how much it could mean for a woman to need her body back. Barbara really wanted to have the surgery for herself and she had the strength of mind and spirit to endure it.

The first surgery, relocating the muscle and preparing for the implants, would be the more difficult. Barbara was frightened going in. But with the smile on her face after recovery, I could see she'd made the right decision. Once again, Barbara felt good about herself as she put this surgery behind her, with just one more to go. I was so proud of her.

Barbara was scheduled to stay in the hospital, which was in Midtown Manhattan, for a few days. Although she had a blood drain and pouch connected to her, by the second day, she was anxious to get out. "Marc, I want to go home ... now!"

"Now? Are you kidding? You have a drain connected to you. The hospital is not going to discharge you."

"I don't care. I can't stay here. This place is disgusting, filthy, noisy, and the nurses are terrible. I'll never recover from the surgery here. So, get me out of here. The health care in this place doesn't exist. I'll get more rest and feel more comfortable at home. If I need anything, my friends will help out."

"Barbara, I just can't get you dressed and take you out. The hospital has to discharge you."

"I don't care how or what you need to do. Just get me out of here!"

So, that's what I did. I went to the administration office, spoke with the administrator in charge, and told her, "I'm leaving with my wife and never coming back." I signed the release forms and discharged Barbara from the hospital, with the drain and pouch still attached to her.

Very carefully, I helped Barbara to the car, and we headed home. Barbara asked, "So, what did you have to do to convince the hospital to discharge me?"

"Well ... actually ... we didn't want them, and I don't think they wanted us either. I wasn't very polite about it."

"Oh, they saw the other side of Marc Gellman?"

"It wasn't a pretty sight," I answered.

Barbara was home about a day when she got a call from a prospective client she had been in contact with for the past several months. The client was ready to list their house for sale. There was one major problem, though. The client wanted to list the house immediately. Barbara was still in bed recovering and still had the drain and pouch.

When I got home from work that evening, Barbara said, "One of my prospective clients called me this afternoon. I don't know what to do. I've been working on getting this listing forever and spent so much time with these people. I guess I'm going to have to give the listing away. I can't take the listing with this drain attached to me, when I need to gather all the information about the house—taking the room measurements, getting listing details, and installing a For Sale sign on the front lawn."

"I'll tell you what," I answered. "I'll go with you and do all the legwork. You can introduce me and tell the homeowner I'm an architect and you rely on me to take all measurements of each room and the house and install the sign. While I gather all those details, you can sit with the homeowner at their kitchen table and go through the written part of the listing."

"But I feel so weak."

"I'll drive and you'll hold my arm as we walk up to the door. Then you'll be on your own to get them to the kitchen and sit down."

On the day for getting the listing, I helped Barbara get dressed. She wore an outfit that camouflaged the drain and pouch. I helped Barbara to the car, put a sign in the trunk, and we were off to the listing. As I drove onto the driveway of the house, I glanced over at Barbara. "Are you ready? Deep breaths."

All went perfectly to plan. The homeowner didn't suspect anything. When we got back into the car, Barbara said, "Now, I have to stop off at my office to turn in this listing. Then, you need to get me back to bed."

"You mean, we need to get back to bed to celebrate the listing?"

"No, silly head, I need to pass out. You get nothing until I get rid of this drain."

At her office, I helped Barbara navigate the process for turning in the listing. Then it was back in the car. As we drove home, Barbara said, "You know what? I'm just thinking. I have a buyer for this house."

"Really!"

"Yes. Get me home first. I need to crash in bed with a nap. After, I'll call my buyer and you and I will plan out how to show them the house."

We planned that out too. And Barbara sold her customer the house. There was little that could stop Barbara. When she set out to accomplish something, she did.

Barbara was such a go-getter, with a beautiful spirit. Her success came from her willingness to listen and learn from others. Over the course of her twenty-seven years working for Zissen Realtors, Barbara met and worked with many accomplished people whom she admired and strived to emulate. There was one person in particular, an older woman named Mary Costanza, twenty-eight years Barbara's senior. Barbara would say, "That Mary Costanza is still going strong into her eighties and she doesn't plan on stopping. She's amazing!" Barbara introduced me to Mary at one of the Zissen functions. Although Barbara would often mention Mary, I had never gotten to know her, beyond that one brief introduction.

Two weeks after I lost Barbara, I received a touching letter from Mary, who was eighty-eight years old at the time.

August 16, 2011

Dear Marc-

How very sad, the loss of Barbara – her physical body, but not her Spirit!

That special Spirit of hers that enabled her to live on for so many years under very difficult circumstances.

I know the love she had for her family and the love you had for her made it all possible.

She wanted so much to live during these years so she could appreciate and love you all!

I know Barbara from being a part-time manager in the Zissen Randolph office. Loved visiting and talking with her!

About three years ago, I had a knee repaired and Barbara sent flowers to me while I was in the hospital. I can still visualize them in my mind.

I have lost three daughters and my beloved husband Anthony many years ago. It takes a while, but we do become happy and appreciative of the blessings life offers and all the good memories – especially of Barbara.

The Lord's Peace be yours

Mary Costanza

(PS: I spoke with Barbara a few months ago.)

I loved this letter from Mary, who didn't know me. Barbara was so into respecting and admiring other people. I don't believe she ever realized how special and courageous a person others saw her to be. Although accomplished and respected as a successful person by our community, by her work associates, and throughout the Zissen Realtor organization, Barbara plodded along in the face of adversity, humbly being herself.

The second surgery for the implants went fine. On the day Barbara came home, when we lay in bed that evening, chilling and staring at the ceiling, I turned and saw tears on Barbara's cheeks.

"Why are you crying? It's all over and we made it. There's no reason to cry anymore."

Barbara answered, "These are happy tears and the only kind we'll have from now on."

We certainly were well deserving of happy tears and hoped for only happy tears from then on. Also, we wanted to believe that the happy tears washed away the memories of our difficult times and we made it through completely unscathed. But we were wounded. And memories of it all would plague us.

There was a change in us. Maybe not one recognizable to friends, but definitely a change. At times, Barbara would become very anxious and often felt it necessary to talk and ramble on when it became quiet, particularly at times when I wanted some quiet. I guessed that the quiet made her feel insecure and she needed to make something happen. For me, the accumulation of our ordeals built up inside me and it intensified my OCD. At times, I would be less understanding and less patient.

I would obsess over things like setting my alarm clock before going to sleep. After several checks, Barbara would say, "The clock is set, my dear. You can safely go to sleep now." When leaving the house, I would have to check several times that I had my keys and my wallet, and that I'd locked the front door. Packing for vacation was torture for me, needing to make sure I didn't forget anything. Barbara would sit on the bed and oversee what I was packing. Otherwise, I would have needed a moving company.

When Barbara's anxiety coincided with my impatience, there'd be one hell of an argument. I admit guilt for doing much of the shouting and being the louder. All this may not sound so terrible and no big deal. Happily married couples do disagree and argue. For Barbara and me, this was all new. But it was just arguing. It would change nothing about us or diminish our love. Barbara would say, "We can't go to bed angry." As simple as that may sound, it worked for us. And our disagreements were quickly over. I had no alternative. Barbara "controlled the electric blanket," was the phrase I used. We didn't have an electric blanket. What Barbara controlled was whether things would get heated up in bed.

In spite of the difficult times that came one after the other, Barbara and I celebrated the many great things we had: our children, our home, and each other. I knew that with Barbara, great things would continue to happen. It wasn't at all as though I was taking a chance and just hoping for the best. I knew, for sure, that our dreams would come true and great things would continue to happen. And you know what? They did.

As I look back at this difficult time, I see the greatness of our love and a romance that had blossomed. Because for better, for worse, Barbara and I were soul mates. Nothing could take away the puppy love we shared.

PART 3

Stories from the Third Day of Shiva

"Marc, how do you have the nerve to do something like that?
Don't you realize that anyone driving by or walking on the
road could see your ass hanging over the balcony?"

CHAPTER 16

All of our silliness

We were a very busy family. I was doing a lot of traveling around the country for my work. The company had operating facilities in about twenty major cities and a consulting business that brought me to more places. While I was busy with work, Barbara had the hard part during the week. She was being a busy realtor, running the house, being a mother to three children. Barbara had all of the responsibilities for getting the kids out of the house in the morning: waking, breakfasting, dressing, and off to school. For after-school activities, Barbara chauffeured the kids to soccer, basketball, and baseball. All these responsibilities, plus a dog.

Barbara's work demands were busiest on the weekends, which is when I took over taking care of the kids. But it was all good and Barbara and I did take advantage of our quality alone time. If we could stay awake after the kids were finally asleep and not marching into our bedroom. Then there were those evenings when we didn't give a shit whether the kids were fully asleep and went at it anyway.

I was able to take Barbara along with me on business trips. My company had a business travel policy that allowed spouses to accompany on a number of business trips, with the company paying the costs. But it was difficult for us to take full advantage of this, with Barbara's work schedule and the kids. I traveled to Baltimore often, a trip that was easy enough for Barbara to come along with me. There were no airports, planes, or different time zones to deal with, and I enjoyed Barbara's company for the long drive.

One time we took the kids with us to Baltimore. While I worked during the day, Barbara toured the Inner Harbor area and the National Aquarium and other sights with them. My company was doing business with the Hyatt Regency Baltimore and the hotel manager accommodated us on the VIP floor.

One day while Barbara was waiting for the hotel elevator with the kids, Brian in a stroller and Jonathan and Kristen standing next to Barbara, one on each side. Boog Powell, who had played for the Baltimore Orioles from 1961 to 1974, happened to walk to the same elevator. A baseball fan, Barbara recognized him. Powell, noticing them, stared at the kids, and then looked up at Barbara and said, "Lady, you have a lot of guts!" You see, it was a nice sunny day in July and Barbara dressed all three kids in T-shirts ... New York Yankee T-shirts.

That evening, when Barbara told me about her encounter, I said, "Barbara, are you crazy? You can't do something like that. This is Baltimore. You're lucky that we're not up in Boston."

Barbara laughed. "I wish I'd had a camera. The look on Boog Powell's face was amazing. Anyway, who are you to talk? You're always doing crazy things, being silly and thinking that everything is funny."

I take full responsibility for Barbara dressing the kids in those T-shirts. That's something that I would do. Married to me, Barbara became infected with my ballsy silliness. And Barbara was right about me. I did find almost everything to be funny. And it was my silliness that made me the perfect match for Barbara. I'm not saying that I was perfect, just a perfect match. However, there's a possibility that Barbara thought I was perfect. When Barbara looked at me, I felt that she thought I was perfect. But maybe not. It is one of those things I wish I had asked her.

Nevertheless, I believe it was my silliness that attracted Barbara to me. She had a difficult childhood. Then I came along. My silliness showed her an easy and happy side, freeing her from her problems at home. For our marriage, the silliness gave us laughter in the midst of pain. The silliness brought us out of our ordeals and helped us to enjoy the good times and not dwell on the difficult times. All the same, I feared there would come a time when the silliness would help us no more. I didn't know how long our silliness will last.

My silliness goes back before I met Barbara, to when I was a young kid. Whether it was real humor or tragedy, I found the humor in everything. It often got me into trouble at school during my kindergarten through ninth grade years at Public School #64, which later became Berriman Junior High School 64.

One time, when I was in third or fourth grade, I was sent to the assistant principal's office for laughing. What did I find so funny? My teacher was lecturing the class about safety rules we needed to observe when we walked through the corridors and, especially, in the stairwells. She was telling the class about a girl who had fallen down a flight of stairs that morning. She described the incident in detail, how the stairs were busy and there was pushing and shoving and how this girl went bouncing down the steps and was seriously hurt.

It was certainly sad to hear about the girl getting hurt. But the picture in my mind of the girl "bouncing" down the steps I found hysterically funny, and I couldn't hold back from laughing out loud. My teacher was angry at my laughing in the middle of her lecture. She asked me what I found so funny. I told her I wasn't really laughing. But as she continued to go on about the incident and describing the fall, I couldn't hold back my laughter.

I was sent to the office of the assistant principal, Miss Hachette. Looking back, I believe Miss Hachette was probably a kind and understanding person and, for sure, was much, much younger than my eight- or nine-year-old mind imagined her to be. Back then, to me, Miss Hachette was a very scary ninety-year-old woman with her gray hair tightly combed back into a bun, who never smiled, was very firm, and had no sense of humor.

As I sat waiting outside her office, I was scared. Eventually, Miss Hachette shouted for me to come in. I shook with fright as she lectured me in a stern voice about how inappropriate it was for me to laugh at such an unfortunate incident. But my problem was about to get worse, as Miss Hachette began to describe the girl's terrible fall. Fearful as I was, as I sat and listened, I kept visualizing the girl bouncing down the steps. I tried to hold back the laughter, but my silliness came over me and I couldn't. The consequence was a note home to my parents and an assignment to write a one-page paper about how inappropriate it was for me to laugh at such things and the importance of safety.

That afternoon, I brought the note home to my mom. As punishment, I wasn't allowed to go out and play with my friends. Instead, I had to sit at the kitchen table and write the paper. As I wrote the paper and continued to picture the incident, I laughed the entire time that I was writing.

I'm not sure that I really learned anything from this punishment, other than to wonder why no one else found the description of the incident funny. It was natural for me to laugh. My heroes were Laurel and Hardy, Abbott and Costello, and The Three Stooges. Their slapstick comedy always had someone being pushed, knocked down, or hit on the head. Nowadays, politically correct activists may consider those entertainers to be offensive. Because nowadays, it's even difficult to defend Rudolph the Red-Nosed Reindeer from being politically incorrect. Luckily for me, those critics weren't around back then. Otherwise, without the influence from those performers, I could have grown up to have a totally different personality. That could have jeopardized my chances with Barbara.

But maybe I would have been silly anyway, and I was meant to be for Barbara. I inherited my laughing reflex from my Aunt Letty, one of my mother's older sisters. Almost every family has someone who has the most incredible, contagious laugh, so distinctive that it causes others to join in the laughter. In my family, that person was my Aunt Letty.

As a young boy, I would sit on the front stoop of our house in Brooklyn with my aunt and we'd people watch. After the people walked past us, I'd come up with something silly to say about the person; the way they walked, the hat or the clothes they wore. And we would laugh! It was more than laughter, it was belly rolls. My aunt would say that although we were being harmlessly silly, it's really not nice to make fun of people. But we did anyway. And there was no one else who I could be sillier with than with my Aunt Letty, until I met Barbara. Although, my aunt was my all-time best laughing partner.

It was easy being silly about making fun of people. This was not politically correct even back then. Barbara's limit on being silly was when I made fun of people. But I could get her going sometimes. I would say to Barbara, "Oh come on. Making fun of people is fun, especially when you focus on what our bodies look like. We're just a funny-looking species."

For a young kid who liked being silly, I used to have fun explaining how our bodily functions take place in the wrong places. For instance, it would be so much easier and convenient if we could pee from the tip of one of our fingers. That way, when we're on a long car ride, we wouldn't have to stop to take a pee. We could just lower the window a few inches and extend the tip of our finger outside and pee. Of course, it couldn't be our pointer finger that could pee. Because we use our pointer finger when we poke at people and that wouldn't be the polite finger to use. And, it certainly couldn't be our right hand, the hand that we shake with. I used to love figuring these things out and carefully thinking them through. It all made sense to me and I truly believed in my own silliness. Even as an adult, I love making up shit like this. Barbara would laugh and say, "Where do you get all this?"

I used to answer, "I read a lot." It was an answer that Barbara found hysterically funny.

Normally, Barbara called me by my name, Marc, and occasionally

Marcus. Coincidentally, I've also been called Marcus by other people over the years. They say it's because my name is spelled with a "c" versus a "k." Marcus is not my name, but I'm fine with it. I kind of like it and I've never corrected anyone. As you can tell from previous chapters, Barbara's favorite name for me was "silly." She had good reason. Sometimes, I called her silly.

It was our silliness that was a thread in the fabric of our marriage. It was our silliness that gave us so much laughter and so much to talk about. It was our silliness that gave us memories. I miss being able to say to Barbara, "Remember when...?" There are so many memories and Barbara is the only one who would have remembered them. We had so many stories of *remember when*....

Remember when .... On one of our vacations, Barbara and I were staying at the Ocean Manor Beach Resort on the Galt Ocean Mile in Fort Lauderdale. The main entrance to the resort was set back from the road and had a long driveway to its porte cochere. Our hotel room was on a low floor, above the main entrance and porte cochere, with a balcony that looked over the driveway.

The first two mornings, I watched Barbara from the balcony as she walked down the driveway to go for her morning coffee. I watched as she walked back up the driveway, returning to the hotel. The third morning, as I watched Barbara, I thought she looked cute, as her head went bopping along, and I got this idea. I decided that I would moon her from the balcony on her way back.

I started laughing out loud at just the thought of doing this. I became very anxious with anticipation, waiting for her to return to the hotel. Then, I spotted Barbara walking along the road. As she turned onto the driveway, I dropped my pants, faced my butt to the driveway, and looked over my shoulder. When I saw her get close enough, I shouted, "Barbara! Look up here." As I stood there with my butt in full view, I looked over my shoulder and saw Barbara with this blushing smile on her face, shaking her head in disbelief.

I was hysterically laughing as Barbara walked into the room. She was giggling. "Marc, how do you have the nerve to do something like that? Don't you realize that anyone driving by or walking on the road could see your ass hanging over the balcony?"

"So what? How did it look? Maybe, I'll be in the local newspaper, with the headline, 'Man Moons Woman from Balcony on the Galt Ocean Mile.'"

"You're too silly."

Remember when ... There was the time when Barbara and I were in Baltimore, during an able-to-get-away-from-the-kids weekend. We were attending a charity event for Mercy Medical Center and drove down on a Thursday evening. The next day I had work-related meetings and Barbara did some sightseeing on her own. On Saturday, the event for the hospital wasn't until the evening. We had a free afternoon for brunch and to stroll the Inner Harbor.

We walked for a while and found a bench along the promenade overlooking the harbor where we were enjoying the sights and doing some people watching. We had been sitting on the bench for only a few minutes when this guy came walking by us with his dog. As we watched the dog, it stopped, pulled back on the leash, and began to take the "taking-a-shit" position. The guy pulled at the leash, but the dog was already starting.

It was a big dog, and it took the biggest shit that I had seen in quite a while. Once the dog was finished relieving itself, the guy pulled on the leash and kept on walking, leaving this big pile of fresh shit in the middle of the promenade. Barbara stood up. "What a pig! That's disgusting! Let's get out of here. I can't sit here staring at that mess."

I started laughing uncontrollably. I could hardly get out the words. "No ... no, let's stay."

"What!" she answered. "No. Come on, let's go! And, what's so funny?"

"Just wait ... let me catch my breath. Listen, silly, let's stay and watch to see if people will step in that shit."

"You're crazy. I'm not staying here. No one is going to step in that."

"Okay, let's see who is right, you or me. Just sit down for a little and let's see."

Barbara sat back down. "I can't believe I'm sitting here watching this."

Within minutes, this guy came strolling along. It looked like he was headed directly for the pile of shit. I just sat there with anticipation. Barbara could barely take it.

"Marc, come on, warn him."

"No! Shh ... be quiet," I answered.

"Someone is going to get angry and punch you in the nose, when they see you laughing."

"Shoosh, be quiet," I answered again.

Hoping for a direct hit, I watched closely as the guy approached the pile of shit. Under my breath, I kept saying, "Don't look down. Don't look down." Fortunately, the guy was distracted by the sights of the harbor. It looked like he going to make a direct hit. As I took a deep breath, the guy stepped directly onto the pile of shit.

I tried to control my laughing. But, when I saw the nauseated and disgusted look on the guy's face as he looked down to see what he had stepped in, I couldn't control myself. To this day, the look on that guy's face is still with me.

Watching the guy being frustrated with trying to get the shit off the bottom and sides of his shoe, was even more comical than him stepping in it. I couldn't stand it anymore. I had to completely turn around on the bench and look the other way. I was laughing so hard my sides hurt and I had to hold on to the bench, not to fall on the ground.

At this point, Barbara was also laughing. She tapped me on the shoulder. "Okay, silly, he's gone. Let's go. You had your laugh for the day."

As I recovered from the laughing and regained my composure, I turned around and looked at the pile of shit. "No, not yet. There's still enough shit left for others to step in."

"Oh, come on!"

Barbara humored me for a little longer, as we stayed to watch a woman and then a family step in it. As we were leaving, I said to

Barbara, "Well, we just witnessed a momentous event, as people changed their luck by stepping in shit."

"I was waiting to hear what your final comment would be. You're too silly."

The experiences that Barbara and I shared together, from funny to sad, are so memorable and made for the fabric of our time together and our relationship. And the stories tell of who we were. As for watching people stepping in shit, well, what can I say? I sure wish my Aunt Letty could have witnessed that with me, our laughter would have fed off each other.

Watching strangers step in shit was definitely an experience that Barbara and I cherished. At least I did. When it came to a good laugh, there were few boundaries for me. This one was a great *remember when*. Barbara, though she thought certain things were crazy, enjoyed how I wouldn't let go of the silliness. It just goes to prove that outgrowing immaturity, and reacting to all situations like a totally mature adult, is highly overrated.

I had so much fun writing this chapter. I had even more fun remembering when Barbara and I were silly together. It was our silliness that helped us to accept the emotional and physical scars that Barbara carried around with her. Today as I look through Shiva Eyes, is it silly for me to think about a brand new *remember when*, like, "Oh, Barbara ... remember when we were so young, we thought we'd live forever."

Barbara and I never outgrew the "kids" inside of us. All of our silliness never grew old and kept our love young. With that our marriage would last for forty years and until we fulfilled our vow: "Till death do us part."

CHAPTER 17

A beautiful sunny day

A s our children grew, they were getting more and more involved in activities, becoming independent, and finding a big world beyond our home. Between school, soccer, basketball, and baseball, they were building their own close circles of friendships and relationships, outside of the circle of friends that Barbara and I had. Also, our children were being invited to spend time in their friends' homes, especially for holidays.

Barbara and I began to realize that our children were confused between our faith and the faith of our neighbors. We did have family get togethers for the Jewish holidays, Passover in the spring and the Jewish High Holidays in the fall. And although we lit candles for eight days of Chanukah, celebrating the festival of lights, Santa did come to our home on Christmas Eve and left toys for Christmas morning. We were an unaffiliated Jewish family, assimilating into a predominately Christian community.

My children's experiences growing up in western Morris County, New Jersey were much different from my childhood in East New York, a predominantly Polish Jewish section of Brooklyn. There was an Orthodox shul located in the middle of the block just two houses away from where my family lived. My grandparents were part of the original group of founders of this shul and, while I was growing up, my dad was the treasurer.

My grandfather died before I was born and my grandmother lived in the apartment next door to us, on the first floor of a four-family house. The other two apartments on the second floor were occupied by tenants. The shul was a major part of my growing up years. When I didn't find my grandmother in her apartment and it was the Sabbath or a holiday, I knew I could find her in shul. Like my family, most of the congregants of the shul were Conservative and observed the "Laws of Kashrut" (keeping a kosher home), although the shul was led by an Orthodox rabbi.

Barbara, growing up on the Grand Concourse, a predominantly Russian Jewish section of The Bronx, had a different experience from mine. Her family was unaffiliated and unobservant. Barbara had not even been in a synagogue until she was eleven, for her cousin's Bar Mitzvah. But it would be Barbara who brought the Jewish faith into our home and who wanted us to make a conscientious effort to expose our children to our faith and the Jewish community.

We didn't have a Bris, the Jewish circumcision ceremony upon which the male child also receives his Hebrew name, for either of our sons. Instead, Barbara had arranged for all three of our children to receive their Hebrew name at a baby naming ceremony in a nearby temple. Wanting to further our children's Jewish experience, we began to discuss an alternative to the public school system and considered enrolling them in a nearby Jewish day school, The Hebrew Academy of Morris County. However, we had no idea of the tuition costs and quickly found out that we couldn't afford to send even one of our children to that school. It was a good thought, but it would be the public school for our kids.

Through a friend, Barbara was introduced to a new friend, whose name was also Barbara. This new friend invited Barbara to the temple where, coincidentally, our kids had their naming ceremony. Temple was a whole new experience for Barbara. Growing up in

The Bronx and later in Jackson Heights, Queens, her circle of close friends was all Jewish. But all of her past Jewish experiences were secular. With all the difficult times we had experienced, Barbara embraced the temple, finding the spirituality in her faith. Also, she met many new friends, became active, joined the sisterhood, and got the kids involved in temple activities and registered in religious school. Although doing this paled in comparison to the experience we wanted for our children from the Jewish day school, we didn't have a choice.

With the kids attending religious school, Barbara decided to join a class for adults who had not attended religious school as a child and had not been a Bar or Bat Mitzvah. It was an adult B'nai Mitzvah class (B'nai being the plural of Bar and Bat), which would culminate with the entire class celebrating together their Bar and Bat Mitzvah.

After two years of classes, the B'nai Mitzvah ceremony in temple was scheduled for May 30, 1987. Barbara and I decided we would have a catered party at our house after the service, for friends and relatives. For music and entertainment, we hired a three-piece band that played klezmer music, called the Hester Street Troupe. I surprised Barbara by hiring a balloon company to install balloons across the front of the house. The company installed the balloons while we were at temple.

One afternoon, a few weeks before the ceremony in temple, when Barbara wasn't home, the kids and I discussed how we would surprise Barbara during the party. We decided that Jonathan would sing the song, "One Singular Sensation," a song from the musical *A Chorus Line*. I was able to get the music track of the song. For several weeks, we secretly rehearsed. We also decided that after Jonathan's song, we would all stand together, and I would honor Barbara with a toast. Weeks in advance of the ceremony in temple, I read the speech Barbara planned to deliver. So, it was easy for me to decide what I wanted to say.

The day of the B'nai Mitzvah was a beautiful sunny day, with bright blue skies. As we got out of the car in the temple parking lot, I held Barbara's hand and said, "The sun is shining down on us."

Barbara smiled. "Yes, it is."

As the kids and I watched the ceremony from our seats in the sanctuary, we were all so proud of Barbara. When it was Barbara's turn to stand up and go to the podium to deliver her speech, I turned to look at my children, now twelve, ten, and six years old. Their mouths were open in awe and their faces were beaming with smiles. It made me quiver a little. Barbara was an incredible role model for our children, and, on this day, it was our turn to honor her.

When we got back to the house, Barbara loved the balloons. Even more, Jonathan did a tear-jerking performance of the song for her. I really mean tear-jerking. Barbara cried through his performance, and so did many of our guests. The lyrics to the song so much described Barbara: "One singular sensation, every little move she makes."

Our house had a large family room with double French doors that opened to a large, enclosed back porch. The party was in these rooms, with the band set up at a corner of the back porch. We had a full house. I gathered the kids together beside me and we stood by the band. Using the band's microphone, I asked everyone to gather around. Barbara gave me a surprised look as if to say, "What's this about?" In an emotional tearful voice, I spoke.

Barbara, over the past few weeks, I've mentioned to the children that we would be making a toast in your honor. We discussed what to say. After some suggestions, the kids said that we shouldn't say certain things, because Mommy will cry. Keeping that in mind, I had some thoughts of what to say since, we've had many tears in our home.

This morning during services, you mentioned that in the face of adversity, which challenged your faith, you found an inner strength to endure. Barbara, the children and I have also benefited from your strength and caring during the many difficult times we've been through. You kept our family together and optimistic and, even at the worst of times, you still had the strength to extend your kindness to others, even strangers, who were in a similar situation. And no matter what was happening, you always kept God in our home.

For this, the children and I are honoring you with this toast. The four of us are very proud of you. You're a special mom and a special wife, and we thank you for giving us this very happy occasion. Le Chaim!

What followed was a few minutes of quiet, as our guests searched for tissues and Barbara came up to give each of us a kiss. Then the band followed with music, playing a hora, a Jewish folk dance done in a circle. It was tight quarters with so many people, but it made for more laughter and celebrating. We even lifted Barbara in a chair in the center of the circle, as everyone danced around her.

It was a beautiful, lovely, fun-filled day. That evening, we were all tired from the long day of events. After turning off the lights, I was practically asleep as soon as my head hit the pillow. Within seconds, I felt Barbara poking me in the back. "No ... I didn't fart," I said.

That may seem like a strange response to Barbara's poking. You see, Barbara would often poke me in the back in the middle of the night, waking me from a deep sleep, and the conversation would go something like this:

"Did you fart?"

"What? I was fast asleep! No, I didn't fart," I would answer.

"Well, you must have farted. It stinks in here!"

"I couldn't have farted. I was fast asleep."

"Marc, you obviously farted in your sleep. Get up and shake out the blanket. And don't fart in bed again."

"It must have been you who farted," I would answer.

"I'm not going to argue with you all night. Get up and shake out the blanket!"

It was so much easier when we had our dog, Pepper. Pepper slept in our room and I was able to blame any farting on the dog.

That night Barbara was poking me, and she turned the light back on. "I'm not asking if you farted. Turn around and look at me. I want to talk."

I rolled over on my side and we faced each other. I was exhausted and just wanted to sleep. I couldn't imagine what Barbara had to say that couldn't wait until the morning and needed me to look at her. But I perked up when I opened my eyes wide enough and saw her smile. Barbara continued, with a loving smile and in a slow mellow voice, just above a whisper.

"Today was a beautiful day."

"Yes, it was," I answered.

"Shush! Don't interrupt me. When I looked down from the bimah, I saw the four of you with big smiles and it made me very happy. Thank you for everything: the balloons, Jonathan's song, the kids' and your toast for me. There were so many nice things that we did and said to each other today. This is the first time that our kids were old enough to see and understand as we publicly expressed our feelings. I want this to be the beginning of how our family communicates and I want us to continue to do this for every occasion that we have the opportunity. Today was a wonderful day for you and me and the kids. I love you."

I smiled and we kissed. Barbara turned off the lights and we fell asleep, cuddled up against each other.

Barbara's Bat Mitzvah was the kickoff to our family's speech-delivering. Over the years, I've saved the many speeches and could probably develop a book based upon family speeches. It would overwhelm this book to include all of them. Instead, I've included excerpts from some.

On Saturday, April 23, 1988, the year after Barbara's Bat Mitzvah, we celebrated Jonathan's Bar Mitzvah. The Friday evening before, the five of us attended the Sabbath service and the rabbi announced Jonathan's Bar Mitzvah for the next morning. As we sat in the congregation that evening, I thought about the five us up on the bimah, and Barbara and me watching our first child become a Bar Mitzvah.

I knew that Jonathan was going to have fun with the excitement and attention. Jonathan was the jokester of the family, often getting in some kind of trouble in school for his silliness. Gee, where did he get that from? But his teachers always liked him and would say,

"Jonathan likes attention and belongs on stage." Jonathan was going to have his special moment on stage as a Bar Mitzvah.

I was reminded of an evening several years before. It was dinnertime, and Jonathan was talking about a talent show being organized at his school. He was nine years old, in fourth grade, and very excited. Kids would be on the stage, in front of the school, and using a microphone. He talked on and on about kids being able to use a microphone.

Barbara and I encouraged dinnertime talk. Listening to the kids talk about their day, school, and friends, was always fun. But that evening, I was half-listening, not paying much attention to what Jonathan was driving at. I couldn't understand how the talent show had anything to do with him, other than being impressed that kids could use the microphone.

Jonathan continued talking about using the microphone and then said, "I told my teacher that I want to be in the talent show."

That caught my attention. "What! You're going to be in the talent show! What are you going to do?"

"I told my teacher that I'm going to sing the song that Michael Jackson sings, 'Beat It.'"

Barbara interjected, "That's very nice!"

Totally caught off guard and surprised, I said, "That is very nice. But you just can't get on stage and sing a song. You have to practice what you're planning to do. This is a big commitment."

"What's a commitment?" Jonathan asked.

"A commitment is that you will need to spend time practicing the song, over and over. If you really want to do this, I'll practice with you each night after dinner."

I wasn't sure if Jonathan would really make the commitment. But he looked forward to each time we rehearsed, and I quickly realized that Jonathan was a real ham. He was always a funny kid. His teachers had told us as much, and now I was realizing for myself that he was a natural at being on stage. His obsession with the microphone was part of his desire to be the center of attention, in front of an audience.

What started off as dinnertime chatter became a family project. Kristen and Brian enjoyed watching us rehearse and were looking forward to seeing Jonathan on stage. Barbara got right into it too. She added much encouragement and made up an outfit for Jonathan: dark sunglasses, white glove, white shirt, red-sequined bow tie, red jacket, and black pants with a white stripe down the side of each leg. We were all pumped up.

One evening while we were rehearsing, a friend of Barbara's, whom Barbara and I secretly nicknamed Yenta, stopped by. Yenta saw Jonathan and me rehearsing, and said, "I heard that Jonathan is going to be in the talent show."

"Yes, he is," I answered.

"You know, Marc ... the kids in the show have real talent. Those kids have been taking private dance, singing, and music lessons. You may be subjecting Jonathan to embarrassment."

It took a lot of self-control for me not to say, "Go fuck yourself." Instead, I tried to be polite.

"Jonathan has real talent and his performance the night of the show will prove it."

"Well ... I'm just trying to be helpful," said Yenta, sounding defensive.

I always believed Yenta to be a jealous, negative person and a bubble buster. Barbara and I always took a positive approach with our kids, encouraging them to reach for what they wanted. If they tried to reach too far, Barbara and I were there to help them succeed and be with them if they should fail.

Barbara and I were open-minded to suggestions from friends and relatives about parenting. But we made our parenting decisions based upon our own choices and paid no attention to any negativity. Barbara and I recognized bad parenting techniques from people, like Yenta, like how to stifle your kids' opportunities and ambitions. We talked about how it was no surprise that Yenta's kids were involved in nothing. Barbara and I would joke, and I would do an imitation of Yenta's kids, saying, "Mom, I want to be in the talent show at my school." And Yenta answering, "You can't be in the show. You have no talent! That show is for kids with talent and you'll embarrass all of us."

For Jonathan's talent show, my family was a team, and no such yenta could burst our bubble. We continued rehearsing. Jonathan looked so cute in the outfit that Barbara had put together.

The night of the show was a blast. Jonathan went onto the stage with poise and confidence, despite the kids with the real talent who performed before his turn. Sitting in the front row were a group of girls from his grade. During Jonathan's performance, they screamed out like fans as he did the moonwalk. At the end of the show, Jonathan won first place. As for Yenta, I wish I had told her to go fuck herself.

April 23, 1988, the day of Jonathan's Bat Mitzvah, was beautiful and sunny, and that morning, we were all excited on our way to temple. Our pride showed, as Barbara and I greeted family and friends as they arrived. As the service was beginning, we took our seats on the bimah. Barbara sat beside me, to my left and next to Jonathan. Kristen and Brian sat to my right and, from the bimah, we looked out at the congregation.

The service began and I felt my emotions come over me, as this event became real. As I looked out at the congregation and saw my parents, I recalled standing on the bimah on the day of my Bar Mitzvah. With my dad standing beside me, I looked up to the balcony, where the women sat in our Orthodox shul, and saw my mother and grandmother.

On this day of Jonathan's Bar Mitzvah, there was no balcony in our temple and my mom and dad sat together. And on this day, it was our son who was becoming a Bar Mitzvah. It was overwhelming for me to believe that we had made it to this moment in time. I felt my eyes tearing up. With all the darkness that we had been through just a few years before, and my fear of

my children losing their mother, the sun was shining down upon us on this day. Barbara made it here with me to our son's Bar Mitzvah. As Jonathan took his place in front of the ark, I felt a quiver through my body. Barbara turned, looked at me, and reached over to hold my hand.

When it was time for Jonathan to deliver his Bar Mitzvah speech, I cried at seeing my little boy step up to the podium, standing so straight, so tall, and so sure of himself. I was so proud and definitely more nervous than he was. That is, if he was nervous at all. Here's a favorite short excerpt of mine from his speech.

> There comes a time when we realize that the world is larger than we ever imagined. We grow to find a world outside of our home and beyond our street and neighborhood and learn of people who are much less fortunate than us.
>
> In a world that has so much wealth, there are so many people who are homeless and hungry. Many of us "fast" for one day for Yom Kippur (The Day of Atonement, the holiest day of the year in Judaism). Just imagine continuing that "fast" for a second day, a week, or even longer. There comes a time when we realize that it is up to each of us to offer help.

A few weeks after the day of his Bar Mitzvah, Jonathan decided that he wanted to join the confirmation class. The class ceremony was on May 18, 1991 and Jonathan was chosen to be one of the speakers to represent the class. This time, Barbara and I sat in the congregation looking up at Jonathan on the bimah. As he stepped up to the podium, he had a serious look on his face. He spoke firmly and with a powerful voice.

> There was fifteen minutes left in the basketball game. It was Mount Olive High School versus Randolph, in the most important game of the year: the championship. The high score between the teams had changed at least ten times in the last forty-five seconds. My team was now losing by two points,

with fifteen seconds left in the game. "Gellman, go in," shouted my couch, with an encouraging voice. I was nervous, because winning the championship might depend on me.

My team had possession. The ball was passed to me. I caught the ball, as the sweat was pouring off my body. I dribbled the ball back behind the three-point line and took my shot. I looked up at the clock. The time was ticking away while the ball was in the air. The crowd was silent, as the time approached one second left in the game, and the ball was headed toward the basket. I watched the ball until ... Swish! It was a three-point shot! The crowd was going wild, screaming, "Gellman ... Gellman!" My teammates lifted me up on their shoulders. I looked up into the stands and saw my mom cheering and my dad crying. It was wonderful.

Then, I felt a teammate poking me in the ribs, as I sat on the bench. "Hey Gellman," he said, "Wake up and stop daydreaming ... we lost." Too bad this was just a dream. Did the dream mean something? Will such an experience ever happen to me?

In the Bible, we are told of a dream with similar meaning that Joseph experienced. Joseph was the son of Jacob. Jacob had twelve sons, but Joseph was his favorite. Jacob would send Joseph into the fields to see if his brothers were doing their job, tending the flocks. He would ask Joseph to report back to him if they were not.

Jacob made Joseph a coat with stripes of different colored cloth. The coat meant that Joseph was the chief of Jacob's sons. Joseph's brothers grew jealous of him.

One night, when Joseph was seventeen years old, he had a dream and described the dream to his brothers. Joseph said, "In my dream, we were tying bundles of grain together. Suddenly your bundles made a circle and bowed down to mine." This dream angered the brothers and they asked, "Do you want us to bow down to you?" At this point in time, they hated Joseph.

Joseph had another dream. In this dream, he said, "The sun, the moon and the eleven stars bowed down to me." He told his father and brothers about the dream. Jacob was angered, and said, "What kind of dream is this? Do you want all of us, even your father and mother, to bow down to you?"

Joseph dreamed that his family would bow down to him. He said that the dream was a message from God to him. People may dream of seeing themselves as being better than everyone else. They may dream of being the captain of a team or of being superior in order to put down others. Joseph's brothers saw him as a person with these selfish motives. But his father, Jacob, saw something else. Jacob saw Joseph's talent. He overlooked the bad in Joseph and focused on the good.

In my dream, my parents were proud of me. They saw only the good. They overlooked the selfishness and arrogance.

Parents seem to see the best in their children. We should be thankful for parents who see the best in us. We dream of being great at things such as basketball. But even if I'm not, my parents always see the best in me. With this support, cooperation, and love from our family, we are able to learn and grow.

We, the Confirmation Class of 5751, are grateful for parents who allow us to dream and see the potential for greatness in each of us! Amen.

As Jonathan spoke, I don't think I took a breath or even blinked. Watching the words flow out of Jonathan's mouth was unbelievable to me. I was looking up at the podium and seeing my kid delivering a speech. That was my kid delivering a speech to a packed congregation. Barbara held on to my hand and was squeezing it. I don't know if she was squeezing it to prevent me from crying or herself. It was a proud moment for a father, as people came up to me to congratulate me after the service. But I felt a little guilty for being given credit. I said, "All the credit goes to Barbara. Between work and business trips, I am hardly home. Barbara does it all."

With a laugh, thinking that I was joking, people would answer, "Well, you must have done something."

And I'd say, "Yeah, maybe."

On May 19, 1990, two years after Jonathan's Bar Mitzvah, we celebrated Kristen's Bat Mitzvah. Once again, it was a beautiful, sunny day, and we were all as excited that morning as we had been just two years before. We were a little more experienced about the routine this time and, with pride, we greeted family and friends. As the service was beginning, we took our seats on the bimah. This time we sat on the other side of the bimah. Barbara sat beside me, to my right and next to Kristen, and Jonathan and Brian sat to my left.

I didn't think that my emotions would swell in the same way they had two years before. After all, this was our second child, and we had already experienced this ceremony. I quickly came to realize that this wasn't going to be a routine event. My little girl was becoming a Bat Mitzvah and there was nothing routine about it at all. My little girl, who came into the world while I was in the hospital parking lot getting Barbara's suitcase out of the car, was going to be reading from the Torah.

The day I met Barbara in the Rockaways, July 4, 1964, was two months before her thirteenth birthday. And it was three days before her thirteenth birthday when I saw Barbara walking to the board-walk with her friends, at the end of that summer. That evening, I so regretted not spending more time getting to know Barbara. Today, twenty-six years later, was the day of our daughter's Bat Mitzvah. Our little girl who used to look so cute in her pigtails. But on this day, the pigtails were long gone, and our little girl was a beautiful, thirteen-year-old young woman.

The sun was shining down upon us, on this day. Barbara made it here with me to our daughter's Bat Mitzvah. I felt a peaceful feeling inside of me; all was perfect and all was fine. There would be no worries on this day.

As for tomorrow, well, that would be for tomorrow. A tomorrow when my obsession with the past would come back to me. It was an obsession, of the cancer of years before, that wouldn't go away. But today was meant to be all about today and, with that thought, my emotions came over me. Barbara turned, looked at me, and reached over to hold my hand.

As Kristen took her place in front of the ark, I looked out at the congregation and down the aisle in the sanctuary. I envisioned the day when Kristen would be a bride, walking down that aisle with Barbara and me. And we'd "give her away" to her bridegroom.

I don't know where that expression comes from: give her away. I intended never to give my daughter away. Kristen would always be my little girl and I wasn't going to hand her over to anyone. Of course, I would give my blessing for my daughter's hand in marriage. Because the groom would need her hand to place a ring on her finger. But that would be it.

Today, Kristen wasn't a bride. She was a Bat Mitzvah. It was tradition in this temple for the mother to deliver a speech and bless the child. At that point in the service, Barbara stood with Kristen at the podium and spoke. I loved Barbara's blessing, especially this small excerpt.

> Kristen, today you assume the responsibilities of a Bat Mitzvah. Daddy and I also believe that this is the time for you to become aware that there is a special person inside of you that only you can find, develop, and be.
>
> The relationship between a mother and daughter is very special. With love, respect, and trust, it is a relationship I cherish deeply. Sometimes, you may feel that I can't relate to anything in your life. I was once a teenager struggling between childhood and adulthood and remember having those same opinions about my mother. As I got older, I realized that our relationship changed and so did we.
>
> From my mother, I learned responsibility, honesty, and the importance of family and caring for others. I always knew that

I could talk to my mom. She would tell me how wonderful it is to have a daughter and wished that I, too, would have a daughter someday. I know that today my mom is looking down on us and smiling at my beautiful daughter. Kristen, I am so proud to be your mother.

Like Jonathan, Kristen continued after her Bat Mitzvah and joined the confirmation class. One evening, while watching TV, Barbara said to me, "Today, I heard that the rabbi is starting an adult confirmation class. I decided that I'm going to join. So far, two of our kids did it. I think that I should too."

I turned to Barbara. "Gee, maybe I should too."

Barbara laughed. "What! Are you joking? Because if you join the class, the rabbi will be shocked, as well as everyone else in the congregation."

Although I supported our children being raised in the Jewish faith, I never felt comfortable in the suburban temple where we were members. The experience and culture were so different from the Orthodox shul that I grew up with in Brooklyn.

The suburban temple was a contemporary style structure built in the mid 1960s. It was later expanded in 1976 and again in 1988. In the sanctuary during services, some congregants wore a skullcap (yarmulke) and some wore a prayer shawl (tallit). The prayer shawls were worn covering the shoulders and were most often new, colorful, and artfully decorated, some with a silver top. The service was mostly in English.

The temple was a big contrast from my shul in Brooklyn. The shul was a tall brick edifice built in the late 1920s and early 1930s, not unlike the many other shuls in Brooklyn. At the sidewalk level, there was a row of four tall, brick columns. Between the columns were tall, wrought iron gates that were kept closed when the shul was not open. When open, it was symbolic of going through the gates to heaven. Just past the gates was a three-story atrium and within the atrium was a wide and tall flight of steps leading to the entrance of the shul, at the level of the sanctuary. Walking up these steps to the sanctuary was symbolic of walking up to God. In the sanctuary, there were stained glass windows, and the ceiling was painted with a mural of ancient times. When in the shul, every male congregant wore a yarmulke. In the sanctuary during services, every male who had been a Bar Mitzvah wore a prayer shawl. Often the prayer shawl was draped over the head. And few to none of the shawls were colorful and new. Most often they were faded and worn from years of use. It was that worn out look that symbolically made the shawls so beautiful. The services were in Hebrew and the chanting of the service by the rabbi and congregation was so very spiritual. I missed all of this; being in the midst of congregants deeply devoted in prayer, sitting beside my dad and brother, and looking up to the balcony and seeing my mom and grandmother.

I found that I couldn't relate to most of the other congregants in our suburban temple. There was one congregant in particular who I often laughed about to Barbara. "What's with that guy?" I'd ask her. On Friday evenings after services, there would be an Oneg Shabbat, a Jewish social gathering with refreshments, in the social room. While everyone was socializing, this guy would be by himself, looking around at everyone with this farbissina face. (Farbissina is the Yiddish word for sourpuss). It was as if he hated everyone and the sight of everyone socializing tortured him. Although he may have been the only really weird person there, I had fun using him as a scapegoat for not wanting to attend services. I would say, "Barbara, I'm not going to services. That guy scares me. I predict that one of these days that guy is going to step away from the wall and start beating the shit out of people."

Laughing, Barbara would answer, "So you're telling me that you don't want to go services tonight."

With mock seriousness, I would reply, "No ... I do want to go. I'm just scared shit of that guy."

I never found my niche in that temple. I didn't join in on any of the temple committees or even the temple brotherhood. At socials, I felt out of place. Even away from temple, it seemed like the only subject that members talked about was temple. No matter where we were, whether in someone's home or out to dinner, there was mostly temple talk. Since I believed people were most likely aware of my feelings and since my appearances at temple were seldom, of course people were going to be shocked to hear about me joining the confirmation class.

Shocking people has always been a love of mine. Nevertheless, I knew I should join the class. It was what Barbara wanted and it would make her happy. Temple was important to Barbara and gave her faith, and faith gave her hope and the strength to endure her health issues. As importantly, I felt like I needed to be a better role model for our kids. I did want them to be proud of their faith and I said to Barbara, "Well, if you're telling me that the rabbi and other people are going to be shocked by me joining the confirmation class, I definitely want to join. I love shocking the shit out of people."

The confirmation class graduation was on May 28, 1993. Each member of the class had a part and prayer to deliver at the service. After the service, several people came up to me to say that they enjoyed seeing the big smile on my face as I watched Barbara step up to the podium and begin her part. An excerpt of Barbara's part:

God, you have blessed me;
With a thoughtful loving husband who has been by my side through good times and bad,
With three wonderful children who fill my heart with pride each and every day,
With a family that respects me, not only as a wife and mother, but as an independent woman, and
With wonderful friends who enrich my life and have become my family.

For me, well, I wasn't much into publicly reciting prayers at that time. Instead, I preferred to just speak my mind about topics. A few weeks before, as we were preparing for the ceremony, Barbara said to me, "You're always into speaking your mind, with your opinion.

Give in for once and throw in some kind of prayer. Marc, this is a religious service."

"Well, actually, during one of the classes, I was reminded of something that, for a very long time, I've wondered about. I got my answer at that class."

During one of the classes, I was reminded of a time when I was about six years old. I was in shul with my dad on one day of the High Holidays: Rosh Hashanah, the celebration of the Jewish New Year. My dad was an usher in shul that morning. I stood with him in the lobby and watched as he directed people. It was kind of boring for a six-year-old, just hanging around watching. But all that would change quickly.

The shul was about full, and services were about to start, when an angry woman came bustling down the stairs from the balcony shouting to my dad, "Mr. Gellman ... Mr. Gellman!"

"What's the matter?" my dad asked.

"I was sitting in a seat and this elderly woman came over and pulled me out of the seat and sat down."

My dad answered, "Okay, let's see what the problem is."

I followed my dad and the angry woman up the steps to the balcony. This was getting exciting. I was hoping for a good fight. When we got onto the balcony, my dad asked, "Which elderly woman was it?"

The angry woman pointed and said, "That elderly woman right there!"

At first, I gulped, but then I laughed. The elderly woman was my grandmother. I was kind of proud. I didn't think my grandmother had it in her. With that, my dad turned to the angry woman and said, "I'm sorry, but there's nothing that I can do about this. That elderly woman is my mother-in-law and that has been her seat for the High Holidays for the past thirty years. You'll have to find another seat."

As a silly kid, I found the entire incident hysterical. The angry woman, still angry, looked for another seat and my dad went back downstairs. As for me, I needed to enjoy the moment, linger a little, and get more details about what happened. I went to my grandmother to ask what had happened. I spoke to my grandmother in English and she would answer in Yiddish.

"Bubbe ... Did you pull a woman out of your seat?'

"Yor." *Yes.*

"Why did you do that?" I asked.

"Ich hab dos geton as du vest visen as du bist a Yid." *I did it so that you will know that you are a Jew.*

I had no idea what pulling that woman out of the seat had anything to do with knowing that I was a Jew. I began to ask again, and my grandmother interrupted me and said, "Snel kum arap tzum tate. Di davenen hoibt zich on." *Hurry up downstairs to papa. The service is beginning.*

I always meant to ask my grandmother about that day. But I never did. The years went by too quickly for me and my grandmother, while I was going from being a young kid to a teenager. Then my grandmother was gone. I always had some regrets for not finding out the answer and felt a loss.

It was almost thirty-eight years later, during one of the confirmation classes, when I figured out what my grandmother meant. During the classes, I rarely spoke or participated. I went to the class, took my seat, listened to the discussions, rarely answered or asked questions, didn't really talk to anyone, and left as soon as the class was over. During one particular class, a topic caught my attention. Suddenly I felt like I found the answer to my question of my grandmother.

Barbara loved the story and said, "Oh, Marc, that story is so beautiful. I have fond memories of my grandfather taking me to the Yankee games. But that's about it. I wish I had the kind of stories you have from when I was six years old."

"Well, you can have fifty percent ownership of this story. Since you own fifty percent of everything else I have."

So often, Barbara returned to talking about her childhood. No matter how many years passed, she was always haunted by her past. I shared my past with her and hoped that stories of my past would become her family stories too. But I understood her pain and didn't know what I could do. Even with all the good we were celebrating, and Barbara being the rock of the family for me and the kids, Barbara couldn't shake off the hurt from her childhood.

As I look through Shiva Eyes and search for answers, I wonder if the pains of Barbara's childhood were gone before she closed her eyes for the last time. I hope so. I want to believe so. But I hurt, thinking that I'll probably never find out. And I hurt even more, thinking that the pains of her childhood probably never did go away.

Barbara asked, "Well, are you going to tell me the answer to your question about your grandmother?"

"You know what, silly head? I'm going to make you wait until the service for you to listen to my part."

While talking about this story with Barbara, out of the air, it came to me about what I would say for the confirmation service. I thought that perhaps no one attending the service would get my point. But that was fine with me, because maybe my grandmother would be listening and that was enough for me. In the service, I proudly delivered my part.

We attended each class, a diverse group of adults with diverse interests, opinions and interpretations. For often, most of us arrived separately and left separately. But together, we searched for guidance in a common mission.

We searched for the way to continue the merits of our ancestors and realized that what we do will make a difference; that the memories of grandparents are memories that children never forget. For me, it is the memory of my elderly grandmother, never giving in to her pain, as she regularly climbed the too-many steps to reach her seat in the balcony of an orthodox shul in Brooklyn.

We search for what's good and pray for the goodness we do, to live on and on. In this mission, we are encouraged by the verse:

"For I Eternal your God am an impassioned God, visiting the guilt of the parents upon the children, upon the third and upon the fourth generations of those who reject Me, but showing kindness to the thousandth generation of those who love me and keep my commandments."

With all my resistance to taking an active part in temple activities, I admit, I did get a lot out of attending the classes. Also, the graduation service was beautiful. I was happy to be a participant. And, I had learned the answer to a question of my grandmother that I had never received the answer to.

Before that day, I never thought of myself as a religious person. But I think to myself, with that speech, perhaps I am. My grandmother was an observant Jew. She observed the Sabbath and every holiday and would take that same seat in the balcony. As a young boy, I spent a lot of time with my grandmother. It was always so easy to find her, she lived right next door. And when she wasn't home, it wasn't difficult for me to figure out where she was. I just had to remind myself what day it was: Sabbath or a holiday. And I would find her in that seat. It was the last seat in the top row in the balcony of the Orthodox shul. At those times, I was reminded that I was a Jew.

As for me, coming to the realization that perhaps I am a religious person, it appeared to me that I might be a very religious person. From my grandmother wanting to make sure that I knew I was a Jew, I learned what my grandmother always knew: "With our faith, we search for what's good and pray for the goodness we do, to live on and on."

Barbara wanted our children to have everything that she didn't as a child: peace, security, and the time to just be a kid, without family conflicts. And an appreciation of our faith. Barbara said that the best part of our adult confirmation ceremony was seeing our children in the congregation watching us celebrating together. Barbara's faith was important to her. My grandmother would have loved Barbara. Or maybe, it was my grandmother who arranged our match.

Finally, on May 13, 1995, eight years after Barbara's Bat Mitzvah, seven years after Jonathan and five years after Kristen, it was Brian's turn. And once again, it was a beautiful, sunny day, and we were all as excited that morning as we had been on the other days. Actually, we were all much more excited, because Brian was the baby of the family; we all still referred to him as "the baby." Plus, Brian was the fussiest. For Jonathan and Kristen's Bar and Bat Mitzvahs, Barbara

made all planning decisions and arrangements and asked them for
some input for the reception party, planned for after the ceremony.
But, with Brian, he needed to be involved in every detail and made
sure that all was going to be his way.

As the service was about to begin, we took our seats on the bimah.
Except for Brian. I looked around, but he wasn't in the sanctuary. In
a panic, I said to Barbara, "Where's Brian?"

"I don't know. Go find him. The service is about to begin."

Barbara wasn't at all worried and kind of laughed. She knew he
was somewhere in the temple. And she knew Brian very well. If any
kid was going to hold up their Bar Mitzvah service for any reason,
it would be Brian. As for me, I was obsessing about where the little
fucker could be.

As I stepped off the bimah, I spotted Brian walking down the
aisle toward me. He had been in the reception room, looking at the
way the tables were arranged. Weeks before, Brian was very specific
about how he wanted the reception room arranged. So, I prepared a
very detailed plan for the room, following Brian's input and seal of
approval, and gave it to the caterer.

As Brian approached me, I said, "Brian, the service is about to
begin. We need to take our seats."

Brian was very calm and matter-of-fact. He intended to get something done before the services started and couldn't give a rat's ass
about inconveniencing anyone.

"Dad. The caterer messed up and didn't follow the layout. We
need to move the tables."

"Not now! We need to take our seats. The service is about to start.
We'll do it afterward."

"No, Dad. We need to do it now."

Well, you don't mess with Brian. He knew how to make us feel
miserable with payback. Brian was always unpunishable. Punishing
Brian for anything was more like punishing ourselves. Brian never
made it through eight days of Chanukah. By the third or fourth
night of hearing Brian complain about each of his presents, Barbara

would cut him off for the rest of the holiday. We felt worse about that punishment than he did.

So, I went with him to the reception room. There we were, as the service was about to begin, in our suits, moving tables around and totally rearranging the room. Once it was exactly to Brian's liking, we returned to the sanctuary. As we stepped onto the bimah, I noticed the sneer on the rabbi's face. The service began.

I didn't mind the sneer on the rabbi's face. I could deal with that more easily than I could deal with Brian. As I sat in my seat, Barbara leaned over and whispered, "Where were you?"

"Don't ask. He's your son," I answered.

By this time, I didn't know how I would feel during the service, or if I wanted to kill this kid. But I was the most emotional this day, more so than on ceremony days past. Brian was the baby of the family and on that day, he was becoming a Bar Mitzvah. I felt a warmth inside of me, as I thought to myself, "Barbara, you did it all. You are our family's role model and your inspiration guided and led the way for our faith to be handed down to the next generation." I guessed Barbara could hear my thoughts. Because at that moment, she reached over and held my hand.

Although it was tradition in this temple for the mother to deliver a speech and bless the child, Barbara wanted me to stand with her and Brian at the podium and take part in the blessing. Here's an excerpt from the end of Barbara's speech and blessing:

Brian, the first time Daddy and I brought you to temple was for your baby-naming ceremony. We chose your two Hebrew names, Ephraim and Yosef. Yoseph was Joseph, the favorite son of Jacob. In Jewish history, Joseph was the famous interpreter of dreams and Ephraim was his youngest son. The story is told in the Torah that when Joseph's father, Jacob, was near death, he gathered his sons together to bless them. He also asked Joseph to bring his two sons, Ephraim and Manasseh, to give them a special blessing. It was tradition to bless the oldest son first, but Jacob chose to bless Joseph's youngest son, Ephraim, first.

He told Joseph that Ephraim was very special and would go on to greatness. Throughout Jewish history, on Shabbat, fathers blessed their sons by saying, "May you be blessed as Ephraim and Manasseh." Daddy and I feel blessed that you are our son.

Brian, you have never been in someone else's shadow. When you were born with curly hair and big brown eyes, you looked different than Jonathan and Kristen. It wasn't long before you expressed your own individuality and made it very clear that you want to do things yourself and in your own way. You've had difficulties but you don't give up and are beginning to recognize the rewards from hard work and perseverance.

Daddy and I love you and are proud of you today and every day. As you take responsibilities of a Jewish adult and affirm your commitment to Judaism, we pray for God to keep you strong with happiness and peace

May the God of our people, the God of the universe, bless you. May the One who has always been our guide inspire you to bring honor to our family and to our people Israel.

We give thanks to you, O Lord our God, Ruler of the universe, for giving us life, for sustaining us and for enabling us to reach this day of joy. Amen.

I was supposed to recite the prayer at the end, along with Barbara. But I was too overcome from Barbara's speech. Instead, I held on to her arm as she so bravely recited the prayer herself.

After the service, our guests were directed from the sanctuary and into the reception room. About one hundred and twenty people attended the reception. Once in the room, I said to Barbara, "Okay, so now I can tell you. Look around. This is what Brian and I were doing before the service. Brian wanted all the tables to be rearranged."

"That's Brian," Barbara answered.

For so many years, everything went well for Barbara and me. Good things were happening for our family and Barbara and I were so much in love. Celebrating Brian's Bar Mitzvah, we were having another beautiful sunny day in our lives. And, when I looked at

Barbara on that day, I saw my wife, an incredible woman. She wore a soft red ensemble that moved when she did. At five feet, six inches tall and slender, with her dark brown hair and eyes, and olive complexion, Barbara was striking in that ensemble.

As a surprise to Barbara, I asked the band to perform "The Lady in Red," a song by Chris de Burgh. At the opportune moment, I led Barbara to the center of the dance floor, and I gestured the band to start. The music began and we danced and when Barbara recognized the song, she smiled.

I am five feet, ten inches tall, and with Barbara in heels, as we danced, we gazed directly into each other's eyes and truly felt the lyrics; that we were alone, it was just Barbara and me. The lyrics couldn't have described the feeling in my heart any better at that moment. I was dancing with the lady in red. A gorgeous, amazing lady with a shining glow around her. The feeling of love encapsulated us.

That's how it was on the dance floor and that's how I felt. I have not forgotten and never will forget the way Barbara looked that day. The feeling of holding her in my arms, as we danced to the words of that song and I saw her smile with her dimples, is a feeling of Barbara I will never forget.

Oh, my. I didn't think that writing this chapter would be so difficult. It did help me to release pent-up emotions that I've carried with me about my family, since I lost Barbara. As I relived this special period in our lives, I see it was a time when my family was blessed with goodness and peace, with the sun shining down upon us. This was the period in time when my family was growing up and when each of us had our turn on stage, able to shine and express our feelings, about our lives, about what we've learned and experienced, about who we are, with so many nice things to say to each other.

The Bar and Bat Mitzvah period of our lives was beautiful. I learned that it's always a beautiful family experience, when the celebration is all about love of family, past and present, and tradition, rather than about competing and trying to "keep up with the Joneses." Or, more ethnically fitting in the case of a Bar Mitzvah, trying to "keep up with the Finkelsteins or the Goldfarbs."

There were times when I didn't realize the impact on me of the simple things in the moment, like Barbara holding my hand. But as I wrote this chapter, looking through Shiva Eyes, I saw my biggest fear during these years. It was wondering how far into the future it would be until I would be looking through Shiva Eyes. Today, as I look through Shiva Eyes, I see the fear I lived with then. I see it as I relive some of the times when Barbara held my hand. At those moments, I was thankful she was with me. It is only now I realize that for thirty years I feared losing Barbara. The fear I lived with was of the day when Barbara would no longer be with me to hold my hand. Maybe the simple things in the moment, weren't simple at all.

I've learned to better understand, appreciate, and re-experience all the splendors and wonders in my life. And if, by chance, this book should be read by others, I do hope this chapter will inspire parents and children to capture the moments, special or not, to express their loving and caring feelings, or to just say nice things to each other. Because such opportunities can pass by quickly.

CHAPTER 18

How about an award

One Saturday afternoon in July 1991, the kids were out somewhere, and Barbara and I were in the kitchen. The house was quiet. I was sitting at the table, relaxing, and looking out the window into the yard. Barbara was rinsing something in the sink. I heard her say, "Marc, next month is August."

I didn't know what that was about. It seemed kind of a strange thing to say out of the blue. I figured that I probably had missed something, and asked, "What did you say?"

"I said that next month is August."

I loved it when Barbara blurted out things like that. It gave me an opportunity to have some fun with her. In mock seriousness, I answered, "Really? You know, you must be right. Because this month is July. In fact, I know for sure that you're right. Next month is really going to be August. How great is that!"

I was still looking out the window.

"Turn around and look at me and stop being silly," Barbara said. "Do you know what next month is?"

"I thought that we just established that it is August?"

"You are so annoying."

I loved being annoying to Barbara. She was so beautiful at those times, with that cute, annoyed look on her face. But I knew my limits with trying to drive her crazy and eased up to give her an answer. "Okay, okay. Next month ... oh yeah ... of course ... It's my birthday. What are you getting for me?"

I went over the limit with that answer. Barbara walked over to me, put her hands on her hips, and with a stern look and an annoyed voice, asked, "And, what else is happening in August?"

"It ... it ... it's our anniversary," I blurted.

"It's a special one!"

"Really?"

"You better stop being so silly and start remembering quickly. I'm getting annoyed."

I figured she was already annoyed with me. I knew that I'd better give up the silliness. "I know, I know. It's our twentieth anniversary."

"Yes, it is," Barbara said with a sweet smile. "So, what would you like for our twentieth anniversary?"

"Gee, let me think. I don't know, haven't thought about it. Well, how about an award?"

The sweet smile on Barbara's face quickly turned to a frown and I knew I was in trouble. I shouldn't have said that. Barbara was pumping me to remember our twentieth wedding anniversary and I was playing with her a little too much. With an indignant look, her hands on her hips, and disappointment in her voice, Barbara asked, "So, you think that you deserve an award for being married to me?"

She was pissed and I knew I was in trouble. I had to quickly backtrack. "No! I was just joking. Unless you really feel I should get an award. But no, I was just joking. Of course, I know it's our special anniversary."

"Well, what would you like to do?" she asked.

"Um ... What day of the week is August 29?"

"It's a Thursday."

"Perfect! I got it. Let's check into a hotel for the weekend. We can order room service and never leave the room for the entire weekend. We don't need to pack or even need a change of clothes, just a toothbrush and a change of underwear. Actually, we may not need a change of underwear either."

That did it. I pushed too far. Barbara had had it with me.

"What? First, you tell me that you deserve an award for being married to me and, with that, you expect me to shack up in a hotel room with you for the weekend. So, tell me—after you last for the first eleven minutes in the room, what will we do for the rest of the weekend?"

"That was a good answer. No, it was a perfect answer," I thought to myself. I deserved it and I knew it. I had lost in this little silliness battle. Barbara put me down and shut me up. She had won and I wasn't a good loser. Because I was never a good loser and couldn't admit defeat. Trying to recapture my pride, I tried to guilt her. "Oh, Barbara. That wasn't a nice thing to say to me. That hurt my feelings."

Barbara was laughing at this point. She knew she had me and planned to rub it in a little. "I hurt your feelings! Are you serious?"

I took a conciliatory deep breath. "Okay, okay. So, what would you like to do?"

Barbara's demeanor quickly changed, her voice growing soft and polite.

"I'd like for you, me, and the kids to go to temple that Friday night for services. It could be a special service dedicated to our anniversary. We can all have a part in the service and the rabbi will do a special blessing in our honor. That's what I'd like to do."

"Wow," I thought to myself. "Barbara sure is letting me off the hook quickly and easily for my wiseass fooling around." Obviously, she was setting me up to get me to agree to this. I figured all I had to do was say yes and all would be good, again. "That sounds great. Good idea. Let's do that."

I really wasn't that crazy about the idea. The hotel idea, which I pulled out of my ass, was kind of appealing. Although Barbara was probably right about the ridiculousness of a lovefest lasting for an entire weekend. A fact that's been said about men, "We always think we want to do it twice, just before we do it once. Then after doing it once, somehow the desire to do it again is gone." Although the eleven-minute remark was insulting, my "getting-an-award" comment made it a well-deserved insult.

Nevertheless, I did have to backtrack and, more importantly, it was obvious that Barbara had already planned this out. I knew it would be nice for all of us to be on the bimah in celebration of this occasion. We could always go to hotels, vacations, or dinners. But having our children together with us, and being honored for an occasion this special, was hard to top. And, again, it made Barbara happy. She smiled when I agreed. Barbara's smile was everything to me.

So, on Friday evening, August 30, we attended a Sabbath service. The rabbi announced to the congregation that this was a special service in honor of our anniversary. The rabbi called Barbara and me up to the bimah and we took our place at the podium.

As I looked out to the congregation, it was heartwarming to see the smiles on the faces of the congregation. Instantly, I realized that Barbara was right. It was amazing to be at the podium in front of the congregation and getting ready to be honored for our anniversary. It was heartwarming to see the smiles on our kids' faces. They were sixteen, fourteen, and ten years old. We were celebrating our twentieth anniversary, a milestone event. Especially for Barbara and me.

At milestones like these, I was haunted by the memories of hearing the cries from Barbara, "Oh, Marc ... I don't want to die." We had made it to this day, and our children were watching us being honored. And in minutes, they would be watching as Barbara and I publicly expressed our love for each other in front of the congregation. Their faces were filled with excited anticipation. For us, as parents, the sight our children at that moment couldn't get much better.

Barbara spoke first. She was such a good and effective speaker. As she spoke, I couldn't take my eyes off her. I gazed at Barbara in wonder. At moments, I felt like it was just the two of us alone in the sanctuary, standing on the bimah, at the podium, and in front of the ark that stored the Torah.

Barbara's speech was lovely. I held back the tears, during the part when she turned to me, looked into my eyes, and said:

> We have had more than our share of sad times. As I awakened after each surgery, there you were, face pale with worry, eyes red from crying, holding my hand and reassuring me that all went well. And then ... always a joke to make me laugh.
>
> Many people asked how I got through that difficult period. It was your love that helped me through. When I was frightened, you held me in your arms. When I was depressed, you made me laugh. I have read that many marriages fall apart when illness strikes, but ours only got stronger.

When Barbara finished, we kissed. Then it was my turn to speak. Afterward, Barbara told me that when it was my turn, she saw this twinkle in my eyes and got concerned about how serious I was going to be. It wouldn't have been the first time that I came out with some pushing-the-envelope, controversial comment. So, some concern on Barbara's part was warranted, as I began.

> I've been mentioning to people at my office that we are celebrating our twentieth wedding anniversary. Some commented that anyone married to the same person for twenty years deserves an award. Although it's nice to receive an award, I'm told by our rabbi that I won't be receiving an award this evening. Just a blessing. But I understand that it is going to be a terrific blessing.

The beginning of my speech went on to be kind of light and got some laughs. I told the story about my mother's ten commandments for being a good husband. Then the tone in my voice mellowed as I began to speak to Barbara from my heart. I ended my speech saying:

Barbara, you've created a good home for our family ... a Jewish home. Not just because it has a mezuzah on the door, but a home where you've strived for peace and harmony. A home in which people respect each other as individuals. A home where great moral qualities are taught by example.

I'm proud to be your husband. You're a special mom and a special wife. I thank you for these past twenty years.

My words were so sincere and so from my heart that it was difficult for me to speak. I forced out the words as I cried through this final part of my speech.

Our children joined us on the bimah and took their place at the podium. Jonathan was the designated speaker.

For both of you, your dream has already come true. You are both nice people, not only to each other but, to everyone else, even people that you don't like. You both do things for us, before thinking about yourself. You are both smart and have good jobs and most importantly, you love each other very much.

The three of us hope that someday we could have a family identical to ours. If there were an award to be given out by someone for "a job well done" for being great parents, a great couple, great friends, and just great people, that award would definitely be given to you. Brian, Kristen, and I want to let you know how much we appreciate what you do for us and thank you. You deserve the best life. We know that you love us, and we love you, too.

After the speeches, we all gathered in front of the rabbi, as he bestowed a special blessing upon us. It was a beautiful way to celebrate our twentieth wedding anniversary, and the best way. Barbara was right and she knew it. I was happy for that. After the service, there was an Oneg Shabbat in the social room. So many people came up to us to congratulate us and the kids.

Much later that evening, I was sitting on the couch in the family room and watching TV. The kids were asleep, and Barbara came over and cuddled up next to me. "Did you have fun tonight?"

"Actually ... it was wonderful."

I noticed that Barbara was holding a large envelope. I immediately thought to myself, "Shit I didn't get anything for her."

"This is something special for you."

"Really? What is it?"

"I'm presenting you with this award," Barbara answered.

I was a little confused and quickly figured that she was playing some kind of joke on me about the whole "award" thing. I took the envelope and pulled out a certificate which read:

****

Society of Splendid Spouses

hereby certifies

Marc Gellman

a

Heavenly Hubby

and thoroughly marvelous mate who's not only my best friend, cherished companion, and faithful lover, but also my very partner in life. I'm sure glad we're on the same side.

PRINCE CHARMING LIVES HERE

B.Mine

SECRETARY

****

I read the certificate twice and stared at it for a few moments, not knowing what to say. When I turned to look at Barbara, I saw in her eyes that this wasn't a joke. This award was proof that I had the most understanding and loving wife that any man could have. I wondered if I deserved her. Feeling embarrassed for having been silly at the wrong time, I gave Barbara a kiss and we went upstairs, where our evening of celebrating our anniversary continued.

CHAPTER 19

Belief in her faith

We had a two-year overlap with our family's Bar and Bat Mitzvah years and our college years. Our Bar Mitzvah years started with Barbara's B'nai Mitzvah in May 1987 and ended with Brian's Bar Mitzvah in May 1995. And our college years started with Jonathan leaving for college in September 1993. During these years, Barbara became increasingly involved with our temple and was installed as President of the temple in September 1994.

For Barbara, belief in her faith and her devoted involvement in our temple had become increasingly important to her. It gave her the faith for healing and forgiveness for any cause of her illness. Barbara brought the spirituality from her temple experiences into the day-to-day lives of our family, with peace of mind, belief in ourselves, and positive spirit.

Barbara's kick-start for increased temple activity began back in 1988. Back then, Barbara was in line for becoming the president of the sisterhood. I so remember our conversation, prior to her becoming the president. I explained to Barbara that based upon my recollection of sisterhood presidents, from when I was a kid in Brooklyn, she didn't qualify.

That conversation happened over dinner one evening. It was just the two of us and Barbara asked, "What do you mean, I don't qualify?"

"You just don't qualify."

Barbara gave me a puzzled look. "What are you talking about? Why?"

"Because, I remember one president of sisterhood, in particular, from when I was a kid. Her name was Rose. She was a few inches taller than you and had a big mouth and big tits. That's how it was back then. All of the women who held that position had those attributes."

The expression on Barbara's face quickly turned from puzzled to rolling her eyes and laughing. Barbara always knew when I was about to make up some sort of silly shit.

"I should have expected that you'd come up with some wild comments about this," she said. "When we were teenagers, I could believe some of the things you would make up. Since then, your spin on things never comes as a surprise to me at all. I can't wait to hear your further explanation. Because I know you too well and I'm sure you have more to say. So, let's hear the rest."

I stood up from the table and began pacing around the kitchen. I wanted to invoke a sense of deep thought and seriousness into the silly shit that I was about to come out with. But there were facts in my message. There really was a powerful-looking president of sisterhood named Rose. And Rose did have a big mouth and big tits. I was just planning to embellish the story a little and add some drama.

"Barbara, listen to me. I'm serious! Had you told me that you wanted to be the president of sisterhood someday, I would have recommended larger implants. Although, you may get disqualified anyway, just because you have breast implants from reconstructive surgery. That's like cheating or falsifying your qualifications and credentials."

"And you're telling me all this with your usual straight face. Silly, after all these years. Tell me—how do you come up with these things and make it sound so serious and sincere?"

I love doing stand-up. I don't tell jokes, just stories. And all my stories are real, based upon my own version of the story. As for Barbara, she was my best audience, ever since that day back as teenagers in the Rockaways. We lay together on a mattress in a vacant hotel room in the Breakers Hotel and Barbara was seeing through my bullshit. During all our years together, it was always a love game between us. So many years later, Barbara was never fooled by me and I always knew it. But I was always persistent.

"Listen, Barbara. This time I'm not joking. You need my advice on this, because some things never change. Back then, being the president of sisterhood required being tall and stout, with a big mouth and big tits. This was the only way that the president of sisterhood could combat being overshadowed by the other big-mouthed women. And especially, the president of the shul, who, back then, would only be a man. Otherwise, the president of sisterhood wouldn't have been able to get anything done her way and the sisterhood would have been at the mercy of what the men wanted the role of the sisterhood to be."

By this point, Barbara was sitting in her seat with a big smile and her arms crossed. In other words, she was enjoying the show, but was believing none of it. Still, with Barbara as my captive audience, I continued.

"Barbara, big women had a better chance, since men are intimated by big women. I remember the expression the men would say, with their heavy Yiddish accents, 'I'm not going to approach that woman. Because I don't want to fall into her mouth.' And, since these men were usually short, their heads were even with the height of the woman's tits and they would worry about being smothered by a pair of big tits."

Barbara rolled her eyes and laughed. "Is that it, or do you have more? Because I can't take any more of this. Just tell me, how long do you plan for this routine to go on? I can tell that you're enjoying yourself. By the way, what about the men who were the presidents of the shul?"

Barbara was a great straight man for me, all the more so because she didn't realize it. Sometimes, I would be about finished with my routine and then she would come out with a question like that.

"Yeah, the men. I'm happy you asked. I couldn't be as vocal about things without your prompting. The presidents were usually short, little old Jewish guys who, for sure, had little dicks."

In disbelief at my answer, Barbara laughed, uncrossed her arms, put her hands on each side of her face, and asked, "Oh, for God's sake. Okay tell me, I can't wait to hear this. Although, I'm not sure I really want to know. How do you know they had little dicks?"

"Because my dad was the treasurer of the shul and he would always refer to the president, by saying, 'He thinks he's a big shot, because he's president. But he's just a little schmuck.' (A Yiddish word, with an original, literal meaning as a vulgar term for penis). Listen, Barbara, trust me. I'm only trying to help prepare you for what you will be facing."

When I did these routines, Barbara would let me go on and on and eventually cut me off. Because, given the opportunity, I could have paced around that kitchen for hours, making shit up and entertaining myself.

Laughing, Barbara answered, "Well, thank you. Have you had your fun for the evening? Now you can load the dishwasher."

I'd had my fun and began to load the dishwasher. Loading the dishwasher was another pastime of mine. I didn't allow anyone else near the dishwasher. With my OCD, I knew that I could pack more dishes into that dishwasher than anyone else. Self-chosen, that job was mine.

Barbara served as the president of sisterhood from 1988 to 1990. Even though she was *not* a big-boned, zaftig, five-foot, ten-inch woman with a big mouth and oversized tits, Barbara was very effective and respected in her position. Which just goes to prove, there are always exceptions to the rule.

In 1994, Barbara was installed as the president of the temple. The installation of her presidency took place during a Sabbath service. As part of the installation, Barbara delivered an acceptance speech. Weeks before, Barbara had discussed her plans for her speech with me. She explained that she wanted the speech to have three messages: a recap of the many warm and wonderful occasions when she had the opportunity to be on the bimah in front of the congregation, an explanation of her observations regarding the behavioral patterns of the congregants with regard to their commitment to the temple, and a report of current events of the anti-Semitism happening in the world outside of temple and how these events will continue, due to the priorities of congregants.

Barbara explained to me that the first two parts of her speech would be safe and asked if the third part was appropriate for a temple installation. Well, she was asking the wrong person whether to include such a political statement. Because making a statement that might be inappropriate never stopped me.

It had been fifty-years since the Holocaust and our suburban Jewish community did react to incidents in the community in the recent years. Nevertheless, I felt that a strong reminder and wake-up call about the threat of anti-Semitism never hurt. With a strong forceful voice, I answered, "Yeah! You walk up to that podium and give 'em hell, Harry!"

"Who's Harry?" she asked.

"Harry Truman. I think he used to give people hell. Now, it's your turn."

As I write this, I realize that even though she asked for my opinion, by this time Barbara had become confident and secure with herself. She was ready to let loose, step forward, and unleash herself from the controls that silenced her during her childhood. I always believed that Barbara had a fire burning inside of her. And now, she was ready to self-ignite that fire. This was going to be the first time that Barbara would, without holding back, deliver a strong statement in public about her position and opinion.

Barbara was a strong person who had endured much and led our family through difficult times. I knew, for sure, she had the conviction to effectively say her piece. On the evening of the Sabbath installation service, Barbara stepped up to the podium and delivered her speech fearlessly and with confidence. Toward the end of her speech, she said:

These are frightening times for our communities. We read articles in the newspapers and magazines about the rise of neo-Nazism in our country. But this year, the promotion of anti-Semitism wasn't just in faraway locations. It wasn't just in remote places where we avoid traveling to. The ugliness of hatred came face-to-face with our children on their college campuses. It was on our television screens and in our communities. For the first time in many years, the words of anti-Semitism have been preached from the pulpit.

Just a few months ago, a paper was published that charged the Jewish people with monumental culpability for the evils of slavery and the slave trade. In a speech at a nearby college, a speaker called Jews "bloodsuckers."

Recently, in our own county, a Holocaust denier ran in the primary for a seat in Congress. The candidate not only denied the existence of the Holocaust but, also suggested that the Nazis tattooed Jews to identify them in much the same way Americans are identified by Social Security numbers. The Jewish community united and waged a successful write-in campaign to put the name of a new candidate on the November ballot, instead. One of our own congregants was the new candidate's campaign manager.

These are frightening times. We must reassess our values. There are congregants who weigh the cost of temple dues because they are reluctant to compromise their lifestyles. We must realize that our lifestyles will be threatened by the rise of anti-Semitism. The hatred cannot be tolerated. It is time to recognize the vital importance of a strong and unified Jewish community. It is time for us all to bond together.

As I take on the challenge of the presidency, I issue a challenge to each of you. Come join me in continuing the dreams of our temple founders and past temple presidents who recognized our temple's importance to our community. Help me to confront the problems we face as a temple and a community. Help me to reach out to congregants who need our help.

As I sat with pride and listened to Barbara deliver her installation speech, I kept thinking to myself, "Wow, that's my wife up there." Barbara often referred to herself as a shy, insecure girl from The Bronx. That evening, she was being installed as the president of our temple and addressing a packed congregation. Barbara no longer was that shy, insecure girl. That pretty girl with the dimples, the girl I met when I was fourteen, had come a long way. Looking around, I saw the congregation listening to Barbara's every word with respect for the accomplished woman she was.

Barbara delivered her speech with controlled confidence and conviction. With the courage of her words, Barbara spoke out about the issues facing our community. Today, twenty-five years later, I read the speech and my eyes are opened to again see the urgency of Barbara's call to reassess our values for action against the roots of anti-Semitism. Because over the course of twenty-five years, nothing has changed, and history shows us that "every generation has reminded us that we are Jews."

During her presidency, Barbara spent a lot of her personal time in temple, sometimes compromising her work schedule in favor of temple. To encourage my attendance in temple, Barbara often asked me to speak to the congregation during a Sabbath service, at times when the rabbi was away on sabbatical or for other reasons. She knew I enjoyed speaking in front of a captive audience and, by getting me involved, congregants could see that I supported Barbara in her role at the temple, which I did.

One evening in August of 1995, Barbara and I were watching TV. I was lying on the couch and Barbara was sitting right behind me when she began speaking about the Selichot service. Selichot is a prayer service that occurs the Saturday evening before Rosh Hashanah, the start of the Jewish High Holidays. I was preoccupied with the TV program and wasn't paying much attention to exactly what she was talking about.

"Marc, as president of the temple, I get to choose who will light the candles on the night of the Selichot service."

"That's nice," I answered.

"So ... I've decided to ask you. Would you like to light the candles?"

"What?" I needed a few seconds for my brain to interpret the question before I answered, "Absolutely not!"

"Why not? You always say yes when I ask you to give a mini-sermon to the congregation. And I always get great reviews about your speeches."

Barbara now had my full attention. She had never before mentioned to me that my speeches had gotten good reviews. I was instantly impressed with myself.

"Barbara, that's different. I like to speak in front of a captive audience, where I can express my opinion about issues and things and people need to be polite and sit and listen to my bullshit. Or act like they're listening. But I wasn't planning to attend the Selichot service, and I'm not interested in attending a service, just to say a prayer and light candles. Ask someone else."

Brushing off the brief conversation, I went back to concentrating on the TV program. But Barbara was always good at catching me at these weak moments, when I was preoccupied with something, in order to finagle a way to get me to do what she wanted. I fell into that trap often. With her perfect timing, Barbara knew how to manipulatively drop morsels of information that would eventually compel me to do exactly what she wanted. She started with a reverse psychology move. "Well, it's probably a bad idea anyway, to have you light the candles."

With that, she caught my attention. I was at her mercy. "Why is it a bad idea?"

"Because, it would be too controversial, and I don't need to hear and deal with the comments that would result from you lighting the candles."

"Wow," I thought to myself. Depending on how controversial it would be or what the controversy would be about, I figured it might be fun going to the service that evening.

"What's so controversial about it?"

"Because only women light the candles. A man has never lit candles at the service. When the president is a man, they've asked their wives or daughters or the president of sisterhood. When the president is a woman, she asks her daughter or someone from sisterhood. You'd be the first man to ever light the candles at a Selichot service, and I'd hear the complaining to no end—"

"Okay, I'll do it," I quickly blurted, before she could finish her sentence.

Women are incredible and just too cunning for us men to compete with. When we want our wives to do something that we know, in advance, that they won't want to do, we just come out and ask. Most often, the answer, "no," comes quickly and we have no recourse or any conceivable idea how to change the no to a yes. But women have men all figured out. They've got their strategy prepared ahead of time, to get us to do whatever they want us to do. Men just don't have a chance against women's instincts, intuition, and subtle cunningness.

Back to the candles. At past services, when the candles were lit, congregants could hardly hear the prayers, since there wasn't a microphone at the candle-lighting location. Being spiteful, and in order to further inflame the potential controversy, I wanted everyone to hear me. I recited the prayer as strongly and loudly as I could. They could hear me all the way to the back of the congregation.

As I left the bimah to go back to my seat, I turned to Barbara. She smiled and gave me a wink. After the service, Barbara told me that as I walked up to light the candles I had a devilish smile on my face. Also, she saw the looks on the faces of some congregants, wondering what was going on with having me light the candles. I loved hearing that, and Barbara knew it. Telling me was her way of rewarding me for lighting the candles.

Barbara served as the president of the temple from 1994 to 1996. After, she remained active as the immediate past president and was appointed to be the temple's representative for Synagogue 2000, a national renewal movement for temples to revitalize prayer and song to attract more members, while sustaining existing membership. With this affiliation and from attending workshops for Synagogue 2000, held in Ojai, California, Barbara met new friends and contacts from other temples around the country and kept in touch by phone and email. And, from the information she learned at the workshops and from her new contacts, Barbara organized and led workshops at our temple.

Things couldn't have been going better for us. With Jonathan and Kristen away at college and Brian in high school, we started to enjoy being almost empty nesters. It was beyond our comprehension that our lives could ever change, and new challenges would take over. And it would be Barbara's belief in her faith that would bring her through the next ordeal. Although she would never lose her faith, Barbara would lose her temple; the house of worship that she loved.

CHAPTER 20

Mommy has cancer

In early February 1997, Barbara began feeling an annoying tingling sensation in her left shoulder. The sensation persisted and our family physician referred Barbara for a surgical consultation. The surgeon performed an electromyography (EMG) procedure to assess the health of muscles and the nerve cells. The test proved negative for any problem.

Over the months that followed, the tingling sensation persisted, on and off. Finally, nine months later, at the beginning of November 1997, Barbara was sent for an MRI and then a CT scan. Both showed a soft tissue mass under the joint where the arm connects to the shoulder, an area where vessels and nerves enter and leave the arm. A biopsy of the tumor was done on November 11. The results confirmed recurrent metastatic breast cancer.

I was at work when Barbara called me. I immediately heard the cry in her voice.

"Oh, Marc ... the results weren't good. The cancer is back. How is it possible to have breast cancer, all these years after having a double mastectomy?"

"I'm leaving the office now. I'm on my way home."

As I pulled into the driveway, I felt overcome with déjà vu. I was back in time, reliving the same moment all over again. I was scared shitless. I think more than the times before, and I didn't know why. Maybe because this cancer had traveled from the breast to another place. Or, maybe I felt our luck had run out and there would be no more miracles for us. I didn't know. I just didn't know what it was that made this time more frightening. I was confused and so very scared. I couldn't handle hearing, once again, Barbara's cry, "Oh, Marc ... I don't want to die." I didn't have the courage to go inside the house. But I had to, and I did. Once again, I made my slow walk into the house, trying to build up any courage to begin to face this news. Barbara ran to me with a cry and a hug and then we sat on the couch in the family room, numb.

Our family physician referred us to an oncologist in Morristown, New Jersey, Dr. Jeffrey Stern. Coincidentally, the oncologist's daughter was a friend of Kristen's from sleepaway camp. Years before, Barbara had said, "Kristen's friend's father is an oncologist in Morristown. I hope I never need to see him, other than as the father of one of Kristen's friends."

Barbara quickly was able to get an appointment with Dr. Stern and we met with him on November 19. As soon we walked into the appointment, Barbara introduced us. Dr. Stern remembered meeting us at the camp, or at least he remembered Kristen. That familiarity and commonality helped to ease the tense appointment for us. At least the doctor wasn't a total stranger.

Dr. Stern gave us more information about the tumor, its size, and where it was located. He described its location as a difficult spot to deal with and suggested two options. He recommended we meet with a medical oncologist and a surgical oncologist in New York City. At the same time, he cautioned us that the surgeon may not recommend surgery. Because of the location of the tumor, the surgery could result in Barbara losing use of her arm. Dr. Stern then explained that if the surgery was out of the question, the alternative would be stem cell transplant.

I didn't know what stem cell transplant was. But Barbara did. As soon as she heard those words, she burst out in tears. I just sat there, confused at what I had missed. Barbara grabbed hold of my hand and cried out, "Oh, Marc ... stem cell is the last resort when there is nothing else that can be done."

Dr. Stern quickly interrupted. "Barbara, we're going to take one step at a time. First you will meet with a surgical oncologist to review the feasibility for surgery and then you will meet with a medical oncologist to talk about stem cell. After, I'll get a report from them and we will meet again to discuss next steps."

To this point, we hadn't mentioned anything to the kids. Our two oldest were away at college, Jonathan at the University of Maryland at College Park and Kristen at the University of Massachusetts at Amherst. Brian was in high school. When we got into the car to go home, Barbara said, "Marc, you need to tell the kids about what's going on. Brian will be home from school when we get there. Tell him first and then call the others."

The house seemed eerily quiet when we walked in. Brian was upstairs in his room. Barbara went to the family room and I began to climb the stairs. My feet felt so very heavy. I couldn't have taken each step any slower. I so wanted to delay having to face what I needed to do, for as many minutes as possible. But I eventually came to Brian's room. He was sitting on the floor doing something when I walked in. When Brian looked up at me, I could see that my being home in the afternoon surprised him. Seeing my face, Brian knew something was up and it wasn't going to be good.

I slowly sat down on the floor and faced Brian. As I looked into his face, it was so difficult for me to speak and hide the fright in my voice. I began to cry. I pushed out the words.

"Mommy is downstairs in the family room ... We just came back from an appointment with a doctor in Morristown ... Mommy has had a tingling in her shoulder for several months and we had it checked out ... We found out that it's a tumor ... and it's malignant."

Brian's eyes began to tear up and in the most weeping voice, he asked, "Mommy has cancer?"

In a voice just above a whisper, I answered, "Yes."

As Brian cried, he repeatedly said, "Mommy has cancer! ... Oh! ... Mommy has cancer ... I've been treating her like shit, and she has cancer ... I've been treating Mommy like shit ... She has cancer."

We continued to sit on the floor, facing each other. I listened as Brian kept repeating over and over, "Mommy has cancer." His voice was haunting. He looked destroyed, reminding himself of his past behavior. After a few moments, I said, "Mommy is downstairs. You can see her. I'm going to my room and call Jonathan and Kristen. They don't know anything yet."

The sounds of Brian's cries have never left me. Twenty-one years later, I can still hear, and feel in my heart, his voice that day.

As slowly as I climbed the stairs to speak with Brian, that's how slowly I dialed the phone to call Jonathan. I called him at his fraternity, but he wasn't there. I left word for him to call me back. Then, I tried Kristen at her sorority. Surprised that I was calling, she quickly caught on that I was crying and, although she didn't know what I was about to tell her, Kristen began to cry too. Hearing her cry made it difficult for me to force the words out. I repeated the words I had used to tell Brian and with that she cried harder and said, "Daddy ... I'm coming home."

I waited a few minutes and tried to call Jonathan again. The kid who answered the phone said he had just seen Jonathan and I heard him shout out asking if anyone else had seen him. I left another message. Fifteen minutes later, another message. Finally, Jonathan called back.

"Hi, Dad. I got a few messages ... is everything okay?"

"No ... it isn't," was all I was able to say, as I began to cry.

Jonathan's voice got very serious, and he began to comfort me, repeatedly saying, "Okay, Dad. Okay, Dad ... slow, Dad ... slow, Dad."

And when I was able to get out the words to tell him, he answered, "I'm coming home."

Until I spoke with the kids, I hadn't cried. I had been able to hold back my emotions to support Barbara. But telling the kids brought it all out of me and I couldn't handle it. Once the crying started, I couldn't stop. When I regained my composure, I went downstairs to the family room and sat beside Barbara. I put my arm around her, and she cuddled up against me with her head against my chest. I began to talk slowly, just above a whisper. "So ... I spoke with the kids. They both said that they're coming home. I told them that you're okay and there's no need to come home, since it is a four-hour drive for each of them."

"Marc, let them come home. Don't discourage them. They just want to see me and make sure that I'm okay. Once they see me, they'll feel better."

"Okay. They're both going to call you later. You can say that you need a hug from them in person and they'll feel better."

The kids did come home and once the initial tears were over, we did have smiles and some laughs over the weekend. Barbara continuously assured the kids that she felt good and she was going to be fine.

That week, Barbara and I attended both consultations that Dr. Stern had recommended. It was clear that the surgery would surely leave Barbara's arm immobile. For that reason, both doctors recommended the stem cell transplant. Barbara and I discussed the options. Regardless of the uncertainty of the outcome, we decided that we wanted to go ahead with the surgery. Barbara and I could accept the handicap, in exchange for certainty that the cancer would be gone.

On December 5, we went to our follow-up appointment with Dr. Stern. He had received reports from both consultations, with their recommendations. Barbara started talking first. "Dr. Stern, we know what the recommendations are and the consequences. But Marc and I have talked about it and we've decided that we'd prefer the surgery and will live with the consequences."

Dr. Stern answered, "Barbara, you've already been through a lot. But you're a young woman, only forty-six; too young to lose the use of your arm. We can't be sure that there isn't another cancer cell some other place in your body. We want to get you many more years without any handicap. I see no role for an aggressive surgical approach and recommend going forward with aggressive induction chemotherapy, with the most active combination regimen and followed by stem cell transplant, followed by focused radiation therapy to any residual mass."

Barbara was very upset. We had thought we had our own plan. But it all changed now. I felt very uneasy. Barbara and I had discussed our options. And we believed that we were making the right decision for us, being fully aware of the possible consequences. Our decision seemed to be so simple. Now, we were being encouraged to undergo a long, drawn-out process of treatments. But we had quickly bonded with Dr. Stern and we trusted him. I asked, "Where would we go for all this?"

Dr. Stern spoke with sincerity, a gentle smile, and a sense of sureness. His personality and his own family made it easy for us to relate to him. Barbara and I felt as if we had known him for years.

Dr. Stern answered, "You're very fortunate that stem cell transplant is being performed here in New Jersey, at Hackensack University Medical Center. Barbara will start off with several months of chemotherapy at Morristown Memorial, under my direction, and then go to Hackensack for stem cell rescue."

"When does all this start?" I asked.

"We can start the chemotherapy in a few days, on the ninth."

I answered, "Dr. Stern, in two weeks, on the twenty-first, is our son's college graduation from the University of Maryland. If Barbara starts the treatment on the ninth, will she be okay for that trip?"

"Yes, you'll be okay for that trip. The chemotherapy will not have built up in your system by the twenty-first, and you can't miss your son's graduation. Barbara, I suggest that you purchase a wig soon. You will lose your hair. I can't predict exactly when. But it will be quick, and you should get prepared ahead of time."

Barbara purchased a wig in preparation for her chemotherapy, which started on December 9. It would be four cycles of induction chemotherapy, high doses in the initial treatment in preparation for the stem cell. Barbara tolerated the early treatments well and a couple of days before the weekend of December 21, we headed down to Maryland, with Kristen and Brian, for Jonathan's graduation.

On the morning of December 21, we opened the curtain in our

hotel room and the sun shone in. We were so excited and walking on air. Barbara was smiling and feeling well. After all, our first child was graduating from college.

I showered first and then Barbara. As I was getting dressed, I heard a shout of distress from Barbara. "Oh, Marc!" As I rushed to the bathroom, the first thing I noticed was Barbara looking into the mirror, with the hair dryer in her hand, and tears running down her cheeks. Then, I saw the hair all over the bathroom, walls, floor, and ceiling.

It was going so well up to that moment. Barbara didn't have a problem while in the shower and shampooing her hair. But, when she began to blow-dry it, much of her hair fell out and the dryer blew her wet hair all over the bathroom. She still had a lot of hair, but it was very thin, and she cried, "Oh, Marc, what am I going to do now?"

"You brought the wig with you, just in case ... right?"

"Yes, I did."

"Okay, so that's what you have the wig for. This is no surprise. The only surprise is ... is that when you started to blow out your hair, you didn't expect to literally blow out your hair."

Barbara's tears changed to a laugh and she said, "Silly ... you are so silly."

"Listen, I'll stand behind you with a towel to catch any hair that blows out, while you blow-dry the rest of your hair. This way we can dry your head and any hair that's left."

After finishing with the hair dryer and to lighten things up, I said, "You know what? The manufacturer of that hair dryer has all kinds of warnings listed on the box. Those bastards should have a warning about the danger for blow-drying hair for people on chemotherapy."

We were able to get some laughs out of this. And we were lucky that Barbara brought the wig with her. The cleanup was so difficult, the hair was wet, and it stuck to everything. When we heard knocking on the door, Barbara became frantic. "Marc, that must be the kids. They're expecting us to have been ready by now. Don't let them in. I can't have them see me like this and I don't want them to know what happened."

"You mean you can't have them see you like this because your hair blew out? Or is it because you're standing there naked?"

I went to the door but didn't open it. Looking through the peep hole, I saw it was the kids and shouted, "Who is it?"

Kristen and Brian answered, "It's us, let us in."

"We're not dressed yet. Mommy and I are still naked and I'm chasing her around the room. We'll meet you in the lobby."

Kristen answered, "Ick. Did you have to tell us that you're still naked together?"

"Well, grow up and go down to the lobby," I answered.

Barbara and I finished getting dressed and then she went into the bathroom to put on the wig. I waited, quite nervous, hoping it would look good. I knew Barbara would be destroyed if there was a problem and would feel that she put a damper on this occasion. She came out from the bathroom, stood, and looked at me. With a sorrowful tone in her voice, Barbara asked, "How do I look?"

I smiled and walked up to her, put my hands on her hips, looked into her eyes, and gave her a soft kiss. For, in my eyes, Barbara could only look one way ... beautiful. And I knew Barbara could see my innermost feelings in my face and feel them in my kiss. She smiled with her dimples, so very cute.

The graduation weekend couldn't have been any more wonderful. We reminisced about it during the long drive home to New Jersey. We talked about how Jonathan led the parade of his class entering the graduation recital, with his arms and hands making the movement like he was raising the roof. When Barbara and I were lying in bed that evening, Barbara said, "I made it through, and I felt fine. Thank you."

"For what?" I asked.

"For cleaning up all my hair in the bathroom. I'm going to Frank tomorrow and have him shave off the rest of my hair. Once again, I'll be totally bald. Are you ready for that?"

Barbara continued with her induction chemotherapy at Morristown Memorial Hospital and finished the four cycles by the end of February 1998. On March 10, she had an apheresis catheter surgically placed on her in preparation for the double high-dose chemotherapy for the pre-stem cell harvesting. She was discharged on March 14. Then, we had to wait until Barbara's white blood cell count reached a certain level for her to begin the stem cell harvesting and rescue, at Hackensack University Medical Center.

From December through April, Barbara was in and out of the hospitals much of the time. As I left for work in the morning and returned home from the hospital around ten at night, I often lost track of caring for Brian, a sixteen-year-old. He was left alone, with Jonathan living on his own and Kristen away at college.

On our way home from one Barbara's discharges from Morristown Memorial, Barbara asked, "What are we doing for dinner? I'm hungry."

I was so happy to hear her say that she was hungry, because most of the time she had no appetite and I had to plead with her to try to eat something. But at that moment, I was so exhausted and couldn't think about what we were going to do for dinner. It took so much energy just to order something from the restaurant and then to go and pick it up. Plus, the thought of eating restaurant food, for yet another evening, was nauseating. "Let's get home first and then I'll figure out dinner."

As we drove onto the driveway, Barbara asked, "What's that big package on the bench in the portico?"

"I don't know. I hope it's something that we can eat. Let me get you into the house first, then I'll bring in that package."

As Barbara sat at the kitchen table, I emptied the package. Inside was a full home-cooked meal: a giant roast chicken, stuffing, mashed potatoes, soup, home-baked bread, homemade jam, and dessert. We salivated at the aroma and the sight of real food. Then I heard Brian walk into the house. "Brian, come here," I shouted.

Brian, being Brian, came at his own pace. I don't know what he was putzing around with in the family room. Finally, after a few minutes, he slowly came up the stairs from the family room to the kitchen and asked, "What's up?"

"We have real food for tonight! A real dinner," I answered.

"Who left this for us?" Barbara wondered. "Look for a note."

I figured there had to be a note somewhere in this package. I checked each item from the package, thinking that maybe a note had been taped to something. I even checked our answering machine for messages. But there was no note or any message on our phone. "This is strange that the food would be waiting for us. Who would have known when we'd be home? There is no note, no message anywhere, and nothing on our answering machine. You know ... this food must have been sent to us from God. It has to have been. It certainly appears that way."

More than a week passed and we still hadn't found out where the food came from. We became more and more certain that it was a gift from God. Then, Brian came home from school one day and told us that a kid in his class had asked him how we enjoyed the food. It turned out that the food was from the Roberts family, an acquaintance of ours in the community. Their son was a classmate of Brian's.

As Brian was telling us this, I recalled that I had seen the Roberts a couple of times that week. Each time in passing, they had a graceful smile and said hello, without any mention of the food. About a week after their son told Brian, I saw the Roberts again and walked over to thank them. They said they were happy to do it and their son wasn't supposed to tell anyone that they had prepared the food.

There was something extra special about that food. Because, as we ate, we could taste the love and kindness coming from someone's heart. We so needed that kind of love. Even so, Barbara and I didn't stop believing that the food was a gift from God, and it was the Roberts family who had volunteered to carry out God's wishes. Because ninety-five percent of people are great.

Through all this, I had the easier part. It was Barbara who had to endure the mental trauma and chemical torture to her body. I've heard of many people, even strong, burly men, who couldn't endure the regimen for stem cell transplant and gave up. But with Barbara, we were able to find some good and fun in it all. After losing her hair, Barbara had a sock hat that she wore in the hospitals. I loved the way she looked in that hat. She looked so cute. When she smiled, the combination of her dimples and that hat was actually a turn-on for me. I would laugh when I came in for a kiss and Barbara would say, "What's so funny?"

My answer would be, "You look so silly in that hat and I like it. You always say that I'm so silly. Well, I really like you being the silly one for a change."

"Don't get too used to it," Barbara would reply. "This hat is going in the garbage when my hair comes back."

"For now, I like the sock hat. When your hair starts coming back, it will be short, and you'll look like Halle Berry. So, it's not all that terrible."

"Why? Do you fantasize being with Halle Berry?"

"No ... not with Halle Berry ... with her look-alike," I answered.

Barbara would ask, "You really love me, right?"

"No," I would answer, "you're too ugly for me."

Barbara would laugh. She knew how I felt about her just by the look in my eyes and when we kissed and snuggled together. And at her darkest and roughest time at Hackensack, Barbara never complained or demanded anything of me. All she asked was for me to cuddle up next to her on the hospital bed. So, I asked a nurse to help me move Barbara a little, so that I could lie beside her. But the nurse advised that because of Barbara's immune system, I was not permitted to lie next to her in bed and all I could do was to place a chair against the bed and hold her hand.

Hearing that, I guess I had a sorrowful, disappointed look on my face. Because about ten minutes later, two nurses pushed a lounge chair/bed into the room and placed it tightly up against Barbara's hospital bed. The nurse explained that the chair/bed could be transformed into many positions. She lowered the back and raised the leg part to resemble the exact position and contour of the hospital bed.

Although they were not allowed to lower the side rail on the hospital bed, the nurse suggested I lay close to the rail and make believe it wasn't there. I did, and after the nurse left the room, I turned to

Barbara. "I'm going to make believe that the rail isn't here and we're both naked. How about you?"

Barbara whispered back, "I'm going to make believe that we're both at home in our own bed."

"And we're both naked?"

"You're so silly."

It had been hard times for my family, with the stress. Sometimes I didn't know where I was, as confusion and exhaustion came over me. From the beginning of November, when we first learned of the test results, it was a difficult six months. It wasn't until April 23, after being away from home with Barbara for the previous ten days, as she finished at Hackensack, when I found a moment to feel some calmness, after settling in at home and helping Barbara to bed. It felt so good to lay next to Barbara knowing that the treatments were over. In minutes, we were both restfully asleep.

But Barbara wasn't all done. On June 2, she had a CT scan to determine if there was any remaining mass in her shoulder. The scan showed a two-centimeter mass still there and she began a schedule of radiation therapy to resolve the remaining mass. And then ... we were all done.

CHAPTER 21

Live ... Love ... Laugh

We were cancer free! Hip-hip-hooray! For eight months, from November 1997 until June 1998, Barbara had been in and out of hospitals, and back and forth for various kinds of treatments. By the end of June, Barbara and I were starting our lives again. It was a new beginning.

Barbara had gone through the stem cell transplant, an extremely difficult course of treatments to endure. We had heard about some people who had quit in the early stages of the treatment, unable to withstand the grueling effects. But Barbara was a fighter and her belief in her faith gave her the strength to focus only on healing.

During most of this period, Barbara was unable to attend temple services. She kept her prayers inside of her. At the beginning of her treatments, friends from temple called. But most of those callers quickly faded away. There were some temple friends who did visit Barbara in the hospitals and kept in touch with me.

Several times over the months of treatments, Barbara asked me if I'd heard from certain people. I hadn't. With almost no outreach to us, Barbara was disappointed with the temple she loved. With the temple where we had celebrated so many wonderful occasions. With the temple where she had devoted so much of herself.

The temple was one of the first things that Barbara talked to me about after being discharged from the hospital in late April. We were quietly relaxing, cuddled up on the couch in the family room, and looking out to the yard. Out of the quietness, Barbara said, "I haven't lost my faith ... only my temple. I need to heal. In order for me to heal, I can't carry any anger. Although I'm done with some friends, I have to move on, with forgiveness. That's the only way I can heal."

In early May 1998, about two weeks after Barbara was discharged from Hackensack, she received a call from a friend from temple. The conversation went like this.

"Hi, Barbara, I was happy to hear that you are home now."

"Yes, I was discharged two weeks ago," Barbara answered.

"Barbara, you've been really good through all this. You remember my friend Cindy, who passed. When Cindy was ill, she was always calling on me to run around with her and help with her kids. But you were considerate of others and held your own. Anyway, a group of us from the temple have chipped in together and will be sending you food. Any day better for you?"

Later that evening, as Barbara was telling me about this conversation, I interrupted her. "I hope you told her to go fuck herself and shove the food up her ass."

Barbara laughed. "That's what I wanted to say. But I didn't." Barbara believed that arguing with those people wasn't going to help her recovery or healing. Barbara needed to find peace with the friends from temple, forgive them, end the dysfunctional friendships, let them go, and move on.

Barbara continued relating the conversation. She had patiently waited for her turn to speak before answering, "Oh, my ... I was wondering when I'd get a call. I want you to know that it wasn't important for the group to wait all these months, until I got home. I'm hardly eating. But Marc and Brian were home, and Marc almost collapsed under the stress of my illness and hospitalization ... and no one cared. Now, it took two weeks for the group of you to get your act together. I can't figure out why my friends were invisible the whole time. Anyway ... we don't need your food. Your help is too little and too late. We are set for food through friends from my office and the parents from Brian's basketball team."

The friend answered, "Well I'm sorry if you feel that your friends have disappointed you."

Barbara politely said goodbye. It was the last time that she wanted anything to do with that so-called friend and the rest of that group. She was disappointed with our temple.

A few days later, when I got home from work that evening, there was a box on the floor in the family room. Barbara was sitting on the couch and I asked, "What's in the box? How come you haven't opened it?"

"I don't know. It was delivered this afternoon. When I noticed that the return address was that novelty-gift store in Randolph, I figured it was some kind of junk. Open it up and let's see."

When I opened the box, I found a card inside. It was from the temple group who planned to send the food a few days earlier. In the box was all kinds of little novelty gifts, pens, note pads. After emptying the box, I asked, "I wonder why they sent us all this crap?"

Barbara answered, "Because, they had already collected the money and when I said I didn't need their food, they sent this. Obviously, they needed to do something to make themselves feel good."

"Okay," I answered. "Where should I put all this shit?"

"I don't want any of it in the house. Just throw it out in the garbage. I want no memory of any of those people. I want to forgive them and forget them."

"Even this pen? Barbara, this looks like a good pen."

"Marc, throw it all out!"

"Well, you should, at the least, send them a note, so they'll know you received this. All you need to write is, 'I received the box of shit that you sent. So, thank you very much, kiss my ass, and goodbye.'"

Barbara laughed and said I needed to let it go. She was calm and accepting of the situation and stressed that we needed to move on.

"Yeah, maybe I should write them a note. But I'm not going to. Just throw it all out and I'm done with those people."

My family had loved our temple, especially Barbara. She had devoted so much of herself and gave respectful recognition to the few original founders who were still around in the late 1990s. Barbara diligently worked, along with most other congregants, to continue the goodness that those founders had aspired the temple to be. Their aspirations were what I had learned at the temple's adult confirmation class. It was what I discovered there, and what my grandmother always knew: "With our faith, we search for what's good and pray for the goodness we do, to live on and on."

But although there was much goodness about the temple, there was an underlying issue that had been festering for several years. Influenced by a group of congregants, there was a growing disdain for the rabbi. And such disdain began to be talked up. It was an issue which some influential congregants, like Barbara, were either unaware of or ignored.

Barbara would ignore and excuse such disdain, saying, "It's nothing more than certain congregants fussing over the rabbi's salary, housing allowance, and other benefits. They're bothered that the rabbi earns so much more than they do, and he has such a sweet benefit package." Barbara believed this to be the root of congregants' issues. But increasingly, congregants began talking down about the rabbi. With a negative spin, they dissected everything that he said and did.

Barbara, along with many other congregants, viewed the rabbi much differently. The rabbi worked, like, seven days a week. And he often had late evening hours, with such things as teaching the adult confirmation classes. On call for so many hours of the day, the rabbi carried around his responsibilities to his congregation on his shoulders all the time. Regardless of this, some congregants felt that the rabbi positioned himself in the middle of temple matters, beyond the boundary of his spiritual responsibilities. And that he attempted to influence and control the temple's board of directors.

About this time, a new cantor was hired, who was liked by some and disliked by others. It developed that the congregants who had disdain for the rabbi, liked the cantor. And congregants who liked the rabbi had disdain for the cantor. As if these goings-on weren't bad enough, this rift was evolving into bigger issues that were to come. Yep, the silliness had begun. Congregants took sides and it was like junior high school once again.

I call it silliness. But the silliness of the conflicting opinions about the clergy caused serious and increasing dissent. Serious enough that the original aspirations of the temple founders were changing, and values were deteriorating quickly. Congregants' priorities for what they wanted out of the temple experience were growing further apart. Suddenly, a wave of congregants was pushing their own opinion about what the spiritual responsibilities of the rabbi should be, versus the cantor's. It was as though the spirituality at the temple was being overshadowed by who should do what and questioning why the rabbi had so much say about the temple. It began to appear that some congregants had been dissatisfied with the spiritual practices of the temple for several years.

As arguments between congregants became the norm at temple, it quickly became obvious that the underlying issues challenging the temple's soul and spirituality were more significant than just conflicting opinions about clergy. Barbara summed up the issues in a letter to the rabbi, dated April 2, 1998, when she wrote, "The temple has become a Bar Mitzvah mill with weekly theme services, designed to hook people into attending. It has become a congregation of parking-lot parents who care little about Judaism. It has become a place where the Jewish spouse in an intermarried couple, already feeling guilt, and unsure of their own Judaism, can have their child be a Bar Mitzvah. This is not what Judaism is about."

The arguing led to shouting at meetings, abandoning civil and orderly discussion. I attended a meeting when a congregant was shouting his anger about temple using vulgar language, disrespectful and unacceptable for a house of God. Even worse, he had his young son with him, and his vulgar language still had no limits. As I witnessed his behavior, I wondered, "Does this man expect the goodness we do to live on and on, with his foul mouth in front of his son?" When I approached a temple board member about such language in temple, he responded, "Marc, it's only words. It wasn't directed at anyone." Certainly, a sad answer.

As immediate past president, Barbara was caught in the downward spiral, as conflicts and infighting became a daily occurrence. The situation had gotten so badly out of control that during a meeting at temple, attended by the rabbi, cantor, temple president, and Barbara, an argument occurred in which the cantor called Barbara, "the bitch from hell."

Barbara and I spoke out publicly about the changes we saw and about the morality that had been lost at temple. In reaction to our outspokenness, an uninformed coward anonymously sent us a very nasty letter. The letter had no signature and no return address. The writer didn't have the courage to challenge me publicly. Instead, wrote a bullying letter to me stating that I was crazy. It went on to state that I had neglected my wife when she needed me the most and that Barbara had to depend on others from the temple to drive her for treatments to New Haven, Connecticut.

The writer was referring to Barbara's first cancer, seventeen years before, when she was treated with radiation therapy. But Barbara didn't commute back and forth to New Haven for treatments. She lived with the Blooms, our friends in New Haven, for all those weeks of treatments. After her treatments, Barbara had follow-up exams with the doctor in New Haven and she had a girlfriend from the temple keep her company for the drive. The exam took minutes and then Barbara and her girlfriend would visit and have lunch with Naomi Bloom.

The writer ended the letter with the statement, "It is obvious the problems of last year at temple have left you bitter. I strongly suggest you seek professional help."

At first reading, Barbara and I found the letter to be quite disturbing. But within minutes, Barbara and I found it quite amusing, laughable, and satisfying. After all, who was the one who really needed professional help, and what kind of sick asshole would write such a letter?

We read the letter again. Now we were hysterically laughing, thinking about this person harboring this feeling toward me and eating their kishkas out for seventeen years. (Kishkas is the Yiddish word for stomach intestine.) Finally, this person had decided to let their frustrations out in an anonymous letter. This was obviously an angry person, who had no life. We showed the letter to several people and the unanimous opinion was that the writer was probably that real weird guy with the farbissina (sourpuss) face. Many of the people at temple thought that they recognized his words and referred to him as a schmuck.

As Barbara and I attended services at other temples, we grew to believe our temple was becoming not a Jewish place to be. For all the years that we were members, our temple had been wonderfully caring, an extended family that cared. We didn't see that any longer. Instead, when illness struck us, we discovered how uncaring the temple had become. To my family, the temple no longer felt like a house of God. It had become an undisciplined inhabited building, where you could flip a coin, and anything goes. The guy with the farbissina face and his cowardly, deranged letter helped us to come to this conclusion.

I resigned my family from our temple and Barbara wrote a letter to the rabbi. An excerpt from that letter reads:

> What terrible shame, that at this terrible time in my life, the temple that I loved has been taken away from me and my family. Instead, the temple has added to the stress of my illness. I hope that the wounds that the community has inflicted on me and my family will eventually heal. In the meantime, we will remain unaffiliated.
>
> I pray to God each and every day that I will once again be well and rid of this cancer. The treatment program is still a long one and I must learn to take one step at a time. These are scary times and now I must carry God with me every day on my own.

Unfortunately for houses of worship, they can be subject to some awful setbacks along the way, caused by conflicts and differences in opinions of clergy and congregants about the ways to practice faith and spirituality. As Barbara wrote in her letter to the rabbi, I believe that's what happened at our temple. During this time, temple etiquette and the temple's mission was forgotten by clergy and congregants, and my family and several others were hurt by the disruption.

It was a brief setback in the overall history of the temple, and I believe that no house of worship, in any denomination, is immune from this happening. My family's sad experience occurred way back in the late 1990s. Today, when I speak to current congregants, I hear about the wonderfulness of the temple. They tell me how clergy and congregants have come and gone over the many years and the wounds of the past have long since healed and been forgotten.

Although this experience left us bitter at the time, it has long since passed. My family has long since moved on and we didn't abandon our Jewishness. Barbara made sure that we continued to keep God in our home and prayed for the goodness we do, to live on and on. And today, our children are affiliated with their own temple, raising our three grandchildren in the Jewish faith.

Also, this experience was a lesson in how we should be more selective about choosing our friends. Sometimes, ignoring our intuition about our friends can come to bite us in the ass. Since ninety-five percent of people are great, we just need to avoid the five percent who are assholes.

I was uncertain about whether I wanted to include this experience in this book. Although it was a very ugly and hurtful time for my family, it is unfair to have any across-the-board negative opinions about houses of worship, from this experience. Nevertheless, I chose to include this experience, since it is a part of my family's history and story.

After Barbara's telephone conversation with a temple friend and the delivery of the gift box a few days later, I began to realize that Barbara was not easily getting beyond the hardship she had experienced. Even though she stressed that we needed to forgive and move on, it was most difficult for her at the times of day when she was alone. I wondered what to do to trigger a burst of sunshine that could remind Barbara about how fortunate we were; to help her transition from the traumatic months of illness to good health; to help her fill the void from the loss of our temple, and to refresh her outlook on the beautiful lives we had and should be looking forward to together.

One Saturday afternoon I went down the road to drop off some clothes at our dry cleaner in Chester, a nearby town. I wandered through the stores on Main Street trying to come up with some ideas and ended up in a jewelry store. As I entered the store and started to browse around, the jeweler asked if she could help. Sounding a little confused, I answered, "I hope so, because I'm not sure what I'm looking for. My wife is recovering from an illness and other problems and I'm looking for something. But I don't know what it is. Maybe something that she could wear all the time?"

The jeweler was bubbly and laughed at my confusion as she glanced around the store for ideas to present to me. Then she smiled and said, "I have it! How about a nice watch? Your wife will wear it all the time, always be looking at it and remembering it's from you."

She showed me the watch display. I looked at all the watches. But none called out to me. They seemed undistinguishable. To me, they were just a bunch of shiny objects that said nothing beyond delivering the time. But I wasn't sure. "Yeah, maybe a watch would be nice. But I don't think it does what I want. I think it could, if you had a watch that could talk and every time my wife looked at it, the watch would say something nice, a nice message, like ... smile. Otherwise, it's just a watch."

The jeweler laughed. I continued to browse around at the display cabinets on my own and then I spotted it. A necklace that read, "Live ... Love ... Laugh." I called the jeweler over and pointed to the necklace in the display. "That's it. I'll take that necklace."

"You know what, that necklace has a message that seems like it talks, and your wife can wear it all the time. It'll become a part of her everyday attire. I wish it was me who had suggested it."

It had been a while since I bought Barbara such a gift. As I watched the jeweler wrap the necklace, I was so excited.

When I got home, Barbara was sitting in the family room. She looked at me. "Why are you smiling, silly? What happened?"

"I bought you something when I was in Chester."

I sat down beside Barbara and handed her the small box. As she unwrapped it, she realized it was from the jewelry store. Barbara got excited and quickly opened the box. Her face lit up and a tear ran down her cheek. I began to choke up a little bit and had no words to say, as I watched Barbara's reaction.

"Oh, Marc, it's beautiful!" She put on the necklace and rushed to look at it in the mirror.

Looking in the mirror, she added, "I'm going to wear this all the time ... and you know what ... from now on, this is going to be my motto."

As Barbara continued to look at the necklace in the mirror, she repeated over and over, "Live ... Love ... Laugh ... Live ... Love ... Laugh." And, from that moment on Barbara did wear the necklace all the time, and the words did become her motto. She reinforced that motto to our children. The motto survived Barbara. In our children's homes, there are signs that read, "Live ... Love ... Laugh."

PART 4

Stories from the Fourth Day of Shiva

"Marc, her name is Sonia. Why do you keep calling her Sun-ya? Stop it already … it's annoying!"

CHAPTER 22

Freeing ourselves

For Barbara and me, there were things in our lives that had changed. But we hadn't changed. We plodded along and stayed the same. A few years had passed since suffering through Barbara's battle with her third cancer, the disappointment with losing our house of worship, and ending our relationships with temple friends. Immediately after all those experiences, we should have sold our home and moved on to reinvent ourselves and make a new beginning, in different surroundings. But we didn't.

In our minds, we wanted to believe that we had moved on and were doing fine. We began to be able to afford more. Two of our kids had graduated from college and were living on their own. With just one more to put through college, we were looking forward to the future years of being empty nesters, on our own once again as we were when we were newlyweds in Jackson Heights, Queens.

Barbara and I had so much going for us. Yet despite all the good that was happening for our family, with special occasions to look forward to, something just didn't feel right. We should have made a clean break from those past experiences and relationships.

Not accepting that things in our lives had changed, and we hadn't changed with them, was holding us back from freeing ourselves to enjoy all the good that was ahead of us.

Even with our children going off on their own, Barbara and I continued to make our lives only about our children. Jonathan moved to his own apartment in Caldwell, New Jersey, about forty minutes away from our home in Flanders. He lived there for about two years and then moved into New York City. Kristen moved into the city too, after college, and it was so much fun to visit the two of them, living nearby to each other on the Manhattan's East Side.

Kristen loved the excitement of living in the city, but Manhattan wasn't for Jonathan. He decided he wanted to move to Florida. Most of our family vacations had been in the Fort Lauderdale area, since my parents had retired to Sunrise, near Fort Lauderdale, in 1981, when the kids were young. With several family trips to Disney World, Florida was a big part of our children's childhood.

I tried to discourage Jonathan from moving away. Our kids had attended out-of-town colleges and it was nice to have everyone back together again. Jonathan was twenty-six years old. To me, Manhattan was an exciting place for a twenty-six-year-old. And important for me, I wanted to keep our family close. Barbara was a lot more accepting than I was. I wasn't accepting it at all. Barbara would say, "Marc, he's twenty-six and independently living on his own. And Florida is a nice place to visit. Give it up. He's planning to move to Florida."

I decided to give it one last shot. On one of Barbara and my visits to Jonathan at his Manhattan apartment, I asked him, "So, why do you want to move? New York City is the greatest city in the world."

"Manhattan is just not for me, Dad. It's too big and too busy. I don't feel comfortable living here. I'd like to move to Florida. We spent so much time down there when I was growing up and I like Florida. Also, I'd like to live nearby to Grandma and Grandpa and see them more often."

I had no comeback for that, and Jonathan had been so very respectful through my attempts to convince him not to move away.

After all, I couldn't hold him back. He was an independent, responsible, grown man. I began to see that he wasn't happy living in Manhattan and wanted something different. I wouldn't try to guilt him into living nearby to us. As a parent, my desire was for my children to be happy. I had just one more question.

"Why do you want to live nearby to Grandma and Grandpa? I got married to Mommy at twenty-two, just to be able to get away from them."

"That's funny, Dad! But seriously, I was thinking of maybe Tampa or some other place. Which part of Florida do you recommend?"

"Well, if you're set on Florida and I can't talk you out of moving, I think you should consider Miami, either the city or the beach. I don't think Tampa is for you and I don't think you'll like any other part of Florida. Miami is really where a lot of action is for young people."

Jonathan took my advice and Miami it was. He lined up a job with a real estate firm in downtown Miami, for May 2001. He was all set workwise. He needed an apartment. Through a friend, Jonathan was introduced to a girl in South Beach, who was looking for a roommate to share an apartment in a building called "The Grand Flamingo." Barbara flew down to Miami with Jonathan and he rented an apartment with the roommate.

On this trip, Jonathan had meetings for his new job and Barbara was on her own one afternoon, to wander around South Beach. She had fond childhood memories of visiting family there and it was very nostalgic for her to be back.

It was a warm, humid day (duh, it was South Beach in May) and Barbara went into a restaurant to get a drink. Jerry's Famous Deli, a Jewish/kosher style delicatessen, on Collins Avenue. Like so many South Beach restaurants, Jerry's had a bar. Barbara decided to sit at the bar and order a "real" drink. This was something that Barbara had never done before, by herself. In fact, this was something the two of us had never done before, even if we were together. But this was South Beach, a happening place that compelled Barbara to be daring. So, she ordered an alcoholic beverage. Barbara was so proud of herself and couldn't wait to call and tell her friend, Felice.

That evening Barbara called home. She was on a high, as she told me all about Jonathan's roommate and the apartment. She was talking cheerfully, quickly, and with a laugh in her voice. I had a good feeling as Barbara spoke. I could picture the big-dimpled smile on her face.

"Marc, I'm happy for Jonathan and to see him happy. South Beach is so beautiful, so alive and so different from the way I remember."

"Wonderful, it will be a nice place to visit, when we visit him and my parents."

"Also, you're not going to believe what I did today. I was walking around and got a little thirsty and I went into this restaurant. It had a bar and I ordered a real drink."

"Wow, good for you! You're such a big girl now."

"Yes, I'm all grown up." Barbara laughed. "I was proud of myself and called Felice to tell her and she said to me, 'You did that! Is there something wrong with you?'"

Barbara paused and then added, "Isn't it weird of her to say something like that?"

"You mean, you called Yenta? Oh, fuck her! Why did you call that jealous idiot anyway? Now you see why the kids can't stand her. And her husband is a pain in my ass too. Just loosen up and have some fun on your own and stop worrying about what anyone else thinks."

Taking a seat at the bar was a good step for Barbara. It was about time for us to step up and begin to reinvent our lives. So often, we fell into the trap of letting our lives be controlled by the opinions of others. That fall, we officially became empty nesters. Brian left for college in September 2000 and we were beginning to take baby steps in creating a new life for ourselves. Yet we still hadn't faced an issue that had been holding us back: how to be us.

After almost thirty years of marriage, we still hadn't found out what "being us" meant. We just knew that was what we wanted to be. During our "once upon a time," when we were living in our newlywed apartment in Jackson Heights, we often talked about the unknowns in our future. After a busy day, in bed after lights out, we'd lie on our backs and face the ceiling, wondering where we would eventually live and buy a house and have kids.

Now, almost thirty years later, many of our questions had been answered. But some of our conversations had not changed. Once again, I began to say, "I don't want to be like everyone we know! I want to be you and me." Barbara laughed and our conversation of almost thirty years ago continued, as if not a day had passed.

Barbara asked, "Are you on that kick again? What is being you and me?"

"I still haven't figured that out. I was hoping that by now, you knew. Because I don't. But that's what I want."

Barbara's answer, almost thirty years later, hadn't changed much. "You can't want something that you still don't know what it is."

"But it is, what I still want," I answered.

Maybe we really had found out what "being us" was. But we were avoiding taking action. Barbara and I were honeymooners during our first four years of marriage, until we had our first child in 1975. And it was twenty-five years later when we began having inklings of feeling like honeymooners again. The big difference was that during our first four years, we were on our own to make our own choices and decisions, with little to no influence from anyone.

Over the years, we had surrounded ourselves with very controlling, opinionated friends. We foolishly let them influence and smother us with their opinions and lifestyles and their standards of what was socially correct. Like Yenta, who had the negative advice about Jonathan being in his school's talent show. She and her husband would always come by to give their opinions when we were doing a project on our home. We'd let their opinions influence exactly what we intended to do. I often felt like saying to them, "Would you get the fuck out of here?" But I didn't. Instead, I listened politely.

We went out of our way to accommodate friends who influenced where we vacationed, movies we saw, and restaurants we went to. We would compromise being us, to avoid hearing shit from our friends. We were fulfilling their desires at the expense of our own desires. I don't exactly know how we attracted such friends. But over the years, they had become fucking pains in the ass, smothering us with their dumb-ass suggestions on everything.

It was long overdue for Barbara and me to get back to being on our own, with friends who weren't negative and overly opinionated. It is so wondrous to be married; to have a soul mate with whom to share experiences and make decisions. It's nice to have close friends, too. But not friends who negatively influence your life. We were beginning to realize that holding on to certain friendships took too much effort and wasn't worth it.

It was time to begin freeing ourselves. And, with an open mind, find a new circle of friends. Maybe by doing this, we could just be us. Even realizing this, Barbara was just not ready to write off some friends. But she did walk up to a bar on her own and proudly order a drink. This was an important step for Barbara; a beginning to freeing herself of the social opinions of others.

Ours was a difficult transition to the mindset of being empty nesters. We were parents, still worrying about how our children were doing, particularly Brian. He was the baby of the family. When Barbara and I spoke with Brian over the phone, he didn't seem totally happy away from home at college in Boston.

Brian once called me at work to tell me that he wanted to transfer to another college, Ohio State. I was in my office when my phone rang, and I answered it myself. When I heard Brian's voice, it scared the shit out of me. He had never before called me at work.

"Dad ... it's no fun, here at Northeastern. My friends from high school are telling me about all the fun and parties that they go to at their colleges. I want to transfer."

I breathed a sigh of relief. There was no problem, no emergency, just whiny bullshit from a kid who had everything. We were busting our asses to scrape together Brian's tuition payment, after having put through our two other kids before him. Now, the little fucker was calling about not having fun at college. Like, I was supposed to feel sorry about that. But I knew it was better to handle this rationally and calmly. This was Brian I was dealing with. The kid who had me moving tables for him before his Bar Mitzvah service.

"Brian, I hear you ... but I'd like you to stay at Northeastern. Mommy and I have been talking about how much you've grown up over the past months. As I speak to you now, I find it hard to believe that I'm speaking to Brian Gellman. You sound so mature, and you've grown so much in this short time. I can only attribute it to your experiences at Northeastern."

Although I joke about Brian and my jokes are truthful, my response to him was sincere.

Brian gave it one more try.

"But, Dad, the cost of tuition at the other colleges is half."

"Brian, the cost of college is not your business. That's a problem for me and your mother."

Brian remained at Northeastern. On June 4, 2001, a couple of weeks before the end of his first school year, we received an email.

Dear Mom and Dad,

I really want to thank you for how much you have given me. I know that I have not shown much gratitude toward the two of you. I'm sorry for that. I want to tell you that you are the greatest friends, as well as the greatest parents a son could have. And anyone is lucky to come into contact with such wonderful people, such as you. I know that Jonathan, Kristen, and I are the luckiest in the world, because we get the privilege to be around you. Your unique qualities have shaped me into the person I have become today and rubbed off on me greatly.

All that you have given me has led up to the best year of my life. This year was the best year of my life, all because of you. You had prepared me so much for going to college and, without your help, this great experience would not have happened.

Mount Olive might not have been the place for me in school. But Northeastern and Boston is the place for me. I wasn't the most positive student in high school, while not utilizing my potential. But here at Northeastern, I have been striving to be the best that I can.

I have learned so much this year and it has been everything that I wished it would be like. This has fulfilled all of my expectations of what college would be like. This is the best investment I think;

in my college education. Because I left Mount Olive so immature
and I'm going to return much smarter and more educated. Even
though I'm upset for leaving this great place, I'm still so very excited to come home. Thank you so much for everything and I love
you so much.

Love, Brian

Wow, being a parent is very rewarding ... most of the time. A
couple of weeks later, Brian came home for the summer. As he was
unpacking in his room, I walked in and asked, "Brian, Mommy and I
were happy to get your email. What changed for you?"

"Oh, I met some friends who I liked, and I did well at school and
made the dean's list and everything. And I know that Mommy told
my teachers at my high school about how I was doing, and you guys
were proud of me."

That response choked me up a little. Getting emotional, I turned
and left his room. He's my son and I love him. And I guessed he
loved us too.

In early July 2001, the family began to discuss two big upcoming milestones: Barbara's fiftieth birthday and our thirtieth wedding
anniversary. Kristen elected herself the organizer of the birthday
party, as long as I agreed to pay for everything. Kristen was living in
an apartment building at the corner of East Forty-Seventh Street and
Second Avenue. There was a nice restaurant on the Second Avenue
side of the building, with a large party room. We all agreed to make
the party at that restaurant. With Kristen living in that building, it
would be easy to get Barbara there for a surprise party.

Kristen negotiated all the arrangements with the restaurant.
Before Kristen signed the contract with the restaurant, she called
me. "Dad, are you sure this is okay for me to sign this contract? This
party is going to be very expensive."

"Of course, it's okay. Sign the contract."

Barbara had survived three cancers. In my mind, there was no cost
too expensive for this birthday; we had good reason to celebrate.

About a hundred friends and relatives were invited, including
three of Barbara's childhood friends she hadn't seen in many years

and a woman, Marge, who had played in a mah-jongg group with Barbara's mother from the late 1950s until 1971. Jonathan was flying up from Florida.

Barbara's birthday was September 12. The party was scheduled for Saturday evening, the eighth. Kristen prepared and mailed the invitations.

****

We invite you to come to a big soiree
We're going to celebrate our mom's birthday!
Although she looks so young, (don't you agree?)
She's turning 50 (and eligible for A.A.R.P.)
Half a century is cause for celebration
Add family and friends and you've got the perfect combination
Although the birthday is no secret, the PARTY'S A SURPRISE!!!
So, getting there by 7:30 p.m. would be very wise
September 8 is the night, so save the date
Reply by August 31 and that would be great
Nino's is the restaurant where the party will be
Come enjoy a Saturday night in New York City
So while she can still eat solid food
Please come join the Gellman Brood
Jonathan's flying in (SHHH!!!) Kristen, Brian, and our Dad
Having you there will make us all glad
There'll be lots of food, laughs, and cheers
We'll toast our mom to another 50 years!

****

As Barbara and I drove to the city that evening, I tried to hold back my excitement. Barbara only knew we were having dinner at Nino's Restaurant that evening for her birthday. She had no idea about the party or that she would be seeing Jonathan. We went to Kristen's apartment first and then down to the restaurant. As we walked into the party and everyone shouted "Surprise!" the look on Barbara's face was priceless. I mean literally priceless. The cost of the party was nothing when I saw the look on her face.

Once things calmed down a little, I gathered the kids and the four of us stood together. Jonathan was the designated family spokesperson to welcome everyone.

I would like to thank everyone for coming tonight. We appreciate it. I know that once my mom overcomes the shock from all of this, she will appreciate it forever.

Take a look around, Mom. These are the faces from all facets of your life. Some of you haven't seen my mom in a while and some of you don't get to see her too often. For those who do, I am pretty sure you won't mind me giving a quick review of her life.

From what I understand, my mom used to be a shy, quiet girl who didn't socialize very much. I'm sure her childhood friends can vouch for that. Well, that has certainly changed. My mom LOVES to talk. In fact, I can't imagine that she ever was a quiet person.

Thirty years ago, last week, my parents got married ... and it's debatable as to which one deserves the award. They didn't waste much time, soon having three kids, now twenty-six, twenty-four and twenty. I live in Miami, Kristen in New York, and the baby—I mean Brian—in Boston. My parents have found new love in New Jersey without kids for most of the year. We know they love us, but they seem a lot happier now.

My mom has become a very successful real estate professional, a successful mom, and a successful wife. At times she appears indestructible, doing many things at once. I guess it isn't that easy having three busy kids, a demanding job, and a husband who is always right.

Although I can't imagine what it's like to be fifty years old. Because ... well, that's old. I'd say my mom looks pretty good. Thanks to her, I have pictures all over my room, of our family. My friends always comment on how beautiful she is and how young she looks. From what I understand, that's always been the case. My mom has a smile that can light up a room and a personality that attracts everyone.

Mom, you deserve this surprise party more than anyone. You are a giver. We wanted to show you how much you are appreciated. It's your birthday, so keep smiling. Sometimes people are like a good wine that only gets better over time. I believe that's the case because we all love you more and more each day. Happy Birthday.

It was fun planning this surprise party for Barbara, with the kids. It was an evening of tears, laughs, and lots of love.

Barbara and I had been discussing how to celebrate our thirtieth wedding anniversary since early July. With the kids and I planning the surprise birthday party, I squashed any talk with Barbara about an anniversary party.

For our thirtieth anniversary, I wanted to do something out of the ordinary. We were empty nesters. It was time for us to get over being safe and to do something that was unlike anything we had ever done in the past. I came across an article about steamboat and riverboat cruises up the Mississippi River and brought up that idea.

At first, Barbara smiled at the idea. Then she looked unsure. "Do you think we'd like doing something like that?"

"I don't know. But it's something different for us and could be fun. We'd have to get more information."

That weekend, we were with friends. They mentioned that they had discussed taking a traditional cruise to celebrate the sale of their family clothing business. Barbara and I mentioned we had been talking about the Mississippi cruises. Our friends immediately made sourpuss faces and, true to form, were very negative. Quelle surprise! We had little in common with them and their kids were older than ours were. We needed to get rid of these dumb bastards. But we didn't, yet. I guess we felt that we needed to be tortured just a teeny bit more.

Most often, the suggestions Barbara and I made were no good to these friends, and everything they wanted to do was always better. I always felt they were the most opinionated, negative people imaginable. They had Barbara convinced about their kind of cruise. I gave in and agreed to the cruise for mid-September.

On the morning of August 29, the day of our thirtieth anniversary, Barbara poked me to wake up. As I turned around, I saw that she had a small package. "It's thirty years, silly. Happy anniversary. This is for you."

I unwrapped the package and it was a trophy cup. On the base, it read:

****

WORLD'S
BEST HUSBAND
Happy 30th!
All my love,
Barbara

****

I laughed. "Does this mean that you feel that I deserve an award for being married to you?"

Barbara laughed. "Don't go there!"

"Okay, well, I have a present for you too. But I didn't wrap it."

I smiled. Then Barbara smiled. Then we kissed. And then....

In mid-September, we went on the cruise with our friends. It was all right. No, it stunk. It was a cheap cruise on a cheap cruise line filled with people dressed like slobs. And all day long, those slobs did nothing else but eat. While other parts of the ship were empty, the buffet lines were always full, even though the food was mediocre. No, the food stunk too.

The cruise might have been better if we had joined the excursion trips, each time the ship docked at a port. But to our friends, everything was too expensive, and they always had a better alternative to the excursions. For me, the best parts of the cruise were when I was alone with Barbara in our room and when I was on my own on the ship's deck, feeling the chilly breeze on my face, drinking a hot chocolate. I also had fun with Barbara at karaoke.

I so regretted giving in and agreeing to take that cruise with those people. It bothered me I'd let this happen. When I agreed to the trip, I figured to myself, "So we'll go on this cruise, what's the big deal anyway?" Even after three cancers, I never gave up hope that Barbara and I would always have forever. But as I sat on the ship's deck feeling the chilly breeze on my face, I began to think that forever was not a guarantee for Barbara and me. I needed to be more selective and better focused at savoring our time together and not be wasteful. I began to feel, by agreeing to this cruise, I had wasted away the opportunity to celebrate a special milestone of ours. And such a milestone might never come again.

After the cruise ship docked at our home port, we drove home with our friends. They dropped us off in front of our house and continued to their home in Blairstown, about twenty minutes west. I couldn't wait to get into our house. I had been holding back my feelings since the first day we got on that ship. By this time, I was totally pissed. The moment we walked into our house and put our luggage down in the family room, I said, "Barbara, we have to talk!" But I couldn't just talk. I was too wound up. I shouted, "Barbara, this should have been a celebration of our thirtieth anniversary, not a contest about how cheaply we can do things."

"I know, I know," Barbara answered.

"Well, never again ... and from now on, those people are your friends, not mine!"

After blowing off a little steam, I could see that this wasn't going to lead to an argument between us. Barbara was also disappointed during the cruise, but was more accepting, trying to make the best of it.

"Marc, listen to me. Listen, okay? I could read your face for the entire cruise. You were really good at holding it in and not saying a word and making the best of it. I felt the same way. We should have done something like the steamboat or something else, and definitely not with them. And we will never go on a vacation with them, ever again."

If Barbara hadn't said this, I could have gone on having a fit. I would have continued fuming with my pent-up frustrations. But Barbara spoke with a warm, loving, and steady calmness. She walked up to me and put her hands on each of my shoulders. As we looked into each other's eyes, Barbara continued. "Marc, we didn't miss out on anything and we did have an anniversary celebration. My birthday party was also a celebration of our thirtieth anniversary and everyone at the party knew that. Jonathan announced our anniversary at the party, and everyone congratulated us. The same people at my birthday party would have been at an anniversary party. So, we did have a special celebration for our anniversary too and it was with our kids."

I was calm. Barbara had brought me down. As I looked into her eyes, I wanted to talk about living a lifestyle like we hadn't before. "But, Barbara—"

"Marc, let me finish. I love you for wanting our thirtieth to be special and not a disappointment. But it was special. The morning of the twenty-ninth, when it was only the two of us, was really everything. We missed out on nothing. I gave you a present and you gave me a present, even though yours wasn't wrapped."

I smiled. But I had a little more venting to do.

"Okay, Barbara. But I am just tired of living our lives dictated by the way that others want to live theirs, and waiting for other people to decide when to start spending some money and starting to live. I believe that those people are cheap and holding on to everything for their old age. By the time they decide to start living, we could be dead."

That evening, Barbara and I stayed up late, talking about what we wanted. We agreed on what we had already known for a long time; there was nothing for us in Flanders anymore and we didn't need the big house. We had fond memories of Flanders, but we should have moved a few years before. The only thing holding us back was Barbara not being ready to move away from her dear friends at work.

We decided to start considering purchasing a home in Florida. Jonathan was living there, and we would be making several trips a year to see him and my parents. Also, my parents were in their eighties and were beginning to need more from us. We felt that we would consider a Florida home as our primary residence and our Flanders home as temporary, until we could decide on a replacement.

We discussed moving into the city, to Manhattan, which could be romantic. We'd be empty nesters, returning to being like the honeymooners we were when we lived in Jackson Heights. But, as we went around and around, we realized that we didn't know what we wanted and had no plans to retire anytime soon. We weren't ready to sell our home in Flanders. A home in Florida would be a good first step.

Barbara and I promised each other that our evening wouldn't amount to a passing, late-night conversation, in reaction to that lousy cruise. We didn't just want to feel better about ourselves, having aired what was troubling us. We intended to make a conscientious effort to begin to reinvent ourselves into a new life, taking advantage of our financial situation and being empty nesters.

The cruise turned out to be an awakening. We hadn't truly moved on after losing our house of worship and we were stuck in kind of a limbo, coasting along. Those friends, being the way they were, did us a big favor. The cruise helped us to identify what we wanted, what we didn't want, what we needed to do, and it brought to light that we were overdue for a much-needed fresh start.

Being confronted with issues gave us specifics to talk about. Our conversation that evening felt like, all of a sudden, we were getting our act together. It felt like we were developing a plan to get a load off our shoulders and discard the old baggage holding us back.

Barbara and I had had a few years of awkwardly coasting along. Maybe even being a little confused about where we were headed, and how to keep our love an everlasting puppy love. Still living in Flanders, our surroundings hadn't changed. To us, Flanders seemed tired, old, and part of our past, and we had occasional sightings of the friends we disliked. Feeling puppy love was challenging amid our stale surroundings, which, to us, no longer felt youthful or vibrant. As we talked, we knew we'd find our way; just when and how were the questions. Barbara and I were unstoppable, because we never lost hope through difficult times. Hope gave us peace within us to love and enabled us to appreciate our beautiful lives.

As I write this book, I've learned that we did keep our love an everlasting puppy love. Back when we lived in Jackson Heights, it was all about us. While raising our three children, making it all about us was challenging, almost impossible, because we loved our kids. But we did get back to making our lives all about us. We reclaimed the youthful feeling from our years back in Jackson Heights. We hadn't lost our frame of mind, our belief that we would live and love forever. And with this book, we will have our forever.

We smiled and sighed with relief. After talking for hours that evening and into the early morning, we felt calm as we went to bed. We knew our love would never grow old and was always going to be fresh and new. And we were set on freeing ourselves, to let ourselves live.

As I finish writing this chapter, looking through Shiva Eyes, I wish we had gone on that steamboat cruise up the Mississippi. Maybe it would have been a trip filled with snafus like our honeymoon, but that would have been another bump in the road that added to our silliness and made us laugh. It could have become one of our stories, a fond memory, another "remember when." Whatever it could have been, I know for sure that it would have been a romantic thirtieth anniversary. Because, it would have been our choice to be us. For Barbara and me, it was the best to be us. Whatever that meant.

CHAPTER 23

Tall hills and deep valleys

Barbara and I loved to visit Jonathan in South Beach. Introducing us to our first restaurant experience along Ocean Drive, Jonathan took us to Larios on the Beach. It was quite a scene, and we felt the South Beach vibe, with the laughter, the great Cuban food, and the *drinking*.

At first, Barbara and I felt out-of-place and outside of our comfort zone. We weren't drinkers and didn't party loudly, to the point of raising the roof. That evening turned out to be a big step forward for us, as we were intent on blending into the South Beach scene.

To start us off, Jonathan ordered a sour apple martini for Barbara and a mojito for me. From that evening on, those became our signature drinks, for all future trips to South Beach. Those became our signature drinks, wherever we went. It was the vitality and free spirit of South Beach that made us want to be part of the excitement of the drinking crowd. Well, real drinkers wouldn't consider us part of their crowd. But we felt good about ourselves, naïvely believing that we had found a new passion: drinking. And it only took one drink to give us a buzz.

319

Jonathan was loving the South Beach lifestyle. He'd decided to look into purchasing a condominium apartment. During our trips to visit him, Jonathan would take us on tours to see the buildings that he was considering. In late December 2003, Jonathan called us and said he had put a deposit on an apartment in a new building under construction. He had fourteen days to back out of the contract and asked if we could come down and help him decide whether he was making a good decision.

Barbara and I flew down the first week in January 2004. The building, called "The Cosmopolitan," was located near the southernmost end of South Beach, on a full square block on Washington Avenue between First and Second Street. The neighborhood, called SoFi, south of Fifth, was up and coming, with many new buildings being planned. In the area north of Fifth Street, South Beach was lively and vibrant, with the art deco hotels along Ocean Drive and Collins Avenue. The area south of Fifth Street was being marketed by the building's developer as an oasis. It was a quiet and tranquil neighborhood, closely surrounded on three sides by water; to the east was the beach and ocean, to the south was Government Cut, the shipping channel leading to the Port of Miami, and to the west was the bay.

The first phase of the building would be ready for move-in starting in May 2004. We toured the site. It was a great location. We could walk just two blocks in three directions and be at the water and walk three blocks north and experience the excitement of South Beach. We were sold on the location in minutes.

Then we went to the sales office to see a model of the building and the interior finishes planned for the kitchens and bathrooms. I had already become very familiar with the building, studying in detail as much as I could by way of my home computer. It didn't take long for me to determine my advice for Jonathan. From the moment we walked into the sales office, Barbara and I began to give each other smiling looks. We both knew that we were going to buy an apartment in this building too. While we were looking at the kitchen cabinets, Jonathan walked away from us. Barbara whispered, "Don't say anything. Let's surprise him."

When Jonathan came back over to us, he asked, "Well, Dad, what do you think?"

"Ask the saleswoman to come over," I answered.

Jonathan had this confused look on his face. He saw me smile to Barbara and her smile back to me and couldn't figure out what was up.

"Is everything okay? Why do you want the saleswoman?"

"Because ... Mommy and I are going to buy an apartment in this building too."

Jonathan was so very excited. As for Barbara and me, we were both over-the-top excited. Both of us had spent our childhood summers in the Rockaways, near the beach, and had been envious of people who were lucky enough to have a home in a vacation or resort location. Now, we were about to become one of those homeowners.

Once we finished negotiating and signing the purchase contract and giving our deposit, Barbara became anxious to immediately call and tell everyone she knew. I quickly thought about it.

"Barbara, just wait. Let's hold off calling and telling anyone. How about the two of us talk and think this through first? I don't think it's going to be a good idea to tell everyone."

That evening over dinner, we talked about what we wanted this apartment to be and not to be. We wanted it to be our home and not a "place"; not just a place near the beach, and not a place for people we knew looking for a free place to stay in Miami. We wanted to replace our need for hotels when visiting Florida, with a home that we didn't have to pack anything for and a bed that only we slept in.

For the first time, we were able to afford a home, a brand-new home, which would be furnished and decorated at a quality better than we'd ever had. When we moved to Flanders, we had little money to furnish and decorate, and when the kids came along, the furnishings always needed to be kid-proof and acceptable to kid wear and tear.

Jonathan was buying a two-bedroom unit. We were buying a

one-bedroom, to ensure there would be no possibility for guests assuming they could stay with us. We planned to fulfill our goal to truly take advantage of being on our own, just Barbara and me. This home was to be our "secret" getaway.

Our decision turned out to be a good one, considering what we quickly learned about the three categories of seasonal dwellers in Florida. The first are the "snowbirds." The snowbirds are people who own or rent an apartment and are there for the entire winter season. The second are the "snowflakes." The snowflakes are people who own or rent an apartment for the entire winter season but go back and forth to their home up north. Then, the third are the "schnor-rer birds." The schnorrer birds are people who don't own or rent an apartment but go back and forth during the winter season and stay with friends and relatives each time. Schnorrer is a Yiddish term for freeloader. Barbara and I planned to be snowflakes. As for the schnorrer birds, they'd have to find someone else to stay with.

Although we told many people that Jonathan had purchased an apartment, Barbara and I told very few that we had too. Jonathan closed and moved into his apartment on May 14, his twenty-ninth birthday. Barbara and I closed on our apartment on June 28 and moved in at the beginning of August. During the months leading up to the move, we were busy buying furniture and clothes. Also, we had to hire contractors for interior work, since the apartment came decorator ready. This meant raw concrete floors and just a prime coat of paint on the walls and ceilings. It was all fun. It was a brand-new apartment being completed and decorated the way we wanted.

Barbara was also busily training for the Avon Walk for Breast Cancer. She signed up for the event in late winter and she was going to be one of more than twenty-seven hundred participants. Barbara was fifty-three at the time and had never taken on such a physical challenge. Almost immediately upon signing up, she began train-ing for the thirty-nine-mile, two-day walk; twenty-six miles the first day and thirteen the second. Barbara walked the streets and roads throughout our township and gradually worked her way up to enduring enough miles to take her through the actual Avon Walk.

While all this was happening, my dad, diagnosed with lymphoma in early January, had been undergoing chemotherapy treatment. He finished treatment by June, and he was so proud to call Barbara and me to let us know that his cancer was, as he described it, in "recession." That was so my dad, cutely describing something with the wrong word. Barbara was on the phone in the kitchen, and I was downstairs in the family room, and when we hung up the phone I could hear her laughing. Barbara knew how much I enjoyed hearing my dad often use the wrong terminology to describe something. Barbara loved my dad so much she never corrected him. His use of the wrong word gave us the material for an endearing conversation, whenever we spoke about my dad. To us, it made him unique, and we never wanted him to change.

"I have to call the kids," I told Barbara. "First, to let them know the good news about the cancer and second, to let them know that their grandpa's cancer is in recession."

Jonathan and Brian were happy about the news and laughed. Kristen had a slightly different reaction.

"Hi Kristen, Grandpa just called with good news. He told us that his cancer is in remission."

"Oh, that's so good!"

I answered, "The only thing is, that when Grandpa called, he told us that his cancer is in recession."

"Ha ha, Grandpa is so funny. Did you correct him and tell him the word is remission?"

"No, why would I do that? Mommy and I think it's funny to hear Grandpa say recession."

Kristen answered, "Dad, you are so mean. Grandpa is going to go to the clubhouse and tell all his friends and everyone is going to laugh at him. I'm going to call him right now and tell him the word is remission."

Jokingly, I answered, "Well, Mommy and I like it when Grandpa is Grandpa. So, if you want to ruin everything, go ahead and call him."

Kristen did call my dad to correct him. Kristen is so caring and loving; that was such a Kristen thing to do. My dad took Kristen's advice very well. But I'm sure that by the time my dad made it to the clubhouse to tell his friends the good news, his cancer was back to being in recession. I'm sure his friends didn't correct him. I'm positive that they didn't laugh at him either. I'm sure that all they said was, "That's good, Ben. Take a seat, you're holding up the poker game."

The Avon Walk was on the weekend of October 2 and 3, 2004. Over a period of two weeks before that weekend, Jonathan had visited my parents a few times. After each visit, Jonathan called to say that he was concerned that there was a change in my dad; he wasn't being himself. But each time Barbara and I spoke with my dad over the phone, he convinced us he was fine. My dad was eighty-five and had been very independent. We figured that it would soon be the time when my parents would need some home-care help.

For work, Jonathan often made sales calls to clients near my parents' home. He assured Barbara and me that he was going to start routinely stopping by to check up on them. On Thursday evening, September 30, Jonathan called me. Barbara and I had just finished dinner and were relaxing in the family room.

"Hey, Dad, I'm with Grandma and Grandpa. Grandpa has lost weight and he's not himself."

"What do you mean that he's not himself?"

"He seems confused and is just not himself. I'm taking him to the hospital and having him checked out."

To my dad, everything was always fine, or okay, or not a problem. To agree to go to the hospital was not like my dad. I knew something had to be seriously wrong for him to agree.

"Is Grandpa okay with that?"

"When I first mentioned going to the hospital, Grandpa was reluctant to go. But he knows something is wrong and finally agreed."

"What about Grandma?"

"Grandma is nervous, but someone is staying with her while we're gone."

"Okay, keep me posted."

I was quite shaken by this phone call. Barbara and I began planning for one of us to quickly get down to Florida to be with my parents. We couldn't put this all on Jonathan. There had to be something terribly concerning for Jonathan to be taking my dad to the hospital and for my dad to agree. Barbara and I just sat, anxiously waiting for Jonathan's call.

Jonathan took my dad to the emergency room at a nearby hospital. Checking in at the emergency room, Jonathan told the staff person that he thought my dad had a stroke. They waited in the emergency room and were eventually taken into triage. The triage nurse did a full assessment and said to Jonathan, "Your grandfather did not have a stroke and checks out fine. This is just aging and, at eighty-five years old, these things happen."

Jonathan answered, "You don't understand. I know my grandfather and I can tell something is definitely wrong."

Finally, Jonathan convinced the nurse that something was wrong. After waiting for four-and-a-half hours, another nurse did more tests and determined that my dad did have a stroke. My dad was admitted to the hospital for more tests.

Jonathan was booked on a flight to New Jersey for the next day, to attend the opening ceremony for the Avon Walk. So, my cousin, Carol, quickly booked a flight down to Florida for the next day, to be with my mom and to meet with the doctors at the hospital.

Bright and early, the morning of Saturday the second, Barbara, Jonathan, Brian, and I drove to New York City for the Avon Walk's opening ceremony, at the South Street Seaport. Kristen was living in Manhattan, so she met us there, along with Barbara's cousin Marsha and our friends Judy and David and their son Evan. We had to be there extra early, because Barbara had been chosen by the Avon Walk committee to be one of the speakers. Being there so early, we were all able to get a spot close to the right of the stage.

Barbara left us to get on stage for the opening ceremony. We all watched anxiously as the ceremony began and nervously waited for Barbara's turn to speak. There were a couple of speakers before her and then Barbara so proudly walked over to the podium. It was an incredible sight to see Barbara, with such poise, so ready to address the sea of people.

My emotions took over. I tried to hold them back, but I could feel them coming. The feeling was too overwhelming for me to control. Seeing Barbara on that stage, at that podium, and so much alive, I cried. It was impossible for me to hold back my tears. For some comfort, I leaned my shoulder against our friend Judy's shoulder; she was sobbing too. I was so proud of Barbara and of the proud confident woman she had become. Barbara began:

Good morning, I am Barbara Gellman from Flanders, New Jersey. Thanks in great part to the support of my family, my friends, and people like you, I am a three-time breast cancer survivor.

This is my first Avon Walk, and, like many of you, I'm both excited and a little anxious. I am also very, very proud. Six years ago, I couldn't walk twenty feet. Today I will aim for twenty-six miles. I don't know if I'll finish the entire distance, and that doesn't really matter to me. I'm here today with my family, my friends and all of you, and I'm going to walk ... because I can!

I am honored to be walking with you this weekend and I am proud to introduce the president of the Avon Foundation.

After the ceremony, we waited to give Barbara a hug and wish her luck, as she began the walk. Jonathan stayed with Kristen and planned to cheer Barbara at several points along the twenty-six mile walk that day. Brian and I left and headed back to New Jersey, deciding to stop off at the mall.

We were in one of the clothing stores, roaming through the aisles. Brian liked to get me in a clothing store. He often complained about the way I dressed. As Brian walked around, he picked things off the rack and said, "Okay, Dad, get this." He didn't ask my opinion, he just said, "Get this." I didn't mind. He had good taste in clothes. And I enjoyed hearing him say something nice about the way I looked, when I would wear something he had picked out for me.

While in the store, my phone rang, and I noticed it was Carol.

"Hi, Marc, how was it this morning?"

"It was pretty incredible. There were so many people and Barbara spoke at the ceremony."

"Where are you now?" Carol asked.

"Brian and I are back in New Jersey in a store. Jonathan and Kristen are in New York. They're planning to meet Barbara at several points of the walk."

While we were busy with the Avon Walk, it was comforting knowing that my parents were in good care with Carol with them. And until this point, Carol sounded fine over the phone. Then, she asked, "Are you able to walk away from Brian and turn your back toward him? I have something to tell you and I don't want him to see the reaction on your face."

Well, that changed everything. I held my breath and answered, "Okay, I'm away from Brian."

"Marc ... it's not good. The doctor who treated your dad last winter for the lymphoma just came into the room to talk with us. He said that your dad was misdiagnosed with lymphoma. He has stage four lung cancer. The doctor said that had your dad been properly diagnosed, he wouldn't have put your dad through the chemotherapy."

I just stood there. It was like my insides fell to the ground. I looked to the floor to make sure I was still standing. As I hung up the phone I glanced around for Brian, to make sure he wasn't coming over to me. I don't remember how I ended that phone call with Carol. I don't know what I said. I had to pull myself together. I didn't want to say anything to my kids until I spoke with Barbara.

The next afternoon, Brian and I drove back to Manhattan to see Barbara cross the finish line and watch her speak at the closing ceremony. She had completed the entire thirty-nine-mile walk, an overwhelmingly exhausting weekend. But Barbara was driven by the excitement of being alongside fellow walkers and survivors, by the speaking parts in the ceremonies and, most of all, by the celebration of being able to physically contribute to the accomplishments of the Avon Walk. For Barbara, participation in the walk was her give-back and appreciation for all those people before her, whose unselfish efforts enabled Barbara to be a survivor. All this inspired and gave

Barbara the stamina she needed. As she crossed the finish line, Barbara's smile glowed with pride.

Again, I watched Barbara walk over to the podium.

> Good afternoon fellow walkers, crew, family, and friends. I am Barbara Gellman from Flanders, New Jersey, and I am a three-time breast cancer survivor.
>
> My first encounter with breast cancer was with the death of my mother. She was only forty-three. I was only thirty when I was diagnosed myself for the first time, and then again, a few years later. During my last struggle, in 1998, my life was saved by a stem cell transplant, a procedure that was unimaginable during my mother's illness. But because somebody didn't give up ... because somebody committed to finding a new way to save more people from the ravages of breast cancer ... because of people like you to keep fighting, no matter what ... I walked with you this weekend. Thank you.
>
> I don't allow myself to look back. I carry the memory of my mother's and my own battles forward, and I look to the future ... for my daughter and for all of your daughters. I'm confident that with this many dedicated people, willing to give so much of themselves, that one day our daughters will no longer need to hear the words that changed my life ... you have breast cancer.
>
> I am so proud to have been a part of this event, and I am honored to introduce the field manager for the Avon Walk for Breast Cancer here in New York.

After the closing ceremony, Barbara seemed fine and still energized. But as soon as we got into the car to head home, the exhaustion hit her. She took off her sneakers, inhaled a deep breath, and slowly breathed out as she sank into the car seat and let her body go limp. I knew the first question she would ask would be about my dad. I started off the conversation, asking, "How do you feel?"

"I feel like I've been energized. I met some of the most incredibly wonderful people who do this walk year after year, even senior citizens, even entire families. Yesterday, along the walk, several people recognized me from the opening ceremony, and they asked if that was my family standing to the right of the stage. When I said yes, they answered, we figured that, because they were all crying."

"Yeah, it was pretty emotional," I answered.

Then, while the kids were talking to each other, Barbara quietly asked, "How's your dad?"

I quietly answered, "Not good. I'll tell you later."

With a sudden, saddened look, she answered, "Oh ... I was afraid you'd say that."

Several years later, Kristen decided to sign up for the Avon Walk for Breast Cancer and eleven of her friends joined the walk with her. The walk was October 20 and 21, 2012; eight years after Barbara participated in the walk and fourteen months after we lost Barbara.

Without Kristen knowing, Brian made several calls to the Avon Walk committee and, with much perseverance and persuasion, was able to arrange for Kristen to be one of the speakers at the opening ceremony.

I'm here to walk, my first Avon Walk. Because my mother was first diagnosed with breast cancer in 1981. It recurred in 1984 and then again in 1997 and then one more time in 2006.

After spending half of her life battling the awful disease, we lost my mom last year; just six weeks shy of her sixtieth birthday. At first, I hesitated to join the Avon Walk. Because I thought it was too soon and my emotions too raw. But then, I realized that my mother, a 2004 Avon walker herself, would never stay home when she had the chance to help others. So, this weekend, I will walk in her footsteps and celebrate the strongest, most courageous, most optimistic, and loving person I've ever known.

My name is Kristen Lebenstein. I'm from Maplewood, New Jersey and I'm in it to end it, in honor and memory of my mother ... Barbara Gellman.

As I watched Kristen walk over to the podium that morning, I began to feel like I was going to lose it. As soon as I heard her begin and say, "I'm here to walk," I did lose it. My emotions overshadowed her speech, and I didn't hear a word she said. It wasn't until many years later, when I began writing this chapter, that I asked Kristen for a copy of her speech. Even after many years, emotionally, her speech wasn't any easier for me to read than it had been to listen to.

Finally reading her speech six-and-a-half years later, I was reminded of my feeling of amazement, watching Kristen take her place at the podium, like Barbara had done several years before. I was so very proud of Kristen that morning in 2012. Four years later, Kristen participated in the Avon Walk in Washington, DC, the weekend of April 3 and 4, 2016, with twenty-two of her friends from Maplewood and Millburn, New Jersey.

After Barbara's Avon Walk, I waited until we were home to tell her about my father. As soon as we were alone, Barbara said, "Tell me about your dad."

"Well, Carol called me yesterday and it's not good. He has lung cancer; stage four. There's nothing that can be done. The doctor is sending him home and arranging for hospice. Carol is staying down there for a few days to get him and my mother settled. She's going to arrange for someone to be with them 24-7. Let's call Carol and figure out when she's coming back and have a plan for who's going down there next. That will be more helpful, than all of us being there at the same time. My parents are going to need continuous support."

Barbara answered, "I'm going to make flight reservations to be down there after Carol comes back. You should plan to be there, after I come back. Maybe the kids should go down there too, while you're there."

At ten o'clock on Sunday evening, October 17, Barbara and I were talking in the family room. By then all of us had been to Florida; Barbara, me and our three kids. I had gotten home earlier that evening. The phone rang. Barbara answered. It was the woman who was caring for my parents. My dad had just passed away.

Tears ran down Barbara's face as she hung up the phone and came over to sit beside me on the couch. Although, this was not at all a surprise, I was in shock. We cuddled up next to each other and Barbara, crying, said, "Oh, Marc. It hurts so much. I am so going to miss your father. I've called him dad for the past thirty-three years ... and he's been my father for all that time."

I sat there in shock. I had just lost my dad. Barbara continued to cry. She had just lost her third parent. Over a short period of time, we had experienced the excitement of South Beach, the emotional Avon Walk, and the sorrow over the loss of a parent. It seemed like our lives were filled with tall hills and deep valleys. A plateau, with maybe a gentle sloping hillside, may have let us enjoy a steady peace. But, we guessed, that's not what life is about, and a steady peace would be too boring. Although, a little boring would have been nice and very welcome.

CHAPTER 24

Everything happens to Barbara

T he December holidays of 2004 and New Year's Eve 2005 would be our first celebrating the holiday season in South Beach. It had been thirty-eight years since our first New Year's Eve together in Times Square in 1967. In the planning for a fun-filled evening for New Year's Eve 2005, Barbara and I didn't expect that we would be captured by the romance of the evening and that we were about to find a new love.

A few days before New Year's, Barbara and I were strolling along Lincoln Road. Our apartment is on Washington Avenue, between First and Second Street. Lincoln Road is a fifteen block walk north on Washington Avenue. Most of Lincoln Road is a pedestrian-only walkway, which spans east and west for eight blocks from Washington Avenue to Alton Road. For the eight blocks, the walkway is lined with retail stores and restaurants, with alfresco dining.

We stopped for dinner and found a lovely table setting on the walkway at The Meat Market Steakhouse, one of the more upscale restaurants on Lincoln Road. During dinner, we began to talk about plans for New Year's Eve.

"Barbara, it's going to be just the two of us, which means we can do whatever we want to do. Let's go to a hotel for dinner that will have music and dancing and we can celebrate the New Year with a ballroom filled with people partying. We'll wear silly-looking hats and just be crazy and have fun. No one will know us, so we can be as uninhibited as we want; screaming and just having a fun time."

"That sounds good to me, except for the screaming part," Barbara answered.

"Why? What's wrong with screaming? Do you have something against screaming? I never knew that about you."

"Okay, silly. I'll look through the *Miami Herald* and see what each hotel is having."

"Barbara, it's just the two of us and our first New Year's alone in years. Please don't look at the prices. Let's have a good time."

Barbara found the Loews Miami Beach Hotel was offering an exciting evening, with a buffet dinner, music and dancing, hats, noisemakers, and a midnight celebration.

"That's exactly what I've been talking about doing for years. How much is it?"

"You told me not to look at the prices. So, I didn't. Should I call and get reservations?"

"Yes, absolutely ... absolutely. But first tell me the price."

Unlike past New Year's Eves, when we dressed scruffy, it was fun getting dressed nicely and a little glitzed up. We were looking forward to going to a hotel. The evening was warm enough for Barbara to wear a sleeveless dress and for me to wear a short-sleeved shirt and slacks. The cool breeze from the ocean made it comfortable to be dressed a little more formally. The Miami weather was perfect for strolling along and observing all the festivities.

It was quite a scene walking the fifteen blocks up Ocean Drive to the Loews. The street was closed to vehicular traffic and each hotel had its dinner tables extending out to the middle of the street. The balance of the street was designated as a pedestrian promenade. Each hotel had outdoor entertainment with either a band or a DJ. Many hotels also had Latin dancers livening up the entertainment. People along the promenade were dancing and singing. For the fifteen blocks, it was one big festival. Barbara and I were lovers holding hands and glancing at each other's smiles.

At the Loews, the lounge and the dining room was lavishly and colorfully decorated. When we were seated at our table, we looked at each other and all we could find to say was, "Wow ... this is nice!" I looked at Barbara. She was beautiful. I took pleasure in her smile, with her dimples so deep. We were always so into each other and loved seeing each other happy. And that evening, we were over-the-top happy.

We didn't know anyone in the restaurant and weren't interested in mingling. It was an evening for just the two of us. We talked, smiled, gazed into each other's eyes, and when we danced, we kissed. The evening was so romantic. We felt good about ourselves, like we were rich being in this hotel. We may not have been rich in money. But we sure were rich in love for each other.

I wish our children could have seen us together that evening. How rare it is for most of us, with all of life's busyness, to take advantage of a special moment and be demonstrative in our love for each other, beyond the boundaries of our bedroom. That evening held a feeling of complete and intense love for Barbara and me; everything around us was of no importance and the display of our love was only about the two of us.

Our waiter came to our table to introduce himself and welcome us to the hotel. Of course, the first thing we ordered was our drinks: sour apple martini and mojito. Then we went into the lounge to dance and after a while we went to the buffet. When we got back to the table, the waiter brought us a bottle of wine, explaining it was part of the dinner. So, we had plenty to drink, and Barbara ordered a second sour apple martini before we started on the bottle of wine.

We danced, drank, and ate, and danced and drank and drank some more. Finally, it was getting close to midnight and we went into the lounge, listened to the music, and danced. At midnight, all hell broke loose, and it was wonderful. After partying, we went back to our table and finished off the bottle of wine.

By one o'clock in the morning, we were tired out and ready to leave. We quickly found that standing up from the table was a problem. We were drunk. Very drunk. We decided that we needed to hold on to each other as we walked, in order not to fall. Leaving the hotel and walking down Ocean Drive was a challenge. The pedestrian promenade still had crowds of people and we were very wobbly on our feet.

Jonathan happened to be at the lower end of Ocean Drive with his girlfriend when he spotted us walking.

"I think I see my parents way over there, through the crowd ... oh yeah ... that's them. There are my parents! Oh, they look kind of unsteady. I think they're drunk."

As we got closer, Jonathan shouted out to us to get our attention. But we heard nothing and didn't respond to him. And he said, "Oh yeah, they're drunk!"

Jonathan came over to us and we began talking to him. But we couldn't make out what he was saying, or what we were saying. As we talked to Jonathan and his girlfriend, they were laughing, and we couldn't figure out what they were laughing about. We also called Kristen and Brian to wish them a happy New Year. The next day, they told us that we were stone-cold drunk.

Somehow, we made it back to our apartment fine. We were able to get mostly undressed and fall into bed. The next morning, we woke up a little hungover and agreed that the night was a success and that it had been quite a while since we had such a romantic evening out.

Over the course of thirty-eight years, from 1967 to 2005, there were only a couple of times that Barbara and I spent New Year's Eve together, alone. And, you know what? Those couple of times were the best. This time, we felt like we had found a new love and we agreed, there is no better new love than with the person you're already in love with.

There was one other time I remember Barbara and me getting that drunk. We were staying at The Breakers Palm Beach and decided to go for dinner at a Mexican restaurant on Clematis Street. We decided to order red sangria and the waitress suggested that we get a pitcher. We had ordered pitchers of sangria in the past, but never one as big as the pitcher that the waitress brought us. This was the size of a pitcher that you'd put out on a table for a party.

We took our time eating our meal and sat for a while after, continuing to drink. Barbara said, "You know, we don't have to finish this whole pitcher." But we did. When we finished paying the bill, getting up from the table was quite a challenge. Leaving the restaurant, we held on to each other and began to call a cab. But decided we were too drunk to get into a cab. There were no benches along the sidewalk, and we had trouble standing. So, we did the next best thing. We sat on the curb, like two drunkards, for about an hour until we felt somewhat sober.

For us, walking after those two episodes of drinking was a challenge. But that was a rarity for us. Most of the time sober, Barbara and I loved our walks in South Beach, especially along Ocean Drive. There was one time in particular when there was an art fair and the street was closed to vehicular traffic. We browsed the sales booths, going from vendor to vendor. Holding hands, we strolled along enjoying the walk and breathing in the warm ocean air. Suddenly, I heard Barbara shout, "Oh, for God's sake!"

"What's the matter?" I asked.

"A bird just shit all over me!"

At first, I didn't notice anything. "What are you talking about?"

With a disgusted look on her face, Barbara let go of my hand, turned to me, spread out her arms, and shouted, "Marc, just look at me! It's in my hair, on my arms and all over me!"

The look on Barbara's face was one of total disgust. She was pissed. I looked her over. Yes, there was bird shit all over her. There was no way for her to clean up. We were a few blocks from our apartment and needed to get home. To me, seeing the bird shit all over Barbara was too funny. As we began to rush home, I had to have some fun with this.

"Wow, that must have been one big fucking bird with diarrhea.

How can that be? I was right next to you, holding your hand and nothing got on me. Let's stop for a minute and let me check."

"What do you have to check yourself for? There's nothing on you. It's all over me ... for God's sake—and stop laughing! Why is it always me?"

As much as I tried, I could never hold back laughing when something happened to Barbara. The combination of whatever it was that happened, and the cutest look on her face of complete disgust, made it impossible for me to keep a straight face. Even when she would shout, "Marc, it's not funny!" I would laugh and eventually, Barbara would catch the laughter and begin to ease up and laugh herself.

Everything happens to Barbara. The five of us, Barbara, me, and the kids, could go out for a family dinner together. If someone's order was going to get screwed up, it would always be Barbara's. If it wasn't a problem with her order, something else would happen to Barbara. Like the time Jonathan took Barbara and me out for dinner to a very upscale restaurant in South Beach, renowned for its presentation of food and exquisite décor. Jonathan had made the reservation a month before and for all that time, Barbara talked about how much she was looking forward to it.

The day came for the dinner and it was fun to anticipate going to this restaurant. Walking into the restaurant, Barbara was in awe of the unique entrance and noticed the glass placemats on the table, as we were being seated. It was truly exciting, until people were seated at the next table. Across the table. I noticed the look on Barbara's face change. "Oh, for God's sake ... Of course, I'd get such a view!"

With our backs facing the neighboring table, neither Jonathan nor I noticed. Barbara had a direct view. The physical appearance of one of the people seated at that table was a difficult sight to take under any circumstance. The person had the misfortune of having several deformities and suffered severe motor skills disorder. It was sad to see. As always, Barbara was a good sport about it, accepted it, and was happy to see that person being out and about and enjoying themselves. That was Barbara, and I loved her for her ways. I could never be as good a person as Barbara was and yet she loved me.

Then there is one of my family's favorite stories about Barbara. It's about when Barbara and I were at the dog park at South Pointe Park in South Beach, with Jonathan's girlfriend's dog, Bella. Barbara and I were standing about one hundred feet apart. Bella was running back and forth between us as she played with the other dogs. All the dogs at the park were friendly and enjoying the freedom of running around the grass.

As all this was going on, I noticed a giant white dog walking toward Barbara. As it approached Barbara from behind, the dog was wagging its tail and seemed friendly. I watched, not expecting anything to happen, as the dog was directly behind Barbara and sniffing around. Then the dog lifted its leg and began peeing on Barbara.

I tried to shout out a warning but couldn't get the words out in time. Although Barbara noticed me gesturing to her, she just stood in her spot, as that dog took the longest piss on her. In seconds, Barbara began to feel the wetness, not realizing what it was. By the time Barbara turned around to see what was happening, the dog had completely emptied its bladder on Barbara.

I put Bella on her leash and hurried over to Barbara. I couldn't hold in the laughter. I truly did try, because Barbara was totally outraged. It was the most incredible sight to witness, probably equal to or funnier than any of the funniest slapstick skits that I saw as a kid, watching Laurel and Hardy or Abbott and Costello.

We walked over to the fountain to get Barbara washed off a little. She took off her shoes and shouted, "Marc, whose dog is that? I am so pissed!"

"Of course you're pissed. That dog pissed all over you. You've been pissed upon, which makes you and all of your clothes pissed."

As she continued to wash at the fountain, Barbara said, "Marc, you better stop laughing. Take these shoes and throw them into that garbage."

"Why?"

"Because they're saturated with piss! I'm not taking them back to the apartment!"

Barbara walked barefoot back to our apartment.

"Barbara, you know, this may have been a once-in-a-lifetime experience. I've heard of people complain about getting shit on by people. But I've never heard of anyone complain about getting pissed on by a dog."

Barbara answered with a laugh and a warning. "Okay, Marc ... enough."

I couldn't get the sight out of my mind. Barbara did laugh with me into the evening. A few minutes after we got into bed and turned off the lights, I started laughing. I couldn't stop thinking about it. Barbara began to laugh again too. "Okay, silly, enough. Let's go to sleep."

"Barbara, a dog pissed on you. That is not a natural occurrence. Please don't expect me to get that picture out of my mind so easily."

The next day on the beach, a couple came over to us and said to Barbara, "You were the topic of our conversation at dinner last night. We saw that dog pee on you."

That was the beginning of a new friendship for Barbara and me. It turned out that Lynn and Elliot also had an apartment in our building. They were about the same age as us and had three children, boy, girl, boy, about the same ages as our kids.

For all the experiences that would prove out that everything happens to Barbara, Barbara always took these misfortunes in stride. As I laughed, Barbara laughed it off too. Through her laughter, she would ask, "Why is it always me?"

And I would answer, "Because you're a silly head."

In addition to all the nutty things that happened to Barbara, I loved to prank her. Or, maybe, I liked to annoy her. When she became annoyed with me, Barbara had this incredibly cute way about her. There was a kind of anger and impatience, always with that underlying cuteness I loved to see. She would say to me, with that dimpled smile, "Okay, enough already."

I truly believe the only reason Barbara put up with me was that she knew it was all out of love. Like, when she had her hands full preparing something at the kitchen sink and I snuck behind her, put my arms around her, and grabbed her ass. Barbara would shout, "You are so annoying! I'm in the middle of doing something!"

As I grabbed at her and kissed the back of her neck, while her hands were full, she would say, "I guess I shouldn't complain. After all these years, you still want to grab me. But can you let me finish what I'm doing?"

"Continue what you're doing," I'd say. "Make believe I'm not here."

One of my pranks that the kids like to talk about involved a woman named Sonia. When we went under contract to purchase the apartment in South Beach, there were many things that had to be done over the several months before the closing. The developer had a person in charge of coordinating the closing; her name was Sonia, pronounced "Sone-ya." After each time I spoke with Sonia, I would update Barbara, and I would pronounce Sonia's name as "Sun-ya."

At first, Barbara would correct me. "Marc, her name is pronounced 'Sone-ya.'"

This went on for several months. Barbara grew annoyed with me. Finally, during one telephone conversation, Barbara shouted, "Marc, her name is Sonia. Why do you keep calling her 'Sun-ya'?"

Calm and annoying as ever, I answered, "Are you sure about that? I really think her name is pronounced, 'Sun-ya.'"

"No, it isn't!" she shouted back. "So, stop it already. It's annoying!"

About an hour later, a thought came to me. I called Jonathan. "Hey, little boy, you're coordinating the closing for your apartment with a woman in the developer's office named Sonia, right?"

"Yes," he answered.

"Well, I've been pronouncing her name as 'Sun-ya' when speaking with Mommy and have been trying to convince Mommy that the name is pronounced that way. So, call Mommy in her office and don't tell her that you and I spoke. Tell her that all is going well with planning for your closing, and you've been coordinating everything with 'Sun-ya.'"

About ten minutes later, Jonathan called me back. "Dad. I think that you better ease up with Mommy. She got really angry."

"Okay. Love you," I answered.

About thirty minutes later, I called Kristen. "Hey, little girl, I've been joking with Mommy about a woman named Sonia. Call Mommy, she's in her office. Make up a story about something and use the name Sonia. But pronounce it as 'Sun-ya.'"

About five minutes later, Kristen called me back. "Dad, Mommy got really angry. I think you better call to apologize. She's totally had it with you. I'm serious. You need to call her and apologize, right now."

"Okay. Love you," I answered.

I thought about what to do. Kristen made it sound like I was in real trouble with Barbara. I believed that I probably was. I had gone a little too far this time. So, I called Brian. "Hey, big guy. Are you still having problems with your cell phone and the phone company?"

"Nope. I finally got it all worked out."

"Did you let Mommy know that? She was concerned."

"I've been meaning to call Mommy and tell her."

"Mommy is in her office now. Please call her and explain how you got it resolved. Most importantly, tell her you were able to get it done because you finally made contact at the phone company with a woman who knew what she was doing, and the woman's name was 'Sun-ya.'"

About three minutes later, my phone rang. It was Barbara. She was laughing. "Okay! Enough already. I give up. You win. You are too silly for me. Did you have enough fun with this? So, if you want to call her Sun-ya, that's fine with me."

"Barbara, why would I do that? Her name is Sonia."

I could go on and on with "Grandma Barbara" stories, as my grandchildren know these stories to be. If it wasn't unfortunate enough that everything happens to Barbara, she had a husband who thought it was all funny. Lucky for me, Barbara knew how much I loved her, with a love that made me silly over her. Our marriage was surely made in heaven. It's the only way to explain how Barbara was able to put up with me for forty years. And being that everything happens to Barbara, I guess I "happened" to her too.

CHAPTER 25

Once upon a time

By the summer of 2006, we'd owned our apartment in South Beach for two years. We had a good taste of condominium apartment living. It was nice not having the responsibilities of maintaining a house: lawn, shrubs, roof, driveway, and on and on. With no stress and worries, Barbara and I always looked forward to the fun of being in South Beach and never looked forward to returning to our house in New Jersey.

When we would arrive in Florida, it was bright and so green and fun to walk into our building and be greeted by the concierge saying, "Welcome back." It was so different on our return to New Jersey. The routine was kind of depressing. After landing in Newark, we'd get the car for the long drive home up a dark, rural country road to the far western suburbs, stop off at a diner for a quick dinner, and pull into our lonely driveway. The house always felt dark and cold and there was no one to greet us or welcome us home.

Barbara and I discussed how senseless it was that we were spending a few weeks out of the year in "paradise" and most of the year living without the amenities we'd learned to enjoy and expect. We decided to actively start looking for something in New Jersey that had much of what we had in South Beach. One early Saturday morning, we started our search in Jersey City and then moved on to Hoboken.

In Hoboken, we parked at the far northern end of the city and began walking downtown on Washington Street. The feeling and the vibe felt good. Walking on Washington Street was a refreshing change from the suburbs. We started out holding hands as we walked. We people-watched and looked into the shops and restaurants. As we warmed up to the neighborhood, I put my arm around Barbara as we continued to walk.

"I think we can fit into this place and have fun living here," she said. We both agreed that it wasn't South Beach, but we began to feel that Hoboken had a unique charm of its own.

Over the next several weeks, we toured all the communities along the Hudson River, from Jersey City to Fort Lee. Hoboken seemed like our only possibility. We identified a new project under construction, called Maxwell Place. There were four buildings planned for this condominium community. The first building was near completion and the second building was scheduled for completion a couple of years later. We began to give Maxwell Place real consideration.

At this point, the real day of reckoning was upon us. Did we really want to sell our house? Were we truly ready to move? The answer was yes, and no. So, we decided to consider the second building, which was scheduled to be completed in 2008 or 2009. By late November 2006, we had identified a specific apartment and planned to be ready to sign a purchase contract within the next couple of weeks.

But that December, we were faced with news that would turn our wonderful world into a horror. Each year in December, Barbara would have her annual checkup with her oncologist. In 2006, it started off with a bone scan on December 1, followed with other tests. By December 13, the summation of all the test results revealed multiple new nodules in her lungs and bones, consistent with metastatic disease.

Dr. Stern called Barbara with the news that there was a recurrence of breast cancer. But he didn't tell her all the details over the phone. Instead, Dr. Stern's call was about scheduling an appointment to see Barbara face-to-face. Of course, I went with Barbara to that appointment.

From Dr. Stern's call, Barbara and I didn't take the initial news too badly. We'd been down this road several times before and we knew that we'd make it through once again. But immediately upon walking into Dr. Stern's office, I saw the look on his face. I knew then that the news was going to be much worse than his description to Barbara over the phone. And we weren't at all remotely prepared for such news.

As Dr. Stern described the several locations of nodules in her bones and in her lungs, Barbara fell to pieces. I sat in total shock and disbelief at what I was hearing. Barbara grabbed onto my arm and cried out repeatedly, "Oh, Marc ... I'm so sorry." Over and over, she cried, "Oh, Marc ... I'm so sorry." Each time she repeated that phrase, I became more and more weakened, as if my strength was being drained out of me.

It was heart-wrenching to see Barbara so devastated and shaking with fright. In all her fright, Barbara's cries were not about herself. Her cries were out of concern for the hardship she felt this news was going to cause me and the kids. She couldn't hold back apologizing.

All I could think about was my dear wife and how different this news was from the past times, when there was only one tumor to be dealt with and the prognosis had promise for a total cure. I was overwhelmed and in shock. I didn't know what to do or say to console Barbara. As fright came over me too, I couldn't stop thinking that this time, I was definitely going to lose Barbara.

Dr. Stern was calming, as he explained that this time there would be no cure, but there were treatments to keep the cancer under control. First, he needed to confirm the kind of cancer that was present in her lungs. On December 19, Barbara was admitted to Morristown Memorial Hospital so that Dr. Max Wertheim could perform a right thoracoscopic segmental resection for a right lung nodule biopsy. The surgeon would make a small incision into

Barbara's back, at her left shoulder, and enter into Barbara's lung, to view the nodules and obtain a biopsy.

After the surgery, Dr. Wertheim called me into his office to discuss his findings. He said that the nodule in Barbara's lung was cancer and there were several such nodules in both lungs.

I didn't know how to take this news. I felt like I'd just lost my wife.

"So, my wife has lung cancer?"

"No, it's stage IV metastatic breast cancer. Your doctor wouldn't have put your wife through this surgery had he been certain it was lung cancer. Now that it's confirmed that it's breast cancer, Dr. Stern will develop a plan for her treatment."

With this news, I should have felt somewhat relieved. If it had been lung cancer, it would have been all over. But it wasn't lung cancer. I could have told myself that it was good news, that it was breast cancer and not some different cancer. But it was stage IV, and, at that moment, I couldn't accept the results as good news.

It was just news. News that sounded so final to me. I couldn't find anything good about it, other than it not being lung cancer. But I needed to prepare to tell Barbara. I rationalized to myself that it was good news. That it wasn't a finality, and we'd have more time for another miracle to happen. I needed to find the hope and faith, like Barbara always had.

In recovery, I sat beside Barbara's bed waiting for her to wake up. When she began to open her eyes, I stood up. When she saw me, I saw her smile a little. I leaned over to give her a kiss and whispered, "Barbara ... some good news. The nodules in your lungs are the same kind of breast cancer. Now Dr. Stern can begin treatment."

Hearing that, her dimples took over her smile. "Good. because I'm planning to live to hold many more babies."

Barbara was able to keep hope. She still had it in her mind that we were going ahead with the apartment in Hoboken. But I couldn't bring myself to think about moving at this point. Barbara had such close relationships with her friends at work and, considering every-thing, I didn't want to take her away from that. I couldn't bring myself to tell her that we weren't going ahead with Hoboken, because her future was questionable. I waited a couple of days as Barbara recovered from the surgery. One evening during dinner, I said, "I don't think that we should go ahead with the move to Hoboken."

"Why not? We want a different lifestyle and the commute is too much for you anymore."

"Yeah, but it's a rough economy and we'd have to sell this house and it's probably not a good time to buy."

I wondered if she bought that excuse. Barbara was no fool. I hoped she didn't read into my real reason. Yes, my commute was becoming pretty tough for me. But the timing didn't seem right, to move to a place where we wouldn't know anyone. I was confused about what to do and the easy decision, for me, was to not move.

One evening, in the middle of all this going on, my company had its holiday party at the Newark Museum. Barbara didn't want to miss the party. She felt it would be a good diversion for both of us to attend. Barbara insisted that cancer wasn't going to completely control her life.

As soon as we walked into the party, we were greeted by the wives of two guys that I worked closely with. The two women were recent breast cancer survivors. Barbara, a twenty-five-year and three-time survivor, was their role model. They were unaware of Barbara's most recent recurrence. Considering their fragility, Barbara didn't want to burst their bubble and chose not to mention anything about our current ordeal.

It was extremely difficult for Barbara and me. The women were all over Barbara, talking about us looking forward to having grandchildren soon. They sincerely had good wishes for Barbara. But underneath those wishes, they viewed Barbara's survival and longevity as hope for their own futures.

The conversation was killing me. I couldn't keep up a good front and engage in the conversation. Barbara looked at me and saw the hurt in my eyes. Barbara did a better job of keeping her composure, while talking with the women. It wasn't until our drive home that we talked about it, and I asked, "So, what do you think?"

"About what?" Barbara asked.

"Well, the party was nice, but those two didn't let up. I know that they're two of the sweetest, nicest people, but their kindness and sincerity was killing me."

"Oh, Marc. They meant well and are happy for us. I quickly realized that you hadn't told anyone in your office. Why haven't you told people?"

I didn't know how to answer Barbara. I'd told Steve, the owner of the company, but no one else. I was confused. I didn't want to have to explain to people what was going on in our lives. I was hoping for something and didn't know what I was hoping for. I just wanted to keep things as normal as possible, without being asked questions about how Barbara was doing or how I was holding up. I'd been through this drill before. And this time, there wasn't going to be a cure. I was in denial.

Barbara was handling it all fine and was accepting that there was no cure this time. She looked beautiful, healthy, and full of smiles. No one was able to tell that there were these little boogers (that's what we called the cancer cells) floating around inside of her. Barbara was ready to fight and stand up to her cancer, while going forward day-to-day, as if there were no cancer. I didn't know if I could ever accept it as well as Barbara. And I didn't know how to tell her about my fears.

As I struggled with how to answer Barbara's question, she beat me to it and answered it herself. "Marc ... it is what it is. Nothing is going to change, and the cancer isn't going away. You need to tell people at work. As far as tonight went, I couldn't bring myself to tell them about me at the party and it was better that they didn't know. It would have soured the whole evening for us and for them. Once you tell everyone at work, they'll hear about it and be able to handle the news at a private time to themselves, rather than at a party."

"It just got to me when they started in with grandchildren and everything else."

"Yeah ... but that didn't bother me at all. I plan on being around for everything."

By spring 2007, Barbara was getting used to the treatments and we were both able to shift our minds to accept that battling cancer was now a permanent part of our life. But new scans showed that the disease was progressing. Dr. Stern recommended a different regimen and wanted us to get a second opinion for next steps. He referred us to Dr. Sandra Abbasi at a medical center in New York City.

On May 7, we met with Dr. Abbasi. The doctor confirmed the planned next steps, which were a series of different chemotherapy treatments. She also discussed with us the possibility of taking part in new clinical trials, in the future. Barbara and I were comforted by the meeting. Dr. Abbasi would go on to play an important role in helping us keep our sanity through the ups and downs of future test results. We felt that we could look forward to many more years, with new discoveries. We felt time was on our side. As for the ongoing doctor appointments and cancer treatments, they became a way of life, just another part of our day-to-day routine.

Driving home from work one evening, I came to realize that we needed to move after all. The traffic on Route 80 was only getting worse. I was getting older. I couldn't take the commute anymore and knew we had to move. Later that evening, while watching TV, I brought up Hoboken to Barbara. "The first building at Maxwell Place in Hoboken is open. Let's take a ride there this Saturday and see how it turned out."

"That's a good idea," Barbara answered. "I still think that we'd be happy in Hoboken."

We went that Saturday and agreed that we'd be happy in Hoboken, specifically with an apartment in Maxwell Place. Barbara was ready to move. However, even though it was my suggestion to take another look at Hoboken, when faced with a decision, I started thinking all over again about the probability of something happening to Barbara. I feared having Barbara distant from her friends, about fifty miles away.

By August 2007, our lives and routine were totally back, and even though it wasn't going away, the cancer seemed like a passing phase. Once again, I asked, "Do you want to go back and look at Maxwell Place again?"

"Of course! You keep having us go back to Hoboken and then you decide to do nothing. You're just like so many of my clients. You're anxious to buy and quickly get cold feet. Let's find an apartment and move. We know what we want."

"Really? We know what we want?" I answered.

For sure, I didn't know what I wanted or what to do. I couldn't take the commute anymore but didn't want to take Barbara away from her work and friends. Barbara was totally on board with moving. And I was on board with moving and keeping Barbara nearby to her work and friends. I wanted both, not one or the other. I wanted both! Depending on the time of the day, I had different thoughts about what to do and what I wanted.

Barbara was certain and answered, "Yes, I know what I want! I want a two-bedroom, two-and-a-half-bathroom apartment with direct views of Manhattan, and nothing less."

"Are you trying to make it more difficult with those demands, because you really don't want to move?"

"Absolutely not! I'm making it easier, by making it totally clear to you, my dear, about everything that I want."

"Well, we'll have to see what the prices are first."

A couple of weekends later, we went back to Maxwell Place. We discussed our budget before we got there. Very quickly, we learned that our budget wasn't going to get us everything Barbara wanted. Barbara conceded her demand for a direct view of Manhattan, exchanging it for an angled view, as long as she could see lots of sky, with unobstructed views from every window.

I wanted Barbara to be happy. It helped that she became a little flexible. I studied the plans for all the apartments and was attracted to a corner penthouse unit, which would have angled views of Manhattan. The unit would have ceiling heights of ten feet, seven inches, with twenty-one windows and a sliding glass door to the balcony, all with glass up to the ceiling, giving the unit incredible, unobstructed views of the sky. It also had two bedrooms, two-and-a-half baths, and an office/den.

We reviewed the apartment with the developer's sales representative. When I heard the price, I got a quick chill and gulped.

Barbara turned to me. "Can we afford this?"

I gulped again and somehow answered, "Yes!"

We went under contract by the end of August 2007 at an amount $550,000 over our original budget. But Barbara was happy. The apartment would be ready for our move-in around early summer 2009.

For Barbara and me, good things were ahead for us, and our future was filled with hope and promise. As the Jewish New Year was about to begin, Barbara sent an email to the kids on September 11, 2007.

Subject: Forward: Happy New Year

Below is a copy of an email I sent out tonight to as many people on my email list I could think of. I hope I did not miss anyone.

I wanted to send you all a special message. Although we do not belong to any temple, you know that I pray each and every day and carry God in my heart. Although this has been such a difficult year in many ways, we have sooo much to be grateful for. I am the luckiest woman on the face of this earth to have such a fantastic family. I love you all sooooo much. **WE** have many celebrations to come. In only a few weeks, a new baby!!!! There will be weddings to go to and babies to hold and I am looking forward to **ALL** of them.

I want to wish you all a Shana Tova; a happy, **HEALTHY** and Sweet New Year!!!!!

Love, Mommy

Below that email to the kids, was the copy of the email Barbara sent to friends and family.

Subject: Happy New Year

Dear Friends and Family:

Marc and I want to take this opportunity to wish you and your families a Shana Tovah; the happiest and sweetest of New Years.

I also want to personally thank each and every one of you for all the love and support and prayers you have given to me and my family. Please know that I value the love and friendship of each and every one of you and am so grateful to have you in my life. Please keep up the prayers. God is listening!! Along with all the trials and tribulations we have been through, we have been blessed with some very good things this year; the incredible news of Kristen and Stephen expecting a baby – our first grandchild, the continuing success of Jonathan's company, Anipath, Brian's new job, and the blessing of healthy, happy children and of course, some good test results. **WE** look forward to many good things to come and wonderful celebrations.

I keep you all in my prayers each day and hope you will continue to keep me and my family in yours.

Again, Shana Tovah and may we **ALL** be written in the Book of Life for another wonderful, sweet, **HEALTHY** New Year.

All my love,

Barbara

In December 2008, Barbara called me while I was at work. "Marc, the rep from Maxwell Place just called and said that our apartment has been sheetrocked. Nothing else is done, but we can go into the apartment this weekend and actually see how the apartment lays out and take measurements."

"Okay, let's do that."

That Saturday was a cold winter day, but sunny. We got to the sales office and a rep escorted us to the apartment. The sheetrocking had been finished earlier that week and dust and extra boards were still all around the apartment. But we were able to walk from room to room. The corner unit had windows that faced south and west, and the afternoon sun was shining brightly into the apartment.

"If you don't snitch on me, I can leave you here," the rep said to us. But there are no lights in the apartment, just temporary lighting in the hallway. Once the sun goes down, it's going to be dark in the apartment. Don't wait for the last minute to leave, because with all of the material laying around on the floors, you could get hurt."

Barbara and I were alone in our new home. We giggled going from room to room. Getting ready to leave, we took an extra peaceful moment to look out the windows that faced west and we leaned back against a knee wall, which would eventually hold the kitchen counter. We were in awe over the beautiful view, as the sun was beginning to set over the cliff of Jersey City Heights.

I turned to look at Barbara and felt my body quiver as I saw tears running down her cheeks. Although my eyes began to tear up too, I attempted to lighten up the moment. "Are you crying because you're happy? Or because you're thinking about how much we're paying for this two-bedroom apartment?"

Barbara answered, "Wow, a poor girl from The Bronx is going to be living in this apartment. Now ... I just need to live."

With that, I put my arm around Barbara and we kissed as we watched the sun continue to set behind the cliff. Barbara's eyes continued to fill with tears. Mine did too, as I heard Barbara's words, "I just need to live," repeating in my mind. We didn't want to leave that spot. It was as if we were meant to remain forever frozen in that spot, with my arm around Barbara. We waited until the very second that the sun was about to completely set behind the cliff and then we left. Standing together in that cold apartment, on that late afternoon in December, was one of the most incredibly romantic and emotional moments of our marriage.

It would be a little more than six years later before I would tell anyone about Barbara and me watching the sunset from the apartment on that day in December. It was at the Bris, the circumcision ceremony, for our grandson. Barbara would not get to meet Jonathan's wife. I know that she would have loved Stacey and, of course, our grandson, Benjamin.

A couple of months before Benjamin was born, Jonathan called me. "Hey, Dad, well, you know that we're having a boy. Stacey and I are planning to have a Bris. We'd like to have it in your apartment, since there are some memories there and lots of pictures."

Benjamin (Ben, my dad's name) was born in February 2015. The Bris was in my apartment. I did all the preparations for this event. The key thing I did was to raise all the window shades up to the ceiling in every room. Barbara wanted an apartment with lots of windows to look out from and see lots of sky. That day, I raised all the shades, so that the sky could look in and see us.

When the mohel, the person who performs Jewish circumcisions, arrived, he asked where I wanted him to perform the ceremony. I set him up to perform the ceremony in the exact same spot where Barbara and I stood to watch the sun set that day back in December 2008.

Back to May 29, 2009. We closed on the apartment and moved in on June 2. Stephen's aunt and uncle, Rona and Rex, lived in Hoboken and invited us to a "welcome to Hoboken" dinner that evening. By dinnertime, Barbara and I were all tired out from the move and too tired to walk to their house. "Barbara, how are we getting to Rona and Rex's? We're urbanites now and we're not supposed to drive to places. Now we have a new lifestyle issue: searching for a parking space if we do drive to some place in town. I'm too tired to walk. Let's take a cab."

Rex offered to drive us home after dinner. But by then, we were a little rested and wanted to hold hands and laugh and take our first walk as residents of Hoboken. We felt young and like true urbanites. It was as if, with a blink of our eyes, our lives were turned back thirty-eight years and we were honeymooners again, back in Jackson Heights.

It was our first night in Hoboken and fun to be getting into bed. We fell asleep quickly and were awakened at about two thirty by a strange noise. I sat up.

Barbara said, "I didn't know you were up. Did that noise wake you too?"

"Yes, what is that?"

It was a beautiful evening, and we had the sliding glass door to the balcony open a little, letting the sounds of the city come in. I got out of bed and went to the dining room windows and looked down to Hudson Street. Barbara followed behind me, asking, "So, what's that noise?"

"It's that garbage truck, picking up the garbage along Hudson Street."

"They pick up the garbage at two thirty in the morning?" Barbara asked.

"I guess it's easier, not having to compete with the traffic during the day. Welcome to the sounds of urban living," I answered. We laughed, went back to bed, and lived happily ever after.

This book is a story, a "once upon a time" a very long time ago, about a boy, born in Brooklyn, and a girl, born in The Bronx, who met and fell in love. They were married and for the first two years, as honeymooners, lived in an apartment in Jackson Heights. Then, they moved from Jackson Heights to New Jersey, had three children, and lived happily ever after.

In most stories, "once upon a time" only comes once. But when they moved to Hoboken, that boy and girl, still so much in love, began a new story. A second "once upon a time." But not a very long time ago. And living happily ever after would only last a little more than two years.

PART 5

Stories from the Fifth Day of Shiva

"Well, silly, I may not know everything about selling real estate. But at least, I haven't called anyone Mrs. Pussy."

CHAPTER 26

We've come full circle

We were busily getting settled in, exploring Hoboken, meeting new neighbors, and having fun with city living. In early July, Barbara mentioned she had been talking with the kids about my sixtieth birthday. They all wanted to make me a surprise party. My birthday was August 22, and it was going to fall out on a Saturday.

I laughed, finding it funny that Barbara was telling me about a surprise party. "Hey, silly head, if you are planning to make me a surprise party, why are you telling me about it?"

"We figured a surprise party would be a challenge. And it would be easier if we told you and you could choose where to have the party."

"So, let me think about this. You're going to have me choose everything, and then make me a surprise party?"

"No, silly. It's not going to be a surprise party anymore."

I was joking around a little, to have some time to get my thoughts together about a party. We had a large, expensive party for Barbara's fiftieth birthday. But I felt differently about that party. Barbara had survived three cancers. To me, that party meant so much more than a celebration of a birthday. It was a celebration of life, making it to a milestone. I didn't think I wanted a party beyond us and the kids, and I asked, "Why? What kind of party are you thinking about?"

"At a restaurant, here in Hoboken, with a private party room that could accommodate about a hundred people. I went over to Tutta Pasta, at Washington and Second Street. They have a very nice room on the second floor, above the restaurant. We already know that the food is good, and it sounded like they can make us a nice party."

"I don't think so. The move here was a big expense, and we still need so much for the apartment and have so many other expenses ahead of us."

"Listen, I already discussed everything with the kids. I want to make this party. You and I have an appointment with Tutta Pasta this Saturday, and you can finalize the plans the way you want. Also, I plan on ordering a cake from the Cake King."

"Shit! How much is that going to cost? Can't we just get a cake from ShopRite?"

"Marc, you better not keep asking about how much everything costs. We're making you a nice party. The kids and I are all excited. So, tell your brain to get excited too."

I didn't see the need for this party. Although I must admit, by the day of the party, I was excited. We got to Tutta Pasta before the guests started to arrive. Barbara arranged for the bartender to begin serving me mojitos as soon as I walked in. The party started off with a cocktail hour. As the guests started to arrive, the younger crowd included me in doing shots. My head was spinning. But it was wild and fun. Then everyone was seated for the dinner.

The party was in the restaurant's private dining room on the second floor, called Danny's Upstairs. During the week, Danny's had an open mic setup for stand-up comedy routines. Having this setup was the main reason Barbara chose this restaurant. Barbara went to the microphone and welcomed everyone. Then, she asked me to come up to the platform to say a few words.

I wasn't expecting to have to say anything. Plus, after the drinks and the shots, I wasn't that steady on my feet. As I walked up to the platform, I wondered what I was going to say. My biggest concern was, am I going to be able to stand without holding on to something? When I stepped onto the platform, I realized that I could hold on to the microphone stand.

Although I didn't have a prepared speech, Kristen was set up to take a video of me as I spoke, so that I would have a recording. As I began to write this chapter, I wasn't sure whether to include what I said at the party. My presentation was a little choppy, I was ad-libbing and drunk. But over the years, my entertaining, either doing some stand-up routine, or leading everyone in a song, became such an expected part of our house parties. Plus, watching the video, I found that in addition to the funny stuff, I also said some sweet things.

My mind was blank at first. But, as soon as I looked out at relatives, friends, Barbara, and my kids, the words seemed to easily flow out of my mouth. "Oh, my ... oh, my ... I think that I need this post to hold me up." I grabbed onto the microphone stand. "That's better ... now I can stand straight."

As I looked out at everyone, I quickly became humbled by the sight. Suddenly I was happy for this party. Barbara and I had moved to Hoboken just a few months before. Now, standing at the microphone, thoughts quickly came to me of so much to reflect on. I had given speeches before and I saw this time as another opportunity to say special things to my family and friends.

> Thank you. Oh my God, what a view. This is really an incredible view to look out and see everybody. And ... a ... a ... really incredible to see people from all parts of my life. It's very nice.

I began speaking slowly and with hesitation, buying some time to gather my what-to-say thoughts. It quickly came to me what I wanted to say from my heart. But I was a little unsure whether it was a time to be serious or silly. Being a little drunk, the silliness poured out first. I figured that it wouldn't be me, without at least a little silliness.

So, I keep being asked by people ... How does it feel to be sixty? I'm not sure what the answer could be. But people ask, how does it feel to be sixty? I always get the feeling that people are asking ... they want to have more information but are ashamed to ask. It's like they want to have more information about what's really going on in this sixty-year-old man. That ... um ... they just ask this general question. How does it feel to be sixty? And, you know, I don't know how to answer that. But if they were more specific and asked something like, does your penis still function? I have to believe that that's an easier question to answer than, how does it feel to be sixty? Because it's specific ... and more about what people have on their minds.

So, if any of you have that question ... my penis is fine. It's very spontaneous, it's very dependable ... and, after all these years, it's still my best friend. Right now, my children, Jonathan, Kristen, and Brian are saying, "I'm so embarrassed." And my son-in-law, Stephen, is saying, "Good for you, Dad."

Everyone was laughing hysterically. I looked at my kids. They were laughing too, with red, embarrassed faces. Barbara was laughing, while shaking her head. Not in disbelief at what I had said. I could read her lips, saying, "You are so silly." In the meantime, I was wondering how to continue. I was quite drunk. Standing up straight and steady was a challenge.

Another question that people could ask—I think I should hold on to this post—I don't think that I could stand without holding on. Another question people could ask is, you know, how are your bodily functions? That's another specific question, rather than, how does it feel to be sixty? It's a question you could answer. How are your bodily functions?

Well, my bodily functions, if anyone has that question about how it is ... it's fine ... an occasional wet fart. You know, for young people, farting is a very highly underrated thing. For young people, farting is a great relief, other than for the people around you. It's better to be the fart-er than being the fart-ee. So ... um ... but, for young people farting is good. But as the years go by, it's a risk that ... you just don't want to go there.

But how does it feel to be sixty? I was reminded that I was sixty, recently ... not so recently ... in July, when we went to visit Jonathan in Florida. I was coming back in the airport and I was reminded of my age, when I was standing on the line and a guy screamed, "Take off your shoes!" Well, that could be easy for many people but, when you're sixty and you're standing up? They don't give you a chair and they don't say, "Oh, excuse me, sir, you're sixty years old. We're going to give you a chair to sit down." They just say, "Take off your shoes!"

They say it nasty, too, and you're afraid to not do it. So, taking off shoes, in a standing up position, for a sixty-year-old man, is not the easiest thing, for many sixty-year-old people. It's particularly difficult because I double-tie my shoes. And the reason that I double-tie my shoes is because if I have to bend down in the morning to tie my shoes, I don't want to have to do it again throughout the course of the day. So, standing on the line and untying my shoes, I was reminded I'm sixty years old.

There's always someone behind me, during this time, who will roll his eyes and make all kinds of gestures. Which, at that moment ... I untie my shoes much slower. Because, you know, being sixty years old, I'm at the airport three hours before the plane takes off. Whereas, the person, usually behind me, who may be thirty years old, he's ready for the plane. So, when they show that they, kind of, can't wait for me to take off my shoes ... I kind of slow it down a little bit. Because, I have all the time in the world.

So, anyway, on this most recent trip to ... actually, I was coming back from Florida. And I made it through the security, and I had everything, except for my shoes. I was waiting and waiting, and I said to the young girl, "Excuse me, I have everything. What's wrong with my shoes?"

She says, "Oh, the machine, it's tied up. It'll be a while."

And I go, "Well, you know, I'm standing here in stocking feet on a cold concrete floor and for a sixty-year-old man, with an enlarged prostate, I can't stand here much longer."

She said, "It'll just be a moment."

I waited a moment and said, "Excuse me, I have to go to the bathroom. I don't think you realize what's going on here. This is enough."

She said, "Well, if you have everything, go to the bathroom and we'll watch your shoes, if that's the only thing you're waiting for."

"Excuse me! Have you ever been in the men's bathroom? The last place that you want to be, in stocking feet, is the men's bathroom."

You know, I understand that women ... that before they go anyplace, they have to go to the bathroom, even if they don't have to go to the bathroom. They want to be ready, and they go to the bathroom and into the stall and neatly do whatever they have to do.

Men are different. You know, we wait until way beyond when we have to go to the bathroom. Our penis is down to our knees before we go to the bathroom. And, when we walk in ... no sooner than we've walked into the door, we're already unzipping ourselves, getting ready. Because we extend way beyond when we have to go to the bathroom, so we can't wait. And I said to the young girl, "Those urinals that are put on the walls are just for show. Men don't pee in those urinals. Men begin peeing as soon as we walk through the door. That's why, when men see another man hurrying in, you don't get in his way."

This young girl just didn't understand.

"Please get me my shoes. I can't go to the bathroom in stocking feet. It could be a mess."

If we make it to the urinal, we're looking at the ceiling and side-to-side and peeing in anything but that urinal. I did get my shoes and made it to the bathroom. And that made me feel sixty years old. No one else in the line seemed to have that problem. I didn't see any other sixty-year-olds on the line, at least they didn't look sixty years old.

By this time, I had gotten my laughs from everyone and the silliness out of me. As I was beginning to feel the emotions of seriousness come over me, I guess the expression on my face changed; the room became totally silent. Thoughts came to me about our children and all that Barbara and I had been through. Now, we had a new start for good things to come, with a new lifestyle. We were urbanites, once again. It was a perfect moment to talk about our children and our love. I began:

Anyway, it really is an unbelievable sight to see everybody, as I stand here and look at faces of people that I've known for many years and some more recently. And so, the question is ... the original question is, how does it feel to be sixty? So, how does it feel to be sixty?

Well, being sixty, I have children who are old enough that I respect what they have to say, and I listen to them. They tell me what to do. They tell me how to live and they're right. They know what it is, and they know what I need.

For example, last week Brian said to me, "Dad, you look like an old man. I'm meeting you at the eyeglass place and we're getting you a new pair of glasses."

And I said, "I don't need new glasses."

He said, "Dad, you need new glasses. You look like an old man."

So, I met with him at the eyeglass place, and he picked them out. Because I couldn't look at the glasses without my glasses and they give you lenses you can't see through. I've learned that my children are smart. I listen to them and they know how to live, and they give good advice. I do appreciate it.

And I'm old enough to have a son that I didn't have to raise. Stephen came to us fully grown ... plus a few inches. I didn't have to send him to college and he's well-behaved. He's the only child that doesn't roll his eyes back into his head while I'm talking to him. Yes, I'm old enough to have that.

I'm old enough to have a grand-dog. My grand-dog, Brewster, was one year old yesterday, August 21. That was a delight. I'm going to see him in a few weeks.

I'm old enough to have a two-and-a-half-foot tall little guy, who comes into the apartment and destroys everything. And, my kids look and say, "Who's Daddy? We don't remember him being like that when we were little. When did he get like that?"

Because Jonah can do anything. Today he was drinking out of a glass. I was so happy watching him drink the glass of water. Then he dropped it and it spilled and broke all over the floor ... and that was okay. That comes with being sixty years old. That this little guy, who's two-and-a-half feet tall, can do anything and he can do whatever he wants.

Then, I took a long pause. I wasn't quite sure if I could get the words that were in my heart spoken from my mouth. I gazed at Barbara and she gave me a sweet smile, shook her head yes, and reached her hand out to me, and I continued with a cry in my voice.

Another thing about being sixty ... I'm old enough to be married thirty-eight years. Next Saturday, a week from today, will be my thirty-eighth wedding anniversary ... and Barbara's too.

That got a big loud applause from everyone. The room quieted down, and I continued to gaze at Barbara and speak as if it were only the two of us. During our forty-six years of puppy love, there were many times when Barbara and I were in a crowd or among many people. So many of those times, I would look at Barbara and feel as if it were just the two of us, as if no one else were there or mattered. This moment was one of those times.

And I'm reminded of thirty-eight years ago, we lived in a two-bedroom apartment in Jackson Heights, Queens. And I used to wait for you until you came home from work, and we'd go out and we'd have fun. We went to the dollar movie, 'cause that's what we could afford. And I remember going out to dinner one night to the Astoria Diner. And after the meal, the check came. We barely had enough money to pay the bill. We were scrounging for the tip. The bill was like $4.25 and we felt so bad that the tip we left was, like, fifteen cents. But between the two of us, that was all that we had in our pockets. That was thirty-eight years ago.

And now, thirty-eight years later, we're living in a two-bedroom apartment in Hoboken. But we don't go to the dollar movie anymore. And if I told you what Barbara paid for shades for the apartment ... It happened to be sixteen thousand dollars.

The mood in the room quickly changed with that statement. It got quite a bit of laughs. With a smile, Barbara had an embarrassed look on her face, and I could read her lips saying, "Oh, for God's sake." So, I figured I'd embarrass her a little more.

At first, I thought that anyone who spends sixteen thousand dollars on shades has to be crazy. But we've had the shades now for six weeks and I love them and in thinking about it ... I still think that anybody who spends sixteen thousand dollars is crazy.

I paused again and the room got quiet. The thoughts in my mind were coming to me fast as a roller coaster. I was going up and down from silliness to seriousness. I had gotten to the point when all my silliness was totally gone, and I continued.

But it's a different life. For the years that we lived in the suburbs, when I'd come home from work, we'd stay in the house and wouldn't go anyplace. And I remember those years, before the children, when we lived in Jackson Heights. When I waited for Barbara at the subway stop, and we went out and we enjoyed.

Now, thirty-eight years later, when I get home from work, we go out and enjoy. We've come full circle and I'm very thankful ... and thankful for all of you for being here. Thank you.

Barbara came up to the platform and gave me a kiss and hug. She had arranged to have a large monitor set up to play a video that she had a photographer make. The video included my very young years, teenage years, adult years, and ended with my grandson, Jonah, saying, "Happy, Happy Birthday."

After, I was so happy that Barbara made me this party. I had a good time and enjoyed being with everyone. I so enjoyed seeing Barbara with a beaming smile, as she thanked everyone for coming and helping to make the occasion so much fun. Sometimes, we let milestones in our lives go by, without any celebration or recognition, or even any acknowledgement. By doing that, we miss out on the happiness from the sharing and the togetherness that comes with celebrating a happy occasion with family and friends.

Actually, I'm happier today than I was back then, that Barbara made the party. Exactly two years and three weeks to the day after my birthday, Barbara would have celebrated her sixtieth birthday. I lost Barbara six weeks before her sixtieth birthday. In a way, I feel like she celebrated her sixtieth along with mine, just two years earlier.

CHAPTER 27

Quality of life and hope

On a Monday evening in mid-October 2009, Barbara mentioned to me that Kristen and Stephen were going to stop by one evening later in the week. A friend of Stephen's from work lived in Hoboken and was leaving the company. Kristen and Stephen were going to meet the friend and others from the office for a drink.

It sounded odd to me that Kristen would come to Hoboken to join in, just for drinks. I asked Barbara if they were having dinner with us and she said, no. They were just stopping by to say hello. The next day, Barbara mentioned to me that they changed their minds and decided to have dinner with us and then go for drinks with friends.

Wednesday evening, Kristen and Stephen came to the apartment. Barbara decided to order in dinner. Brian joined us too. During dinner, I asked Stephen about his friend's reasons for leaving the company. We discussed that a while. For some reason, the whole thing didn't sound convincing. I felt like something was up.

"You're just going for drinks? Your friends couldn't, at the least, make it a farewell dinner? And how come you didn't arrange to do this in Manhattan after work? Anyway, you're going for drinks. Be careful driving home."

Stephen answered, "Oh, no, I'm not driving. Kristen will drive home. She can't drink, because she's pregnant."

Barbara immediately jumped up with this big smile, shouting, "Are you serious?" I just sat there trying to process what was just said. I wasn't sure what I'd heard. It wasn't until Barbara started hugging and kissing the two of them, did I realize what Stephen had said. I continued sitting there, surprised and a little bewildered.

This news would change our plans for a vacation to Disney. For several months, Barbara had been trying to firm up the best time for that vacation with our first grandchild, Jonah. She so wanted the trip to be as soon as possible, but at an age that Jonah would understand what it was about. Stephen didn't want to go during the summer in the heat. Barbara talked about the spring of 2010.

People advised that at two-and-a-half years old, Jonah was a little young to appreciate Disney. So, Barbara began thinking about going in the fall of 2010. Jonah would almost be three. But now, with a new baby on the way, those plans needed to be postponed. Barbara began to think about how soon to go after the baby was born, with Kristen's due date in June 2010.

Barbara decided the best time for Disney would be the spring of 2011. Jonah would be almost three-and-a-half and the baby would be nine or ten months. People advised that Jonah, at three-and-a-half, would still be too young and the baby wouldn't get anything out of the trip. Barbara's response was, "So we'll go again a year later and then again a year after that."

Barbara was racing the clock, which was ticking away. We never lost hope for a longer future together and we didn't change our life-style because of Barbara's illness. But when it came to making plans for taking our grandchildren to Disney, Barbara did not want to take the chance of missing the opportunity for a trip of a lifetime.

Barbara announced the new schedule for the Disney trip, and we didn't have to think any more about it, at that time. Now, it was all about the arrival of another grandchild. Barbara so needed to focus on this gift of a new life in our family. She so often asked me if I was happy about the news. But I knew she was really asking if she was going to be all right. I would say, "Of course, I'm happy! And this will give you more things to plan for."

Barbara would answer, "So, I'm not going anywhere other than sticking around to be with our grandchildren and I'm going to be all right? Just tell me that."

"Yes, you're going to be all right," I answered.

"You promise?"

"Yes, I promise."

In my heart, I knew that I was promising something I had no control over. I always had the feeling that Barbara believed I had more information that I wasn't telling her. By asking me this while looking me straight in the eyes, she believed that I was telling the truth and that I knew for a fact that all would be all right. But I didn't. All I had was hope that new treatments would come on the market.

Barbara knew I was constantly doing research on the Internet. I always told her of new treatments and therapies being worked on and the vast number of alternative drug treatments. What I didn't have the courage to tell her was that there were a finite number of drugs. Although there were new drugs coming on the market, I always feared the day when Barbara would exhaust the list and there would be no more available in time for her.

I learned that each protocol had a life-term of several months or a couple of years. Then the cancer would become immune to the treatment and more aggressive. The doctors would tell Barbara, if the drug doesn't work, they had another. I knew the supply wasn't endless and so did Barbara. But she didn't ask, and I needed to keep hope in my heart and on my face for Barbara. I never wanted her to feel that I would ever give up on her. Hope was so important to our quality of life, and hope was important as we looked forward to the birth of our second grandchild.

CHAPTER 28

This can't be our last New Year's Eve

The winter holidays of 2009 came. Barbara and I were back in South Beach. Lynn and Elliot were there too. Lynn and her friend from Michigan were busily planning for New Year's Eve 2010 and keeping Barbara in the loop, so we could join them too. But, as much as we loved their company and we knew we would have a blast, Barbara and I weren't sure if we wanted to join them.

The year before, we had a wonderfully wild time with that group at a restaurant called Taverna Opa. But Barbara and I wanted to spend this New Year's Eve differently, just the two of us. Also, we didn't want to go far. Although, as long as we stayed in South Beach, nothing was that far away. I'm not sure why, but we wanted something different. We just didn't know what we wanted the different to be.

As I write this chapter, I think about how Barbara and I would wonder what the "different" was that we were so often looking for. Was it really having three kids, because friends and relatives had two? Or moving to New Jersey, because everyone else was moving to Long

Island? Also, there were those talks we had about wanting to be "us." Was this the different that we were after?

I can see now that Barbara and I always knew the answer and we always attained the different. As I look through Shiva Eyes, it is so clear to me. So, what was the different? It was simply being ourselves. It was not being followers, and not accepting what others did as a necessary path for us. Different was being the us that we wanted to be. Because when we gazed into each other's eyes, we could always find us and the confidence in our belief that there was nothing we could ever do more perfectly than be ourselves. Although there would be uncertainty in what we wanted the different to be, our experiences always turned out to be the way we wanted them. And we always saw the different ... through our eyes.

For something close, we decided to go to a steakhouse on Washington Avenue, directly across the street from our building. Red, the Steakhouse Miami Beach offered a special evening for New Year's. We could have dinner in the restaurant and go up to the roof deck of the building after dinner, for drinks. From the roof deck, we would be able to watch three fireworks going on at once: from the beach at Lummus Park, from Bay Side in Miami, and from Biscayne Bay. We agreed, this was what we wanted to do.

New Year's Eve came, and it seemed so calm and peaceful to the two of us. I think it seemed that way because we weren't looking for anything to be special or to meet other people or to try to get drunk. We weren't looking for it to be anything other than a night for just the two of us.

We did get dressed up for dinner, but there was no pressure about anything. All we had to do was cross the street and New Year's Eve would begin. Dinner at Red was great. The prices were high, but it was New Year's Eve, and this was South Beach. Barbara noticed that Red had Kobe steak on the menu, but no price. Barbara said she didn't care what the price was. Kobe steak was what we were having.

When it came time to order, Barbara inquired about the price of the steak. A surprised look sprung across her face. The price was outrageous.

"I don't think so," I said calmly, hoping she would agree, So, we ordered our drinks and had a great dinner and dessert too. The restaurant was packed. It was wonderful to be surrounded by young lovers celebrating their New Year's Eve. These young people were us, thirty years ago. It was so beautiful to see and be in the middle of.

After dinner we took the elevator to the roof. I don't do well on roofs, perhaps part of my OCD. As we stepped off the elevator and out to the roof, I asked, "This is fun?"

"Oh, come on. We can get a little closer to the edge."

"Okay. But no drinks. I'm dizzy enough from just being up here. I don't need to add to my dizziness."

Nothing else was important beyond the fact that we were together. I began to frighten myself, wondering why I felt this way. Did my intuition know something? Would this be our last New Year's Eve? Why had we put so much into wanting this night to be peaceful and just the two of us? The whole feeling thing made me anxious, and I had to calm myself down. "This can't be our last New Year's Eve," I thought to myself. "Barbara looks so good, so beautiful. In a few months we'll have a new grandchild." No, it was just too soon for *us* to end.

I surprised myself, as a calm came over me on that roof. It was Barbara's smile. She was so happy. We had so much to look forward to and we enjoyed the scenery of the young romance that surrounded us. Barbara finally eased me over to the parapet wall and we looked out at the beautiful, exciting South Beach scenery. We could see in all directions and it was romantic.

We began to kiss. Well actually, we began to make out. For God's sake, we were fifty-eight and sixty years old and married for thirty-eight years. But that night, up on that roof, we were like two horny teenagers again in Far Rockaway, Queens. Even though I was beginning to feel the arthritis in my knees from all the standing.

We kissed and we kissed, and we looked into each other's eyes. Nothing needed to be said. It was all in the kisses. I began to hold Barbara closer and closer, as I lowered my hands to hold her ass.

Forehead to forehead and looking into each other's eyes, Barbara softly asked me, "What do you think you're doing?"

"I'm holding your ass."

"Marc, we're on this roof with all these young couples. We are going to look like fools. So, take your hands off my ass."

"Nope. We need to be a role model. I'm never going to see these people again and who cares what anyone thinks. Screw them. Besides, I always grab your ass in public."

"Um ... that was forty years ago."

"Well, we're doing a lot of talking about this subject and in the meantime, I've had my hands on your ass the whole time. So, everyone probably noticed by now. So, they've either gotten over the sight or have learned something," I answered, as we continued kissing and I kept my hands on her ass.

Then, in our romantic moment, we began to hear the fireworks. It was spectacular. After the fireworks, we took the elevator down to the lobby, crossed the street to our building, and finished the evening making love.

There is much hype about makeup sex. But our true and devoted love, our hope to be together for eternity, and our feeling that there would never be anyone else, made for the best sex. That night felt like it was our first time, and we had a lifetime ahead of us.

Even though we started with no idea what we wanted, that New Year's Eve was everything we wanted it to be. It was romantic and we needed to say little to each other. Everything that needed saying was in our gaze into each other's eyes, and, of course, holding on to Barbara's ass on that rooftop.

The next day, we met Lynn and Elliot at the pool. Barbara asked them how their night was.

"Not so great," Elliot said. "And so expensive that I feel like I was robbed."

They knew of our plans and Barbara told them we had a very enjoyable evening. She didn't tell them about us making out on the roof.

The next day we left South Beach, heading back home to New Jersey and back to reality. Barbara was due for blood work in January.

CHAPTER 29

When does it end?

Barbara had been suffering for several months with a pain in the left side of her neck and shoulder. Thinking it was an ear infection or fluid draining in her left ear, Barbara went to an ear, nose, and throat doctor, but the pain persisted.

On a Saturday evening in mid-January 2010, Barbara and I went to dinner with a neighbor from our building. It was a cold winter evening and we bundled up for our walk to the restaurant, called 10th and Willow, which is also the location.

It was a fun evening. The restaurant was one of our favorites in Hoboken. The food is good, the drinks are great, and we were usually the oldest people in the restaurant. The front of the restaurant has a bar setup with counter-height tables and stools and the back room has a dining room. The restaurant gets kind of noisy as the evening progresses and a younger, mostly singles crowd takes over.

There was something rejuvenating about being around young people; Barbara and I just never felt we were getting older. Now, in Hoboken, our friends were younger, our new interests felt youthful, and our teenage kind of love seemed unending. It was fun being in that youthful environment with friends that evening. If we had we been alone, there would have been some touchy-feely at the table, with a few words from Barbara, such as, "Would you stop it?"

But I wouldn't have stopped, because if you want to feel young, you can't always reserve intimacy for the privacy of your home. Doing that classifies you as an adult and being an adult brings on too many responsibilities, ailments, and thoughts about the future. If you want to stay young, you have to think about now and believe you're going to live forever.

Dying is not for the young, and Barbara and I needed to be young. We needed to be back in the 1960s, sipping our black-and-white ice cream sodas at Jahn's. When we were teenagers, we would go to Jahn's after a movie. Jahn's was a popular ice cream restaurant and had several locations in the boroughs. We often went to the one near Eighty-Second Street in Jackson Heights or met friends from Forest Hills at the one on Queens Boulevard.

Jahn's made the best black-and-white ice cream sodas. I loved making fun of Barbara as she drank hers. Each time that she sipped her soda, her dimples would get so deep on her cheeks. When she wasn't paying attention, I would put my finger into her dimple. Barbara would say, "Stop being so silly. You're making me feel self-conscious." She was so cute with her dimples when she sipped the drink, and I couldn't help staring at her. She really liked my silliness.

The evening at 10th and Willow was all good, although Barbara did say that her neck hurt. As we were leaving the restaurant, the pain worsened. We were reminded of our life's reality. Suddenly, Barbara was almost crying from the pain, saying, "Get me home!" I asked if I should call a cab. Barbara answered, "Just hold me and let's walk quickly."

I put my arm around her and held her up as we walked quickly back to our building. In the elevator, Barbara was doubled over in pain. Our neighbors were so concerned and didn't know what they could do to be of help. I told them that she'd take a painkiller and I'd get her to bed.

The next morning, Barbara said the pain was not as bad and she would call Dr. Stern's office on Monday for an appointment. Later that week, she saw Dr. Stern. Barbara described the pain and told Dr. Stern she was having trouble with her speech and her tongue was a little crooked. Dr. Stern ordered the usual blood tests, plus a bone scan, an MRI of her spine, and an MRI of her brain.

Barbara called me from the car after her appointment. I was so busy working while listening to her, I didn't hear all the details. Then, I heard, "Oh, Marc. He ordered an MRI of my brain."

"Oh." I tried to sound calm.

"What are we going to do if it's in my brain?"

"What did Dr. Stern say?"

"He said we have to check everything in order to determine what is causing my tongue to be crooked."

"Okay ... so let's just have all checked."

"But, what if it's in my brain?"

"You'll get the necessary treatment like you've had in the past. Okay? I'll see you tonight."

I hung up the phone and stared at the wall in my office. My mind was a blank and I stared and stared at the wall. After a few moments, I began to think, an MRI of her brain meant another doctor, another specialist, another opinion, and someone else to tell us something about what the next treatment would be.

"When does it end? When do we reach the point when we can just go on and on? Or do we have to take our last breath to have peace? I'm not ready for this. Aren't wives supposed to outlive their husbands? Barbara is so much stronger than me. Is that why she was the one chosen to go through this?"

A few days later, Barbara had the tests and at the end of January, she had the results. Barbara called me at work with the results, shouting with joy. "The MRI of my brain is fine! Are you happy?"

"Of cause I'm happy. I didn't think that there would be a problem."

"However, my tumor markers are up, and Dr. Stern is taking me off the Gemzar and is going to start me on Navelbine. Also, he wants me to make an appointment with a neurosurgical specialist about my tongue. I want you to go with me for that."

"Yeah, I'll go with you. This is such good news. We'll celebrate when I get home."

"Oh? Where are you taking me?" Barbara asked.

"Nowhere, we'll celebrate in our bedroom. See you later, alligator."

Barbara laughed. Through the phone, I could feel in my heart the smile on her face as she answered, "See you in a while, crocodile."

CHAPTER 30

I always had it all

B arbara scheduled her appointment with the neurosurgical specialist for February 4, 2010. It was a late-afternoon appointment in Morristown. A neighbor drove Barbara to the appointment, and I met them at the doctor's office. As usual, the doctor's schedule was running late. We became anxious, wondering what new episode this doctor was going to unleash into our lives.

Finally, we were called in to the see the doctor and went through the usual routine of describing Barbara's health history and our life's experiences with cancer. The doctor reviewed the MRI of Barbara's spine, a copy of which Barbara brought with her to this appointment. Then, he performed a physical examination.

Throughout the appointment, I hung on every question and every comment from the doctor. I kept my focus on his face, his eyes, and his expressions. It didn't seem to me that he was able to pinpoint the problem causing the pain in Barbara's neck. But, when she mentioned her tongue being twisted, I saw a look cross his face, as if he had determined the cause.

The doctor said he needed a few minutes, excused himself, and left the exam room. Barbara looked at me, concerned. "What do you think?"

I answered, "I think he figured out the problem and from the look on his face, he knows the remedy."

So, you think it's good?" Barbara asked.

"I think he knows what needs to be done and that makes it good."

The doctor returned to the exam room.

"I see what's causing the problem. As soon as you mentioned the problem with your tongue, I knew the cause of the neck pain. Come with me and I'll show you everything on the MRI."

We followed the doctor and he showed us Barbara's MRI and began identifying all the tumors along Barbara's spine. I don't think he realized that we hadn't seen these pictures and were not prepared to be shown so much information. As the doctor described the film, Barbara's knees weakened, and she held on to my arm. This was shocking and Barbara said, "I'm going back to the exam room and you can continue with my husband."

Pointing to the MRI, the doctor showed me a tumor on the cervical spine C1. He said that if that tumor received radiation, he was sure the problem would be resolved. Then he described a treatment called CyberKnife, in which the radiation is pinpointed to a specific spot. This was good news.

We returned to the exam room and I found Barbara very frightened. Not just because of the uncertainty of what was coming, but from seeing all those tumors along her spine. To reassure her, I quickly put a smile on my face and said, "Barbara, it's good news. There is a specific tumor causing the problem and it can be dealt with."

Then, the doctor described the CyberKnife procedure that would be performed at Overlook Hospital. We both felt relieved. Hope was back. We met with the doctor at Overlook Hospital who would perform the CyberKnife. We liked him and his staff and all was good.

The treatment went well and we were back on track, looking forward to the birth of our second grandchild, due on June 14. We decided to get in a trip to South Beach during the last week of May and returned to New Jersey on May 31. Our timing was perfect.

Drew Rachel was born three days later, on June 3. The ordeal of the past few months was behind us.

It was a long wait at the hospital that day for Drew to arrive. It took the two of us to entertain Jonah, a two-and-a-half-year-old who was rambunctious while waiting in the lobby for hours. Drew was born in the afternoon and we stayed at the hospital into the evening.

During the drive home, Barbara talked and talked. We couldn't stop chattering about our beautiful granddaughter. I just listened as I drove, dreading any serious conversation. Then, Barbara blurted out, "We have it all." I agreed and smiled at her. And then she said, "Now, I just need to live." Nothing else was said until we got home.

We were both exhausted from the day. I dropped down on the living room couch and turned on the TV. Barbara hurried to the computer to email the news to her world. At 10:11pm, she wrote:

> It's a girl!!!! Kristen gave birth to a baby girl today. Thursday, June 3, 2010 at 3:11pm. Drew Rachel weighed in at 8 lbs. 1 oz. and is absolutely gorgeous!!! Her very proud Daddy, Steve, and her extremely proud big brother, Jonah, are ecstatic as are we all!!! Enjoy these pictures which I was just too tired to put captions on. I think they are self-explanatory!!! We are exhausted from a busy day. Love to all of you from all of us.

After, Barbara came into the living room, sat down next to me, and held on to my arm. "We have everything, right?"

"Yes, we do," I answered.

"Look at me when you say that."

I looked at Barbara and said, "Yes, we have everything."

She asked, "And good health too?"

I could only get out one word. "Yes."

It was the first time I had ever heard Barbara talk about having everything. The fact is, married to Barbara, I always had everything. To Barbara, the grass was never greener someplace else. She held no jealousy nor envy about anyone or anything. To Barbara, whatever we had at any point during our marriage was all we needed. It was everything.

Barbara's courage and optimism brought her through all her bouts with cancer and kept our marriage and family together. She always accepted difficult and troubled times and did whatever was needed for us to make it through.

As Barbara sat beside me on the couch that evening, I could see that we truly did have everything. It was at that very moment, after all the years of our marriage, that I came to realize, with Barbara, I always had it all. At that very moment, "all" meant having Barbara holding on to me and her knowing I would never leave or give up on her struggle to live. To me, "all" was seeing Barbara's smile, filled with hope ... and her dimples. From that moment on, I knew I would need nothing else, until the day I would lose her.

It had been several months since Barbara's last appointment with Dr. Abbasi. On June 28, 2010, I received an email from Dr. Abbasi.

Hi. Just checking in. How is she doing?

The next day, I emailed back.

> Hi, Dr. Abbasi:
>
> This is so very much appreciated. Barbara is tolerating the Navelbine okay. Her hair has grown back, but she complains about fatigue with hemoglobin between 10.0-11.2. For a long period, prior to March 2007, Barbara would suffer from a continuous dry cough. When she started Zeloda, in the spring of 2007, that coughing stopped. As Zeloda was approaching its end, the coughing came back. At this point, Barbara has many episodes, when she coughs continuously.
>
> Recent events are, as follows:
>
> | | | |
> |---|---|---|
> | 1. February 3, 2010 | Last Gemzar | |
> | 2. February 23, 2010 | Micro port put in | |
> | 3. March 3, 2010 | Started Navelbine | |
> | 4. March 10-12, 2010 | CyberKnife procedure for tumor in cervical spine C1-C2 (Barbara had suffered from pain in her neck and shoulder for several months. After this procedure, the pain is no longer.) | |

I have attached a chart of some of Barbara's blood results. The CA27.29 is steady, but much higher than it was when she was on Zeloda. The CEA has come down a little, but also not as low as it was on Zeloda.

Barbara continues to get Zometa.

Thanks,

Marc

That evening, while I was in the family room relaxing and watching TV, my mind drifted a bit. I thought about my email to Dr. Abbasi. I realized that Dr. Abbasi's email asked, "How is she doing?" The doctor wasn't asking for a report. I guessed that I was losing my perspective. Barbara's health care had become so procedural and regimented. I was forgetting how to view and understand our situation from a human perspective. I was reminded that doctors are people. People with families. People who are loving and caring and that was where Dr. Abbasi was coming from. She was simply asking, in a loving and caring way, "How is she doing?'

The next day, I emailed Dr. Abbasi again.

Hi, Dr. Abbasi:

I just noticed that I didn't actually answer your question. Other than my yesterday's email, Barbara is doing well. To look at her, no one can tell what she is going through and she looks healthier than other women her age. Also, she is loving our second grandchild, now three weeks old ... and ... we're both loving living in Hoboken.

Thanks,

Marc

CHAPTER 31

Time passing became my worst enemy

We left for South Beach on July 2, 2010, for the week. It was our second Fourth of July living in Hoboken and once again we missed out on the fireworks on the Hudson. We didn't know that fireworks would be happening on the Hudson when we made our travel plans and we were so disappointed to miss them. Especially since our neighbors invited us and several other neighbors to a Fourth of July party on their roof-deck, in direct view of the fireworks. Barbara and I agreed that next year, if the fireworks were taking place on the Hudson, we were staying in Hoboken.

This was our second summer in Hoboken. Barbara and I were loving it. City living was great for us. We talked about it one time, and Barbara said, "I think that we are really apartment people." She was right. Our house in the suburbs worked for our family. But for just the two of us, an urban apartment was better.

It was a new beginning for us, with no more responsibilities for a house that had multiple levels, a lot of land, and the monotonous outdoor scenery of people working on their lawns for hours. I used to be one of those people. But by the late 1980s, I was done and hired someone to do that work.

During our later years in Flanders, our interests and lifestyle gradually changed from those of our friends and neighbors. By the time we moved to Hoboken, there was only one couple left we still socialized with, Mary Ellen and Carl. Our circle of people completely changed from when we had our house parties for Chanukah, with a usual invitation list of ninety people.

Our perspective on the suburbs also changed. We began to feel that a private home was not so private. Neighbors see more of you, like when you get a new car or have something done to your house. It seemed apartment living was more private and yet our apartment friends were just an elevator ride away. In the suburbs, when a home sold in the neighborhood, our neighbors, knowing that Barbara was a realtor, would ask that obnoxious question, "*What's* moving in?" We were so tired of it all and happy we had said goodbye to the suburbs.

After we moved, Barbara delayed leaving the Zissen Office in Randolph. She didn't want to leave her friends. After a year of commuting, Barbara transferred offices and began working at Zissen's Hoboken office. It was a big change for her, after twenty-six years. Now, Barbara's biggest complaint was finding parking while showing houses and apartments. And she missed her Randolph office friends.

Barbara was slowing down with work. It became increasingly difficult for her to get around to show properties. Barbara was used to the suburban way of showing properties. She found the transition very difficult. Well, that's what we blamed for her slowing down. We didn't talk about it being her health, or her continuous struggle with tolerating the side effects of the treatments. The more Barbara reduced her work hours, the more time she spent with our grandchildren, Jonah and Drew. In them, she would live forever. Tuesdays became Barbara's day with Jonah and Drew. This gave Kristen the day off to do things for herself, and the kids were all Barbara's.

Barbara would continually say that she wouldn't be working much longer, and I continually encouraged her not to stop. With her working, I could believe that she would continue to be active, feel good, and look forward to working with new customers. As I think back to this time, I realize that I didn't know what to believe, what I wanted, or what I needed to do to keep our lifestyle and our routine as normal as possible. I wanted to feel like there was a future for us.

It was a scary and confusing time for me. I didn't understand why I felt so much more scared than the times before. With Barbara's first cancer, Jonathan was six years old, Kristen was four, and Brian was two months. With the second cancer, our children were nine, seven, and three. With the third, Jonathan and Kristen were away at college and Brian was in high school. It seemed like I was so much stronger during those times. This time around, as in those times, Barbara made sure that everything felt normal, with no sad faces around her. She didn't complain. To everyone all around us, all was wonderful.

I believed that Barbara always looked forward to the challenge of working with customers. She was a people person and got energized when meeting new customers. The energy that came from her work with customers was keeping our lifestyle as normal as possible, giving us a belief in a future.

For Barbara and me, work was great dinnertime talk. I'd hear about her customers and we'd each talk about our day's adventures. It was what we did for all of our marriage. It worked for us, and I didn't want it to change. The stories of her experiences with customers ranged from heartwarming to hysterical, like the time Barbara was showing a house in Blairstown. While touring the acres of property, Barbara spotted a bear. The customers were so excited to see a bear on the property and remained calm while watching the bear prowling around. But Barbara, a Jewish girl from The Bronx, took off running back to the car. I couldn't stop laughing as she described how frightening it was to her and I pictured her frantically running. Barbara's best stories were of the thrill she got when visiting a happy customer, after they moved into the home she sold to them.

Barbara and I always had much to talk about, particularly our work experiences. Barbara's stories were so different from the stories that I had from the years when I sold homes in The Bronx, while attending college. Selling real estate, starting at eighteen years old, was an adventure and education for me and I always shared my daily experiences and snafus with Barbara.

We never considered our day's activities boring, or ordinary. There was always something that stood out from each of our days that we could talk or laugh about. I remember the first week I started working for a realtor, the broker gave me a stack of index cards. He told me to call the people on each card and tell them about a one-bedroom apartment that we had for rent and ask if they were interested. I was new at doing this, and practiced ahead of time, saying, "Hello, this is Marc Gellman from Royal Key Real Estate. We have you listed as looking for a one-bedroom apartment. Are you still interested?"

Well, I grasped that very easily and started calling people. My only problem was, I had difficulty pronouncing of some of the names. Growing up in the East New York section of Brooklyn, with names like Schwartz, Cohen, and Goldberg, I wasn't used to the names in the predominantly Italian Baychester neighborhood in the northeast Bronx. So, when I came to the card with the name "Pucci," I had no idea that it was pronounced "Poochie." I dialed the phone and a woman answered. I started, "Hello Mrs. Pussy."

The woman said, "Excuse me!"

"Hello, are you Mrs. Pussy?"

She answered, "And ... who are you?"

"I'm Marc Gellman from Royal Key Real Estate. We have you listed as looking for a one-bedroom apartment. Are you still interested?"

The woman answered, "I'm no longer interested in moving and my name is pronounced 'Poochie.'"

I didn't realize what I had called the woman, until I hung up the phone. I quickly called Barbara. "I just called this woman who was looking for a one-bedroom apartment and I called her Mrs. Pussy. How would you have pronounced P-U-C-C-I?"

Barbara replied, "You are so silly."

Barbara loved that story and years later, when I would laugh at something she did, Barbara would say to me, "Well, silly, I may not know everything about selling real estate. But at least, I haven't called anyone Mrs. Pussy!"

Barbara was such a good realtor. She loved people. I was so proud of her reputation in our community as a good, honest, and well-meaning businesswoman. But the thrill of being with Jonah and Drew was drawing Barbara away from working. She just wanted to play grandma and with that, I was frightened.

For all of our marriage, Barbara was always juggling so many activities: family, work, temple, running the house, cooking, social activities, and on and on. She was always on the go. To look at Barbara at that point in our lives, she was so beautiful and looked so healthy. I couldn't let myself accept what was going on inside of her. I was so concerned about where her mind was. I wondered, was she scared too? How could she not be? Was she ready to stop fighting? It wasn't obvious and I couldn't see her fright when I looked into her eyes.

Barbara made two deals while with Zissen's Hoboken office. For her first deal, she was the listing agent for a one-bedroom apartment in our building. The other deal was the sale of a two-story penthouse apartment, which ended her career with a bang. At the Randolph office, I believe the most expensive sale she was involved with was around $800,000, expensive for New Jersey's western suburban residential market. Her average home sale was around $400,000. Barbara sold the Hoboken penthouse for $2,300,000. This was by far the biggest sale of her career. I was so proud of her. I could tell that it would be her last.

Barbara was talking more and more about being with Jonah and Drew and our fun conversations swapping real estate stories were happening less and less often. She was spending more time in the apartment and visiting our grandchildren and less time at her office. As I saw the changes in Barbara's daily routine, time began to go by too fast for me. Friday afternoons began to feel like they were coming along the day after Monday. I couldn't slow down time, and time passing became my worst enemy.

At this point, Monday, back-to-work day, was my favorite day of the week. Monday was like a new beginning and the start of another week with Barbara. It was difficult for me when people would start talking on Mondays about plans for the weekend. I wanted to say, "Hey, it's only Monday! Slow it down! The weekend is far away." But quickly, it was Friday afternoon again and my time with Barbara was ticking away.

It pains me to think that Barbara might have had similar thoughts. But when I got home to her, I never knew it from her smile. We talked about our day and always talked about tomorrow. I wished that each tomorrow would take a long time to arrive, and that Fridays would take forever. "Today" was always too good and I never wanted it to end.

As I wrote this chapter, I struggled to understand my fears and the changes that were happening to Barbara, during the spring and summer of 2010. As I sat at my desk on Monday evening, January 26, 2015, it was about three-and-a-half years since I lost Barbara. I was obsessing, trying to figure out what was happening back then. I paced back and forth, going from sitting at my desk to staring out the living room window, but came to no understanding of this frightening and disorienting time in our lives.

Looking out of the window through Shiva Eyes, I only saw the cold darkness of the winter evening, adding to my confusion and loneliness. For all of our lives together, Barbara and I were always totally in sync with each other. What was going on with us, back in the spring and summer of 2010? Our minds, our plans, and our aspirations seemed to have been going in different directions. But why? I didn't know.

That evening in 2015, the weather report advised of a major snowstorm. I hate snow, but that storm I welcomed. It was a good reason to stay home the next day and chill and maybe figure out whatever it was that was dragging me down. It felt like a free day and I planned to go through the den and start cleaning up files. I had accumulated so much paperwork, notes, and copies of bills and I felt better, planning the time to clean up the mess.

As I did the cleanup the next day, I found so much that I didn't need to keep. I also found Barbara's Day-Timer wallet, with her Day-Timer from May 2010. I think, if I had found that wallet at another time, its contents wouldn't have helped me as much. I looked in the pocket of the wallet and found three things. The first was a picture of Barbara and me from 1967, at my high school prom. I stared and stared at the picture for about an hour, reliving that night at the prom.

I attended my sophomore year at Franklin K. Lane high school and my junior and senior years at Samuel J. Tilden. I didn't have lots of friends at Tilden, located in the East Flatbush section of Brooklyn. I was new to the neighborhood and spent most of my time working after school at the Big Apple Supermarket on Church Avenue, dating Barbara in Jackson Heights on weekends, and spending my summers in Far Rockaway.

I did know some girls at Tilden. I liked them, and they would ask me to hang out with them. I would say that I had a girlfriend. Since they never saw me with Barbara, the girls didn't believe me. I heard the sarcasm in their voices as they said, "You say you have a girlfriend, but we've never seen her. I bet you're not interested in girls."

A little embarrassed, I answered, "Nope. I like girls. It's just that I have a girlfriend."

To which they responded, "Okay, then let's get together this weekend."

To me, no girl at Tilden came close to being as cute and as pretty as Barbara. It was Barbara I wanted to be with over the weekend.

Finally, at the end of my senior year, I was going to prove to everyone that I really did have a girlfriend. I told everyone I was bringing her to the prom. The night of the prom, Barbara's mom drove Barbara to Brooklyn, to save me the trip of driving all the way to Jackson

Heights, only to come back to Brooklyn. When I saw Barbara, I knew that my high school friends were going to drool. She wore this incredible red gown, which looked hot in contrast to her olive complexion and dark hair, up in curls. She was some hot-looking date!

I borrowed my dad's car to go to the prom at El Caribe in the Mill Basin section of Brooklyn. I couldn't wait to walk into the prom with Barbara. Practically as soon as we walked in, my friends pulled me to the side, and asked, "Who is that girl? She's not your girlfriend."

A big smirk broke out across my face.

"Yep, she is."

They still didn't believe me. But when the slow dancing started and they saw the way Barbara and I held on to each other and kissed on the dance floor, no one doubted that she was my girlfriend. The prom was great. But I couldn't wait for the prom to be over to drive Barbara home and make out in the car.

With snow falling outside my Hoboken windows on that January day in 2015, I continued to stare at that picture. I couldn't put it down. It was as if I were at the prom again and I could still feel Barbara in my arms, as we danced and kissed on the dance floor that night. We were so very young and so much in love, a love that would last for the next forty-four years.

Behind the prom picture was a printed card with this poem:

> If I were a bird, I could sing so pretty
> If I were the sun, I could shine so bright
> If I were a flower, I could stand so graceful
>   I am not a bird, the sun or a flower
>   But I am a Cancer Survivor
> And thank God that
> I can hear the birds
> I can feel the sun
> I can see the flowers

Behind that poem was another poem that Barbara must have cut out from something.

One night I dreamed I was walking along
the beach with the Lord. Scenes from my
life flashed across the sky. In each, I
noticed footprints in the sand. Sometimes
there were two sets of footprints;
other times there was only one.
During the lowest times of my
life I could see only one set of footprints,
so, I said, "Lord, you promised me,
that you would walk with me always.
Why, when I have needed you most,
would you leave me?"
The Lord replied, "My precious child,
I love you and would never leave you,
The times when you have seen only one set
of footprints, it was then I carried you."

After finding the Day-Timer, I realized why this chapter was so difficult for me to write and why I struggled to understand where I was going with this chapter. I understood so much more now, as I sat alone in the quiet of my apartment, thinking and staring at the walls and the pictures displayed around me. Because staring at that prom picture, I felt how much in love we were and the love we had. Barbara and I were truly one.

As I write this particular paragraph, it is three years and six months after Barbara passed away. I realize that I'm still grieving for Barbara. In the last couple of weeks, my grieving grew more intense. Staring at that picture, I felt so empty inside, knowing I would never kiss her lips or hold her again. All I have is pictures and unanswered questions. Did Barbara feel that she had the fullest and richest life, even though it was cut short? Did she feel robbed? Did she die in peace? Was she scared? When will I ever accept that she's gone? When will I ever stop picturing the grave beside Barbara, where I'll eventually be? And, how long do I have to wait until I'm with Barbara once again? Most importantly, could I have handled it all differently and better? Was Barbara just going along with how I wanted us to live our lives during this time? Or was she truly happy and didn't want for anything to be done any other way?

As I sit alone and reminisce in my mind, I'm beginning to understand why I encouraged Barbara to continue to work. Why I resisted change, why I was scared, troubled, and confused. This fourth cancer was different than the first three. Each time before, we had the hope that she could be cured of the disease. The fourth time, there would be no cure. I remember the time Barbara said something like, "How could the doctors predict a ten-year life expectancy? That's a long time and so much can happen and change."

At the time, I made this out to be just a passing question, going in one ear and out the other. Since Barbara wasn't asking for an answer, I tried to make nothing of it. However, I can still, so vividly, recall the question. So, it obviously didn't go in one ear and out the other. Instead, I stored it away in my heart, ever since that day. Back then, I never asked about and avoided any discussion of life expectancy predictions. I couldn't accept the possibility of losing Barbara. I wouldn't have been able to look into her eyes if my hope was gone.

Now, as I sit alone in thought, I can hear how Barbara spoke those words so matter-of-factly. At the time, I didn't question exactly what she was talking about, or what the ten years had to do with anything. I think now about the two telephone conversations I had with a nurse oncologist. The first was a little more than a year after Barbara was diagnosed with metastatic breast cancer that had spread to her lungs. I don't remember the reason why I called the nurse. As the nurse was answering my questions, she purposely interjected a prediction into the conversation. "Barbara will be okay. She'll have time with her grandchild."

I understood the statement, but I let it go right by me. I didn't want any more information about what her statement implied. I feared hearing about any predictions of Barbara's life expectancy. Interrupting the nurse, I quickly continued with my questions. About six months later, I had occasion to speak on the phone with the nurse. Once again, the nurse said, "Barbara will have time with her grandchild."

I hesitated. This time I asked, "How much time?"

"Two to ten years," the nurse answered.

It was information I never wanted to have. As I sit here now, I realize that at some point, probably shortly after she was diagnosed, Barbara must have asked Dr. Stern how long she had. Knowing Barbara, in her mind she must have automatically processed the two to ten years as a sure ten years. And she probably believed that ten years was enough time to fight and win the battle. Surely, with ten years, some cure would be discovered in time to save her life.

I never told Barbara, or anyone, about my telephone conversations with the nurse. When the kids or anyone else asked me if I asked the doctors about her prognosis, I always told them that Barbara would need treatments for the rest of her life to keep things under control.

I ignored any information about the possibility of Barbara dying. I dreaded ever having to face Barbara and discuss that she was dying and how much time she would have left. Barbara and I never talked about her dying, only about her living. I hoped that when the end did come, she would just close her eyes knowing that I never gave up on her.

I see now that Barbara knew it was time to make changes in our lives and move on, to give all her attention to the kids. I was the one who wasn't ready to accept change. But she was incredible and kept on rolling with the punches. Barbara did whatever she needed to do in order to have a rich and happy life.

The prom picture was a portrait of our young love, taken at a time when it seemed like we would live forever. I so believe that having that picture with her, Barbara saw herself back in time, each time she looked at it, and thought about how our love was still young and unchanged. The poems, which she kept close to her, are so telling of Barbara. She was so accepting, so optimistic, so positive, and so strong. She had so much faith.

Barbara wasn't just going along with what I wanted. She was doing what was best for the both of us. As much as I felt that I had to protect her from her knowing that she was dying, Barbara was the one protecting me, during that frightening and difficult time. I understand it all now.

PART 6

Stories from the Sixth Day of Shiva

*"Let's finish off this wonderful evening. How about if I
pull over to the side of the road and we make out?"*

CHAPTER 32

I wish I had asked her

We were back in South Beach from the end of December 2010 until after the New Year. Our friends Lynn and Elliott were there, too, and we spent much of our time with them. It was the coldest winter stay that we ever had over our years in South Beach. For several of the evenings, the four of us went out for dinner wearing winter coats that we'd brought south with us, and even kept our hoods up. It was freezing and the first time that we used the heat in the apartment. It was a good opportunity to test that the heating system actually worked.

Barbara and Lynn began planning for New Year's Eve. We had so many options. I reminded Barbara of our incredible first New Year's Eve in South Beach, after we bought our apartment. So, Barbara called the Loews Hotel to see if the hotel was having its New Year's buffet again, and it was. I suggested we go there. Lynn agreed and we made reservations.

It was a little chilly, New Year's Eve, walking from our building to the Loews. But it wasn't going to change our plans. We walked up

Ocean Drive and decided to stop at the Hotel Victor along the way. We ordered drinks, not expecting the size of the drinks to be anything different from the usual. When our order came, Elliott became hysterical as the waitress placed four giant goblets on the table.

"What the hell are those?" I asked.

"These are the drinks you ordered," the waitress replied.

Elliott laughed as he said to me, "The look on your face when you saw the drinks. Now, I can't wait to see the look on your face when we get the bill."

Elliott had us all laughing at the ridiculousness of the four of us sipping away at those giant drinks. It set the tone for an "anything goes, let's just have fun" evening. The drinks tasted great, and the hotel atmosphere made it worth the more than one-hundred-dollar bill for the four drinks.

We'd barely finished our drinks when it was off to the Loews for dinner and more drinks. After dinner, we went to the lounge to listen to the band and to celebrate bringing in the New Year, 2011. It was 2011, the year that we were going to be celebrating our fortieth wedding anniversary. Barbara mentioned to me that the kids were planning some kind of a surprise for our fortieth.

"Oh, what is the surprise?" I asked.

"I don't know, silly. It's a surprise!"

"Okay with me. I just hope they give us a heads-up on how much the surprise is going to cost us."

Forty years. We were married so very young. We always thought we'd easily make our fiftieth wedding anniversary. Now, as we continued with hope, I wondered if we'd make our fortieth.

This was the forty-third New Year's Eve that Barbara and I spent together between New Year's 1966 and 2011. We missed being together for New Year's 1966, because we broke up a few weeks before and got back together a couple of weeks after New Year's. We missed 1968, when Barbara visited her grandfather in Florida over the holidays.

For bringing in 1967, the first New Year's Eve that we celebrated together, we decided to go it alone with plans to be at Times Square.

I saved up money for us to have dinner at one of the Manhattan steakhouses near Times Square. After dinner, we hung out in the crowd waiting to watch the ball drop.

It was so cold that night. We held on to each other to try and keep warm and make sure we wouldn't lose each other in the crowd. While standing and waiting for midnight, I had an idea. I suggested we might be warmer if we opened our coats, hugged our bodies close together, and exchanged body heat. So, we tried that. After a few minutes, Barbara asked, "Do you really think this feels warmer?"

"No," I answered, "but it feels really good."

"It doesn't feel good for me," Barbara answered.

"Okay, get a little closer and then tell me what you feel."

We were both still virgins, but not so innocent. We thought we were being quite bad with the things we did. Looking back at that era, I realize how much it sexually sucked to be teenagers in the 1960s. The twenty-first century would have been much more fun for us, or at least the 1990s. We definitely missed out during our teenage years.

I confess, though, we made up for it after we were married. I could never keep my hands off Barbara. At any opportunity, we were peeling off our clothes. I so remember a particular Sunday afternoon in a July, when the kids were, like, ten, eight, and four years old. They were playing with friends outside the house. Barbara and I started going at it in the family room. Barbara said, "We better stop. The kids can walk right in on us."

"You go upstairs and get naked. I'll check out what the kids are up to and be right there."

I ran outside and saw the kids playing with their friends at a neighbor's house down the block. I ran back inside and up to the bedroom. As I tore my clothes off, I said, "The kids are down the block at the O'Connor's. They should be busy for a while."

After not such a quickie, Barbara said, "Go check on the kids." I quickly got dressed and ran outside. I could see all three of them still playing at the O'Connor's. I came back into the house. "They're all still playing. We should do this afternoon thing more often." And we did. Very often.

On that frigid New Year's Eve in 1967, we eventually closed our coats and went back to hugging. It was so exciting to be in Times Square at midnight, and we kissed while being shoved and pushed by the crowds. Somehow, even with the temperature dropping, we felt warmer. Barbara's smile, with those red cheeks and red nose from the cold, was too cute. I remember kissing her and thinking, "This is my girlfriend and I think she's the prettiest girl in all of Times Square tonight."

As I was thinking this and staring at her, Barbara looked into my eyes and asked, "Do you love me?"

Our first date was almost a year and a half earlier, in August 1965, and we didn't live close to each other. It was a tedious trip for me from East Flatbush in Brooklyn to Jackson Heights, Queens. I would take the Utica Avenue bus to the train on Eastern Parkway, to Forty-Second Street, Manhattan, and change for the Flushing Line train to Jackson Heights to the Junction Boulevard stop. Then, I walked about six blocks to Barbara's apartment building.

Living at such a distance from each other, and being young teenagers, our relationship was on-and-off for that year and a half. We were boyfriend-girlfriend on and off and went steady on and off. At one point, I gave Barbara my ID bracelet. This was the thing to do in the 1960s to show that you were going steady. Barbara gave it back to me during one of the times that we were "off." We were so young, just having fun, beginning to do some sexual exploring with a lot of touchy-feely. But we were mostly "on." After periods of being apart, we always came back to each other with a closer relationship.

We had never spoken about love. This was the first time the word "love" came up. I looked into Barbara's eyes a little confused, not knowing what to say. I knew I had real feelings for her. But was it love? At that moment, it seemed like she couldn't have picked a better time to ask.

I felt so adult, taking Barbara to Manhattan and to an expensive restaurant. It was so romantic, sexy, and arousing to think that I could be in love. Her question made it obvious, she was in love with me. We were in the middle of a crowd of strangers. It was as if we were on an island. Although the crowd was around us, it felt like we were all alone. I answered, "Yes ... But I think you're ugly."

Barbara replied, "Why do you have to be so silly all the time? Just answer me. Do you love me? And don't just say, yes. Tell me if you love me."

I felt a weird feeling, like a fit of seriousness came over me. At that age, I was seldom serious. Being silly was me. My favorite expression was, "Take off your clothes. I want to talk to you." I wasn't even able to be romantically serious. I could feel my heart beating and shivers throughout my body. I could hear nothing around me, and my eyes were inches from hers. I said, "Yes ... I do love you."

The serious look on Barbara's face quickly changed into a sweet smile and we kissed our first kiss knowing that we were in love with each other. Whether it was true love or just puppy love, it didn't matter. That love would never feel any different from that day until the day I lost Barbara. It may have been at that very moment, when the two teenagers who we were became one. We kissed in the middle of the crowd. We forgot about how cold it was. I felt like I was soaring. The feeling of flying couldn't be any more incredible than the feeling I had when I realized that I was in love with Barbara, at that very moment when I said, "Yes ... I do love you."

I thought to myself, "This isn't just talk. I really do love this girl." As I write this, I so regret that I didn't say it more often during all the years that followed. At every New Year's Eve, when we kissed, I always thought about that kiss at Times Square. I wonder now if Barbara thought about that kiss too. I hope she did. I wish I had asked her.

For some of our teenage years, we hung out with friends for New Year's. Barbara and I weren't drinkers. But it was fun to see our friends trying to get drunk. When we were married and moved to Flanders, we quickly became friendly with our neighbors. The New Year's Eves in Flanders were house parties, and they were fun. As the years went by, some of the neighbors moved away and our friend circle changed. The house parties grew old. It was much more fun with the original group of neighbors, when everyone was younger, and the evening was all about playing fun games and laughing.

The newness and the spark of partying in the suburbs were gone, as the games and laughter changed to sitting around and chatting. For Barbara and me, too much of the chatting was about retirement and moving to fifty-five and older communities, neither of which held any interest for us. Other than the tradition of watching TV at midnight and watching the ball come down in Times Square, the evening was just another social get together.

As the years passed, New Year's Eve eventually became going to dinner with friends at the same Chinese restaurant, then to the movies, then to watch fireworks in Morristown at midnight, and then to a diner for dessert. These evenings were always so dull, since this was also our routine for Christmas Eve, just one week before, except without the fireworks.

That routine was fine for me on Christmas Eve. It was at least something to do, considering there are few entertainment options for Jewish people on that night. I don't know if Jewish people's activities on Christmas Eve are the same in all parts of the United States. But growing up in New York City and living most of my married life in New Jersey, I found this to be the routine for Jewish people on Christmas Eve: Chinese food, movies, and apple pie at a diner. There were several Christmas Eves when Barbara and I were invited to a friend's house and it was fun. But for most Christmas Eves, we stayed true to the typical Jewish New Yorker routine.

In the New York area, many restaurants used to close on Christmas Eve, except for Chinese restaurants. Barbara and I joked that restaurant owners were probably preparing by saying, "Let's get the chow mein ready. Our customers will all be Jewish tonight." My Aunt Mollie used to call it "charmagne." In fact, growing up in Brooklyn, in the 1950s and 60s, it seemed like everyone called it charmagne. I wonder if it was an intentional way of disguising a non-kosher food. Chow mein doesn't seem to be the special Chinese dish it used to be, when I was growing up in Brooklyn. And, I definitely haven't heard it called charmagne since then.

On those dull New Year's Eves, going to watch fireworks in Morristown was awful. It didn't have to be awful, but we did it the cheap way. You see, each New Year's Eve, Morristown had a "First Night." If you bought tickets, it was a night of several different venues in town, in several locations. Ticketholders went from event to event, which culminated with people gathering at the town's square for direct views of the fireworks at midnight. If, like us, you didn't buy tickets, you stood freezing your ass off in a poorly lit parking lot, just outside of town, waiting for the fireworks to begin.

Anyway, it was the same routine each year and I found the evening annoying. When we began planning for New Year's Eve, Barbara and I would talk about going to a hotel, to a celebration like Guy Lombardo had on TV when we were kids. But when Barbara would discuss this idea with friends, it became less about what Barbara and I wanted to do for New Year's Eve and more about what our circle of friends chose.

The plans would result in an argument between Barbara and me. Barbara was so much more willing to be accommodating and flexible than I was, to give in to what our friends wanted to do. Even more annoying, this would happen throughout the year, not just for New Year's Eve.

The kids continually told us that we needed to get a life. We finally recognized that the kids were right. We could afford better, and it was time for us to move on. Barbara and I had faced so many challenges in our lives. It was over the course of these New Year's Eves that we began to recognize we shouldn't pass on opportunities to celebrate occasions and events to the fullest.

At this point, in South Beach, those dull years were long behind us. Now it was New Year's Eve 2011, and it was midnight. The lounge at the Loews was filled with music and cheerful celebration. Barbara looked at me and smiled with a loving look on her face, as we slowly kissed. We said nothing. I could feel that we were both thinking about how wonderfully blessed we had been and thankful we were, for the past year.

My eyes were inches from Barbara's, as they had been at Times Square on our first New Year's, forty-four years before. Looking into her eyes, I could sense that she was wishing for another year. For sure, I was too. In the middle of all the celebrating around us, Barbara asked, "This is going to be a good year, right?"

"Yes," I answered.

It was always difficult for me to get the words out when she asked such questions. Barbara always breathed a sigh of relief when I gave her a positive answer and she found peace in that. But over the years, the questions pained me more and more each time she asked. Barbara's prognosis wasn't improving. As time passed, my answers felt like increasingly bigger lies. I wondered if Barbara believed me less and less. Did she wonder if my answers were only telling her what she wanted to hear? It was a question I hoped Barbara would never ask me. Because I would have lied.

For me, the evening was so wonderful, and Barbara looked so beautiful. Although I noticed for the first time that evening that speaking was a little more challenging for her and her tongue was a little more twisted. At another time, observing these changes in Barbara would have brought me down. But not that night. That evening, nothing could bring me down. Barbara was smiling and, with that, I could smile too.

There are so many reasons to be thankful that we bought the apartment in South Beach. We met new friends and had new experiences. During this later period in our marriage, the years wouldn't have been as fulfilling if we hadn't begun to live our lives our way. Buying the South Beach apartment was a new beginning of the next phase of our lives and the apartment became our "secret" getaway. We called it paradise.

It was the excitement of South Beach and the New Year's Eves there that set the tone for making these years particularly special. It was on that night each year, when we came out of our shell, spread our wings, and became something that we weren't: free-spirited.

This was something that we so needed to experience, even if it was just for that one night each year. On these New Year's Eves, whether we were alone or with friends, it became all about what we wanted, and doing whatever it took to make each year we had together a celebration. Each year, our celebration included calling our kids so they could hear our happiness and know that their encouragement and support had worked.

By 2011, we had owned our apartment for seven New Year's Eves. We didn't spend 2007 in South Beach, after Barbara had surgery in December 2006. So, this was our sixth New Year's in South Beach. And it would be Barbara's last.

CHAPTER 33

There was a plan ... once again

We left paradise on Sunday, January 2, 2011. Like always, as we were closing the apartment door, Barbara said, "Goodbye apartment, be back soon!" It was always sad to leave South Beach and say goodbye to Jonathan and his dog, Brewster. We'd had a great time. It was also nice to be getting back to our apartment in Hoboken.

I had been quite anxious before this trip to South Beach. We were so very busy during the trip and it kept my mind occupied. But we were going back to New Jersey now and my anxiety was building up again. Barbara had gone for scans back in November and the results were very concerning. I just couldn't shake off the anxiety.

In December 2006, when Barbara was diagnosed with metastatic breast cancer in her lungs and bone, her scans also showed a lesion in her liver. The lesion was identified as probably being a hemangioma, a collection of blood vessels. But over the next twelve months of Barbara's treatments, the reports from periodic scans indicated that the lesion had gradually gone away. Since a collection of blood vessels would not have suddenly gone away, in December 2007, the lesion was reclassified as a resolving metastasis.

At that time, for Barbara, this was great news. Although the hemangioma was reclassified as a metastasis, the metastasis was gone. But this news caused me to think, "Oh, shit, are there any more of those little buggers floating around in her liver that are below the resolution of the scans?" It would have been better if it were a hemangioma, as originally identified. I kept my thoughts to myself. Because this was good news, back then. The lesion was gone. It wasn't necessary to raise concerns.

Since December 2007, there had been no evidence of any cancer in the liver. Now, the scans from November 2010 showed three lesions. Dr. Stern reviewed the report with us. Barbara felt comfortable that Dr. Stern would plan the next steps and consult with Dr. Abbasi. Back in November, rather than concerning herself about the results of the scans or giving any thought to what Dr. Stern and Dr. Abbasi had planned for her treatment, Barbara was more occupied with preparing for Thanksgiving and being in South Beach for the winter holidays.

After almost thirty years and being a three-time cancer survivor, for Barbara, her life had become all about *now*. The results of the scans and what was to be tomorrow was less important. So back in November, Barbara preferred to deal with the latest news after the holidays and she put off her next appointment with Dr. Abbasi until mid-January.

Now we were back in Hoboken and I was quite anxious about our appointment. On January 13, I wrote:

> Dear Dr. Abbasi:
>
> My wife, Barbara Gellman, has an appointment with you on January 18 at 1 p.m. In preparation for that appointment, I have attached the following:
>
> 1. Schedule of the individual abnormal blood results for the periods of April 16, 2007 to January 5, 2011.
>
> 2. Blood work results from January 5, 2011.
>
> 3. CT Abdomen with IV Contrast   11/15/10*****

4. CT Pelvis with IV Contrast   11/15/10
5. CT Thorax with IV Contrast   11/15/10
6. CT Soft Tissue Neck with IV Contrast   11/15/10
7. CT Chest W71260   7/12/10
8. CT Abdomen W74160   7/12/10
9. CT CSpine W072125   7/12/10

*****Of much concern is the CT Abdomen, 11/15/10, which states a new finding, as: "Low Attenuation Foci in the right lobe of the Liver and in the dome of the Liver," a total of three, which are new. A summary of the history of the Liver is as follows:**

1. 12/13/06 CT AbdomenW74160: There is a focus of low attenuation in the right dome measuring 7 mm. This may represent a hemangioma.

2. 12/3/06 PET TMRW CT Neck to Thigh: The Liver demonstrates a 7 mm well circumscribed focus in the dome which is better seen on contrast CT.

3. 4/11/07 CT Abdomen: There is low attenuation within the dome of the Liver which is unchanged since the previous study.

4. 7/9/07 CT Abdomen W74160: There is 5.0 mm low attenuation lesion at the left hepatic dome on image #51 which is smaller than seen previously which suggests interval improvement of a hepatic metastasis. No other hepatic lesions are identified.

5. 12/7/07 CT Abdomen W74160: The previously noted hypodensity in the right lobe of the liver superiorly is no longer noted suggesting it may have represented a resolving metastasis. There is no evidence of a space occupying lesion within the liver or spleen.

6. 6/17/08 CT Abdomen W74160: The liver enhances homogeneously, as does the spleen.

We'll see you on the eighteenth.

Thanks,

Marc Gellman

Our appointment with Dr. Abbasi was at one o'clock. I had several work-related meetings scheduled that day, also in New York City. Barbara came to work with me and sat in at all my meetings. It wasn't unusual for Barbara to spend the workday with me when she had a doctor's appointment in New York. People at my workplace were used to seeing Barbara occasionally showing up with me at meetings. Barbara would often participate at these meetings and afterward give me her opinion. Other than the doctor's appointment, it was always a fun day to have Barbara with me.

The best part of the day was going to lunch, when Barbara would bust me. "Is this all you do? It seems like you have lots of fun. No wonder you like to go to work."

"Well, if you want to join in with the fun," I'd answer, "you should come to work with me more often. You could be my driver."

There was one time when Barbara was my driver for the day. To get ideas for a canopy for one of my company's buildings, I wanted to visit several buildings with canopies, at locations scattered around Manhattan. Barbara agreed to come to work with me that day and be my driver. Without her doing the driving, I'd have needed to park illegally at each location, while racing to look at the canopies and take pictures. Or I'd have needed to search for parking facilities, which would have taken up too much time. At the end of that day, I asked if she wanted to be my driver more often. Barbara laughed and turned me down. I loved having her company that day.

I sometimes wonder what it would have been like for Barbara and me to have our own business. We worked together so well at solving life's issues and making decisions. Also, we couldn't stand to be apart. We talked to each other several times during each workday. It would have been so wonderful, had we worked our own business together.

We kind of did have our own business, with the few residential rentals that we owned. In late 1984, Barbara and I began talking about working together on a business. We thought about purchasing residential homes for rental income. Our plan was to continually buy homes each time we saved enough cash for the down payment. We put our plan into action and during 1985 and 1986, we bought two one-family and one two-family rental properties. Our plan was to continue buying, but we didn't.

That changed in 2001, when we bought another one-family in a foreclosure sale. Unlike the other properties, this home was a gut renovation. It was a major project for us, but we had a great time working out the details of the renovation. After that, we lost interest in purchasing more properties for rentals. Since we only acquired these few rental properties, we didn't have enough to make it a full-time business. But the properties continually had issues and required our joint problem solving, and for Barbara and me, that worked.

These rental properties became family projects and we each had our own role. Barbara dealt with tenant issues. She handled the renting and all tenant communications and coordinated the work when we needed a plumber or electrician. I handled the handyman chores and renovation. Much of this work, such as general repairs, kitchen, bathroom, and deck renovations, I was able to do myself. When I needed a hand, Jonathan, Kristen, and Brian pitched in to help me on such projects.

People I knew offered to be my partner in my small real estate ventures. I always answered, "I already have a partner, my wife. And she's the only partner I'll ever have." Barbara and I were the closest of partners in everything we did. And we were the best of partners as we sat close together holding hands, awaiting our appointment with Dr. Abbasi.

While we waited in the lobby to be called for our appointment, my mind was racing, wondering what questions I wanted to ask and how I would pose the questions without upsetting Barbara. There was one worry that I couldn't stop from spinning around in my mind: that we were coming to the end of available treatments. I hoped that Dr. Abbasi would tell us of new breakthroughs I didn't know about. I kept thinking about the only two drugs that I knew of that were left, Ixempra and Eribulin. According to my research, these were administered after all other treatments have been exhausted. I so didn't want to hear the doctor mention either one of these drugs. But if she did, I wondered, how I would ask about what comes next?

As we waited in the lobby, Barbara talked about our trip to Disney World. She had firmed up all the plans the week before with Kristen and Stephen. We would be leaving Saturday, March 12. By that time, Jonah would be almost three-and-a-half and Drew, nine months. This was going to be Barbara's dream-come-true trip. She felt for certain there was nothing Dr. Abbasi was going to tell us that would stop that trip from happening as planned. It was the most important thing to Barbara, as everything in our lives was becoming all about *now*.

As much as I wanted to believe that Barbara was so accepting, each time we confronted problem test results, I knew she was living with great worry. Barbara was so good at holding herself together, putting on a positive front, and mentally leaving things for tomorrow that were out of our control and couldn't, in any way, be fixed today. Barbara came across as if she were depending on me to keep our lives focused on the positive, and maybe to some extent she was depending on me. But it was really Barbara leading us to find peace, with our difficult circumstance. And now, she talked about Disney World, as we waited to see the doctor.

Margie, Dr. Abbasi's assistant, called us into the office. Throughout the physical, Barbara was chitchatting away with Dr. Abbasi, talking about living in Hoboken, our grandchildren, and our upcoming trip to Disney World. Dr. Abbasi reviewed the reports with us and commented on how great Barbara looked. She advised that the treatments with Navelbine should continue a little longer and then go on to Ixempra. Barbara was listening and responded with, "Okay."

I gulped and held back the feeling of panic inside of me. I had been obsessing over the probability of hearing the doctor say Ixempra. When she did, I didn't want to ask what would come after. There was no reason for me to ask. I knew it would be Eribulin and, after that, there would be nothing. But I didn't want the appointment to end. I wanted to hear Dr. Abbasi say more, even though I didn't know what that more could possibly be. I asked, "What comes after the Ixempra?"

Dr. Abbasi answered, "I'd like you to begin Ixempra soon for six months and then six months of Eribulin. After that, I recommend a particular clinical trial that has been getting good results. If you want to do that, I will get the paperwork done now, for you to start the clinical trial next year."

Barbara listened attentively. The whole conversation scared the hell out of me, hearing about Ixempra and Eribulin. But there was now a window of hope in hearing about the clinical trial. Dr. Abbasi was thinking far in advance. She wanted to get Barbara enrolled now for a trial more than twelve months away. That gave me some peace. More importantly, Barbara was excited and optimistic. Her hopeful smile was all I needed to see.

With a plan we left Dr. Abbasi's office going, literally, on our merry way. When we got into the elevator, we kissed. As we kissed, I said, "Barbara, security can see us on the camera. Let's do this when we get home."

"Who cares what security can see? And let's do 'what' when we get home?"

Barbara had this big smile, with her dimples so cute. I devilishly smiled back. We were on a high at that moment and kissing in the elevator the way we were, with no other worries in mind, seemed so very naughty. Because all that mattered at that moment, for Barbara and me, was that once again there was a plan.

From January until March, our conversations pretty much became all about our trip to Disney World. We left for Disney on Saturday, March 12. As usual, we split up and took separate flights. I was never a happy airline passenger. With my OCD, I'd stress for weeks before any flight, thinking about being squeezed into the small passenger space. But it was a specific flight that caused me to never want to fly with Barbara.

We had two kids at the time. Jonathan was four and Kristen was two. We were on a flight coming home from a vacation at Disney World. For me, it was the roughest flight imaginable, with frightening turbulence. At one point during the flight, I said to Barbara, "If we make it off this plane alive, we will never fly together again."

After the kids were grown and it was just Barbara and me on a flight, Barbara asked, "Why do we still have to fly separately? You're always crazed about flying. Wouldn't you be more comfortable if I were sitting next to you?"

"Barbara, we started out with nothing. We've worked so hard for what we have. If something happens, at least one of us should be left to enjoy what we have."

I said that believing it would be Barbara left with everything, not me. Also, I was always such a nervous, anxious airline passenger. I felt that Barbara would be better off on a calm comfortable flight without me. After I lost Barbara, my fear of flying was gone. I could march onto the plane like a true soldier. I was impressed with my newfound bravery. But it wasn't bravery. It was that my worst nightmare had already happened.

So, we split up for our trip to Disney World. Barbara, Kristen, and Drew were on one flight. Stephen, Jonah, and I were on another. Jonah was so excited about going on an airplane to, as he called it, "Flordida."

Jonah, at three-and-a-half, was taking it all in. He got to meet Woody, from *Toy Story*. It doesn't get better than that for a three-and-a-half-year-old. Drew, at nine months, looked at the sights and parades with an amazed look, as if to say, "Wow, this is incredible!" And Barbara ... well ... Barbara got her dream of bringing her grandchildren to Disney World. At this time in her life, it was hard for anything else to top that.

After our time at Disney, we all drove down to South Beach. The kids stayed at a hotel near our apartment and had a fun two days. They left the day before Barbara and me. We helped load them into the van at the hotel. As the van drove off to the airport, Barbara and I waved to them from the curb shouting, "See you back in New Jersey."

After waving them off, Barbara turned to me. "Jonah wasn't too young for this trip and Drew was fine too. Marc, I'm telling you now. We're doing this Disney trip again next year and I want Jonathan and Brian to join us too."

"Okay," I said. "That sounds like a plan."

CHAPTER 34

Pancakes for dinner

n 2011, Daylight Savings Time started while we were at Disney World. We returned to New Jersey on March 20, the first day of spring. I was back to work on Monday the twenty-first. When I got home from work that day, Barbara had all the window shades fully raised. It was our second spring in the Hoboken apartment.

Neither of us were fans of winter. We loved spring and being in the apartment with an extra hour of afternoon daylight. When getting home from work at this time of year, I often said, "It feels too early for dinner."

Barbara would answer, "Do you want to go for a walk first?"

I would say, "No, let's get naked. Why put off for later when we're tired, what we can do now?"

Barbara sometimes agreed. But more often, we went for a walk. Even in our home in Flanders, we looked forward to the start of Daylight Savings Time. After the winter months of arriving home in the dark, our home was suddenly brighter and more cheerful. I remember one time when the kids were young; it was the first Monday after we turned the clocks back over the weekend. I was heading home from work at the usual time. When I pulled into the driveway, the kids were playing in our front yard. As I got out of the car, Jonathan had a puzzled look on his face. "Daddy," he asked, "how come you're home so early?"

After each winter, I wasn't used to being home in the daylight. It was so refreshing. Once we became empty nesters, the house was quiet. It was just the two of us to talk, be silly, and chill. Barbara would tell me to quickly change my clothes for dinner, because we're going for a walk afterward and getting some fresh air. The months of hibernating in the house after work, to avoid the dark and cold, were over. This time of year was a favorite of ours for enjoying time together. We loved what spring was all about. And spring was what we so much needed; another shining beginning, giving hope for good things to happen.

In the years that followed, after I lost Barbara, this time of year was especially difficult for me. Getting home on the first workday of Daylight Savings Time, I grieved for my loss. My knees felt weak and I rushed to the couch. As I sat, I stared out at the sun-filled apartment and asked out loud, "Oh, Barbara ... where are you?" I got no answer. I was so alone. I could feel the new season, a new shining beginning. But without Barbara, the apartment was empty and the quiet was heart-wrenching. Each year, the start of Daylight Savings Time is one of the many times when I miss Barbara most of all.

We had a busy spring schedule ahead of us. On top of everything else, the three-year lease on Barbara's car was ending. We were living in Flanders when we leased the car. I remember signing the lease agreement and wondering if Barbara would survive the length of the lease. Now, with more uncertainty from the results of the recent scans, I needed to decide what to do.

Barbara put me on the spot when she asked, "Should we just extend the current lease for another six months?" Those were her words. But what I could feel her really asking was something more like, "Am I going to be here, and does it pay to get another three-year lease?"

My mind raced to give a quick and spontaneous response. I

wondered if this was the right time for me to start that "life" conversation I'd been avoiding. However, it was a conversation I knew I didn't have in me to start. I so dreaded the possibility of ever hearing Barbara say, "We need to talk about our future and what's going to be." I so hoped that such a conversation would never happen, so our time together could peacefully end, without ever losing the hope in Barbara's eyes.

What do I do? I quickly raced through so many questions in my mind. Do I give her an answer based upon a good business decision? How could I tell her that there is so much uncertainty about the future and maybe we should just extend the current lease? Or do I tell her what she wanted to hear? Why is this so difficult? It's just a car, what am I trying to do? I let my heart lead the way. "No ... no, turn the car in and get a new car with a three-year lease like the current lease."

Barbara answered, "You think that's what we should do?"

"Absolutely!"

I could tell Barbara really felt it made more sense to extend the current lease. But I didn't want to decide what to do based upon a business decision. I kept thinking to myself, it's just a car and it's going to make Barbara happy to get a new one.

At this point, we had been married for over thirty-nine-and-a-half years. For all of those years, I had always shopped for a car with Barbara. For a woman, purchasing a car is often not a pleasant experience. The salespeople assume that women know nothing about cars.

I always hated going to the dealerships. The salespeople asked me for details about what I wanted. I would tell them, I don't know. "This car is for my wife," I'd say. "Ask her." They would quickly turn to Barbara and then continue directing the questions to me. I guess that many car salespeople assume that the man will be making the decisions. The entire experience was so annoying. I said to Barbara, "I think that you should call the salesman that we worked with three years ago and meet with him yourself. His name was Perry, right? He'll work with you."

Barbara did exactly that. On the way home from the dealer,

Barbara called me. She was so excited. "I decided on the Infiniti SUV and Perry has one in the color and with all of the details I want. I saw it on the lot and sat in it and it is gorgeous. I turn in my car and pick up the new one the day after tomorrow."

This car was so extra special to Barbara. It felt so good to see that getting the new car and a three-year lease brought her so much happiness. It was the first time in our marriage that Barbara negotiated the entire transaction and selected everything that she wanted, without me seeing the car and influencing her decisions. Barbara was surely more than capable of leasing a car. But in the past, she didn't feel comfortable working with car salespeople. I don't know why that field is dominated by men who are ignoramuses.

Our first trip with the car was in early April, when we attended a cousin's wedding at Temple Israel in Lawrence, Long Island. It was a black-tie affair and Barbara was planning to wear a strapless black gown. The morning of the wedding, she said, "I hope the dress fits. The last time I wore it, it was tight."

When she got the dress on, Barbara called me to zip her up and she told me to do it carefully and not to force it. I was able to zip it up quite easily and I said, "That's so great, you must have lost weight."

Barbara answered, "Do you really think that's so great?"

I made like I didn't hear her response and instead asked, "Are you wearing underwear under that dress?"

"Of course I'm wearing underwear!"

With a devilish intonation, I said, "Well, that's your loss."

"Oh, stop being so silly," she said, laughing.

Barbara looked so beautiful in that gown. In the past, all she'd have needed to do was to give me a wink and we would have been late to the wedding. But spontaneous things like that didn't happen for us anymore. Five years of treatments had taken away Barbara's feeling for lust. Although we hadn't stopped making love, it was different. The act of "making love" may suggest the term "having sex." But the term having sex doesn't suggest the act of making love. Now our making love was all about our intimacy.

Barbara came up to me as I began to put on my bow tie. "Before

I put on my lipstick, give me a kiss." We kissed and looked into each other's eyes. I could tell she was concerned that she had lost some weight. But that was a problem for another day. For tonight, we were going to a wedding, and not just any wedding. It was a Long Island wedding and Barbara intended to party.

Barbara was scheduled for new scans to be taken a week later. It was a frightening time, and I was worried about the results. But I didn't think about that as we drove to Long Island. All I could think about was walking into the temple with my beautiful wife. There would be no other woman there as beautiful as she was. Although it was forty-four years later, the feeling would be no different than when I walked into my high school prom with Barbara. Over the years, we grew older. However, in my eyes, Barbara didn't.

I was looking forward to the music and our dancing. Barbara and I were usually the first on the dance floor and often the last to be seated. We arrived at the temple a little early. By the time the ceremony and cocktail hour were over, Barbara was feeling a little tired. As we found our seats in the ballroom, the band was playing. I gestured to Barbara to dance. She looked at me and sighed.

"Okay," I said, "let's rest."

Then, Barbara stood up. As usual, we were the first on the dance floor. We danced throughout the evening. Barbara held on to me and I wondered if at the end of the evening, the last dance would truly be our last.

Driving home after the wedding, Barbara was already planning our next activity. She talked about throwing a cocktail party for our Hoboken neighbors. By this time, we'd been living in the apartment for twenty-three months. We'd made many new friends. Barbara really wasn't up to making the party. But that wasn't going to stop her. Barbara asked Judy if she would help, and Judy volunteered Bruce to join in helping.

Barbara would often make parties and do everything. She relied on me for little. Especially after the first party she made for our neighbors, when we moved to Flanders. At the last minute, Barbara noticed that we needed more soda and she asked me to go to the supermarket. I rarely went to the supermarket and probably had never bought soda before. I couldn't believe the price for a liter bottle of soda. I bought everything on Barbara's list. But when I got home, I had a fit and said to Barbara, "Holy crap, the price for a bottle of soda is ridiculous. After this party and unless we're planning for another party, from now on, the only beverage in this house will be water."

Barbara answered, "Okay, I'm not buying soda anymore. We'll drink water and the supermarket is now off limits to you."

The outcome of my fit wasn't so bad. After all, our children grew up drinking water only and I got out of errands to the supermarket. Supermarket errands were only one of many chores that I was able to get out of, during our marriage.

I used to think that I outsmarted Barbara. Eventually, I found out that she would get back at me. Several years after I lost Barbara, I was talking to Jonathan about Barbara and he happened to say, "Well, Dad, I'm sure that you know how Mommy used to get back at you, when you would do something she didn't like."

"I don't know what you're talking about," I answered.

"You mean you don't know that Mommy used to make you pancakes for dinner, just to get back at you?"

I hated pancakes for dinner. When I got home from work and Barbara was serving pancakes, I would ask, "What else are we having?"

Barbara's answer was always, "That's it. That's what we're having for dinner."

As I grew more and more annoyed, she remained perfectly calm and told me, "Well, that's all we have tonight. Let your brain tell your stomach that you're full."

For all the times that we argued, I thought Barbara just let me scream it off and then she would move on. I never knew she had her ways of getting back at me. I now wonder what other things she did. Barbara wasn't a spiteful person, at all. I was learning that she had her ways of getting satisfaction, while letting me think I won an argument. When, in truth, I'd lost and unknowingly paid the consequences. The crazy thing is that during our forty years of marriage, I never figured that out.

The lesson doesn't do any good for me now, except to give me a smile and make me think that I probably deserved pancakes for dinner much more often. I do hope Barbara knew that she got her payback. I'm sure she knew. Barbara was too smart to think otherwise.

The cocktail party for our neighbors in Hoboken was on a Saturday evening in the middle of April. Barbara prepared her usual specialties, baked clams and shrimp scampi. She always had a variety of hors d'oeuvres that she was known for. It had been a while since Barbara had made such a party. This was the first one in Hoboken and this cocktail party was a success. Barbara was so pleased.

A couple of days after the party, I received an email from Dr. Abbasi. Her office had been finalizing the arrangements for Barbara to be accepted into the clinical trial scheduled for the following spring. The email read:

> Hi:
>
> I spoke with Dr. Stern. I want to test Barbara's old tumor for the presence of a protein that is the target of a new antibody. In order to do this, I need for her to give me permission (consent form) to test the old tumor. If this is ok, will send by email for you and her to read.
>
> Sandra

I wrote back:

> Hi, Dr. Abbasi:
>
> This is totally fine with me and Barbara, to test the old tumor tissue. Please send by email for us to read.
>
> Thanks, Marc

Dr. Abbasi wrote:

> Hi:
>
> Here it is. If you agree we need to send one more form to you also (HIPPA). I am cc'ing Christina, who is our coordinator on this.

All the paperwork for the clinical trial was complete and submitted. Now, with much praying, we hoped that the test results would come out positive. It would take a few weeks to get the results.

For the first Saturday in May, we had a busy day scheduled. In the early afternoon, we had a charity event on the Lower East Side of Manhattan for Animal Haven, a nonprofit organization that finds homes for abandoned cats and dogs. After that, we had a birthday party to attend in Midtown Manhattan.

Barbara was feeling a little sluggish that morning and I asked her if she wanted to skip the Animal Haven event and rest up for the birthday party. Barbara never wanted to miss out on anything. "Nope," she said. "I'll get myself together and I'll be fine."

We drove into Manhattan. It was a nice, sunny, comfortable day and when we were a couple of blocks from the location of the event, I spotted a parking space. "Park there," Barbara said. "I'll hold on to you and we can take a slow walk." It was a lovely walk on the streets of the Lower East Side. The quaint neighborhood was bustling with activity. People were enjoying the day and the local shops. As we walked, Barbara said, "This feels so good."

At the event, a friend came up to me and said, "Barbara looks so beautiful, in spite of all that she's going through. She's an amazing woman. But how is she really doing?"

"She hasn't given up smiling," I answered. "She's doing as good as the smile on her face."

After the event, we headed up to Midtown for an early evening birthday party. The party was in the lobby of an office building; an out-of-the-ordinary space for a birthday party, which made the party unique and fun. The lobby was transformed into a party space with food stations, cocktail tables, music, and dancing. After going through the saying-hello-to-people stage of the party, Barbara and I found our way to a table. By this point, Barbara was quite tired from the day's activities and I brought her something from the buffet.

A work friend of mine, Tony, joined us at our table with his wife, Rena. Barbara so liked Tony and Rena. They were a young, fun couple, whose wedding we attended nine years before. They were married in a church in Bensonhurst, Brooklyn and their wedding reception was in Midtown Manhattan. We were living in Flanders at the time, and it was a long trip from Flanders to the church in Brooklyn and then to the restaurant in Manhattan.

A few days before, Barbara asked, "What time will we need to leave to get to the wedding?"

I answered, "It's going to be a long trip with Sunday traffic, to get to that section of Brooklyn. We'll have to go through Staten Island and over the Verrazano Bridge. I heard that many people are skipping the church and just attending the reception."

Barbara answered, "Really! That's awful. The ceremony at the church 'is' the wedding. I don't care how long the trip is, we can't miss the wedding. I'm sure the bride will be looking around for familiar faces, during her shining moment as she walks down the aisle. I hope people change their minds and attend the ceremony."

The traffic that day was horrible. Making it across the Goethals Bridge took much longer than expected and we still had to go through Staten Island and across the Verrazano Bridge. Running out of time, we were getting quite anxious that we had traveled so far, and it seemed like we were going to miss the wedding. As we neared the church, it turned out we were only a little late. Barbara said, "Drop me off in front and I'll run in and you park the car."

I answered, "Okay. I just have to pee first and put on my tie."

Barbara said, "Just park the car and bring your tie with you. You'll put it on when you're seated and there's no time for you to pee."

I made it to the seat next to Barbara just as the procession down the aisle began. We'd made it just in time and I put on my tie, as I meditated to get my heart rate to slow down. I would have been totally fine after a few minutes in my seat, if I had taken that much-needed pee.

It was a beautiful ceremony and it was so nice to see the smiles on the faces of the newlyweds. When we got back in the car and on our way to the reception, Barbara said, "It was a trip to get here, but I'm so happy that we made it to the church. I so enjoyed being at the ceremony. I felt badly for Tony and Rena that more people didn't attend. But they were happy to see us there and I enjoyed seeing the glow in their smiles."

I answered, "I enjoyed it too. It would have been even better if I didn't have to pee. My dick was exploding and practically hanging down to my knee by the time the ceremony was over."

Barbara answered, "You are so silly."

For Barbara, no matter how cumbersome the trip to the church was, it was the right thing to do. Barbara was always compassionate and empathetic toward others, without looking for or expecting anything in return. About two weeks after I lost Barbara, I received the sweetest note from Rena.

> Dear Marc,
>
> I want you to know how my heart saddened to hear about Barbara. I have to tell you, that of all the people I've met at Cosmo, you and your wife made the greatest impression on me. You have always been so kind, easygoing, and loving that my heart is truly torn for you. I must say that you are among the minority of special couples who inspire novices like me to see the brighter side of things. God gave you the perfect partner, because you are special people, and for that, we must be grateful. So many people spend a lifetime lost, searching for that someone to join them in their journey. You had that, and I know that life will be very hard now, but she will always be with you, souls connected for an eternity.
>
> I will continue to pray for you and your family, and I know that being such a good, gentle soul, you will find beauty in life even through the mourning. May God bless you always, and I send you love and blessings.
>
> With Deepest Sympathy,
>
> Rena Pinto

Barbara believed that an act of compassion is, somehow or some way, always returned. There are many ways that compassion can be returned, often in ways that we may never know or realize. I know that Barbara would appreciate that the compassion she showed to Tony and Rena was, in fact, returned. It was returned to me, during my time of sorrow.

At the birthday party, we were having fun at the table with Tony and Rena, as the music switched to some of the old classics. Tony said to us, "This is your kind of music. Why aren't you dancing?" As we listened to the music, it was difficult for Barbara and me to sit it out. But it had been a long day for Barbara and she really wasn't up for it.

Like many people we knew, Tony wasn't aware of Barbara's health situation. Certainly, by just looking at her, it was almost impossible for anyone to recognize that she had any health issues. Tony began to coax us, saying, "Come on, guys, get up and dance." So, we did. We danced to just two songs and that was enough.

To anyone watching us dancing, I'm sure that it looked like Barbara and I must be so much in love ... and we were. I remember the moment so clearly, looking into Barbara's eyes and seeing her warm smile. I could feel her love for me, and I knew she could feel my love for her. The moment was so beautiful and romantic. I was thankful for Tony's persistence. We so loved to dance. This dance would be our last.

A few days later, we attended an event for an annual gala for Friends of the Hudson River Park. We took the ferry near our apartment to get to the city. My choice would have been to drive. Barbara was always reminding me that we were now urbanites and urbanites use means of transportation other than their cars to get places.

The event started at the park on Twelfth Avenue, at Twenty-Third and Twenty-Fourth Streets. There was a cocktail hour and guests were able to stroll through the park. Our apartment in Hoboken is directly across the Hudson River from the park. Barbara and I walked up to the river. It was fun to see our building from the New York City side of the Hudson. We kept saying to each other, "I still can't believe that we live there."

After the cocktail hour, guests were directed to Tunnel, a nightclub located a few blocks from the park at Twelfth Avenue and Twenty-Sixth Street, for dinner. Barbara and I had attended so many events, affairs, and galas in the city over the years. But now it was so much easier because we didn't have that long drive into the city and back to the suburbs. Instead, Barbara held on to my arm as we walked along the Hudson River back to the ferry terminal after the dinner. The evening's experience was so very different for us and, in minutes, when we got back to the Hoboken side, we looked across the river at the park. Barbara said, "Let's walk out to the end of the pier and get a better look at where we were." It was so exciting for us. Our lives seemed so enchanted.

When I'm reminded of times like this, I wish that our children could have seen us together. As they read this book someday, I hope they can imagine how Barbara and I looked as we danced our last dance and how we looked as we stood on that pier, with our arms around each other. During our children's growing-up years, I know they heard us argue too many times and not just about pancakes for dinner. I hope they will find in this book how much in love we truly were.

On May 10, I emailed Dr. Abbasi:

> Dear Dr. Abbasi:
>
> My wife, Barbara Gellman, has an appointment with you this Thursday, May 12 at 3:30 p.m. In preparation for that appointment, I have attached copies of the following:
>
> 1. Schedule of the individual abnormal blood results for the period of April 16, 2007 to April 13, 2011.
> 2. Blood work results from April 13, 2011.
> 3. Pet W CT Neck To Thigh 78815　　　4/11/11
> 4. Ct Chest W 71260　　　4/11/11
>   (findings Thorax, Abdomen, Pelvis)
>
> We'll see you on the twelfth.
>
> Thanks,
>
> Marc Gellman

Barbara came to work with me on the twelfth and we spent the day visiting projects that I was involved with in Manhattan. We toured a building that my company was considering purchasing, at Second Avenue and 127th Street. It was a fun day and kind of took our minds off our anxiety about the doctor's appointment, which wasn't until later that afternoon. We were so fearful of finding out about another potential ordeal for us, considering that Barbara was having difficulty speaking, as her tongue was increasingly getting more twisted.

At the appointment, Dr. Abbasi examined Barbara and she suggested an MRI of the brain. Barbara said, "We're going on vacation next week to South Beach and I have an appointment with a neurosurgeon on June 1. I want to leave for vacation with a clear mind and do whatever needs to be done when we get back."

We made it through the appointment without any conclusive bad news. But I saw the concern in Dr. Abbasi's face. I could feel a sudden fright coming over me and felt my insides quiver. But Barbara seemed relieved. She was only concentrating on our upcoming vacation. We both knew from experience that whatever the next hurdle was, it didn't have to be faced in any hurry. Certainly a few weeks would make no difference. On the next day, Friday, May 13, I received an email from Dr. Abbasi.

> Hi:
>
> Barbara's tumor is + which means she is a candidate for the trial, when the time comes.
>
> Have a good weekend.

I wrote back:

> Hi, Dr. Abbasi:
>
> Great news for a Friday evening. Have a great weekend too.
>
> Thanks,
>
> Marc

On May 19, the day before we were leaving for South Beach, we attended a luncheon at the New York Hilton Midtown. Dr. Abbasi was one of the honorees. Later that afternoon, I received an email.

> From: Sandra Abbasi
>
> Subject: Thank you
>
> ... for coming to the event today. I appreciated your support.
>
> All the best, Sandra

I wrote back:

> ... and we were so proud to be there. Near the end of your speech, you mentioned that you are a weeper. That's why we love you.
>
> Thanks,
>
> Marc Gellman

Dr. Abbasi wrote back:

> It is a job hazard though ...

CHAPTER 35

Ninety-five percent of people are great

On May 20, 2011, we left for South Beach. This trip was a bit different. In the past, Barbara dragged me all over the place; we had to go here there and everywhere. For this trip, Barbara held on to my arm as we walked along Lincoln Road and Ocean Drive. It was a casual stroll, as we window-shopped past stores. It was also probably the first time that Barbara didn't buy anything for herself. Instead, she convinced me to buy a couple of shirts at the Tommy Bahama store on Lincoln Road. I told her I didn't need any new shirts, but Barbara picked out a couple that she liked. When I asked about something for her, Barbara answered, "No, I don't need anything."

As we prepared to leave South Beach on Sunday, May 29, Barbara was going through the routine of getting things in the apartment closed and put away. As always, before locking the door, Barbara took a last look into the apartment and said, "Goodbye, apartment

433

... See you soon." We had plans to come back in a month. But this trip would be Barbara's last.

In the years that followed, before I locked the door, I could hear Barbara saying, "Goodbye, apartment ... See you soon." And each time, I felt the queasiness in my stomach and weakness in my knees and I couldn't help saying out loud, "Barbara ... where are you?"

We left paradise and were back to reality in Hoboken. Barbara's appointment with the neurosurgeon was on Wednesday. For me, this was going to be one of the more frightening medical visits. Barbara was becoming weaker, her speech more obstructed. My feeling grew more real that the cancer had most likely spread to her brain. I'd had a flash of this fear at our appointment with Dr. Abbasi, when she suggested an MRI of the brain. But a week after that appointment, we left for South Beach. While we were away, denial took over and I brushed those fears aside. I couldn't accept that this trip to South Beach could be our last. Even though Barbara was hinting to me each time we shopped, when she would say, "No, I don't need anything."

There was so much unknown and this time I couldn't find information on the Internet that would give me some kind of heads-up. All I could do was wait to hear what the doctor would advise. And as I expected, the doctor quickly scheduled an MRI of her brain. For Barbara and me, our only comfort was that the weekend came. With that, we had a reprieve from hearing any news.

We were having a relaxing Saturday and Sunday. Early Sunday afternoon, I went out to the pier and stared at the Hudson River for a while. It seemed to be a peaceful day. When I got back to the apartment, Barbara was sitting on the couch, with a blind stare on her face as she spoke on the phone. When she saw me, I heard her say, "Hold on, here's Marc." She gestured to me to take the phone. "It's Dr. Stern."

"Hello, Doctor."

"Marc ... I was telling Barbara the results of the MRI. The cancer has now become more aggressive and has spread to her brain."

Since we got back from South Beach, Barbara had gotten even weaker and her speech even more obstructed. I had become certain that this was going to be the outcome of the MRI. But expecting the worst didn't make it any easier to hear the results. I was stunned. I quickly thought to myself, "No, this isn't happening. I'm not ready for this. What do we do? How do I tell the kids? What do I say to Barbara?"

I looked at Barbara. She had a blank look on her face and was staring blindly in the other direction. I heard Dr. Stern ask, "Hello … hello, Marc? Are you there?"

"Yes, Doctor. What do we do now?"

Dr. Stern replied, "I've spoken to the neurosurgeon and we discussed either whole brain radiation or surgery to remove the tumor. From my discussion with him, I believe the whole brain radiation is what he is going to recommend. But he needs to see Barbara and the MRI to make that determination. It is difficult to get an appointment with this doctor. So, you need to call his office first thing in the morning. Tell his staff of my conversation with the doctor and that you need an appointment for this week."

"Okay, Dr. Stern, I'll call in the morning."

"Marc, also, this doctor is out-of-network."

"Oh my," I answered. "Should we also go to an in-network doctor, for a second opinion?"

"No, Marc. If Barbara is going to need the brain surgery, this is the doctor you want."

"Okay, Doctor, I'll let you know when I have the appointment."

I was going to do whatever Dr. Stern advised. Barbara loved him. In addition to his professional accomplishments and our trust that his treatments kept Barbara alive, Dr. Stern was such an incredibly wonderful person. We had no regrets and were thankful for how he got us through the too-many difficult years.

After I lost Barbara, there were people who asked, "Did her oncologist give her the proper care and treatments?" My standard answer to that question became, "Even good doctors lose patients." I've witnessed the doctors who give so much to their patients, even when the loss is inevitable. It's unbelievable to me how these doctors can continually take on new battles. I loved Dr. Stern too.

I hung up the phone and sat beside Barbara on the couch. She looked directly into my eyes and asked, "What are we going to do?"

With my arm around her, Barbara rested her head on my shoulder. I was trying to process what Dr. Stern had said. Over and over, I was reliving seeing Barbara's face when I walked into the apartment and she handed me the phone. My heart was breaking, and we sat in silence for a few minutes. I didn't know what to say. I didn't know what to do.

All kinds of thoughts flashed through my mind. This has to be Barbara's decision. Doesn't it? Why is she asking me? Can't she tell me what she wants to do? I'm her husband. I don't want to lose her. I don't want to make the wrong decision. We always made decisions together. But this cancer is in her brain. I want to try anything. Can I force her to have someone drill a hole in her head? Most importantly, what does she want? I think I know what I want. I want to do anything to save my wife. But what does she want?

I feared that Barbara was tired and wanted the struggle to be over. That was something I could not accept. But I thought, "How could I force something against her wishes?" With a few deep breaths, I calmed down some of the confusion in my mind, and answered, "Barbara, we're going to do the same thing we've always done, take one step at a time. I'll call the neurosurgeon tomorrow morning and get an appointment."

Sobbing, Barbara lifted her head from my shoulder, looked into my eyes, and said, "As soon as I noticed that it was Dr. Stern calling me on a Sunday, I knew it was going to be something terrible that he was going to say. Oh, Marc ... they're going to drill a hole in my head."

"We don't know that yet. Dr. Stern is saying that it may be whole brain radiation."

"But if it turns out that I need brain surgery, what's that going to cost?" Barbara asked.

"Well, we're going to do whatever it takes. We have no choice."

"Oh, Marc, it's in my brain. I'm scared," she said with a trembling voice.

As I held my arm around her, she was shaking, as if a chill was going through her body. Each time that Barbara would say "Oh, Marc," my heart broke. Her every sentence started with, "Oh, Marc." All I could do was to look into her eyes and comfort her, letting her know that I would never give up on her. I tried to ease her emotional pain. Although I knew I was doing a poor job in concealing that my heart was breaking.

Barbara felt so very guilty about what she was doing to me. I so wished it was me instead of her. Her life from childhood faced so many adversities. She deserved better. She deserved more time. She deserved to see more grandchildren.

Barbara and I were dating when I started working at age sixteen. Two years later, Barbara started to work too. We both worked a lifetime and put in our dues to get what we had. Barbara was being robbed of the rest of her life and what would have been the easy years, when we would reap the rewards of a lifetime of striving to get ahead. I felt so very guilty that Barbara was being cheated and I would be left with everything that was ours. I had to keep it together. Even though this time, my strong-willed wife had the look of defeat on her face.

Barbara asked me to call Judy and ask if she could come up to our apartment. Judy was a social worker for a hospice company. She was the first neighbor that we met in Hoboken. Over the past two years, Judy and her husband, Bruce, had become very dear friends of ours.

When Judy answered, I immediately said, "We just got a call from the doctor about the test results. Can you come up?"

Before I had a chance to finish my sentence, Judy answered, "I'll be right there."

"Just come in. The door will be unlocked."

Within minutes, Judy walked into our apartment and Barbara rushed to her with open arms for a hug. I heard Barbara say, "I guess it was meant to be that we met and became friends. Because you work for hospice and I'm going to need hospice."

Judy calmed us down and we discussed next steps. The first step would be to decide when to tell the kids. Judy suggested that we use today to get ourselves together and to call the kids tomorrow.

"Okay," I said, "as soon as I get to the office tomorrow, I'll call the neurosurgeon and make the appointment. Then I'll call the kids."

I called the neurosurgeon's office the next day and was able to get an appointment for Friday, June 10. It was only Monday and it felt like it would be a long week, until Friday. I sat back and took a deep breath before calling the kids. This was the kind of call that I had to do too often over the years. And this one was going to be the most difficult.

I must have sat at my desk for more than a half hour, thinking about what I was going to say. For most of that half hour, I just sat, staring around, and thinking about nothing. Stress had so fiercely built up inside me. I couldn't take it. I needed to let go, go limp, and take a free fall, and land wherever I was meant to land. It worked. My mind became a blank as I stared into space. All thoughts seemed to have left me. I felt light and airy, as my mind drifted and floated around with nothing.

Finally, I was ready to make the first call. It would be to Jonathan. I decided my second call would be to Stephen. I needed help with these calls and figured it would be easier on me for Jonathan to call Brian and for Stephen to tell Kristen. Also, I planned to talk more about radiation therapy, rather than surgery. I felt that the kids needed to be brought up-to-date slowly with how we got to where we were, before getting into the discussion about brain surgery.

As I was writing this chapter, I called and asked Jonathan to write about his recollection of my call back then. Jonathan wrote:

> Dad, you called to tell me that the cancer had spread to Mommy's brain and you were planning doctor visits, particularly with a doctor who specialized in radiation treatment. You were going to consider all options and expressed some optimism that radiation might be able to address it and/or shrink the cancer enough to stop it from spreading any further. Though, it didn't sound very convincing to me ... more of a positive attitude approach to keep us and Mommy from panic.

Of my three children, Jonathan was always the most challenging for me to be able to convince to have hope. He would go along with the positive talk that Barbara would be okay, but I knew Jonathan was aware that each bad turn brought us closer to the time when he would lose his mother. He was often pushing Barbara and me to do things sooner rather than later. When we were buying our apartment in Hoboken, the four-building complex was being developed in four phases. When the first building was ready for occupancy, Barbara and I decided to wait for the second building, which was to be ready in two years. Jonathan tried to convince us to buy in the first building.

In hindsight, I question if we should have done what Jonathan advised. I like to think we did the right thing. We didn't want to live our lives based on the assumption that Barbara was dying, with the mindset that we had a limited amount of time to get as much in as possible. Rather, we wanted to live our lives with a lifestyle based upon Barbara living. We loved our lives and having each other to wake up with each morning. It was as simple as that.

When I spoke with Jonathan on the phone about the radiation therapy, I asked him to call Brian to share the news. I also told Jonathan I was going to call Stephen, and tell Stephen to share the news with Kristen.

As I did with Jonathan, I called and asked Stephen to write about his recollection of my call back then. Stephen wrote:

> Dad ... when you called me and said that the cancer had spread to the brain, I felt, for the first time, hope for even keeping things just status quo for a little longer was gone. The different options were unimaginable (brain surgery). When I told Kristen, I felt so badly for her. She was destroyed by the news and kept asking for confirmation that she could be optimistic about the results for each option. For the first time, I couldn't tell her that things were going to get better.

I depended on Jonathan to speak with Kristen and Brian and talk them through what was happening. I knew that Jonathan, rather than I, could keep the conversation positive, without minimizing the severity of Barbara's condition. Jonathan wrote about his conversations.

I spoke with Brian and Kristen, who asked me repeatedly if Mommy was going to be okay. I even got into an argument with Kristen, who pressed me for answers, as I kept telling her that I didn't know. I said that it is definitely not good at all, but that I didn't know what would happen. They both asked if it meant that Mommy was going to die. I again said that I didn't know. Kristen was persistent, and just wanted me to say that all would be okay. I wouldn't do that and insisted that I didn't know. Brian seemed to better understand and was more accepting of the possibilities and probable outcome. He also understood and was accepting when I said that I didn't know what was going to happen. After speaking with Kristen and Brian, I called Mommy. She was upbeat, positive, and reassured me that this was all part of her road to recovery.

All these phone calls happened quickly on Monday morning. I thought that waiting for our appointment on Friday would seem like forever. But as usual, the week was passing by very quickly. And, to me, so was Barbara's life. All that kept going through my mind was, "I'm losing her." As much as I had hope for the chance that all would go well and we'd have more time, I could only think of the worst. "I'm losing her." I so didn't want Barbara to see that in my face. If nothing else, I wished for just a few more years. This is exactly what I wished when the cancer had metastasized almost five years earlier. I felt as if my original wish had come true and there weren't going to be any more extensions.

Friday came and we were waiting to be called into our appointment. I could see the fright on Barbara's face. I knew it was time for some silliness to ease the stress. Barbara would get angry with me when I got silly at such serious times. Most often, I eventually got a smile from her and got those dimples to show. I started to talk about the funny thoughts that were going through my mind.

"So, what do you think this doctor is going to look and sound like? We have never met with a brain surgeon. For sure, we know what a brain surgeon doesn't look like. Since, we've often heard 'doofus' people being referred to as not being a brain surgeon."

With a confused look on her face, Barbara answered, "What are you talking about?"

"I'm talking about when people are referring to an idiot person and say, 'Well, he's no brain surgeon.'"

"What does that have to do with anything?" Barbara asked, sounding a little annoyed.

"Well, we're meeting with a brain surgeon in a few minutes and I'm trying to figure out what to expect."

"What are you expecting to need to expect?" Barbara asked with a laugh in her voice.

"That's why I'm bringing this up ... I'm trying to get prepared for what to expect."

"You are so silly," Barbara answered, her dimples now showing.

"You know what, Barbara? We've never met a rocket scientist either. I wonder if a brain surgeon looks and sounds anything like a rocket scientist. Just like a brain surgeon, we know many people who are definitely not rocket scientists."

The silliness of these thoughts got me and Barbara through the wait. As we were called into the doctor's office, I said to Barbara, "Okay, this is exciting. We're finally going to get to see what a brain surgeon really looks and sounds like."

Barbara answered, "You are so silly."

The doctor gave us a warm greeting as we entered his office. He asked about us, how long we'd been married, about our children. Then he told us a little about himself and that he was going to review the MRI with us. He seemed like a regular guy and he made me feel relatively comfortable. My only concern was that he didn't look like a person who was at all handy enough to be drilling holes in people's head. I just couldn't help from having these silly thoughts. I needed to have these thoughts, because I had never been so frightened.

He began by saying that there were three tumors on Barbara's brain, one larger and two smaller ones. So, surgery was not a preferred option. He recommended whole brain radiation and said that breast cancer on the brain reacts well to radiation. He advised that there was a good chance that the smaller tumors would resolve, and possibly the larger one too, and that thirty days after the radiation, they'd take another MRI. If any part of the larger tumor was left, at that point, we would consider surgery.

Once again, there was hope. As we left the doctor's office, Barbara was still asking me, "So, they still have to drill a hole in my head?"

I answered, "That determination is thirty days away. We'll deal with that then. More importantly, I don't think that I trust this guy to do the drilling. He doesn't appear to me to be a handy type of person at all. I just don't see him with a drill in his hand. So, I'm going to do that part of the surgery."

Barbara looked at me with the most loving smile. She knew I would do anything for her. For now, Barbara was scheduled for fourteen radiation treatments, starting on June 16.

When we got home, Barbara sent an email to several of our neighbors explaining her health condition. A couple of neighbors already knew, but most didn't. This would be the first time that Barbara would go public with her health history to our neighbors in Hoboken. Barbara always looked so well. No one could detect that she had any health issues.

In her email, Barbara described that she was scheduled for fourteen treatments in Summit, about thirty minutes from Hoboken, and each treatment would take about ten minutes, starting on June 16 and ending on July 6. She hoped to be able to get neighbors to drive her to and from some of the treatments.

Barbara started to get responses from neighbors saying that they would be happy to help and they advised which days they were available. Then she received an email from a neighbor, Elias, who wrote that he'd like to make things easier for Barbara, by her not having to think about who was doing the driving each day. He volunteered to drive all fourteen days. Other neighbors began volunteering to bring dinner each night.

The support that we were getting from neighbors, whom we had only known for a short period of time, was heartwarming. Barbara and I were so fortunate. There were always people who gave us support. We never felt alone during our difficult times. I've grown to truly believe that, in my world, ninety-five percent of people are great. There may be different levels of great. Like some people may be great and others may be super-great. But, regardless of the level of great that people may be, ninety-five percent are great. As for the remaining five percent of people, they're assholes.

CHAPTER 36

I felt so alone

Barbara got herself mentally psyched and all set to begin the radiation treatments on Thursday, June 16, 2011. She had the driving schedule all worked out with Elias and was anxious to start. Elias was so very considerate. He called the night before and said to Barbara that there was no need for her to meet him in the parking garage, that he'd wait at the front entrance to the building. The first morning, Barbara went down to the lobby and Elias was parked at the curb and ready to go.

Elias owned a Mercedes SUV. But he was driving his partner's car that morning. He felt Barbara would be more comfortable. Barbara described the car as the biggest and most comfortable Mercedes she'd ever seen. When she got into the car, Barbara found a small package on her seat.

"What's this?" she asked.

Elias answered, "That's a high-protein, organic nutritional shake for you to build up your strength."

There would be a shake on her seat each day. Elias couldn't have been any sweeter and kinder in making these trips each day easy and comfortable for Barbara.

After the initial shock of hearing about the tumors in her brain just a couple of weeks before, Barbara accepted the challenge she was dealt. Leaving the hospital after the first treatment, Barbara called me from the car. She was so excited. "All went well! Elias and I are headed back to Hoboken. I feel good and have only thirteen more treatments to go. I'm going to get through this."

Barbara approached the ordeal with incredible courage, putting on a strong front for our family and friends. But I could see the pain in her smile, even when her dimples were showing. Barbara didn't want anyone to worry. It was more like she didn't want to see the look of doom in people's faces or the sound of doom in their voices. Once again, it was Barbara who was our family's strength.

Barbara began to email relatives and friends about what she was going through. I found one of the emails. It was to Doug and Cheryl. We met Doug and Cheryl in August 1972, when Barbara and I were on vacation celebrating our one-year wedding anniversary. We had been friends with them ever since. When Barbara was at the hospital in Philadelphia for her surgery, Doug surprised me and stayed with me during the surgery. Barbara wrote:

> Figured I would write out this letter and explain easier than on the phone.
>
> It's been a rough few months. As I think you know, I am on a permanent chemo regimen and will be for a long, long time, I hope. The chemo changes as it becomes less effective. Seems to last about a year and then we switch. Most have not been too bad, but the latest one which we started in April has been very taxing. Two days after I started it, and having nothing to do with it, I wound up with an attack of what they call ischemic colitis, a very painful abdominal bleeding situation. I wound up in the hospital for four days on pure liquids and then had a colonoscopy, another assault on my body. Needless to say, I was whooped when I got out of there. The doctor then decided to do a PET scan and MRI and found three lesions (breast cancer) in my brain – scary shit!! It

is not brain cancer, but breast cancer which travelled. The doctors tell me that breast cancer on the brain responds well to radiation.

Anyway, we went through a few weeks of seeing specialist doctors who are conferring with each other. They have decided to go the route of radiation for fourteen treatments to the brain and after a month or so, will repeat the MRI to see if they need to surgically remove one. I hope not. Brain surgery sure doesn't sound like fun. Although the surgeon tells me this is an easy one, easy for him to say. Anyway, we have made some great friends here in the building and one of them who works at home takes me to treatment every day in Summit, which is one half hour away. The treatment takes ten minutes and then we turn around and come home and I take a nap. After radiation, I go back on chemo.

The kids have been so supportive. They are adults now and want to be treated that way. Jonathan flew up for Father's Day weekend and Marc and I spent the day with the kids.

Sad to have to write all this bad news but wanted to update you. My tongue got twisted from one of the procedures and makes it frustrating to speak on the phone. We love you guys so much and as soon as I feel up to just hanging for a few hours, I will let you know right away. I promise.

Love,

Barbara

The radiologist advised Barbara that once the radiation treatments started her hair would begin to fall out. Unfortunately, this wasn't a new experience for her. This would be the third time. In past times, Barbara would hide her emotional pain and she strived to disguise any physical changes resulting from the treatments. When Barbara lost her hair from the first two times of chemotherapy, after each time, she discarded her wig and happily proclaimed, "I don't plan on needing a wig ever again!" So, she didn't have one on hand for this time. She bought a new one.

I think wigs have their purpose and can be attractive. But I hated the wigs on Barbara. I knew that wearing the wig was uncomfortable for her and I tried to convince her that she didn't need to do it for me. She felt it would be easier on the kids. In the past, she would say,

"What do you want me to do, wear a hat all the time?" She did wear a hat when going through stem cell transplant. But this time it was summer. So, a hat wasn't an option.

Having her hair begin to fall out once again was devastating for Barbara. She knew from the past times that it was best to quickly get her head shaved, rather than suffer the miserable process of the spotty, gradual hair loss. Barbara called a salon on Hudson Street, about ten blocks south of our apartment. She spoke with a beautician and explained her situation and asked if she could have her hair cut in complete privacy. The beautician offered to start his workday early the next morning and open the salon before hours. He would lock the door after Barbara got there so that no one could walk in on them.

Barbara made the appointment and asked me to drive her on my way to work. When we drove up in front of the salon, Barbara insisted that I go to work, and she'd walk home. She said, "I just want to be alone. I'm fine."

When she walked into the salon, the beautician was waiting for her with a bouquet of flowers. Barbara told me that he was so sweet, as she cried the whole time. When the cut was done, he wouldn't accept any payment. Barbara told me, "He just wished me much luck, gave me a big hug, and kissed me goodbye."

He was a total stranger who touched Barbara's life, with no expectations of receiving anything in return. Such people really do receive something in return; the gift of feeling good about themselves for what they can do for others. This man extended his kindness to Barbara, whom he would never see again. He was surely a member of the ninety-five percent of people who are great.

Barbara did well with the schedule of treatments and the daily routine, which tired her out. We had quiet evenings and relaxed in the apartment. Friends and neighbors in the building came to our aid and arranged an alternating schedule for bringing us dinners. I worked out my schedule so that I was always home for dinner.

One evening I had a meeting scheduled for nine o'clock at one of the company's properties in Manhattan. I called Barbara that afternoon of June 29. "Hi, I'm coming home for dinner. But I have to go into Manhattan afterward, for a short meeting. I'm meeting with Joe at our building on First Avenue at nine o'clock. We have to meet at that time, because we're looking at samples of lighting for the exterior signage and it won't be completely dark until then."

Barbara answered, "That sounds like fun. I'll go with you. I haven't seen Joe in a while."

"Not necessary, it's going to be just a quick look. So, I'll come home, have dinner with you and leave at eight-fifteen to meet Joe. It'll be quick and I'll be right home."

Barbara said, "You sure? I have no problem going with you."

I didn't know what to do. Barbara often came with me on such assignments. But she was weak after the tenth treatment and it was a hot, humid evening. I thought it best that I go by myself. After dinner, Barbara asked me again, "You sure you're okay going without me?"

"This is going to be a quick one. I'll be back quickly," I answered.

As I drove into Manhattan, I felt so guilty that I didn't take Barbara along with me. I didn't know what the right thing was to do. Barbara often came with me on these evening and weekend trips to look at buildings and company projects. She knew many of the people I worked with, and they expected to see Barbara with me.

Barbara was particularly familiar with this building on First Avenue. She had been there with me several times to tour the building, during the different phases of its renovation. A few months earlier, Barbara had come with me to decide which columns on the facade would be best to install flag signs. It was in February, on a cold, rainy, miserable evening. I held a large umbrella over the both of us, which barely sheltered us from the freezing rain as we trudged through the icy slush, walking up and down First Avenue. We were looking at the building from different views, angles, and distances.

"For God's sake," Barbara asked, "How many more times are we going to walk back and forth? We already decided which columns the signs should go on."

"I'm not quite sure if we chose the right columns. Let's take a look at the building from across the street and confirm that we are right."

"Okay," Barbara answered. "But I hope you have plans to take me for a great dinner, after walking through this mess."

"No problem. I already decided where to go. There's an Italian restaurant on 109th Street, just off First Avenue."

"After all this, you're taking me to a restaurant in this neighborhood. Have you ever been there?"

"No, but I heard the food is good."

I finally felt certain of the locations for the signage, and we began walking to the restaurant. Barbara reluctantly came with me through the slushy sidewalks. We stood out front of the restaurant and Barbara took one look and said, "Oh, no ... no ... definitely no!"

The restaurant was on the ground floor of a disheveled looking four-story walk-up tenement apartment building, probably over a hundred years old. Many of the old New York City apartment buildings have charm and distinctive, beautiful qualities. This one didn't. Perhaps on a nice sunny day, there is a quaint, appealing look to this late-nineteenth, early-twentieth century building. But on this rainy, slushy, messy, and miserably cold evening, the outside appearance of the restaurant wasn't an inviting sight. I said to Barbara, "Our boots and bottom of our pants are soaked and we're both freezing and hungry. I'll wait here out front and you go inside and take a look and tell me what you want to do."

Barbara went into the restaurant and came out with a smile on her face. "Marc, it's a quaint, old-style restaurant with tablecloths and old people doing the cooking."

We went in and were seated. Because of the bad weather, the restaurant was pretty much empty. Barbara had this big smile on her face, and I asked, "Are you happy because you're with me, or just because we're out of the freezing rain?"

Barbara answered, "It smells really good in here. I have a feeling that the food is going to be incredible."

It was. Barbara said it was the best shrimp scampi she ever had.

"I bet their desserts are good too."

"Oh, we're not having dessert here. There's a French pastry shop around the corner."

"What? A French pastry shop in this neighborhood? We're in Harlem, right? Are you joking?"

"Nope, I'm not joking. I planned a perfect evening, with a romantic walk in the freezing rain, followed by a wonderful dinner and to-die-for dessert."

After dinner and dessert, we got back to the car and we kissed. Driving home, Barbara said, "Nice evening. I'm happy I came along."

"Yeah, there's nothing like a romantic walk in freezing rain!"

Barbara laughed. "What was so romantic about it?"

"Well, we were both snuggled under the umbrella and I caught a few feels, just to keep our blood circulating. Let's finish off this wonderful evening. How about if I pull over to the side of the road and we make out?"

"You're as horny as a toad. How about if we just get home," Barbara answered.

"I'm just thinking about doing it for you in appreciation for coming along with me tonight. Also, you're probably pretty horny too, since you brought up the horny thing first. Actually, I'm only horny from hearing you say it. I was fine before you brought it up."

"You are so silly," she answered, laughing.

I went on, saying, "It'll be like I'm taking you home after a date, and we park before I walk you home. And in the car, it'll be like old times when we did things we weren't supposed to do."

The look on her face stopped my rambling for a moment, and I asked, "What are you smiling about?"

"I love you," she answered.

We never outgrew the feeling that we were doing things that we weren't supposed to do. When we looked romantically into each other's eyes, we were always teenagers again. I don't believe that our lust in lovemaking would have ever grown old, had it not been for the side effects of her treatments. I know for sure that my lust for Barbara will never end.

We always had so much fun together when Barbara came on assignments with me; like the time we stopped off at one o'clock in the morning to look at a sample of a light sconce that had been installed that week on a building in the Inwood neighborhood of Manhattan. We made this stop on the way home from Midtown Manhattan, after attending a black-tie wedding. We got the strangest looks from the overnight staff as we walked into the sales lobby. I was dressed in a tuxedo and Barbara in a black gown. Or like the many times, after babysitting for our grandchildren in Maplewood, New Jersey, we took the long way home to Flanders by way of Manhattan to look at projects that I was working on. The long way home added more than fifty miles to our ride home.

I don't know of any other wife who would have considered these work-related excursions fun. Or of any other wife who would have put up with a husband who considers an "evening out" with his wife as an opportunity to look at buildings being renovated. I truly believe we were one of the chosen to have had a marriage arranged directly from heaven.

We beat the odds that said our marriage would end in divorce, because we met and got married so very young. It might be very simple, how our marriage survived all odds. We never outgrew being horny teenagers, doing things we weren't supposed to do. Or we were just able to escape the pressures of life so often and slip into total silliness. We so loved acting and calling each other silly. Being like horny teenagers was a bonus. It all worked for us.

That evening in June, driving into Manhattan to meet Joe, I felt so alone. I missed Barbara so much, not having her with me even for this small assignment. I couldn't get out of my mind the look on her face as I left the apartment. I kept thinking that she must be disappointed. I was so angry with myself.

It was after rush hour and I was able to make it through the Lincoln Tunnel and across town to the East Side very quickly. As I drove up First Avenue to the building, I saw Joe waiting out front. I turned onto the side street alongside the building and drove to the parking lot around back. As I walked around to the front, Joe spotted me.

"Where's Barbara? Is she with you?"

"No," I answered, "I'm alone this time."

CHAPTER 37

Two puppy lovers

I t was Friday, July 1, 2011. Barbara had her twelfth treatment that morning. Afterward, she wanted to chill out, not think about next week's final two treatments, and forget about the world over the Fourth of July weekend. I got home early that day and found Barbara sitting on the couch. The setting was kind of odd. The apartment was quiet, the television was off, and Barbara wasn't reading anything. She was sitting on the couch and staring toward the window.

I sat down next to her and asked, "So ... what are you up to?"

"Oh, I'm just looking out the window and enjoying my view and feeling no worries. I want this to be a weekend of no cares. Karen dropped off dinner for us. But let's go down and sit on our bench."

There is a park, next to our building, that is a peninsula extending out into the Hudson River, with benches at the farthest tip. The spot is so very peaceful. Barbara and I laid claim to one particular bench, which became a haven for us. We could talk about the view of New York City, the boats on the river, and just sit and hold hands. It was a place of no worries and only peace. When no one was nearby, we would kiss.

The first time that we sat on that bench was an evening in June 2009, soon after we moved to Hoboken. We looked at the Manhattan skyline and couldn't believe that we lived in this exciting place. It was the beginning of our new lifestyle. We felt like we did when we lived in Jackson Heights, newlyweds in our first apartment and so much in love. As the sun set, we watched New York City turn golden, with the direct sun shining on the facades of the buildings. The view truly does turn into the "Gold Coast" and we were fascinated to live here.

Shortly after dark, we moved up to the sixth-floor roof deck in our building, which has direct views of the city. There are lounge chairs on the deck and we took two chairs and placed them side by side and lay down. It was about nine o'clock.

"This is so beautiful," Barbara said. "Are you happy?"

"It doesn't get better than this," I answered.

Barbara asked, "Do you love me?"

"No, you're ugly."

"Oh, stop it. You do love me. You wanted this apartment for me, even though we can't afford it."

"Where did you get the idea that we can't afford this apartment?" I answered.

"So, we can afford to live here forever?" Barbara asked.

"Probably not. But we may be able to get by if we tell the kids that from now on, they're on their own, if we don't get a dog, and if we don't have any more kids. By the way, are you on the pill? I refuse to use a condom anymore."

"My dear, not to worry. Chemo took care of the need for birth control ten years ago."

"Good, because we can't afford condoms or pills."

"You are so silly," Barbara answered.

As we looked up at the stars, we talked and fell asleep on those lounge chairs. It felt good sleeping in that evening air. Until I felt

Barbara tugging on my arm, saying, "Wake up, it's eleven o'clock. Let's go upstairs."

"Oh, let's sleep down here for the night."

"Get up. We can't sleep here. People are going to look out of their windows and wonder, who are those two crazy people? Also, I need to go to the bathroom."

"That's your problem. I plan to pee in the bushes."

"You're crazy. Let's go," Barbara said, laughing.

Of course, we did go back to our apartment that night. But it wouldn't be the only time that we fell asleep on those lounge chairs.

Saturday morning, July 2, I felt Barbara poking me to wake up, asking, "Are you up?"

"I am now, being that you keep poking me. Just give me a minute to wake up and I'll go wash up and come back to bed and we can fuck."

Barbara answered, "It looks like a beautiful day outside. I want to go out for dinner tonight. Nearby, just the two of us. But I want to dress up a little. I'm going to wear a dress and I'd like you to wear slacks and a nice shirt."

"Okay, but are we fucking now or not?"

"We're not. Let's get up."

I had been lying on my side facing away from Barbara. I turned over.

"So, you woke me up, just to tell me that you want to go out for dinner tonight?"

"Yes," she answered.

I moved closer to Barbara. We kissed and I looked into her loving, warm brown eyes. As my mood changed from silliness to seriousness, I said, "Okay, we'll dress up and go out for dinner, just you and me. But I don't want you to wear the wig. It'll be just you and me and we'll be ourselves."

"You want me to walk around outside, with no wig?"

"Yes."

We kissed and Barbara said, "You do love me."

I don't know what was on Barbara's mind that morning; her kisses felt so loving. Or what brought about her hurry to wake me and tell me of her plans for dinner, just the two of us and dressed up. But I know what was on my mind that morning as we kissed. It was, "How much longer will I have her? And eventually, when I turn over each morning, what will I see?"

That evening, as we picked a restaurant in the neighborhood, Barbara asked, "So, you don't want me to wear the wig?"

"Nope. No wig."

"Let's go to Casual Thai," Barbara said.

"Do you want me to call a cab?" I asked. Barbara had become frail and weakened.

"We don't need a cab. It's only four blocks and it's beautiful outside. We'll take a slow walk."

As we walked down Washington Street, Barbara said, "It really feels so good walking in the fresh air, without a hat or that wig."

Barbara hadn't had much of an appetite over the past week. But when we ordered our food, Barbara said, "I'm actually very hungry." As we ate our dinner, I could see that Barbara was enjoying her meal for a change and we laughed together about her regained appetite. I was so happy about how much she enjoyed dinner that I tipped the waiter more than fifty percent.

Leaving the restaurant, I asked, "Do you want me to call a cab?"

"No, I feel so good. I'll hold on to you and we'll walk slowly."

The look on Barbara's face was soothing to me. Smiling and laughing as we walked up Washington Street, with her cute dimples, Barbara's face had a glow. I could feel that she'd found hope, once again. On that walk home, we could feel each other's vibe. Regardless of the medical report, we could truly believe that all was going to be fine. The evening couldn't have been any better and we were surely having a weekend of no worries and no cares.

That evening wasn't just a dinner out. It was a date. A date for two puppy lovers whose first date was forty-six years before. I have no way of calculating the number of dates we had over those many years. But this one was different from all the others. Because this one would be our last.

Back in the apartment on the couch, we cuddled, kissed, and just looked into each other's eyes. That was our lovemaking for that evening. And each kiss felt like our first. It was as if we were teenagers again on the couch in Barbara's parents' apartment. It was back to being so innocent, when kissing was as far as we would go. I guess we both needed to feel like we were back in the past, to a time when there could be no end to our love, and we would have forever.

That Monday was the Fourth of July. The fireworks were on the Hudson River and the barges were adjacent to our building. We were invited to a party hosted by our neighbors, Elias and Milija. Their apartment has a large roof deck, with direct views of the river. Barbara and I had been looking forward to this party. It was a fun evening seeing so many of our neighbors, and Elias and Milija were the best hosts.

The fireworks began and Barbara and I stood with our arms around each other. The view was so magnificent. I turned to smile at Barbara. I saw she was crying. We had been living in Hoboken for twenty-five months and met so many nice people. I could feel the pain of her thinking that she would miss out on the life that we dreamt of, and this would be her last Fourth of July. I held her tighter as we watched the fireworks, with tears running down her face.

After the fireworks, dinner was served. Barbara regained her composure and seemed to be having a good time. We mingled separately among our friends. After a while, Judy came up to me and said, "Goodnight. Bruce and I are going to leave. Barbara is tired and we'll walk her to your apartment."

"That's all right. You don't have to do that. I'll leave too," I answered.

Judy said, "No. Barbara wants you to stay and come home when you're ready."

I looked to Barbara. She was on the other side of the roof deck. With a loving smile, Barbara mouthed to me, "You stay." I smiled back and watched as she left with Judy and Bruce.

I don't know how to describe the feeling that overcame me. I felt weak and so alone, knowing Barbara wanted me to stay. This was a first. We always left a party together. I felt that all the hope we had built up over the weekend was gone and Barbara was setting me free to be on my own. Having lived with my parents until I was married at twenty-two and been married for almost forty years, I had never chosen to be on my own. Now, the choice to be on my own wasn't going to be mine.

PART 7

Stories from the Seventh Day of Shiva

As I was still looking down, crying, "Oh my God,"
I heard Barbara say, "Stop saying, 'Oh my God.'
You're scaring me." I looked up, and Barbara was smiling
at me. When I saw those dimples, I smiled back.

CHAPTER 38

I know

Barbara's last treatment was on Wednesday, July 6. Elias drove her to the hospital, and I left work to meet them and be with Barbara for the treatment and the meeting with the radiologist. I had been waiting a few minutes when they drove up to the front of the hospital. Elias gave Barbara a kiss and wished her good luck for her final treatment.

As we sat in the waiting room, Barbara and I held hands and smiled. This part of the latest episode was over. We would have a one-month breather, before knowing the outcome of these treatments. After the treatment, we met with the radiologist and nursing staff. Everyone was wearing their smiles on this last day. They even gave Barbara a certificate for completing all her treatments. They were all so kind and sincere and wished Barbara luck.

As I watched the staff interacting with Barbara, I wondered if they were thinking to themselves, "Will Barbara be one of our lucky patients?" It's difficult for me to understand how people can perform such a job, day after day. But then again, ninety-five percent of people are great. These folks are obviously a part of the ninety-five percenters.

One of the nurses asked Barbara, "Where's your son? I always see him sitting in the waiting room so patiently waiting for you. I was surprised not to see him here today." The nurse was referring to Elias. Barbara didn't correct her and just answered, "He dropped me off and went home. My husband met us here to be with me for my last treatment."

Barbara couldn't wait to leave the hospital. As we walked to the parking garage, she held tightly on to my arm. As we drove away from the hospital grounds, Barbara breathed a sigh of relief. "Well ... I'm happy that's over."

"Me too!" I proclaimed.

For all the times, through all the years, when we finished a series of treatments, Barbara and I celebrated with laughs, jokes, and beaming smiles. This time was different. Although we talked in the car on the way home, there wasn't any celebrating. Barbara seemed to be having personality swings, being herself and not, as she stared out of the front window. She went back and forth from smiling to an expressionless blank stare. And even when she did smile, I couldn't get her fully engaged. She was so very different from her usual smiley, bubbly self after being finished with a treatment. Something was going on with her. I couldn't figure out what it was.

The next morning, Barbara was back to herself and I happily left for work. That evening when I came home, I found her cheerful. As soon as I walked into the apartment, she greeted me with a big hug and said, "Let's sit down. I have a few questions."

"Where's dinner? I'm starving," I answered.

"Don't worry, Barbara Kalman is dropping off dinner tonight. Just sit down," she said.

"Okay ... I'm sitting. But I'm still starving!"

Barbara quickly blurted, "So, when do we go to see Stern and I don't remember what Stern said what comes next."

Suddenly, I saw that she wasn't herself again. Barbara was cheerful and smiling. But her speech and manner of speaking concerned me.

"We have an appointment with Dr. Stern on the thirteenth, next Wednesday," I answered.

Barbara quickly answered, "So, we see Stern and what is Stern going to say? So, Stern is going to say what comes next."

As I looked at Barbara, I thought to myself, "Oh my God! What did the treatments do to my wife?" Never before had she referred to her doctor as "Stern." When Barbara called me after her routine appointments with Dr. Stern, I sometimes jokingly asked, "So, what did Jeffrey have to say today?" But most often, it would be, "Dr. Stern." This referring to "Stern" was not like Barbara at all. As the evening progressed, she seemed to be lost, confused, and disoriented.

The next morning was a Friday. As we awoke, Barbara seemed better. We cuddled in bed and kissed, and I said, "You weren't yourself last night. Are you okay?"

"Yeah, I don't know about last night. I can think clearer now. Maybe I should call for an appointment with Dr. Stern?"

"Well, that's much better. Last night you were calling him 'Stern.' How about if I call him when I get to the office? Maybe I can get an appointment with him for Monday."

As soon as I got to the office, I called Dr. Stern. I told him that Barbara was confused and disoriented at times. Dr. Stern said, "Bring her in on Monday morning. I'll tell my staff to expect you. I'll run some tests and examine her whenever you get here."

Over the weekend, Barbara exhibited more personality swings. There were times when she seemed fine and times when she became confused and lost. I was very anxious. I could hardly wait until Monday. On Monday, Dr. Stern examined Barbara. Then he met with me. "Marc, I want to admit Barbara into the hospital and start running tests and monitor her. Take Barbara down to the emergency room and we'll start the process of getting her admitted."

Barbara was assigned a bed in one of the emergency rooms. By this time, Kristen and Brian were with us. We joked and played games to pass the time, as we waited for Barbara to be moved to a patient room.

It was early afternoon. Dr. Stern came by and called me out of the room to talk. "Marc, I have the results of her blood work. Her tumor markers have spiked way up."

Then, Dr. Stern paused, and I watched the expression on his face become very somber. It became obvious to me that I was about to hear the worst.

"Marc, when I reviewed the results of tests and exams with Barbara, she changed the conversation to talking about her children and grandchildren. I think that you saw that happen during the times when you were with Barbara at appointments with me. Fortunately for Barbara, she is a strong person. She is a fighter, who is able to hold on to hope and ignore the negative prognosis. But it should not be surprising to you that we have come to this point."

Then, Dr. Stern paused again and said, "I'm not ready to place her on hospice yet. I want to monitor her condition this week, while she's here in the hospital."

"Thank you, Doctor," was all I could get out. I could find no other words to say.

As I stood outside of the room, I felt lost, helpless, and confused about what to do. The news was certainly not a surprise to me. Through all our years together, Barbara and I could come around to accepting difficult and upsetting news and, with hope, move forward together. This time, for the first time, I was on my own. I had no one to discuss how to move forward, while facing no hope.

As I continued to turn over in my mind what Dr. Stern had said, my head was spinning. "This is it! I'm definitely going to lose her, and it is going to be soon. How am I going to accept that it is the end of us? I'm not ready to tell the kids. How do I tell the kids? How do I go back into the room?" But I did go back into the room and found them having fun, playing Words with Friends on Barbara's iPad. I joined in.

Jonathan came up from Florida, the next day, Tuesday. We all visited Barbara at different times that day. I told the kids I wanted all of us to be together to visit Barbara on Wednesday. I wanted to break the news to them when we were all face-to-face. I called Kristen Tuesday evening. "Tomorrow afternoon, Mommy is being moved to a room on the cancer floor. I'm going to be with her for the move. I'd like for all of us to be with Mommy at the same time. Brian told me that he'll be there in the afternoon."

"Okay. Jonathan is with me. So, we'll see you there," Kristen answered.

"What about Stephen? I'd like him to be at the hospital too."

"Steve is planning to be there," Kristen answered.

"Okay, I'll call you in the morning to confirm."

The next morning, I called Kristen. "Are we all set for all of us to be at the hospital this afternoon?"

Kristen answered, "Yes, all set."

"Stephen too?"

"Yes, we'll all be there."

"Okay, see you later," I answered.

When I got to the hospital, I found Barbara in a very angry mood and I said, "Barbara, you're being moved to a nicer and more comfortable room."

"I don't want to move. I want to go home," she insisted.

"You'll be home by the end of the week. Dr. Stern needs to monitor you for two more days."

When I wheeled her into the other room, Barbara refused to get out of the wheelchair. She kept insisting that it wasn't her room and she wanted to go home. Eventually, I helped her to stand up from the wheelchair and held her in my arms. Barbara stared into my eyes. I could feel my eyes filling with tears. As her eyes filled with tears, too, I wondered what she was able to tell from the expression on my face. Could she tell that this was the end? Could she tell that my heart was breaking? I hoped she could tell how much I loved her and how much I cared.

As we looked into each other's eyes, I could see and feel that she was frightened. Barbara had had enough. She just wanted to go home. With a sob in my voice, I whispered, "Please, Barbara, just two more days and then home. Please smile for me and show me your dimples. The kids will be here soon. Let's be happy for them. We've always sheltered them from our pain. Let's do it again."

For all of our marriage, I was always able to make Barbara laugh, even during the most difficult times. This time, I hoped for a smile. Barbara did smile. But she had sad puppy dog eyes. I helped her onto the bed.

The kids all arrived at the hospital at about the same time. While they were with Barbara, I scouted for a lounge where I could talk to the kids in private. When I got back to Barbara's room, she had fallen asleep. It seemed like the right time to break the news. I was so very nervous and tried to hold myself together. I wanted this to be about me being supportive of my children, rather than my children being supportive of me. "Listen," I said, "while Mommy is sleeping, let's all go to one of the lounge rooms."

When I was in the lounge a few minutes earlier, it had been empty. But now there was a guy in the lounge. Hoping the man would leave soon, I became anxious as Kristen began to politely engage the man in a conversation. He began telling Kristen about his daughter and her medical history. It was sad, but I just wanted him to leave. This was not the time for my kids to reach out to hear someone else's problems. I was about to lay horrible news on them. Eventually, the man left. I quickly closed the door behind him, took a deep breath, and began. "Okay, let's all talk," I said, to get their attention. I could see in their faces that they knew something was up.

"I spoke with Dr. Stern and things are not good. Mommy is not doing well." I looked at Jonathan and I could tell that he knew I was finally going to be real about Barbara's condition.

"Mommy's blood tests show that her tumor markers have taken a sudden spike up. The cancer is throughout her body, in her bones, lungs, liver, spine, and brain. You know that for almost five years now, Mommy has been getting treatments that have been able to keep the growth and spread under some control. That's not working anymore. This is the end. There is nothing else that can be done. There is no other treatment for her. She's not going to get any better than you see her now and her condition is going to get worse. Mommy is not going to make it ... and she doesn't have much longer. I know that each of you really knew that this was not going to go on for much longer, even though Mommy and I never gave up hope."

One of the kids asked, "How much longer?"

"I don't know. Dr. Stern said that he's not ready to place her on hospice. But we need to plan for the funeral ... and we need to make the arrangements soon."

I looked toward Stephen. "Making the funeral arrangements is going to be difficult for all of us, including you. But I'm hoping that you can do it. Please tell me if this is a problem for you and I will totally understand. Because I'll be relying on you to select the funeral home and make all arrangements, including selecting the casket and making all other decisions. I trust all your decisions. It's totally okay if this is at all any kind of problem for you or if you need help."

Stephen answered, "Don't worry, Dad. I'll take care of everything. I'll call my father tonight, when Kristen and I get home, and ask him to come with me."

I looked to my children.

One of them asked, "What will the doctors do for Mommy now?"

"Mommy will be discharged from the hospital Friday morning. She may get treatments of a drug called Eribulin, for some period of time. But nothing is going to change the outcome. Mommy is not going to survive this."

Telling my kids was horrible. I wanted to be gently convincing and yet, not give them any false hope. I looked at their faces and hoped they could accept what was to come. Even though I wasn't sure that I was ready to accept that my wife was dying. I felt like I was just going through the motions. I began to understand that even at the worst of times, with absolutely no possibility of a change for the better, there is always some kind of hope that we try to hold on to.

We went back to Barbara's room. She was still asleep. I suggested to the kids that we find the hospital cafeteria. None of us had an appetite. We sat together and there wasn't much to say. Brian was quite upset. "I feel so bad that I let Mommy down. She is never going to see me become something. Jonathan, you have a home and a business and Kristen, you have a home and a family. I have nothing. I wish I had something about me that she could be proud of."

"Brian," I answered, "Mommy has always been proud of each of you. It never mattered to her how much you had or how much you did."

Brian thought he hadn't had the opportunity to prove himself to Barbara. But he shined in her eyes. Barbara loved being Brian's mom. In Barbara's professional and personal activities in our township and neighboring townships, she met many families with children, similar in ages to ours. When she met a kid around Brian's age, Barbara would say, "My son is around your age. Do you know Brian Gellman?"

Most often the answer was, "Yes, I know Brian."

That answer became a joke in our family. So often, we heard someone say, "I know Brian." Somehow, Brian got around. He was one of those kids who everyone knew, and people seemed to remember him for years.

Of our three children, Brian was the challenge. There were so many times I was at my wit's end with him. But it was Barbara who could accept any troubled situation in stride and say, "Well, that's Brian." There were times when Barbara was driven to tears over Brian and still, she would say, "Well, that's Brian." There was nothing Brian could do to compromise his mother's love and support for him.

Oh, Barbara ... you would be so proud of Brian. He truly is a kind-hearted, sensitive, and good person. He lived with me after you were gone, even though he had his own apartment just twelve blocks away. He did the cooking and errands, while searching for a job, and even took me to ShopRite and showed me how to shop. It was wonderful to have him living with me, but so unfair. After two-and-a-half months, I decided that I needed to let Brian go and live his own life. I needed him, but it was time for me to be on my own.

One evening after dinner, I said to Brian, "I think it's time that you move into your apartment and start living your own life. I need to start depending less on my children."

"Okay, Dad," he answered. "I can move into my apartment this weekend. I'll stay in my apartment four days a week and stay with you three days a week."

I answered, "I think it's time for me to be full-time on my own. I really want you to have your own life."

Brian had a concerned look on his face, and answered, "Do you want me to move out because my room is a mess?"

"I'm sure your room is a mess, which is the reason we keep your door closed and I never go in there. But no, that's not the reason. You really should have your own life."

Brian answered, "Is it because my wash is still in the dryer?"

"Absolutely not. But since you mentioned it, please get your shit out of the dryer. I really want everyone to get back to their own lives and not be saddled with me."

Barbara, Brian did move into his apartment that weekend. It was the first time I was alone. It was so difficult, and I missed Brian so very much. I needed him and wondered if I should have agreed to the four-day and three-day option. But I knew that I made the right decision for Brian. So often he sends me a text message, asking, "How was your day?"

Several years later, I was at work, in a meeting in the conference room. During the meeting, I heard my phone beep. While continuing with the meeting, I looked at my phone and noticed that it was a text message from Brian, which read, "You're a great dad!"

I wondered about the text and what I had done. I hadn't seen Brian in two weeks and tried to figure out what I'd done to prompt him to send me such a text. I sent a text message back to him, asking, "Why, what did I do?"

I quickly got back a response. "Nothing... I just wanted to tell you that you're a great dad."

For a father, it doesn't get much better than that. A parent's pride is about more than the material things our children accomplish. It's about the people they become. I am so proud of the person that Brian has grown to be. You did good, Barbara. You did good.

We all left the hospital cafeteria and spent some time with Barbara that evening. The next day, I got busy screening various home health care companies that could provide help with Barbara on weekdays, when I was at work. I got lucky, fast. I found an incredibly organized company that had a branch office in Weehawken, a town just north of Hoboken. I made arrangements for their service to start on Monday, July 18.

Our neighbor Judy suggested that I gather all jewelry and other valuable items in the apartment and give them to the kids or get a safety deposit box. Several different people from the health care company would be coming and going, and Judy warned that items could start to disappear. I took her advice and gathered all of Barbara's jewelry. I decided to go to the bank and rent a safety deposit box. Barbara wasn't into jewelry and didn't have a lot. But certainly, the jewelry had some monetary value and, more importantly, priceless sentimental value.

At the bank, a clerk assigned me a box and directed me to a private room to transfer the items. Until this point, I had been going through the motions to get the jewelry secured. But then, it became so real. As I packed the box with Barbara's personal jewelry, I held her gold ankle bracelet with little hearts, her necklace with a heart and diamond chips, and her silver-gold watch with diamond chips. I gave all these pieces to Barbara for her birthdays when we were teenagers, more than forty years ago.

As I looked at the jewelry, I could picture Barbara's face at the very moments when I gave each of these pieces her. Then I held her engagement ring and wedding band. I felt guilty for taking Barbara's treasured possessions away from her at her most vulnerable time. Barbara didn't know what I was doing. I felt like I was doing something behind her back and acting as if she were already gone. When I called the bank clerk over to lock the box, I tried to smile. I held back my emotions until I got back into the car. I was hurting and filled with pain and I cried for my dear wife.

Friday morning, I brought Barbara home from the hospital. Knowing the kids would keep her company, she suggested I go to work. Brian was in the apartment. Fortunately, he was living with us at the time and able to cover most of the household needs, shopping,

cooking, and so much more. Kristen was coming over in the afternoon, bringing Jonah and Drew and Jonathan.

I left for work. It was midafternoon when the executive adminis-
trative assistant, Aurelius, called me out of a meeting to say, "Marc,
you have to go home! Your family needs you."

On the phone, Jonathan explained what had happened. Barbara
was in bed and Jonah and Drew started jumping on the bed, laughing and playing. At first, Barbara was smiling, but then she wanted
them to stop. Suddenly, Barbara wanted out of the apartment.
Jonathan took her for a walk, just the two of them. Barbara became
confused and disoriented and led Jonathan to the parking garage.
As they walked around the garage, Barbara would stop and pause,
staring at things for minutes at a time. She then brought Jonathan
to the building's courtyard, where he watched as Barbara sat on a
bench and stared at the flowers. She did not want to leave. Jonathan
phoned Brian and told him where they were. Brian came down to the
courtyard and Jonathan went back to the apartment to phone me.

I rushed back to Hoboken. When I got to the apartment, Jonathan pointed to Barbara from the window. I saw Barbara sitting in
the courtyard; Brian was there with her. She refused to come back to
the apartment and wouldn't talk to anyone.

I went down to the courtyard, brought over a chair, and sat in
front of Barbara. But she wouldn't acknowledge that I was there. She
looked the other way. No matter how I moved in front of her, she
looked away. I held her hands and pleaded, "Barbara, come with me.
Please come with me." She didn't respond, as I continued pleading
with her.

Suddenly, Barbara turned and looked at me. The expression on
her face changed from frightened to a warm and loving, yet saddened, look. She seemed to have awakened from a dark dream and I
felt that she was back with me. We gazed into each other's eyes, as I
put my hands on her waist and helped her to stand. Then, I put my
arms around her. All this time, Barbara was gazing into my eyes, as
I gazed into hers. We stood in this position for about a minute and

then, in a sobbing voice, Barbara whispered to me, "I know." Then she put her arms around me too.

We embraced, gazing into each other's eyes. Hearing Barbara say, "I know," said it all. My emotions overcame me. This was our goodbye to each other. It was the goodbye that I could never say. Now, Barbara had made it so easy. Because with those two words, Barbara was telling me that she knew it was the end. Neither of us needed anything more to be said. After almost forty years of marriage, the look in our eyes and the feeling in our hearts were communicating better than any spoken word. And after almost thirty years of living with cancer, it was at this moment when we were finally at peace. We had reached the point of acceptance and we did it together.

After a few minutes, I said, "Barbara … let's go home." She held on tightly to my arm as we walked to the elevator and to our apartment. I felt such pride that Barbara was my wife. Of all our great walks together, this would be our last.

CHAPTER 39

A person of faith

On Monday morning, July 18, representatives from the home health care company showed up, ready to go. I was quite nervous, not knowing how Barbara was going to react to having someone with her all day. Barbara was so independent and used to doing for herself. No matter how fragile she was after surgeries and treatments, she would always say to me, "You go to work. I'm totally fine." It was difficult for me to accept that she wasn't fine anymore.

Two women came that morning: the health care nurse, to record and prepare a schedule of all that needed to happen, and Miriam, the health care aide. Miriam, a wife and mother of young children, lived with her family in Weehawken, a town just north of Hoboken. The moment I saw her, I breathed a sigh of relief. Miriam had such a warm, loving smile and she warmed up to Barbara immediately.

I felt so fortunate that the health care company got it right, just from the information I'd given them over the phone the Thursday before. I'd been hearing so many horror stories, and I truly believed that once again we were being blessed. Miriam would arrive each morning, Monday through Friday, before I left for work, and care for Barbara until I got home. I would care for Barbara over the weekend, with help from the kids.

That Wednesday, Barbara had a scheduled appointment with Dr. Stern for an examination and a treatment of Eribulin. Brian drove Barbara and Miriam and I met them at the hospital. Kristen met us there too.

While Barbara was getting the treatment, Dr. Stern came to the treatment area and asked to speak with me in his office. I asked Kristen to come with me. In Dr. Stern's office were pictures of his family. Kristen had attended summer camp with his daughter and asked, "How is Lauren?"

There was some friendly talk. Then Dr. Stern changed the subject. "Marc, the treatment that Barbara is getting today could be difficult for her, considering her weakened condition. I don't feel that continuing this treatment is of benefit."

I knew what Dr. Stern was suggesting. It was a drain on Barbara to bring her to the hospital, and the treatment wasn't going to change the prognosis. But Kristen wasn't giving up yet and wanted the treatments to continue. So, I let Kristen do the talking.

"Will these treatments give my mom more time?"

Dr. Stern answered, "This isn't a miracle drug, and her quality of life is slipping away quickly."

In a pleading voice, Kristen answered, "Dr. Stern ... August 29 will be my parent's fortieth wedding anniversary. September 12 will by my mom's sixtieth birthday. I have a party planned for August 6 to celebrate. That's only two-and-a-half weeks away. I so much want my mom to make it to that party."

This kind of conversation must be one of the most difficult for a doctor. Kristen's plea was so heart-wrenching. I looked to Dr. Stern and saw the pain on his face, as he looked to me to answer my daughter. I turned to Kristen and could only get my words out above a whisper.

"Kristen ... it's not going to happen. You're going to have to cancel the party."

Kristen pleaded, "But ... can we just continue the treatments and see?"

Dr. Stern answered, "I can lower the dosage, to make it easier for your mom to tolerate."

I turned again to Kristen. "Kristen, listen to me. Even with continuing with some of the treatments, Mommy will not be in any condition to go to a party. This party is kind of a surprise, since we have no idea what you have planned or who is coming. But you will have to tell everyone that it is cancelled."

With a sob in her voice, Kristen sighed, "Okay."

Each day, Barbara's condition grew worse. I slept little, and the strain on me was difficult. After Miriam left on Friday, with the weekend ahead, I realized that I needed additional help. The kids came over on Saturday and while Barbara was asleep, we talked. I explained that we needed help around-the-clock and on weekends.

I waited too long to get live-in help and it took its toll on my family. We reached out to friends and relatives for advice on what to do and if they knew of someone. Two different sources recommended a woman living in Brooklyn and her references were very comforting. Her name was Rosey. Brian volunteered to call Rosey, interview her over the phone, and find out if she could start the coming week.

Brian left the room and called Rosey. When he returned, Brian said, "Okay, I spoke with Rosey and she seemed very nice over the phone. Tomorrow, Rosey is taking the train to Hoboken. I'm going to pick her up at the station and bring her here. So, we should all be here tomorrow to interview her and get her started. Are we all okay with that?"

The next day, we waited in the living room for Brian and Rosey to arrive. Barbara sat on the couch and we explained to her what was happening. When they came in, Brian announced, "Everyone, this is Rosey," and we introduced ourselves.

Rosey immediately sat on the couch beside Barbara. As Rosey told us about herself, she was totally focused on Barbara. It was easy to warm up to Rosey. We decided she would start on Tuesday.

Miriam was scheduled to come on Monday, and it would be her last day. I felt badly giving her such short notice, after just a week. When I told her of our plans, Miriam couldn't have been any more understanding and made it so easy for me.

On Tuesday morning, Rosey, a five-foot, two-inch, powerhouse Trinidadian woman, arrived at our apartment and brought her care, her love, and her vast experience into our home with a running start. She took immediate control and organization of the household, the cooking, the cleaning, the wash, all while caring for Barbara. Most importantly, Rosey quickly became part of our family. For my family, Rosey was a blessing.

Rosey gave me a strict order. She told me if there was a problem in the middle of the night to shout out to her for help. She said, "Marc, you need your sleep. So, call me whenever." She knew I was constantly waking up throughout the night to check on Barbara.

One night, I reached over and patted Barbara's side of the bed. She wasn't there. I jumped up and called to her. She answered from the bathroom. I found her sitting on the toilet not able to get up. I asked, "Why didn't you call me?"

"I've been calling you. You didn't hear me."

I don't know how long she was sitting there. I helped her back to the bed and said, "The next time, don't go by yourself. Reach over and tap me and I'll take you."

The next night, Barbara tapped me. I jumped up, hurried to her side of the bed, helped her up, and held on to her, as we walked. Then, I waited to help her get back into bed. The next night, as I walked with her to the bathroom, Barbara let out a groan of anguish. When I turned to look at her, I saw her eyes roll as she fainted in my arms. I held on to her, dragged her to the toilet, and sat her down.

She was limp. I got down on my knees and held her seated on the toilet. I thought I was losing her. My heart was racing, as I tried to catch my breath to call Rosey. With my arms extended up to brace Barbara, I was looking down with my forehead on her knees. My mind was repeating the thought, "Don't die, don't die." I repeatedly cried out loud, "Oh my God! Oh my God! Oh my God!"

As I was looking down, crying, "Oh my God," I heard Barbara say, "Stop saying 'Oh my God.' You're scaring me."

I looked up, and Barbara was smiling at me. When I saw those dimples, I smiled back. To me, the look of her sweet smile was saying, "Calm down. Everything is going to be all right." All it took to make me smile was to see Barbara happy and believing that everything would be all right. And at that moment, whatever being "all right" meant, didn't matter. Because for a short while, my wife was back, with a clear mind and no confusion, and I could dream that she wasn't dying. Barbara could dream too. Even though this episode would be short, it was so wonderful to dream together once again, and for Barbara to experience a moment of happiness in the middle of the darkness.

With much relief, I gazed into Barbara's eyes. "You're so silly," she said. We laughed and when we locked into each other's smile, we felt like teenagers again, with silliness and puppy love. I said, "Okay, well, that was frightening. Next time I'm not going to get you up from the bed so quickly. You'll sit up first, wait a minute to get your bearings, and we'll do it slower."

I helped Barbara up and back to the bed. I sat beside her and we kissed and there was even a feeling of lust. With almost forty years of marriage behind us, I was certain that Barbara felt that way. I know for sure that I did. For both of us, during these few moments, cancer was of no concern. Barbara seemed to be totally back. She was her whole self, and her face was as cute as the first time I saw her in Far Rockaway in 1964, forty-seven years before. As we continued to enjoy the moment, Barbara asked, "Why did you bring me back to bed? I still have to go to the bathroom."

We laughed and I helped Barbara back into the bathroom. That evening was the last time I had Barbara totally back with me, the last time we laughed together, and the last time we felt like teenagers again. Our silly kind of love made us the oldest teenagers, and the youngest members of AARP. Within a couple of days, walking became too difficult for Barbara and we used the wheelchair.

That Saturday was a beautiful, sunny summer day. All the kids were over, and everyone wanted to take Barbara down to the pier for some fresh air and get a break from the apartment. I told everyone to go ahead downstairs without me. I just wanted to lie down on the couch in total peace and quiet.

The kids and Rosey, along with Jonah and Drew, wheeled Barbara down to the pier. Jonathan told me later they found a nice spot to sit on benches, under a covered area, and Barbara sat in the wheelchair and stared at the Manhattan skyline. They kept active with Jonah and Drew and tried to engage Barbara in their playing. But Barbara continued staring off into the distance for almost the entire time, until they brought her back upstairs.

Staring at objects and scenery had become much of what Barbara would do, since I brought her home from the hospital just two weeks before. Barbara so enjoyed the view from our living room windows and when she sat on the couch, she stared with concentration. During our marriage, there were two other times Barbara stared like this. In 2004, after my dad died, we moved my mom back up north from Florida and placed my parents' condo apartment for sale, with all furnishings. Before the sale closed, Barbara and I made a trip to Florida for a final search of the apartment to make sure that we hadn't left valuables. I even moved furniture around to check every corner. It paid off, because behind the television unit I found my dad's pool cue.

As I combed the apartment, Barbara sat in each room, looked around, and stared. The apartment offered many memories of happy times. I could tell she was visualizing all the wonderful times we had visiting my parents with our children in that apartment. As tears ran down her cheeks, Barbara was trying to cast the memories and the feeling of being in that apartment in her mind, to take with her and keep forever. It was the first time, in our thirty-two-year marriage, that we were faced with such finality.

The other time was in 2009, when we moved from our home in Flanders, after living there for thirty-six years. We were twenty-three and twenty-one when we moved to Flanders. It was the home where we grew up together, fell more in love, and where we brought home our three babies. As the movers came, Barbara went from room to room. With tears in her eyes, she took in the feeling of the goodness that took place in the kind of home that she strived for, for our family.

Now, over the past couple of weeks, as Barbara stared from our windows at the views in Hoboken, I could see that she was taking in as much of the scenery as she could. It seemed to me that she stared at objects and scenery rather than at us. I believe that Barbara knew she would never see these objects and scenery again. But Barbara was a person of faith and knew that she'd see all of us again someday.

As I watched my wife's life gradually coming to an end, I was reminded of an article that I read many years before. The article was adapted from a rabbi's keynote address at a Union for Reform Judaism Biennial, in Dallas. In the article, the rabbi states:

> Many of us have forgotten that the afterlife is a fundamental tenet in Judaism. No major Jewish movement has ever denied belief in life after death. Reform Judaism did reject the notion of *tehiyat hameitim*, the resurrection of the dead, but each of our platforms has affirmed belief in the immortality of our souls. Nevertheless, we have chosen to abandon the most hopeful belief in Jewish tradition in nearly every Reform pulpit, and thus in nearly every Jewish heart. And because of our forgetting, I have seen Jews die with less serenity, grace, and hope and with more agony, than Christians who believe in heaven.

He goes on to say:

> In the face of our finitude, only religion can offer hope – hope that the good in us will win and hope that we will not be separated forever from those we love.

Remembering this article helped me to understand and accept Barbara's last weeks. She was such an incredible person of faith and person of strength. From Barbara during this time, there were no complaints, no sad face, and no feeling sorry for herself. Because of her faith, Barbara made this time of sorrow easier on our family. As importantly, she made it easier on herself with the belief that the love was not coming to an end and her goodness would reward her with the gift to take the love with her. Barbara was dying with serenity, grace, and hope, and would die with peace. It was Barbara's faith that gave me the hope to believe that if I wished with all my heart, Barbara and I would be together again someday.

When the kids brought her back upstairs to the apartment, Barbara was smiling. I was smiling too, after being sacked out on the couch while they were gone. But that evening, Barbara took a turn for the worse. For a couple of days, she had been having periods of gasping for breath. That Saturday evening was the worst. The kids helped as Rosey and I got Barbara onto the bed and calmed her panicking, while she gasped heavily for air. Jonathan and Brian decided to call 911 and told the police that their mother couldn't breathe. By the time the police arrived, Rosey and I were able to get her calm and under control.

There were a few minutes in between everything that evening, when Barbara came out of her confusion a little and asked how long she had been out. But Barbara's condition continued to get worse. Around midnight, I called Dr. Stern's office to speak with the doctor on-call. I explained that Barbara was having discomfort and had seemed to be uncomfortable breathing. He recommended giving Barbara the drug Roxanol.

Jonathan listened to my call with the doctor. When I hung up, he said, "Dad, you didn't fully describe Mommy's condition."

"Okay, I think it will be better if you speak with the doctor," I answered.

Jonathan paged the doctor and described that Barbara was in severe distress. I heard Jonathan say, "Okay, Doctor, I'll explain it to my dad and have him call."

Jonathan turned to me. "Dad, you need to call hospice and make arrangements for them to take over. I know that you have their twenty-four-hour contact information. You need to call hospice now and then hospice will call the doctor for authorization and proceed. The doctor said that he'll be waiting for a call from hospice."

A hospice representative called me back and confirmed that they had authorization to proceed with their care and advised that a nurse would arrive at ten on Sunday, the next morning. I was on the phone with the rep for quite a while answering questions. One question was about my faith. The rep asked if I wished for their rabbi to reach out to me. I answered, "Yes ... that would be wonderful."

Early the next morning, the phone rang. When I answered, I heard, "Hello, this is Rabbi Kraus. I'm the hospice rabbi."

"Hello, Rabbi. Thank you for calling."

"I'm so sorry to hear that your wife isn't doing well. I'm here for you and can visit you in your home. When will it be convenient for you?"

"As soon as possible. All of my children are here with me."

The rabbi answered, "I have to make a stop first. I'll be there before noon."

"Thank you, Rabbi."

We were all sitting around the dining room table, waiting for the rabbi. Our neighbor Judy was with us too. When the rabbi arrived, he asked if he could visit with Barbara first. He went into the bedroom and closed the door. A few minutes later, he came out and sat at the head of the table. He reached over and put his hand over mine.

Jonathan was the first to speak. "Rabbi, my mom loved her faith. Is there a prayer that you can say for her at this time?"

"Yes ... and I already did."

The rabbi spoke with us for a while. He was very comforting and offered advice, but I was so numb that I don't remember what he said. Nevertheless, I was so pleased that I agreed to have him visit us. After the rabbi left, I heard one of the kids say, "Wow, I never met a gay rabbi before."

"What did you say?" I asked.

"The rabbi is gay," they answered.

"How do you know that he's gay?"

"Dad! He was wearing a rainbow bracelet and he talked about his partner."

"Well, I didn't notice and he's one of the nicest rabbis that I've ever met."

The hospice nurse arrived and began coordinating the ordering of supplies to be delivered. She went over with Rosey the schedule and how to administer the medication. Judy and another neighbor, Barbara K., who is a doctor, were there to help too.

I was overwhelmed with all that was going on. But Rosey was doing well coordinating with the nurse, with support from Judy and Barbara K. I was in the bedroom with them when the nurse said that she ordered a hospital bed. They began to discuss where to place it in the bedroom.

It all was too much for me. I went into the living room and sat on the couch. Barbara K. followed me into the living room and sat next to me.

"... And how are you doing?" she asked.

"I'm doing." I sighed. "But I don't really want her in a hospital bed."

"Marc, she'll be more comfortable, and you'll be more comfortable. You need to get your rest too."

"But I don't know how much longer I'll have her sleeping beside me."

"Marc, the bed can be adjusted to be aligned with your bed and you'll have her right beside you."

"It won't be the same. I really want her right next to me."

Barbara K. quickly popped up from the couch and went into the bedroom. I heard her say, "We have a change in plans and will need to cancel the hospital bed. They have all kinds of pillows and we can use the pillows to get her in different comfortable positions."

For now, with all that was happening, I would still have Barbara sleeping beside me.

CHAPTER 40

Say something

The morning of Monday, August 1, 2011 was warm and sunny. Rosey came into the bedroom and helped Barbara out of bed. As Barbara stood up, Rosey put her hands on Barbara's hips to keep her steady. She looked up into Barbara's eyes and said, "Barbara, stand up tall. I want to see you smile and be thankful. God has given you the gift of another day and it's a beautiful day."

Rosey helped Barbara with showering and breakfast. Afterward, Barbara stayed in bed most of that day. As the day went by, she seemed to be drifting away. That evening, as I sat on the couch, Rosey came over and sat beside me.

"Marc ... I think it would be better for you to sleep on the couch tonight."

"I understand. But I want to be with Barbara. She may wake up and need help. I don't want her to be alone."

"Marc, you make sure to call out to me for anything."

"I will."

Later that night, as I turned off the lights in our room, I cuddled close to Barbara and whispered under my breath, "You will never sleep alone and even when you're gone, I will always feel you beside me." So many thoughts were going through my mind, except the thought of saying goodbye. Barbara would leave me without either of us saying goodbye.

As I listened to her every breath, I didn't think I'd be able to fall asleep. But listening to the rhythm of her breathing put me to sleep. I woke up several times during the night. Each time, I checked to make sure that her breathing tube was properly in her nostrils and fell back asleep.

The next morning came quickly. I turned off my alarm before it was about to ring. I kissed Barbara on her cheek. I was happy to see that she looked better than the night before and she was sleeping comfortably.

That morning, I had a previously scheduled appointment in Manhattan, just three-and-a-half miles from our apartment. I had planned to cancel the meeting. But that morning, Barbara really did look fine to me. I knew that if she were awake, Barbara would tell me to go to the meeting. I decided to go.

At about eleven thirty, I left the meeting and was heading to my office in Newark. As I entered the Lincoln Tunnel, I called home to find out how things were. Jonathan answered the phone. "Dad, the hospice nurse is here. She said that Mommy will be gone within the next hour and a half."

Before Jonathan could explain more, I blurted, "I'll be home in five minutes!"

When I got home, all the kids, Judy, Rosey, and the nurse were in the bedroom with Barbara. From the foot of the bed, I crawled onto the bed and next to Barbara and lay there with my arm over her. Through the corner of my eye, I saw Judy directing everyone out of the bedroom. She closed the door behind her.

I lay beside Barbara, just staring at her face. She looked so beautiful. I still wasn't ready for her to die. I just wanted her to open her eyes and say something, one more time. She wouldn't have to speak. I could do all the talking and her eyes could answer me. But she didn't open her eyes and my staring and her breathing kind of put me in a trance and I fell asleep beside her. I still hadn't caught up on my lack of sleep, from prior nights. I woke up two hours later to the sound of her breathing, with my arm still over her.

I came out from the bedroom and the nurse went in to check on Barbara. The nurse came out and said, "I'm going to leave. Barbara's condition seems to be stable. Please call me with any changes and I'll come back."

We were all just hanging out and waiting. At about four o'clock, the phone rang.

"Hello, Marc. This is Doctor Stern. How is Barbara?"

"Well, the hospice nurse was here waiting. She didn't expect Barbara to hang on so long. So, she eventually left and will come back."

"Marc, she's a fighter. Please call me and keep me up-to-date."

At about four thirty, Kristen said to me, "Dad ... Mommy is really holding on. Maybe you should tell her to relax and tell her that it is okay to let go."

I took a deep breath and gave her my answer reluctantly. "Okay."

I went into the bedroom, sat at Barbara's side, and leaned over. My cheek was touching her cheek. My wife was a strong-willed person, who knew what she wanted. I just couldn't bring myself to give her permission to die. It would have to be on her terms, not mine.

Over the course of Barbara's thirty-year battle with cancer, we would discuss what next medical steps to choose. But Barbara always made the final decision, and I would support her choice. Now, I was cheek-to-cheek with Barbara, once again, to give her support. As I closed my eyes, I whispered into her ear. "Barbara ... can you hear me? Dream with me. Let's dream that we're down in South Beach. Can you feel the warmth of the Florida sun upon us? We're sitting on our sand chairs, right at the water's edge. It's so beautiful and we're laughing, as we look out at the calm ocean. There are no waves today. The ocean is like a lake and so very calm and clear that we can see the bottom and the water can't be anymore turquoise in color than it is today. It's all so beautiful and we're happy, laughing, and so thankful for all that we have."

As I picked up my head and opened my eyes, I saw a tear on Barbara's cheek. I felt a sense of peace knowing that she could hear me, and she could let her emotions show. Then I saw a tear fall to her cheek, and then another tear, and I realized that the tears were mine. I so wished that she heard me. I truly believe that she did.

In the months and years that followed this day, it often happens that certain music and songs bring me back to being with Barbara. It is music that reminds me of specific times and events. I feel Barbara with me and am reminded of where we were and what we were doing when we heard those songs. A little over a year later, on September 23, 2012, I was alone in the apartment and had the radio on. I was doing chores, when I realized the song playing was "Unforgettable," by Natalie Cole and her dad, Nat King Cole.

I began listening to the words. It so described the feelings inside of me about my memories of Barbara. She is so unforgettable. The words reminded me of her love, which still envelops me, and of the warm feeling my memory of her brings to me. Wherever Barbara is, I hope she's been remembering me too.

As I listened, I found myself dancing in the middle of the living room. With my eyes closed, I embraced myself. But in my mind, my arms were embracing Barbara around her waist. I could feel her arms around my shoulders. It was how we danced as teenagers. When the song ended, I opened my eyes. Barbara was gone. I sat on the couch and stared out the window. For certain, a forty-year marriage doesn't fade away. It continues on and the grieving never ends.

There is one song in particular that brings me back to that moment in our bedroom, when I sat beside Barbara and whispered into her ear. More than two years later, in the fall of 2013, I was driving through Jersey City Heights, on my way home from work. I had the radio on and the first line to a song caught my attention. The song, which I hadn't heard before, was by A Great Big World and Christina Aguilera. I pulled over to the side of the road. As I wiped the tears from my eyes, I listened to the words to "Say Something."

The song instantly brought me back to August 2, the day Barbara died. As I spoke to Barbara on that day, I so wished that she'd say something to me. Or give me a sign that she could hear me. That she knew I so wished to be with her, and I would go anywhere along with her on her journey. That if I didn't do all that I could, it was because it was all beyond my capability. And how helpless and small I felt that it was all over, and I couldn't do any more for her. Barbara and I never actually said goodbye. Whispering into her ear as she was leaving me, I hope she was able to dream along with me of the beauty we shared. I wish she had said something.

In those moments in our bedroom, I continued sitting by Barbara's side and whispering into her ear about South Beach, while Barbara's breathing continued strong and her facial expression remained intense, with her arms clenched up to her chest. We all kept walking in and out of the bedroom to check on her and just hung around, waiting.

At around eight fifteen that evening, Rosey said to me, "Marc ... it's going to be very soon." Rosey brought a chair into the bedroom and sat at the foot of the bed. At eight thirty, I heard Rosey shout, "Marc, come in here!" Barbara had stopped breathing. I called the kids to the bedroom. As we stood and looked at Barbara, I didn't know what to think or feel. Barbara looked so much at peace, relaxed, serene, and so beautiful.

One of the kids called Judy, another called the hospice nurse, another called Dr. Stern's office, and I called the funeral chapel. When Judy came into the bedroom, she checked Barbara's pulse and then disconnected the oxygen. Judy asked Rosey to clean Barbara and Rosey asked us to leave the bedroom and she closed the door.

A few minutes later, Rosey opened the bedroom door. "Marc ... please come in here." I went into the bedroom. Rosey closed the door behind me, and said, "Her nightgown is saturated and soiled. I need help getting it off, so that I can sponge bathe her. Are you all right with helping me do this?"

I've never been comfortable with looking at a person who is deceased. I didn't even look at my dad in his casket. But this was my wife. Looking at her and being able to touch her was something I didn't want to end.

I said to Rosey, "The nightgown is so dirty. Let's pull it down off of her, rather than over her head."

We struggled to get the nightgown off. "Marc, go to the kitchen and get scissors and we'll cut the nightgown off of her."

"I don't want to do that. The kids will be wondering what's going on in here that I need scissors. I'm sure that we can stretch it and get it off. We're throwing it out anyway."

We did get the nightgown off and as Rosey bathed Barbara, I looked through the dresser for a specific nightgown. I was looking for a black nightgown, it went so well with Barbara's olive skin. Rosey set up the bed and we called Judy and the kids into the bedroom.

When the representatives from the funeral parlor arrived, they told us to take our time in our final moments with Barbara. After a few minutes, I said to the kids, "Okay ... let's go." I turned to Barbara. "See you later, alligator ... see you in a while, crocodile."

I felt drained, lost, confused. I didn't have it in me to call and talk to anyone over the phone. I left that to the kids. All I could do was to send an email to a few people.

> From: Marc Gellman
>
> Sent: Tuesday, August 02, 2011 11:41pm
>
> Subject: Barbara
>
> After a thirty-year fight with cancer, my dear Barbara passed this evening at 8:30 p.m.

After, I went to the couch. Rosey sat beside me and in a most compassionate way, asked, "Marc, how are you doing?"

"I'm okay. It's not like this was a surprise. And Barbara's suffering is over."

Rosey answered, "And your suffering for your loss is just beginning, but your worries will be over. You should try to go to sleep."

As I got into bed, I couldn't take my eyes off the empty side. I kept trying to picture Barbara there. I couldn't stop thinking that this is the way it would be forever. The emptiness of the bed frightened me. I repeatedly whispered, "Barbara ... where are you? Show me those dimples."

Barbara's life was taken from me. There would be no more night-time snuggling in bed on a cold winter night. No more waking up in the morning and watching her sleep. When we were newlyweds and I woke up before Barbara, I would get close to her face and stare at her and think about how beautiful and cute she was. Barbara would sense my staring and wake up annoyed but smiling, and say, "Stop it. I'm not ready to get up." But I just wanted to stare at her and tell her how silly she looked while sleeping. She would wake up from my annoyance and we would talk, get silly, and start the day with more than just a kiss.

This night, I was frightened, staring at the emptiness and not having Barbara to talk to. No longer would we talk about our first kiss in the lobby of the Breakers Hotel in Far Rockaway in 1965. Or talk about when we were driving to a vacation in the Poconos and Jonathan, who was four years old, asked, "Where are were going?" I told him to the Poconos, and he answered, "Daddy, I'll poke you in the nose."

Or talk about when we walked on the boardwalk in Wildwood, New Jersey with Jonathan and Kristen, after buying ice cream. Kristen was in her stroller and we didn't realize that she had fallen asleep, with her face in her ice cream. A lady came up to us and said, "Your little girl has fallen asleep in her ice cream."

Or talk about when Brian, at four years old, ran into an elevator in a hotel in Hollywood, Florida and the door closed before the rest of us got into the elevator. It was frightening hearing Brian screaming from inside the elevator. But afterward, we all laughed remembering the sound of his screaming gradually fading away, as the elevator descended.

Most of all, I wondered if I did all I could for Barbara. Should we have talked more about the end? I know that we communicated the finality with our eyes and our hearts. But during the last few days when she was conscious, should we have said goodbye? Should we have said to each other, "See you later, alligator ... see you in a while, crocodile?"

I thought about the week before. We were in bed and Barbara reached over and touched my face. Through her touch, the love was going back and forth between us. She smiled at me. But in her smile, I could see her concern for me and guilt that she was leaving. Barbara knew how much I depended on her. I could tell she was worried about how I was going to get along without her. I wondered if Barbara felt she was letting me down. Now, just a week later, I lay in bed alone. I missed Barbara so much already and it hurt. My mind went from one thought to the next, until somehow, I fell asleep.

The next morning, I awoke and stared at her side of the bed, trying so hard to imagine Barbara still there. I dragged myself out of bed to shave and shower. Rosey was getting the apartment in order, going through medical supplies that needed to be discarded and giving Brian instructions for what needed to be returned, like the wheelchair. We spent the morning and early afternoon doing errands. Then, Rosey packed her suitcase and said, "Marc, I'm all done. What else to you need me to do?"

"Oh, Rosey, I surely hoped and thought that you would be with us for much longer than a week. Although, it does feel like you have been with us much longer. You so quickly became part of our family and I truly believe that we were blessed with you."

"Thank you. Brian is driving me to the train. I'll see you tomorrow. I will be attending the service at the funeral chapel."

After packing for our week's stay at Kristen and Stephen's home in Maplewood, Brian and I left Hoboken. Jonathan had left Hoboken the night before with Kristen. The plan was for all of us to be together this night and meet with the rabbi. The next morning was the funeral and after, we would all stay at their home for seven days of Shiva, the period of mourning.

CHAPTER 41

Smiling through the tears

It was Thursday morning, August 4, 2011. I was overwhelmed, as I entered the sanctuary at the funeral chapel with my children. There were more than three hundred people in attendance. The rabbi began the service and then looked to me to deliver the eulogy. As I spoke, I could hear sobbing and sniffling. After, when I got back to my seat, Brian leaned toward me and whispered in my ear, "Dad ... that was the best speech that you have ever given."

Brian's words were the best thing I could have heard at that moment. I so much wanted to give honor and tribute to Barbara, for everyone to hear. Then, Jonathan and Brian went up to the podium together. Jonathan spoke first.

When I decided to move to Miami, my mom promised not to let more than two months go by without seeing me. And she always made sure that was the case.

As most people know, my parents did not fly together. My mom would take an early morning flight. My dad would drop my mom off at the airport, on the way to work, and take a late evening flight. Once arriving in Miami, one of my mom's first tasks was to go to Publix. She would load up on groceries for the week. And every single time, she would get groceries for me too. She wanted to be sure that I was eating well and that I had what I needed.

And then, my mom and I had our special date nights. We would meet at the corner of our building and walk together, often holding hands or I would put my arm around her, as we headed to Monty's for happy hour, which was our favorite date night spot. My mom loved that it was a cool local spot with music, lots of people, and the opportunity for us to spend quality alone time together. We would always load up at the raw bar and get our favorite drink, called the Pain Killer, which was loaded with alcohol, but tasted good. Most times, we would each have one drink. But there were times when we both went for the second. And, I can remember one time having to help my mom up to her apartment and tuck her into bed, because she was extra tipsy.

After spending time talking, eating, and enjoying each other's company, we would walk home together. My mom would often hold on to my arm, or even hold my hand, as we walked home.

We loved our date nights and we loved each other so much. My mom loved her husband, children, family, and friends with all of her heart.

Brian spoke next.

My mom was the best! Everyone loved her. My friends wrote, in my high school senior yearbook, about her being the greatest, even before acknowledging me. My mom was a fighter, who I compare to, *The Little Engine That Could.* While she was battling her cancer, she would approach each challenge slow and steady. Each time she overcame a challenge, my mom enjoyed her time cruising downhill. She never gave up hope and taught us to live, love, and laugh. My mom was the best mom, and it shows how great she was by the number of people who are here today to show their respects.

Kristen and Stephen went up to the podium. Kristen began:

If you look at my mom's Facebook page, her title is "mother." She always identified herself as a mother, grandmother, and wife before she identified herself as anything else, no matter her job.

Hulk Hogan, The Incredible Hulk, Rocky Balboa ... They had nothing on my mom. I've been told, over the past few months and years, by so many people that my mom is their hero, how strong she is, and what an amazing woman she is. It is so difficult to put into words what kind of woman she really was because "amazing," "heroic," "strong," don't do her justice.

I spoke to my mom ten times a day. I'm one of those people who need their mom's approval and advice on anything, from buying something for the kids, buying something at the grocery store, or how many cups equals a pint, stuff like that. She also knew I couldn't make a decision on anything ... anything. No matter the question, she always answered me, never annoyed, and with a laugh.

In 2004, my mom participated in a two-day, thirty-nine-mile walk to raise money for breast cancer. She had a goal of raising a certain amount of money and destroyed it. At that time, she was a three-time breast cancer survivor and was asked to speak at the events opening and closing ceremony, in front of thousands of people. Her words resonate in my ears, since that morning: "My name is Barbara Gellman and I'm a three-time breast cancer survivor!" The crowd of thousands roared and the proudest five people were standing off to the side, though quiet, so filled with excitement, so proud that that she was ours. I was then, was before, and will be forever, so proud to be Barbara Gellman's daughter.

The day Steve and I told my parents that we were pregnant

with Jonah is at the top of my list of best days of my life. My mom longed to be a grandma. It felt like the minute Jonah was born, my mom began planning a trip she had dreamt about doing, a trip to Disney World with her family, her grandkids. I was so excited when we were finally getting to go. I let her pick everything and do anything. Some people dream of Italy, some people dream of Africa. My mom dreamt of Disney World and no matter where I go or what I do in my life that was the best trip of my life. She spoke about it with Jonah every possible second, she could, on the phone, in person, before and after. I could talk about the trip for years, because there were so many special moments; one of her favorites being the ride "It's a Small World." She loved listening to Jonah sing the song to the ride.

In these last few weeks, I longed for my mom. Just to tell her I won a game of mah-jongg, to tell her what class Jonah was going to be in next year, just to tell her the little things. It's those conversations I'll miss the most. I may not have gotten these moments in, during the last few weeks, but I did get few precious moments that I'll never forget ... seeing her face when Jonah and Drew walked in the door, seeing her reaction to pure happiness when Jonah told her, "I love you more than candy, Grandma," having her reach out for my face and rub my ear which was especially "her" thing. I will never stop feeling the warmth of her hand as it touched my face and ear ... one of the best feelings in the world.

The other day my friend said such a smart thing to me. She said, "This is going to be hard, but because of your mom, you will get through it. She gave you the strength to get through tough times." I truly believe that the only way we could get through this, is because of my mom. Her strength and courage that she passed on to us and her sense of family, is going to be what gets us through this rough time, after Shiva is over.

On the day my mom passed, the hospice nurse decided to stay when she came to visit her. She thought she'd pass early afternoon, but my mom's heart ... beat on with strength. She wouldn't give up. She was a fighter and I will always remember her that way.

I love you, Mommy, you are my hero, my strength, and everything I am. I am ... because of what you taught me. I will miss you so much.

Then, Stephen spoke.

I met Mom almost nine years ago. It was on a Saturday night for the dreaded, "Introduce My Boyfriend to My Parents" dinner. It is easy for me to say that I remember the evening as hitting it off with Mom immediately. But at the same time, it's impossible for me to remember it any differently.

Never have I taken for granted how lucky I am. I've often heard stories from friends, co-workers, relatives, griping about their mothers-in-law. Yet their experiences are foreign to me. Mom and I had such an easy relationship. We got each other. We both got Kristen and I had someone on my side; a mother-in-law on her son-in-law's side ... let me repeat that ... a mother-in-law on her son-in-law's side. Her trust in people, serenely sweet disposition, honesty, and warm smile drew people to her. Such an awesome woman, she was so cool.

Behind her endless veil of syrupy sweetness, Mom stood on an enormous mountain of fearless courage. I can only echo what everyone has said here. Her fight has been astounding yet does not define her. She defines herself. All of us will miss Mom so much and we have to promise ourselves to remember her and talk about her. It's what will continue to keep her with us. Mom, you are with me forever. I love you.

After our eulogies, the rabbi stepped up to the podium, recited prayers, and spoke about Barbara and his meeting with me and the kids, the night before. In particular, he said, "Marc, as we spoke last night about Barbara, it was obvious that you were not only very much in love with her. You were also very proud of her."

The rabbi was so perceptive and so right. I was so very proud of Barbara. When I first met her, she was a shy girl from a poor family. Her shyness was in part from being intimidated by friends whose families were financially much better off than hers, and who could afford to do such things as planning to attend out-of-town colleges. Her friends seemed to have stable families, while Barbara lived in a home where finances were always shaky and there was much arguing and, eventually, a divorce.

Growing up, Barbara was silenced by dominating relatives, who seemed to dictate how things were to be done in her parents' home. When reminiscing about her childhood years, Barbara described the times when she asked her mother for something and her grandmother interjected, saying, "I wouldn't give it to her if she stood on her head!"

When Barbara was nineteen and her brother was thirteen, her mother died. They were left with practically no money and no plans for care for her younger brother. Yet, Barbara was always able to keep herself together and smile through it all.

Barbara would often say to me that I changed her; that she was too unsure of herself to speak up or approach people. She used to say to me, "I was a poor girl from The Bronx who learned what it takes to speak my mind, from a boy I met from Brooklyn." But it wasn't me. Barbara was always able to chart her own course. It was her decision to shed herself of the negative surroundings of her past. After we were married, those friends who seemed to have so much more during her growing-up years, now appeared to have nothing over Barbara. And as for the relatives who would dominate her family's decisions, it was Barbara's choice to move away from them and start a new life.

Through the years, I didn't give much thought about being proud of Barbara. I just was. She was the person that I tried to be. Barbara could handle difficult situations, accept the outcome, and move on. She did that all her life. Barbara was a survivor. She was the person who could be married to me for almost forty years and put up with my shenanigans and OCD, with always a smile. I so miss listening to Barbara giving speeches in temple or speaking after being honored by organizations and from work for her accomplishments and contributions. After such occasions, Barbara would say, "I was looking around at the audience while I was speaking, but all I could see was the big smile of pride on your face."

I would answer, "That wasn't pride. That was gas. I was smiling, thinking about the poor people seated nearby to me."

"No, no. You were smiling because you are proud of me."

After being silly, I would fess up and say, "Yes. I am proud of you!"

That day at the funeral chapel, I hoped Barbara could see the pride on my face. I was smiling through the tears, as my children spoke from their hearts to more than three hundred people, who came to pay their respects to Barbara Karen Gellman.

After the memorial service, my children surrounded and held on to me, as we walked out of the funeral chapel to the limo. I sat in the front seat, next to the driver, and the kids sat in the seats behind. As I looked out of the front window, I stared at the hearse and could see the top of the coffin. I was oblivious to everything going on around me. All I heard was the thought in my mind, over and over again, "Oh Barbara! Oh Barbara!" It was unbelievable to me that this funeral was for my wife and we were leaving to go to the cemetery.

After the burial service, we got back into the limo and headed to Kristen and Stephen's home to begin the seven days of Shiva. The house was quite crowded, as many people came back after the cemetery; others who had been at the funeral chapel were there too. The rabbi led the Shiva service. My children and I followed the rabbi in reciting the Mourner's Kaddish. I had recited this prayer seven years before, for my dad, and that was difficult. But reciting the prayer for my wife, as my children recited the prayer for their mother, was ripping my heart out.

At the end of the service, I gestured to the rabbi that I wanted to say a few things. I talked about Barbara and me. Some of the stories were funny and people did laugh, even though my voice cracked and

I couldn't hold back my emotions. After that day, I continued to tell stories and did so for each of the seven days of Shiva.

On the seventh day, Kristen said to me, "Dad, you have to write a book of all the stories about you and Mommy."

"Oh, Kristen, what am I going to write about?"

Kristen answered, "There were so many people who came each day to listen to you speak, after the service. The stories are interesting. I want you to write a book."

"I wouldn't know where to start," I answered.

"You can start by writing about your eulogy. That could be chapter one. Dad, so many people asked if they could have a copy of the eulogy."

In a tired voice, I answered, "Kristen, I can't discuss this anymore, right now," "Let's take the traditional walk around the neighborhood and Shiva will be over."

It is tradition at the end of this period of mourning to "get up" from sitting Shiva and begin to get back to normalcy. The walk through the neighborhood by the mourners is done so that neighbors will see you; it shows the community that you are back. So, that's what my children and I did. It was so comforting to be surrounded by relatives and friends who consoled us for the seven days. But now, it felt so good for us to get out and be on our own again. Although, we did it with trepidation, knowing we were facing a new beginning.

Jonathan went back to Florida, Brian and I back to Hoboken, and Kristen and Stephen got their house back. While driving back to Hoboken, I said to Brian, "When we get home, we need to go to the supermarket and to the cleaners."

"What do you have to go to the cleaners for?" Brian asked.

"I brought all of my bedding there, before we left last week."

"Dad, when we get home, let's bring our stuff to the apartment and then I want you and me to sit and relax in the park by the water a little bit. We can do those other things later."

"Okay, whatever you want."

Walking into the apartment was depressing. It was so empty. In my mind, I could hear Barbara's voice. Brian and I went down to sit by the water and we watched the boats on the Hudson River. It was a weekday afternoon and the waterfront was peaceful and quiet.

After about an hour, Brian asked, "You okay, Dad?"

"I can't believe that I'm sitting here without your mother."

"I know, Dad. Let's go to the supermarket and the cleaners and we'll get the apartment back in shape."

Back in the apartment, I went through the motions of putting the bedding back on the bed, while other things were going through my mind. Later, when I came back into the bedroom, I was struck by the sight of the bed. I realized that the sheet and pillowcases, which had a vibrant red pattern, were the set that Barbara died on. I stared at the bed and thought about changing the bedding. But I decided to leave it. It felt comforting to look at. The bedding was Barbara's favorite. It was as if Barbara made the bed for me and was saying, "Don't worry, I'm not leaving you." I so much wanted to feel that Barbara was with me.

Brian and I relaxed that evening. Eventually, I said, "Okay, big guy. I'm going to bed. Tomorrow, I'm going back to work for a few hours."

"Are you okay, Dad?"

"I'm fine. Good night. I love you."

"Goodnight, Dad. Love you."

In bed, I stared at Barbara's pillow and whispered, "So, this is the way it's going to be forever." After all our teenage years of dating, our engagement, and our forty years of marriage, I didn't know how I was going to accept that it was all over, and Barbara was not lying beside me. Even with the ordeals of cancer that spanned thirty years, I felt that I lost her so quickly.

I pictured her face and how she looked as she slept. I could still feel her beside me. As much as I imagined Barbara lying beside me, I was in disbelief that it could be over. I whispered over and over, "Barbara ... where are you, where are you?" I wondered if something was destined to happen to me, so that we could be together again. I pictured the empty grave beside Barbara that would be for me.

My mind couldn't stop racing. I continued to stare at her pillow and think about how young we were when we got married. In the early years, Barbara and I joked about someday celebrating our seventieth wedding anniversary and being two old farts, dribbling on ourselves. That was a milestone that seemed so easy to achieve, back then. But we only made it a little more than halfway there.

Growing old together wasn't going to happen. I felt some comfort, as I began to think about our marriage and how we would have grown old in age, but not in mind and spirit. Barbara and I had something special going for us throughout our marriage. We didn't grow old together. We stayed young together. I know with all of my heart that if we had made it to our seventieth anniversary, Barbara and I would still be as silly as we were on the day we were married. Our kiss on our seventieth anniversary would have been with the same intense puppy love as our kiss on New Year's Eve 1967, in Times Square. We were two horny teenagers back then, something we never outgrew.

I turned onto my back and stared at the ceiling. I thought about the first four years of our marriage, before we had kids. Those years were so precious, and that time became the seed from which our young love continued to grow, for forty years.

I often suggest to newlyweds to hold off having children right away and to take advantage of the freedom and spontaneity that young couples without children enjoy. It's not that I regret having children and starting a family. But the first phase of a marriage, the newlywed phase, is underrated and sometimes quickly skipped over. Nowadays, people are older when they get married and feel pressure to start a family right away. They miss out on their only chance to be alone, when they are young, healthy, and energized. It's a loss of a rich life experience. Because there is no guarantee that there will be that opportunity to be empty nesters again, years later.

As newlyweds, Barbara and I were so young and horny, we couldn't keep our hands off each other. It was difficult for us to get used to the fact that we could go all the way with sex, and it was socially acceptable. As newlyweds, there was no longer any need to get away and hide what we were doing from anyone, even my parents. We could do it in the comfort of our own apartment, make it last as long as we wanted, and didn't need to hurry to get dressed. Actually, most often, we didn't get dressed afterward. We went about the apartment naked and slept naked too. It was quite a novelty for us.

Barbara and I had Jewish parents who drilled into us, during our teenage years, that it was wrong to be sexually active before marriage. Even after we were married, we couldn't shake off the years of lecturing from our parents about sex. It was this mindset that made each time more exciting. To us, each time always felt like the first.

For Barbara and me, it was still puppy love. The wedding rings on our fingers didn't change us. Puppy love may be the description of the best kind of love. Don't believe the naysayers who define puppy love as a teenage infatuation. For Barbara and me, it was a true love and maybe the best kind of love. Puppy love is young and innocent, with silliness and excitement that is so intense. It's a love that doesn't tire, because it feels never-ending, like a teenager's view on life. And if you're lucky, like Barbara and I, the intensity of puppy love can last until "death do you part."

As I lay in bed that evening, I pictured Barbara's face the first time I met her in Far Rockaway, Queens. I thought about how Barbara and I became the model for a romance that can survive horrific news and the darkest of times. I smiled. Because even though our time together was cut short, we had the romance of a lifetime.

I closed my eyes. I hoped and wanted to believe that Barbara had a good life. I believe that she felt she did. As I held on to that thought, my mind stopped racing, peace came over me, and somehow, I fell asleep.

PART 8

After the Seventh Day of Shiva

"Well, if that's the case, we need to give people more to talk about. I think that while we're walking down the street, I should be squeezing your ass. And stopping to make out a little and maybe with a little grinding going on."

CHAPTER 42

Going for a walk

For several months after Barbara's death, it was difficult for me to go for walks around the streets of Hoboken, even in the company of others. The weekend after getting up from sitting Shiva, my neighbors Judy and Bruce invited me to get out of my apartment and join them in a walk with their dog. The company of my friends was nice. It felt good to get out of the apartment. But the whole thing was very weird. My knees felt weak and my stomach a little queasy.

Back then, I couldn't explain why going for walks was weird and uncomfortable. As I write this chapter, I can think more clearly. I think about how Barbara and I were one. And how overnight, I became one half of what I was.

For some reason, I was frightened outside of the apartment, even though the fresh air felt good. I felt better in the apartment. Brian was staying with me and his company was comforting. I was okay much of the time at work, where I was distracted and busy. But the drive to work, and especially the drive home, were awful. No longer having Barbara to speak with from the car, I felt lost as I drove. I think that no matter where I was or what I was doing, I felt lost.

About a week later, on a Saturday evening, my employer sponsored an event for employees at the new soccer stadium in Harrison, New Jersey. We could bring family members to the event. I brought Brian. We took the train to Harrison, just a few stops from Hoboken. It was nice when we arrived in Harrison and walked the couple of blocks to the stadium. But again, it was weird. My knees felt weak and the queasy feeling came over me again. For the almost thirty-eight years that I worked for this company, Barbara always accompanied me to such events. Now I thought, "What is Brian doing here with me? I miss Barbara."

My apartment was the safe haven for me. Despite the warnings people gave me about the psychological effects of having a family member die in the apartment, it felt safe and comfortable. I didn't change anything in the apartment. When I sat on the couch, albeit alone, I felt Barbara with me. It was easy to look up at the pictures and see her. During the evenings, I occupied myself with the many chores I had inherited from Barbara. Gee, she did so much to run the household. But when I left the apartment to walk around the neighborhood, well … it was just very difficult. Brian coaxed me out of the apartment often. It still never felt right.

That Thanksgiving would be a difficult one for my family. Thanksgiving was one of Barbara's special holidays and she had her own menu that was so very different from others. Yes, we had the traditional turkey, but Barbara's stuffing, broccoli casserole, mashed potatoes, were all so Barbara. And her apple pie, well, that was always the highlight of the evening.

Barbara's apple pie was well known in our community. She coached people on how to follow her recipe. The feedback she always got was, "Yes, Barbara, I followed your apple pie recipe. But it didn't turn out as good as your pies." A couple of times in our temple, the sisterhood sold Barbara's apple pies as a fundraiser. Barbara organized a group of women at the temple and they purchased all the ingredients. They took orders from the congregation and Barbara supervised the mass production of her apple pie. They always sold out. Barbara printed the recipe for those who helped out, but everyone who tried their hand at it said, "It didn't turn out as good as when Barbara was supervising us."

For this Thanksgiving, the kids felt we should all be together. We all agreed that this Thanksgiving would have its sadness. Brian suggested a change of scenery. After all the years of Thanksgiving up north, and he suggested celebrating with Jonathan in South Beach. That would be a change. Kristen decided she and Brian would go shopping after arriving in South Beach and they would do all the cooking the way Barbara would have done it, even the apple pie. We were all set to go, and all reservations were made.

The middle of November was a low point for me. I don't know why. I had made it through the many events after Barbara died: my birthday, the day of our fortieth wedding anniversary, Brian's birthday, Barbara's birthday, and the Jewish holidays. But the middle of November just came over me. As a person who doesn't like to fly anyway, I wasn't about to get on a plane for Florida. I asked Kristen to cancel my trip. The kids were very disappointed. Kristen wanted to wait a few days before canceling the plans. I urged the kids to go ahead with the plans without me, that I'd be okay and wanted to stay home and rest. But the kids were not going to leave me alone for the holiday. They hoped that I would snap out of it. I couldn't. Kristen canceled the plans.

Kristen didn't want to have Thanksgiving in her home, where we had it for the past two years. Before then, Barbara and I had Thanksgiving in our home. When we moved to the Hoboken apartment, we moved the tradition to Kristen and Stephen's house. Kristen said that it would just be too emotionally difficult to have it in her home this year.

Hearing that we were available, Stephen's aunt and uncle invited us to their home. They were having their traditional Thanksgiving celebration with family and some friends and invited us to join them. We all loved Rona and Rex and, of course, we said yes. Jonathan was going through a difficult time too and decided to spend

Thanksgiving with cousins in Florida. It was awkward that we were split up. The whole thing was awkward, even though we were trying to make the best of things.

Kristen called me the day before and said that she would pick me up, on the way to Rona and Rex's. The weather forecast was for a very mild Thanksgiving Day and Rona and Rex live in Hoboken, about ten blocks away. "No need to pick me up," I said, "I'll walk." Kristen made it clear that she would be picking me up in front of my building.

Thanksgiving morning Brian called and said that he was coming over to my apartment and would walk with me to Rona and Rex's. I understood that this was going to be a difficult day for us, but for heaven's sake, I insisted, I could walk the ten blocks myself. Brian said he wanted to hang out with me a little and then we'd walk over together. I called Kristen and told her it was going to be a nice day, and the plan was that Brian and I would meet her at Rona and Rex's.

It was a nice day. Rona and Rex are great hosts and there is always too much food and drink. But that's what Thanksgiving is, a day with family and overeating.

Right after dinner, Brian was ready to leave. I decided to stay a little longer. Kristen said she would drive me back to my apartment. About a half hour later, we said our goodbyes and left. I helped load the kids into the car and then told Kristen that it was such a mild and nice evening that I wanted to walk off some of the meal. She pressed me about wanting to drive me home and asked, "Dad, will you be okay?"

"I'm a big boy and it will be an easy walk in Hoboken."

As I waved goodbye to Jonah and Drew, the car pulled away. I began my walk home. All was fine, until I got about a half-block. Then emotions came over me, with weak knees and a queasy stomach. It was not a pleasant walk. The scenery was fine. Other people were walking on the street and all seemed good. The evening at Rona and Rex's had been very nice. But something was missing. As I walked, I didn't have anyone holding on to my arm. It was a painful realization.

I felt like sitting on a step of one of the row houses along the street and crying, as emotions came over me.

Suddenly, I'd forgotten the day's fun festivities. I became confused about where I was. I wanted to get home quickly, to my safe haven. At that moment, the grief of Barbara not being with me was overwhelming. For almost forty years, Barbara walked with me from such occasions. All I could think, as I whispered under my breath, was, "Barbara ... where are you? You're supposed to be holding on to my arm. You held my arm to keep your pace as you walked in heels. You also reinforced my balance as I walked with you. I'm walking by myself now and feel a little wobbly. I'm not used to walking alone."

Suddenly, I realized why my children didn't want me to walk home alone and why Brian met me at my apartment to walk with me. I always knew I was so fortunate to be blessed with children who are so very kind, caring, sensitive, and smart. I'm reminded of the time when a cousin said to me, "I'm envious of you."

I answered, "What? You're envious of me?"

"Yes, I'm envious of the relationship that you have with your children."

"Why? You have a good relationship with your children too."

He answered, "I taught my son everything he knows. Now he thinks he's smarter than me."

I answered, "That's the difference between you and me. Because I taught my children everything I know. And I know, for sure, that they are smarter than me."

I truly believe that I tried to do my best for my children and hoped that my best was more than just good enough. Nowadays, my children often call me for advice. Perhaps, I didn't do so badly. Jonathan once forwarded me a copy of an email that he had sent to somebody. In it, he wrote, "Much of what I have learned throughout my life, both personally and professionally, has come from my father. He set the example, and we all learned that family, faith, and community are the essentials in life. Hard work, dedication, and perseverance have also been instilled in us."

I made it home to my apartment that Thanksgiving evening. I

was alone, but I could feel Barbara. I sat on the couch and thought things out, as I sat and grieved. I understood why walking the neighborhood had been so difficult. I knew I missed Barbara and realized that walking with Barbara had been so very underrated in my mind. I guess we both took our walks for granted. Barbara and I believed our time would never come to an end; we always had forever for going on walks together.

As I sat alone in my apartment, in the complete silence, I remembered our walks. It was at that moment that those walks became so much more special. I guess Barbara and I were walkers, and we never changed our walking patterns over the course of forty years. Barbara walked to my right and for informal strolls, we either held hands or I would place my arm around Barbara's waist and her arm would be around my shoulders. For formal walking, with Barbara in heels, she held on to my arm. We didn't plan these positions. It was just natural for us. When Barbara and I walked together, we always held on to each other. We'd often hear comments from people about how much we always looked like we were in love. That was because we were.

When we walked, I was Barbara's hero. She held on to my arm and I felt like I was her strength and protector. But even as Barbara helped me to feel strong, holding on to my arm, she knew that she was the one holding me up and guiding us to where we were going. It worked for us that I was the designated protector. But I confess: it was Barbara, walking beside me, who was the stronger.

Several years after Barbara died, I came across a woman's profile on an Internet dating site. The caption in her profile read, "The way to a man's heart is through his stomach." Then, her profile included several pictures of dishes that she cooked. I don't know who it was who originally came up with that saying. It's dumb and the most unromantic way that a woman can think about a man.

There is little simpler and more romantic than to understand that the way to a man's heart is for him to feel like a hero. All it may take is for a woman to hold on to her man's arm. After all, if women weren't holding on to a man's arm to guide the way as they walked, a man could walk in the wrong direction, slip on a banana peel, or even step in dog shit. Even as women continue to fight for rights and equality in the workplace and business, there can be, should be, and are different rules for the workplace, versus flirting and romance while going for a walk.

When we were teenagers Barbara and I always took the time during our walks for some, even a lot of, making out and grabbing. Even with people around, kissing in the middle of a walk never stopped us. When we walked, we got smiles from people and heard, "You two look so cute together." I guess the way we felt about each other showed.

When we lived in Jackson Heights, Barbara would take the Flushing line train to and from work to her job in Manhattan. In the mornings, she would make the long walk to the train station at Ninetieth Street and Roosevelt Avenue. In the evenings, I often waited for her at the Eighty-Second Street station. That station was a longer walk from our apartment on Ninety-Third Street, but Eighty-Second Street was a retail shopping street, and the walk was more interesting.

I'd arrive at the station earlier than Barbara's train, which was elevated above Roosevelt Avenue. I waited for Barbara and watched as train after train passed, until I saw Barbara at the top of the platform, coming down the stairs. As we embraced, I'm sure it appeared to anyone inconceivable that we had only been apart since the morning. It was the best part of our day because we'd be together until the next morning. And if it was a Friday night? Well, that was over the top.

We walked along Eighty-Second Street and window-shopped. We had little money. But the long walk was part of our evening together and we could talk about our day.

A few weeks before we moved to Flanders, Barbara and I were doing our window-shopping on Eighty-Second Street. As we passed a pet store, I noticed that one of the dogs was looking at me from the window display

"Barbara, let's hold up for a while. That dog is looking at me."

Barbara answered, "Stop being so silly. That dog is not looking at you."

We kept walking. After a few paces, I stopped.

"Okay, watch me. I'm going to walk back, and you'll see that the dog is looking at me."

"Oh, stop it! That dog is not looking at you."

I went back and, sure enough, the dog looked at me. Barbara laughed and said, "You're nuts."

I wanted to go into the store and see the dog's reaction to me. When I picked up the dog, I couldn't help but say, "Let's buy this dog. It really likes me." Then the dog licked Barbara's face and we were done. We left our apartment for a walk and came back with a puppy. Pepper was a great dog and, years later, immediately loved our children, as we brought each home from the hospital. Pepper even loved Brian, who would do anything to annoy that dog.

I recalled our walk on 108th Street in Forest Hills, Queens, on a cold winter evening. We were both bundled up in our coats and scarves. Barbara's face was sticking out from the fur-trimmed hood of her coat. As we walked by a kosher delicatessen, we decided we wanted something, but didn't know what. Barbara was so bundled up already and didn't want to go inside. I suggested getting a knish to share as we walked.

I went into the delicatessen and Barbara stood outside looking into the store window. The knishes were right up front, and I told the elderly gentlemen at the counter that I wanted one to go. He started to wrap the knish and then looked out the window and saw Barbara looking in. He asked, "Is that girl with you?"

"Yes, we're sharing the knish."

The elderly man said, "She is so beautiful, where did you find such a beautiful girl?"

"Jackson Heights," I answered.

"And look at those beautiful dimples," he added.

At this point, Barbara could tell we were talking about her and she smiled. I went back outside with the knish and the man smiled at us. As we walked away, Barbara asked, "What were you two talking about?"

"That old man said that you're ugly."

Barbara looked at me and said, "I don't think so." With the knish in hand, we stopped for a kiss.

When we lived in Flanders, we enjoyed our walks around the development of homes. We had fun seeing the different seasons and the upgrades to houses each season. We knew many people in the community. We took different routes and would usually see someone we knew along the way and we'd stop to talk.

A friend of ours, Helene, once mentioned to Barbara that she had met a neighbor of ours and she had said to our neighbor, "Oh, you live on Brewster Place. My friends, Barbara and Marc, live on that street."

Our neighbor answered, "Oh, those two. I see Barbara and Marc all the time. They're always taking walks and they hold hands like they think that they're still teenagers in high school."

I can relate to that statement. If it appeared that we thought we were still teenagers, that's because Barbara and I never really grew up. We liked talking baby talk and our nickname for each other was "silly." Yes, when either of us called the other, we both responded to the name "silly."

I always found humor in things that might not really be funny. I was usually able to get Barbara into the silliness of a situation. Like the time Barbara and I were in Bed Bath & Beyond, which I called "Bed Bath and Go Further." Barbara always got annoyed with me when I changed the names of things.

I didn't like to shop, and Barbara would hurry through stores to keep me interested, trying to engage me in whatever she was looking for. She was in the candle aisle and called me over to smell one of the candles. I really didn't care what the candle smelled like. I just wanted to leave. So, I smelled the candle and Barbara asked what I thought. I answered, a little louder than she appreciated, "It smells like vagina." A woman, nearby in the aisle, obviously heard me and strained to look at us through the corner of her eye, trying not to be obvious. This only fueled our silliness. Barbara pulled me by the arm, and we left the store.

Barbara's reaction and the look on her face was so funny to me. All

I could do was laugh and when we were outside the store, the silliness overcame the two of us. The shopping was over, but we had fun. Silly was a perfect name for us. We never did outgrow it. Just like we never outgrew the love that we had as teenagers. Maybe it was just puppy love that we never outgrew. The love I saw when I looked into Barbara's eyes. It was a young love that helped us to ignore the presence of any sorrow.

In Flanders, we had neighbors around the corner who were a little older than we were. We had heard that their marriage was not going well. Sometimes, when Barbara and I walked past their house, we'd see the husband sitting out front. Most often, he looked like he was in a daze. He never said hello. It was as if he didn't notice us walking by his house. We'd debate whether he was drunk or on drugs.

One day, Barbara happened to meet the wife at the A&P and the wife told Barbara that she was getting a divorce and her husband had already moved out. Barbara told her how sad that was and was sorry to hear such news and asked how her children were taking it. The neighbor said that her children weren't surprised and had said, "After all, we never saw you and Daddy walking down the street like the Gellmans do. They are always holding hands."

That night when I got home, Barbara told me about these neighbors getting a divorce. "They are getting a divorce because of us."

I asked, "What did we do? I hardly know them."

"Their kids said they should get a divorce, because they don't hold hands like we do."

"What?"

"I'm just joking. But obviously, we are being watched, as we walk around the neighborhood."

"Well, if that's the case, we need to give people more to talk about. I think that while we're walking down the street, I should be squeezing your ass. And stopping to make out a little and maybe with a little grinding going on."

Barbara answered, "I don't think so. We can stick to holding hands. That seems to be creating enough gossip."

Walks on the beach, any beach, always brought us back to our teenage years. We talked about the Rockaways, during those walks. It was where we were young and started our loving and the memories were so special. The beach brought us back to those years and at any age we were teenagers again with "forever" ahead of us. This was the feeling that we had even through our later years. Even through the darkest of news, we felt we would have forever.

There was a special walk that is a cherished memory for me. My employer purchased tickets for me to attend a charity event with Barbara, at the Rock Center Café at the ice-skating rink at Rockefeller Center. We parked at a parking garage on Forty-Fourth Street and walked to the restaurant on Fiftieth Street. It was a fun evening. Over the course of our marriage, some of the nicest places that I took Barbara were arranged by my employer.

The event was on a weekday and as the evening progressed, we started to tire, so we left. There is an elevator from the restaurant and ice-skating rink level to the street level. We took the elevator up to the street-level lobby. It was pouring outside, the wind was howling, and the rain was going in all directions. What to do? We were dressed up for this semiformal and had no umbrella.

We decided to wait for a taxi. Surely a taxi will come down this street, we thought. But it was late in the evening, and a weeknight, and no taxis were coming. We hurried the half-block to Fifth Avenue, sure we'd get a taxi on that street. We huddled against the recess of a storefront watching for a taxi. But there were no taxis on Fifth Avenue, either.

We agreed that we could be standing there all night waiting and decided to make a run for it to the parking garage. If a taxi happened to come along, we'd take it. So, as quickly as Barbara could run in heels, we started hurriedly down Fifth Avenue, alongside the buildings for whatever kind of protection we could get. The storm was so fierce that after about a half-block, we were soaked through and through. I felt Barbara pull my arm and say, "Why are we rushing? We can't get any wetter than we already are."

With that said, we stopped in our tracks, looked at each other, and laughed. Barbara's mascara was running down her face. Our hair was completely flat. Barbara held on to my arm and we began to stroll very slowly, laughing and looking at each other all the way back to the parking garage. When we got into the car, we could hear the squish on the seats. We kissed and drove home.

Too many of us often rush through things in our lives, without understanding why we're in a rush. I talked about our walk in the rain on one of the nights of Shiva. Several of Kristen and Stephen's friends were there, young couples with young children. I suggested that they all try to slow things down in their lives and take the time to think about if whatever they are rushing to is worth the rush. I asked, "Can you get to where you want to be by taking it a little slower?"

We can savor the precious moments that come upon us during our lives. We just need to slow things down and pause in order to recognize those precious moments, even if it's just a walk in the rain. Clothes can be washed or replaced. But nothing will replace precious moments with our spouse. "Going for a walk" is very underrated. I so miss my walks with Barbara.

CHAPTER 43

Memories of grandparents

The transition to becoming the lone parent to our children had its difficulties. Barbara was the family mediator and peacemaker. She kept us close. We were having our spats and disagreements and the anger inside each of us at our loss was not helping to keep our family together. Having celebrated Thanksgiving separately, Jonathan in Florida and the rest of us in New Jersey, wasn't easy on us. It increased the tension and made the situation worse.

Kristen stepped up and tried to diffuse the issues that had left us empty and wanting for something. But we weren't all together. Although we wanted this Thanksgiving to be different, to spare us the pain that Barbara was gone from the holiday, it was just too different.

After much confusion about how to ease our grieving, the kids decided that we had cheated ourselves out of our family Thanksgiving and Barbara would not have wanted that for us. They decided that we should have Thanksgiving at Kristen and Stephen's after all, except we'd celebrate it on Christmas Day, when Jonathan would be in New Jersey. Jonathan made plans to travel to New Jersey, arriving on December 23 and returning to Miami on the twenty-seventh.

The kids would prepare all of Barbara's recipes. And there was an added bonus. The year before, for Thanksgiving 2010, Barbara baked her apple cakes. She was overzealous that year and there was one cake left over. Barbara had suggested that Kristen freeze the cake. "We'll save it for a special occasion and when we're all together again," she'd said. That special occasion never came for Barbara. So here we were a year later, and the cake was still in Kristen's freezer. The kids prepared the meal from Barbara's recipes, except for the apple cake. Because we had the one that Barbara prepared the year before.

I guess this was a special occasion after all. Barbara would have been so happy. We were all together, all healthy. Brian had started a new job and moved into his own apartment. Jonathan traveled up from Florida to spend the weekend with us. Kristen and Stephen, as always, were so warm and welcoming in their home and Jonah and Drew were so cute. As I looked at my family around the dinner table that evening, I thought to myself, "You did good, Barbara, you did good. This is certainly a special occasion that you wished for us to have. And that extra cake that you baked last year, well, that was meant to be."

The cake was larger than we could finish that evening. Kristen sent us home with large pieces of the leftovers. Several evenings later, I still had apple cake. But I couldn't throw out any leftovers. This cake wouldn't go to waste each evening. As I sat alone in my apartment, I said out loud, "Barbara, for a cake that is a year old, I feel like you just served it to me."

I knew there was no time soon that I would get used to being without Barbara. That wasn't so terrible, because I didn't want to get used to it. But I began to realize I needed to start accepting that she wasn't sitting beside me, holding my hand. She wasn't coming back.

Barbara was in my memories and in my broken heart. I could see her in my children's faces. But the closest I could get to touching her was a hug from my children. Jonah and Drew seemed to have some signs of little dimples on their cheeks. I don't know if the dimples will get larger or stay with them as they grow. But for now, I look at my grandchildren and see the gift of those dimples from Barbara.

One Sunday, I joined Kristen, Stephen, and their kids at a Hibachi restaurant in Mountainside. There was a wishing well at the restaurant. Kristen gave Jonah and Drew pennies to throw into the well and told them to make a wish. Drew was too young to understand, but Jonah said that he wished, "I hope we can see Grandma again." A few days later, they went to a sushi restaurant. Once again Kristen gave the kids pennies to throw into the wishing well. Jonah threw a penny into the well and then turned to Kristen. "I want to whisper to you what I wished." He then said, "I wished we could play with Grandma."

Kristen texted me what Jonah had said. I read that text message over and over. I had often wondered over the past months, how much better off my family would be if it had been me who died, instead of Barbara. Barbara spoke with the children so much more often than I did. She also had her weekly routine of spending a day caring for Jonah and Drew. This gave Kristen a day off to do chores or have a little time for herself. More importantly, the weekly routine developed a loving relationship between Barbara and the children. Being a grandmother was so dear to Barbara and she savored the time she spent with Jonah and Drew.

Drew was only fourteen months when Barbara died and Jonah was forty-five months old. But Jonah would not forget her. He talked about when Barbara and I took him to the Liberty Science Center. A year after we took him there, he asked Jonathan to take him there too. He told Jonathan about the fun he had with Grandma and Grandpa and even remembered particulars of the trip.

Jonah talked about the family trip to Disney World and about wanting to go to the Museum of Natural History. Barbara had mentioned to Jonah that she bought tickets to go to the museum and he was looking forward to it. But like so many other plans Barbara had, we ran out of time for the museum. Now Jonah was asking his Uncle Jonathan, "Can you take me to the Museum of Natural History?" Such memories and impressions weren't forgotten.

About a month after Barbara died, Kristen had personalized photo books made, one for Jonah and one for Drew. Drew was too young to realize what the book was about. But Jonah had an immediate attachment to his, which was titled *Grandma and Jonah*. The following April, it was Jonah's turn at preschool for "Show and Share." Jonah brought the photo book to show his class. I wished I had been in the class to see Jonah. But I did see a picture of Jonah standing in the front of his classroom showing the book. He had it open to a page which had a large picture of him and Barbara.

I so wished Barbara could be here to see Jonah and Drew grow up and for other grandchildren to come. It is so beautiful that Jonah has these memories. Because memories of grandparents are wonderful memories that children never forget.

CHAPTER 44

Give me a sign

I became busy with starting a life for myself. I got out of the doldrums that I sank into in November. During her last month, Barbara was concerned about my well-being. She would say to neighbors that I looked worn down and she was worried about me. Barbara and I never discussed that she was dying. Instead, she showed concern for me. I believe that Barbara did accept her own mortality. She had taken care of me for forty years and I know she feared more about how I would get along without her than her own death.

My neighbors in Hoboken were the best. But I didn't want to become a sympathy case. I needed them to be my neighbors and friends, not my caregivers. I accepted invitations to spend social time with friends, but the taking care of me needed to be done by me.

I had lost a lot of weight during the past months and my clothes showed it. I was hesitant to buy new clothes. I figured I was beginning to come back to myself and the weight would come back, too, so why run out and buy a new wardrobe or alter the clothes I had.

My eating habits had changed. I no longer had the nervous

munchies every evening after dinner. For some reason, I felt different. An air of calm seemed to come over me. I was finding solace. Everything seemed so light and easy and I didn't know why. It was as if I woke up one morning and things seemed brighter. Even in my grief, I could see the sun shining. I no longer hurried home after work, because there was no one waiting for me. I could mosey around, didn't have the obligation to meet deadlines, and only had to answer to myself.

After continuously losing weight, it seemed that I finally bottomed out, but I wasn't gaining it back. I was tired of wearing my pants like hip-huggers and bunched up around my ankles. My belts were of no help; I was at the last notch. It was time to find a tailor and it was time for some new clothes.

In mid-December, when I wore a suit to our condominium building's holiday party, it confirmed that I had to do something about my clothes. I walked around the entire evening holding up my pants and my jacket just hung on me. I felt self-conscious, but my friends and neighbors knew what I had been through and were happy that I attended the party, no matter how I looked.

I was distracted from my self-consciousness about my clothes when a young neighbor approached me to speak about her love for Barbara. Barbara only lived in the building for twenty-six months. But for Barbara, that was plenty of time to leave an impression and touch the lives of others. Making such an impression on others so quickly was so Barbara.

It was nearing the end of the evening and people were beginning to leave the party. The young neighbor approached me and asked if we could go outside of the room to talk. Melanie was one of the first neighbors that Barbara and I met when we moved into the building. It was an easy introduction. Melanie had the biggest Great Dane that Barbara and I had ever seen. Bekum was not only big, but also a very handsome and very lovable dog. We always enjoyed meeting with Melanie on one of her walks with Bekum. I'm being terrible for describing Bekum before talking about Melanie. Melanie was single. She had a lovely, friendly, perpetual smile and talked softly and calmly.

Melanie said that she had tried to approach me several times over the past several months. But she found it too difficult to express her feelings to me. Her friends knew she wanted to talk and coaxed her to approach me that evening. I could see that she was very nervous and as she started to speak, tears filled her eyes. Melanie held her hands to her mouth. "I can't," she said as she sobbed.

I grabbed hold of both of her hands and stood looking at her in wonder about what could have gotten her so emotional.

Then, she said, "I've wanted to speak with you, but it has been so difficult for me to say what I want to tell you. I need to tell you how much Barbara meant to me and how much she did for me. I hardly knew Barbara. But she was so wonderful, loving, and caring to me."

As I listened, I squeezed her hands to give her reassurance and strength to continue telling me her story. I didn't want what she had to say about Barbara to end. Although I went to the party that night to just party, this moment was the high point for me. I wanted to hear about Barbara. And what Melanie had to say about Barbara was so accurate. Our conversation brought a fresh wave of grief for all I had lost. Yet, I continued to listen and, at that moment, I wanted the grieving to continue.

It was difficult for me to remember all the details of what Melanie had said to me that evening. I asked her to write it for me.

> I had the opportunity to get to know Barbara during my maternity when I was going through a very hard time. I was disappointed in my family and the lack of their support during the hardest time of my life. My mom was not there for me physically or emotionally. And it was a time in my life that I needed her the most. I had this beautiful baby girl, my angel Chloe, who enriched my life, yet there was still such a void. I felt very alone.
>
> During that time, I would see Barbara during the day. She was such a bright spot in my day. She was my sunshine amidst all the clouds. She was always so happy and nice, and I felt as though she really cared about me and Chloe. I knew that she was genuine in her concern. I opened up to Barbara and shared my unhappiness. She never passed judgment, but rather she was so supportive and made me feel not so alone anymore. She invited me into

her home many times and she always wanted to introduce me to her daughter and new granddaughter, Drew, who was born two weeks before Chloe. She touched my life in such a way that I will always remember her kind and sincere way during the most wonderful and hardest time in my life.

What I want you to know is that I regret not taking Barbara up on her many offers to come into your home and into your lives. My sadness and depression prevented me from knowing Barbara even more. I wish I had said yes to spending afternoons with her. But even without that, I knew that she was an amazing woman with a heart of gold and a wonderful mother. She touched my life and I will always have a special place in my heart for Barbara. I will forever be thankful for having the chance to know her.

Thank you for asking me to be a part of your memories.

Love,

Melanie

That night, I walked home from the party with Judy and other friends. I mentioned to Judy what Melanie had said. Judy asked if I was okay and if it upset my evening. I told her I was okay and happy with what I heard.

Back alone at the apartment, I sat and grieved. But I felt good about the impression Barbara left on people. I sat and sat and then turned the situation around looking for some kind of humor in it, as I so often did throughout forty years with Barbara. I said out loud, "Barbara, how wonderful you were to people. That was so nice, the way you extended yourself to Melanie. You are so special."

Then I shouted, "But Barbara, what about me? After all, look at me in this suit. How ridiculous do I look? I walked around the entire evening at the party with one hand holding up my pants and with my underwear sagging. How could you let me leave the apartment looking like this? Stop laughing! It's not funny, or maybe it's a little funny. Okay, I'll go shopping, but you'll have to give me a sign of what's going to look good on me."

Getting new clothes on my own was adventurous for someone like me. It may sound simple, but not for someone who never had to do that himself. It was a big change in my life. I knew I would feel better wearing clothes that fit. My anxiety about going shopping was insignificant compared to the worries of the past thirty years.

My worst nightmare had happened. I was alone to start a life, without burdening my children. The children continually asked how I was doing. I began to tell them, "Everything is all right and I'm okay." They didn't believe me. But I told them that anyway, even though it wasn't so.

I went to the Short Hills Mall the day after Christmas. For a non-shopper, that was pretty brave. The mall was packed with shoppers. Brooks Brothers was so busy, and their special sale left the store in shambles. It was impossible for the store to have enough staff to help the crowds of people. The pants were strewn all over the top of the display table and I weeded through, looking for anything that was my new size, as I whispered under my breath, "Okay, Barbara, give me a sign for which three pair of pants you like. Please, don't expect me to do this on my own."

CHAPTER 45

Barbara was blessed

I became adventurous shopping for clothes. I still hadn't become adventurous in the apartment. There was still so much that I hadn't looked through.

I attended a neighbor's party in mid-December. It was a real funny invitation. A young couple Barbara and I were friendly with in the building threw a party for their dog's fourth birthday. The invitation was not only for people. They also invited people with their dogs, if they had one. I was thinking of borrowing a dog to bring to the party but decided to go it alone.

I could have had a dog to bring to the party, if I'd followed through on a business concept that I had thirty-five years before. I had an idea for starting a rent-a-dog business. At the time, there was a growing number of families with both husband and wife working. It's difficult enough for two working parents to care for their children. Having a pet added to the already excessive responsibilities.

I thought about how wonderful it would be for such families to have a dog, just for weekends or for certain weekdays. Families could reserve a specific dog, or they could get a different one each time. I approached my friend Tony with the idea. Tony and Michele bred beagles and I thought they would be perfect partners for the business. When I told Tony about the idea, he told me that I was nuts. That was the end of that business idea.

There were about twelve couples who brought their dogs to the party and several who came by themselves, like I did. It was a fun party with all these dogs in the apartment. They had a birthday cake for the dogs to share and Boomer looked cute in his party hat. It was the first party of its kind that I had attended. Welcome to urban living and the new generation of thirtysomethings. I really love these people. Barbara, you would have had a blast at this party.

At the party, some people were talking about the kitchen cabinets and how nice the large cabinet was above the refrigerator. I listened and said, "I have that same type of cabinet in my kitchen." They asked if I found it convenient to have. "I don't know," I answered. "I have no idea what's in it."

I hadn't looked in such places in the apartment. But as soon as I got back to my apartment that evening, I looked to see what was in that cabinet. "Oh, Barbara, so this is where the candlesticks are."

I was wondering what happened to them. And there was much more. I guess that when Barbara was failing and we were getting in hired help, she packed things away. I had no reason to look in such places. I grabbed a stepladder, went through the cabinet, and took out some of Barbara's favorite pieces, which she displayed over the years. It felt good to find this stuff. Some of it was from Barbara's mother and from her grandmother. Someday it will all go to Kristen, as per Barbara's will.

Several years earlier, Jonathan broke off an engagement four-and-a-half weeks before the wedding. After that happened, Barbara changed her will, leaving all her jewelry and dishes to Kristen. But for now, I enjoy having it, and Barbara would be so happy that I have it on display.

Finding these material things was comforting. Seeing Barbara's clothing was not. Just after Barbara's death, it was difficult to go into the closet and see all of her clothes, much of what she wore when she was ill. These were her personal possessions and it was just too difficult for me to go through them. I kept telling myself, "There is no need to keep the clothes. She's not coming back."

Kristen and Stephen were visiting one Sunday, and I asked Kristen to please empty the closet. It became difficult for Kristen. After a while she asked if this was a job she could finish another time. She looked at my face and said, "Okay, okay ... I'll take it all out now." Kristen eventually took all of Barbara's clothing from the apartment, keeping some for herself and donating the rest.

It was difficult for me to discard anything that had Barbara's handwriting. For example, there was a grocery list on the counter. I looked at the list and could visualize Barbara writing it. It was so personal in her handwriting and I didn't want to let it go. I spoke to my therapist and he advised that things like this need to be discarded. He explained that having a shrine of such items is not healthy. He told me, you have other, more important things that are in her handwriting. But I really didn't. Her handwriting was in the checkbook, on the calendar, and little notes of hers here and there, but I didn't have something special in her handwriting. I so wanted to hold on to anything that was as personal as her handwriting. I could look at her handwriting and imagine that she wrote it minutes ago. It made me feel as if she were still here.

I looked through Barbara's pocketbook and found two fortunes she had saved from fortune cookies. Barbara always liked to read the fortune cookies and wanted to believe that they were a sign of her future. The first fortune read, "When you can't naturally feel upbeat, it can sometimes help to act as if you did." I was surprised and saddened and found this fortune out of character for Barbara to have kept. Barbara had lived the past thirty years so positive about living. She was so full of hope, with no false pretenses in her belief that we'd beat this cancer together. There were times when I could see the stress on her face. There were times she would ask for a hug and say, "Everything is going to be okay, right?"

I would answer, "Yes." And a smile would come through her concern.

I was upset to find such a fortune and to be reminded that there were times when Barbara could only pretend to be optimistic. I kind of wished I hadn't found that fortune and been reminded that she was so pained. It took me several weeks to convince myself that it couldn't have been a total act for thirty years. Barbara was a positive person. I hoped that I gave her the comfort that I would always be with her, searching for a way to live, love, and laugh.

The second fortune read, "You will be blessed with longevity." Barbara so wanted to live and was always ready to put up a fight. Over the years, we saw so many doctors and specialists and went for second opinions and consultations. Always when we met a doctor for the first time, Barbara would look the doctor straight in the eye and say, "I want to live."

The reaction was always a nice smile with a response, "We are going to do the best for you."

Barbara would always say, "I'll do anything and go through whatever it takes."

In the months before Barbara died, I closely watched the doctors' interactions with Barbara. The signs of hope I had seen from so many doctors over the past thirty years were gone. Rather, we heard quick statements, we're going to do this and we're going to do that. It was fine for Barbara, who had the will and optimism to handle anything. But it was so painful to see the hope in the specialists' eyes fade away.

It was five months since I lost Barbara. There were still many things in the apartment that I hadn't gone through. One day I was looking for something I believed was in a cabinet in the office. I opened the door and saw that this was the cabinet where Barbara kept many of the picture albums of the family that she had put together over the years. I hadn't investigated this cabinet before and I spotted a small book that had a colorful cover, different from the large picture albums. I opened the book and realized it was a diary from Barbara's trip to Italy.

During the early summer of 2000, a group of our friends began planning a vacation to Italy for that September. Barbara wanted us to join the other four couples. But I couldn't go on such a trip. Just talking about it, my OCD kicked in and I began obsessing about the long airline flight. Barbara was so understanding. She really wanted to go along with the group of friends but didn't try to pressure me at all. Instead, she said, "If it were going to be just two other couples going, I would feel that I was tagging along with them. With four other couples, I'll be fine and fit right in. Would you have a problem if I go without you?"

"I think you should go. You'll have a good time. Won't you be touring in Switzerland as well as Italy?"

"Yes, we will," she answered.

"Good! Bring me home a cuckoo clock."

Barbara never mentioned that she had kept a diary of that trip. I skimmed through the pages and glanced at what was written. I became anxious seeing her handwriting. As I skimmed through the book, I could hear Barbara's voice talking to me about the trip.

Barbara told me all about the trip when she returned from Italy. But I didn't listen to all the details. Barbara often accused me of not listening when she talked. I would use the excuse that I was hard of hearing. Barbara would say, "Don't give me that BS." That was always an easy excuse for me. I used it so often that she bought me T-shirts that read, "Selective Hearing, it works for me," and, "My wife says that I don't listen to a thing she says, at least I think that's what she says."

In public, people would laugh when they saw me wearing those shirts. I would forget that I was wearing the shirts and wonder why people were laughing or staring at my chest. Some people commented, "I guess your wife bought that shirt for you." Barbara and I had an honest marriage. I didn't mind wearing the shirts. We both knew that I was full of it. It was good to know that she realized the truth about me, so that I didn't have to pretend I was someone other than myself.

But after Barbara was gone, she got back at me for all those years of my selective hearing. I would talk to Barbara after she was gone and, of course, she never answered me. I felt I was talking to myself, while hoping for an answer, a sign, or something. On a trip to South Beach, I noticed that the cleaning service forgot to mop the balcony floor. It got grimy between trips and needed to be mopped, so as not to track the dirt throughout the apartment. Barbara always mopped the balcony floor when she first arrived, and the tile sparkled.

I looked at the floor, which looked grimy. From inside the

apartment, I rubbed my hand over the floor, and said, "Oh, shit. Barbara ... I can't walk out on the balcony. The cleaning service forgot to mop the floor. What do I need to get this clean? Where's the mop? Where's the bucket?"

After searching around, I continued, "Okay, Barbara, I found the mop and bucket in the air conditioning closet. I think you kept the cleaning stuff under the sink in the kitchen. Barbara, tell me what I need to use. Okay, so don't answer me. At least, can you lead my hand to the right stuff? Okay, I guess you're refusing to do that too. Let me see. I see vinegar. Yes! I remember you would use that. I see distilled water. Barbara, what did you use distilled water for, and what is distilled water? It's probably for cleaning the tile, right? Oh, there's ammonia. I'll need that too ... I think."

I filled the bucket with water, added the distilled water, vinegar, and ammonia. I began to use the mop, but it broke. I got a rag and got down on my knees to begin washing the floor. "Ouch ... Barbara ... these tiles are a killer on the knees."

Then I remembered that I used to feel badly watching Barbara wash the floors on her knees. So I bought knee guards for her. "Okay, Barbara, where are those knee guards that I bought for you?"

I looked around and found them under the sink and went back to washing the floor. I was so proud of myself, finding everything. "Okay, Barbara, I'm all done. But why isn't the tile shining, like when you did it? I wish you would answer and tell me of any steps that I missed. Are you even listening to me? And by the way—I'm sorry for all those years of my selective hearing."

I began to read the diary of Barbara's trip to Italy. But after the first few sentences, I put the diary back into the cabinet. I wasn't ready to read it. Although, it was comforting to know that I had something of Barbara's, in her own words and handwriting.

I guess that the fortune from the cookie came true. Barbara was "blessed with longevity." Because, that diary is Barbara's forever, and this book is our forever.

CHAPTER 46

I miss you

A month later, I went back to the cabinet for Barbara's diary of her trip to Italy and brought it into the living room. I sat on the couch, got comfortable, and set up to read. As I read, I could hear Barbara's voice reading to me. She wrote so much about the details of each day of the trip. It was comforting to read about her dream trip. The parts that gave me pause were when she wrote of the kids and me, back home in New Jersey.

I was happy to see that Barbara didn't write about us every day and that she was so busy on the trip and doing for herself. But she did write of us, and I picked out those sentences from each day that she mentioned us.

> Day 2 – Monday, September 11
>
> It will be weird spending my birthday without Marc and the kids.
> I miss them already.

I recall that on this day, I wondered if Barbara would call the next day. To me, it was more than just weird spending September 12, 2000, without Barbara.

Day 3 – Tuesday, September 12

A phone call home to Marc and Kristen. I wish I could have spoken to Jonathan and Brian.

That day was Barbara's birthday; she was forty-nine. I think that this may have been the only birthday that we were apart since she turned fourteen. The fact we weren't together that day feels emptier today than it did back then. Barbara and I always thought that we'd have an endless number of birthdays to spend together. But we missed that day and now there are no more to spend together. That specific birthday seems more important to me today than it did in September 2000.

Day 6 - Friday, September 15

I have thought of Marc and the children all day as today they left for Boston. I'm having a great time, but today and tomorrow, my thoughts will be with them and move-in day at Northeastern. I wish I could have been there as well, but know they will all do fine without me there.

Barbara made her plans for the Italy trip months before we knew of Brian's move-in day at college. Move-in day is such a special experience for the entire family, upon a child becoming a college freshman.

We were all together to move Jonathan into college. Jonathan, the one who went to sleepaway camp for only a four-and-a-half-week season, was nervous about his separation from family. As the day went by and our leaving grew closer, Barbara and I saw the look on Jonathan's face begin to change. He did perk up a little when we passed the football cheerleaders in practice.

Later that afternoon, when Barbara and the kids were putting the final touches on Jonathan's dorm room, I walked down the hall to stretch. As I passed a room, I recognized one of the cheerleaders from earlier that afternoon. I looked in and said, "Hi."

She turned and said hi back and then asked, "Do you happen to have Scotch tape?"

I answered, "Oh, yes, go down the hall and see my son. He has

Scotch tape." She did and they talked. We all soon left, and Barbara cried in the car as we drove off, leaving Jonathan at the curb with a sulking look on his face. He later told us that right after we left, he went to that cheerleader's room.

With Kristen, move-in day was much different. Kristen is an organizer. She was ready for college and making new friends. With her personality, it was much easier to leave her curbside. But Barbara cried anyway.

Day 7–Saturday, September 16

I thought of Marc and the kids all day today. I hope all went smoothly on move-in day. I missed being there. As I write this at 12:30 a.m., Marc and the kids have probably left Boston. That would be 6:30 p.m. EST. I wonder how the goodbyes went. Probably it was best that I was not there to shed my tears. I hope that Marc and the kids were able to control theirs. I hope all Brian's stuff fit in and that he likes his roommate, Jose, and his room. I can't wait to talk to Brian when I get home. By Saturday night, he will be all settled in his room and will have gone to his first classes. I know he will be fine. I can't wait to visit on parents' weekend.

It will be very lonely for Marc this week at home with nobody at home. I miss him dearly. He would not have liked a trip like this, but it is a lot of fun.

We had arrived in Boston the night before move-in day and stayed at a hotel, nearby to the college campus. We didn't get much sleep that night. The kids, although adults, were fooling around. Barbara would have kept us under control and stopped the silliness. Always being the instigator, I could only encourage the silliness.

All worked out well that Barbara wasn't there, because Brian hated his dorm room. By the time Barbara came home, Brian had already negotiated a move into a better room, and he was happy with the college.

Day 10 – Tuesday, September 19

Today I felt homesick. It is so far away, and I don't like the idea that I can't just pick up the phone and call. I miss talking to Jonathan, Kristen, and Brian.

This is so mother-like. For Barbara, it was always all about her family.

> Day 11 – Wednesday, September 20
>
> Brian's first day of school. I pray that all goes well and that he likes his classes and does well. I will be thinking of him all day. I can't wait to hear about everything. I will call tonight.

Barbara was on her dream trip, but nothing could tear her from the worries of parenthood. My children were so blessed to have her.

> Day 12 –Thursday, September 21
>
> I miss Marc and the kids. He would have hated the crowds, the lack of time to rest, and the schedule, but he would have loved the food.

Yes, I would have hated the crowds and mostly the airplane flight. It wasn't until now that I miss being with Barbara on that trip.

> Day 13 – Friday, September 22
>
> I can't believe I've been away for two weeks. In some regard, it seems like I've been here forever. I miss home and Marc and the kids. Yet, it all seems like I just got here. Now that the trip is over, I can't wait to get home and hug and kiss Marc and speak to Jonathan, Kristen, and Brian.

Today, as I grieve, I can't wait until that someday when, once again, I'll be together with Barbara for that hug and kiss.

Barbara concluded her diary of the trip with a recap of her favorite parts. She also wrote:

> All-in-all, it was a fabulous trip. I am so grateful to be able to have enjoyed this journey to Italy – a dream come true. Thank God for my good health, for my wonderful, fantastic, special husband who let me go on this fantastic trip. His love and unselfishness are very special indeed and I treasure him and thank God for his love every day.

Oh, Barbara. I am so grateful, too. Thank you for this journey that started when I was fourteen and you were twelve. I treasure you and our love and am so thankful for the true love that we had and the puppy love that went on for a lifetime. It was surely puppy love that we never outgrew, and it began at a time when we believed we would live forever. It's the best kind of love, because it's a love with no strings attached, no responsibilities, no fear or concern for the future. It's a pure love that made us hurt inside when apart and made our forty-year marriage magical, romantic, and filled with life, even with a thirty-year struggle with cancer.

For our twentieth wedding anniversary, I joked about my deserving an award. Sincerely, I was just joking. But, as I thought about the two of us on August 29, 2011, the day that would have been our fortieth wedding anniversary, I came to realize that it was you who was truly deserving of an award.

See you later, alligator.

Okay, I'll say it for you.

See you in a while, crocodile.

I miss you and I truly believe that we will be together again someday. This isn't the end of our storybook lives. It's the beginning.

EPILOGUE

I searched deep into my soul as I made my way through writing this book, to understand the courage and frame of mind that helped Barbara to thrive through the difficult times. I so needed to prove to myself that she felt good about her life, her accomplishments, and her legacy.

I obsessed over searching for answers to such questions as: Did Barbara feel that she had a full life? What else could I have done for her? Barbara left me without us saying goodbye. Should we have said goodbye? Most importantly, despite all the difficult times, did Barbara have a life filled with the greatest happiness that, by far, overshadowed the difficult times? So often, I believed I had found the answers. As I thought further, I was always uncertain.

In my apartment I have a framed picture of Barbara, taken when she was about four years old. She was a beautiful child, with a smile so innocent and pure. It is the smile that I always saw in Barbara, even as an adult. After I lost Barbara, I stared into that picture and was pained thinking about what that sweet-faced little girl had to endure during her lifetime. In my grief, I asked: Did she have the kind of life that someone so innocent deserved? Shouldn't her life have been as sweet as her face? Barbara was so deserving of good things. Was the outcome fair?

It turns out the answers I was searching for had been in front of me all along. Several years ago, Barbara came across a postcard that she noticed in a store, which she framed and placed on our bedroom dresser. I now remember Barbara saying to me, at that time, "This postcard best describes us." On the front of the postcard is a picture of a beach scene showing a heart shape etched in the sand. Leaving the heart shape are two sets of footprints in the sand. The footprints lead to a couple walking along the water's edge. The caption below the picture reads, "Every day we share is special."

That framed postcard on my dresser had the single answer to my questions. I didn't pay much attention to the postcard or to what Barbara was saying at the time. Obviously, I saw the postcard all the time, but never took real notice of the picture or interpreted its meaning. I took it as just two people walking on the beach. Sad, how we easily overlook and miss out on the important things right in front of us.

The couple on that postcard could easily be Barbara and me. We so often walked along the shore, holding hands, and Barbara would often stop to inscribe something in the sand, like a message or a heart shape.

The answer to Barbara's courage and frame of mind had been in front of me for years. It was in that picture on the postcard of a couple and the caption below. "Every day we share is special." Barbara had placed that postcard on our dresser years before, leaving it for me, knowing that someday I would take a closer look, perhaps after she was gone, and I would be reminded of our lives together.

Barbara knew me too well. She had cared for me in life and prepared me for living after her death, knowing I would obsess with questions about her happiness. And I did. With that postcard, Barbara summed up our forty-year marriage. The caption says it all.

During each difficult time, Barbara lived for the moment. Her time became all about what was special in her life, at that moment.

Since I was with Barbara every day, by leaving that postcard on the dresser, she was telling me, "Every day we shared was special" and that her life was special. Surely, no one can ask for a better life than one in which every day is special.

It's been several years and my family's grieving for our loss of Barbara doesn't seem to have lessened. I don't believe it ever will. But I'm hoping that memorializing Barbara's memory in this book will help us understand that when she left us, she was at peace with her destiny.

When I spoke on one of the nights of Shiva, I asked Kristen to keep Barbara's memory alive in her children, as best she could. I asked for there to always be a picture of Barbara in her children's rooms and for her to talk to them of Barbara, so that their grand-mother's memory would live on.

Drew was only fourteen months old when Barbara passed. Other than Kristen talking about Barbara's picture in her room, Drew remembering Barbara holding her is not likely. But Jonah was three years and nine months old, and I have hope that he will remember the feel of Barbara's love. Barbara so much wanted to be a grandmother and I so much want her memory to live on in our grandchildren.

Our family is doing well. Kristen, following in Barbara's footsteps, became a real estate sales associate for a company in Millburn, New Jersey. Kristen and Stephen sold their house in Maplewood, a house that Barbara helped them find, and moved to Millburn. Kristen cried when they moved. But Jonah and Drew told Kristen that they'd have new memories in their new home.

Jonathan lived in South Beach for many years and built up his career there. But after Barbara passed, he felt alone and missed being with the family. He moved back to New Jersey and rented an apartment in Hoboken, near me. On Facebook, Kristen had been in contact with a woman that she knew when they were kids at summer camp. Kristen asked Stacey if she remembered Jonathan. Jonathan and Stacey had their first date on November 29, 2012. They got engaged on July 6, 2013 and were married on April 12, 2014. Their son Benjamin was born in February 2015. The three of them now live, with their dog Brewster, in their home in Millburn. Kristen was their realtor.

Brian moved to his own apartment in Hoboken after Barbara passed. He had always been nearby to me. He has had various jobs and a small business and has been involved in several basketball and soccer coaching activities. In the summer of 2019, Brian accepted a job in Arizona. He lives in Old Scottsdale. I miss him so very much. He's an independent, grown man now. But to me, he's still the baby of the family. And in addition to him calling me often, I get a text from Brian every few days asking, "How was your day today?"

As for me, in February 2014, Kristen convinced me to sign up on a dating site: Match.com. After a few months, I signed up on J-Date too. I've been on many dates and have discovered that I had something that so few people ever had: an incredibly wonderful marriage.

I'm hopeful that I will find that special someone to be in my life, once again. But what I may never have again, and miss, is starting a conversation with two words, as I did with Barbara, or hearing Barbara starting with those same two words: "Remember when...."

I don't have Barbara to reminisce with. That's one of the many losses that comes with losing a spouse, after a long marriage. But I can read about us in this book, which I wrote looking through Shiva Eyes. Ahh ... writing this book, looking through Shiva Eyes. It was with the heartfelt emotion of looking through Shiva Eyes that I was able to see and relive all the goodness of our life together. During my writing, I felt Barbara with me. And maybe, when I read aloud, Barbara can hear me.

So often, hearing a song on the radio helps me to reminisce about the times I had with Barbara. To me, the song "Through the Years," by Kenny Rogers, tells the story of our marriage and always brings a tear.

I wrote in the first sentence of Chapter One, "I think I was always attracted to girls. Maybe even as far back as when I was in diapers." I went on to write, "I could be playing a game on the sidewalk with my friends, pitching bottle caps or playing stoopball, and be totally engrossed in the game. But, when a cute girl with dark brown hair, dark brown eyes, and an olive complexion walked by, I would instantly forget about the game and stare at her."

After forty-six years of puppy love, when I think back on my childhood years before Barbara, it seems like I was always looking for her. Even as a young kid it was as if Barbara was always there with me, and I wanted to find her. As if she were, always, the only one I cared for, even before I met her. Once I did find Barbara, there was nothing that could come between our love, and there was nothing that we couldn't do together.

Barbara and I had a beautiful life together, a life that we both cherished and loved. Through the years, the good times and difficult times, the laughter and tears, our love got better and stronger. Every day we shared was special.

Barbara will continue to live within me until I close my eyes for the final time. Then I will lie beside her once again.

About the author

After a lifetime of working for others, Marc Gellman now works for himself. After more than forty years focused on architectural design and real estate development projects, Marc has launched several new careers: writing books, performing stand-up comedy routines, and creating and starring in "Benjamin's Grandpa" videos.

His future outlook is all about accomplishing the fun stuff he always dreamed of doing. "In my youth, I was a silly kid. Life's challenges and experiences influenced me to become a (mostly) serious-minded adult, and conformity was the only way to survive in the corporate world. With no one to answer to any longer, it's time for the silly me to come out ... with maybe just a little seriousness now and then."

Marc grew up in the East New York section of Brooklyn, New York in the 1950s and '60s, and most of his world existed on the block where he lived. During the summers, his family—mom, dad, and older brother—vacationed in the Rockaways of Queens, NY, a summertime beach community, with a mix of bungalows, three-story rooming houses, and grandmas who played mah-jongg on sandy front porches.

On the day of his sixteenth birthday, Marc started his working career as a clerk at the Big Apple Supermarket on Church Avenue, Brooklyn. He earned maybe $1.25 an hour and made extra money from a side business he cooked up, ferrying groceries home from the market for elderly customers. He earned enough for a standing

Saturday night date with Barbara, with pocket money left over for the week.

As a young boy, Marc developed an interest in watching the construction of buildings. He would excitedly visit the site of anything being built in his neighborhood after school and monitor the construction progress each day, and he went on to attend a school of architecture.

While attending college, Marc became a licensed real estate salesperson, selling homes in the Northeast Bronx and later in Woodhaven, Queens. He married one week after his twenty-second birthday, two weeks before Barbara's twentieth birthday.

After graduation, the couple moved to a rural New Jersey northwest suburb, where they raised their three children. At first, Marc worked for a home builder and later grew his career at a management and design consulting firm. Now ... he's a proud author, a stand-up comedian, and grandpa to three grandkids.

Printed in the USA
CPSIA information can be obtained
at www.ICGtesting.com
LVHW022336180923
758554LV00028B/165/J

9 781737 522300